# Changing Men
# in Southern Africa

# Changing Men
# in Southern Africa

edited by Robert Morrell

UNIVERSITY OF NATAL PRESS
Pietermaritzburg

ZED BOOKS LTD
London & New York

University of Natal Press
Private Bag X01
Scottsville 3209
South Africa
E-mail: books@nu.ac.za

Zed Books Ltd
7 Cynthia Street
London N1 9JF
*and* Room 400, 175 Fifth Avenue
New York NY 10010

ISBN 0 86980 990 3 (University of Natal Press  Hardcover)
ISBN 0 86980 983 0 (University of Natal Press  Softcover)
ISBN 1 85649 915 4 (Zed Books Ltd  Hardcover)
ISBN 1 85649 916 2 (Zed Books Ltd  Softcover)

First published in 2001

Distributed in the United States exclusively by Palgrave, a division of St Martin's Press LLC, 175 Fifth Avenue, New York, NY 10010

UK Cataloguing-in-Publication Data is available from the British Library

US CIP has been applied for

Editor: Andrea Nattrass
Cover designer: Evan Oberholster

Designed and typeset by the University of Natal Press
Printed and bound by Natal Witness Commercial Printers (Pty) Ltd
Pietermaritzburg

# Contents

# Acknowledgements

This book could not have been assembled without the support, encouragement and intellectual generosity of many people. First and foremost are the contributors – I thank them for their patience and commitment. Bob Connell is the inspiration behind this book which was edited and written in Durban. It is to my friends here that I owe a great debt of gratitude. They have been my intellectual and emotional cocoon. They include Geoff Schreiner, Alan Rycroft, Vishnu Padayachee, David Johnson, Cathy Burns, Keith Breckenridge, Mike Hart, Doug Hindson, Jenny Robinson, Tim Quinlan, Harald Witt and the Durban gender reading group of the mid-1990s. Fran Fearnley was a constant source of encouragement and practical advice.

My parents, Richard and Bridget, and my brother, Christopher, by example focused me on this labour. Georgina Hamilton was a loving companion in the years it took to produce this book. My sister, Penny, who has been a treasured ear and voice, constant, for twenty years does not know how much of this book is hers. The book is for my daughters, Tamarin and Ashleigh, who have inspired me by their being.

This book was engineered by Michael Kimmel's energy. Glenn Cowley from the University of Natal Press and Robert Molteno from Zed Press made it happen. Andrea Nattrass was a marvellously diligent editor, and Margie Ramsay fashioned the index. The cover is the creation of Evan Oberholster and reflects his talent, humour and South African origins.

I would like to acknowledge the support of the British Council, the HSRC (now the NRF) and the University of Natal who helped financially to support some of the constituent parts of this project.

For various illustrations and photographs thanks are extended to Pat Flanagan and *ZigZag Surfing Magazine*, *Work in Progress*, and Zapiro.

# Note on Terminology

This book uses a language of race developed by and in opposition to the racist nomenclature of apartheid. Under the Population Registration Act of 1950 all persons in South Africa were designated to belong to one of the following 'races': white, Bantu, coloured and Asian. These terms (and the Act itself) were contested but the power of the state before 1990 and the ongoing legacy of apartheid has meant that they still have force and descriptive power. Over time they have mutated: Bantu has become 'African' or 'black'; Asian has become 'Indian'.

In some registers racial classifications are insulting and unnecessary. While having sympathy for this point of view, the editor has decided to give race its social and analytical weight by using the following descriptors: white, coloured, African (when referring to people formerly classified as Bantu), Indian, and black (when referring to people who are not white).

The term 'black' is contentious as it is used in many different ways partly as a result of the influence of the Black Consciousness Movement. In the late 1960s and 70s the Movement attempted to develop a race consciousness on the basis of a rejection of European values and colonial oppression. It was the Black Consciousness Movement that described all people of colour as 'black'.

# Preface

In the mid-1990s I was engaged in writing a doctoral dissertation on the white settlers of colonial Natal.[1] In the process I began to develop an interest in issues of masculinity, not least because I realised that the people I was studying were by and large men. In time I began to see the connections between the racialised political and economic power of white settlers and constructions of masculinity. These connections were in some cases causal (for example, in the development of a colonial militarism), and in other cases shaped the form of social activity (for example, the gendered use of leisure time and playing of sports). It became apparent that the history of South Africa sorely lacked a gender perspective which went beyond the examination of women. By the 1990s studies of women in South African historiography were much in evidence and richly detailed. They showed how women had been left out of history and that they were oppressed. Existing gender literature, however, remained effectively synonymous with the study of women.

In 1997 I organised a Colloquium on Masculinities in Southern Africa at the University of Natal.[2] Leading gender theorists specialising in the critical study of men took part, including Bob Connell from Australia, Debbie Epstein and Jeff Hearn from Britain, and Michael Kimmel from the United States. Historians of gender and masculinity in Africa, William Beinart, John Tosh and Luise White also attended. In addition, a gender activist from Norway, Jorgen Lorentzen, was present. In all, 29 papers were presented, most of them by South African scholars. The intention of the Colloquium was to develop a more conscious and theoretically informed understanding of masculinity in South African history and society.

In 1998 I edited a special issue of the *Journal of Southern African Studies* (Volume 24, Number 4) on Masculinities in Southern Africa. Apart from an overview written by myself, the issue contained nine articles by authors who had presented papers at the Colloquium. The focus of the special issue was on South African history and covered a range of themes. Not surprisingly, a number of articles dealt with violence. Keith Breckenridge considered the racialised violence found on the gold mines. Sandra Swart argued that the 1914 Afrikaner Rebellion was caused by, amongst other things, an attempt by marginalised Afrikaans-speaking farmers to reclaim a Republican masculinity and with it their dignity and the life they had lost in the wake of the South African War (1899–1902) and the formation of the Union government (1910). Anne Mager discussed generational violence and changing conceptions of masculinity amongst Africans in the 1950s. Clive Glaser showed how notions of territoriality were central to the understanding of masculinity amongst urban African youth in the 1960s and how such notions infused the social organisation of gangs and promoted violent rivalry between these gangs. Katie Mooney investigated the sub-cultural viol-ence of white 'ducktail' gangs in the 1950s. The gendered nature of work in the nursing profession was the subject of Catherine Burns's article. Nursing was 'women's work' and the introduction of African men to expand the provision of health services floundered on this rock. Two articles dealt with masculinity and the environment. William Beinart challenged the idea that early colonial male explorers inevitably laid waste the environment and imposed rigid, modernist frames of understanding on the new land-scape. Malcolm Draper charted the way in which different, and sometimes contradictory, understandings of masculinity interacted with the conservation policies of two prominent pioneer conservationists in KwaZulu-Natal in the apartheid era. Homo-phobia was the concern of Marc Epprecht as he investigated the relationship of Robert Mugabe's public homophobia with the understandings of sex and sexuality amongst Zimbabwe's people. He argues that the importation of West-ern ideas about sexuality has constructed a framework which inadequately captures indigenous understandings of homosexuality. Epprecht does not think it helps to describe Zimbabweans as 'homophobic' as this attributes to them prejudices, whereas the situation is more about the absence of a language – an 'unsaying'. In all of these articles, race and class are important concepts and themes which constantly remind the reader of the impact of conquest, colonialism and capitalism on gender relations. These historical realities also expose the flaws inherent in the thinking that all men have the same, essential, masculine identity.

The present book is the second (and final) phase in disseminating the work of the Colloquium. Its focus is contemporary. Most of the contributions are concerned with the last twenty years of the twentieth century, although some delve into the early apartheid era. The majority of the chapters originated in presentations to the Colloquium. The remainder were solicited from scholars who either were not able to attend the Colloquium, or whose work on men and masculinity only came to my attention after the Colloquium had been concluded.

In the international arena masculinity as a social problem, and as a key component in the gender question, has become increasingly politically visible since the mid-1970s. Pioneering work in the mid-1970s and early 80s by activists such as Michael Kimmel (of the National Organisation for Men against Sexism [NOMAS], in the United States) and Michael Kaufman in Canada has matured to the extent that governments and international agencies worldwide now acknowledge the importance of considering masculinity and working critically with men.

One of the reasons for this increased awareness has been the emergence of a New Men's Movement as an ally to the feminist movement. Organising in the developed world, this new movement emerged in the early 1980s to promote gender change and to involve men in this change. Unlike the Men's Movement which was largely a reaction to feminism and attempted to defend the privileges of men, the New Men's Movement organised men to participate in a programme designed to identify the nature of men's power over women and to work towards gender equality. Initially this was taken up most vigorously by consciousness-raising groups which discussed the masculine identities of their members and attempted to develop new ways of understanding masculinity. This inward-focusing impulse was in time accompanied by a more public and political engagement with issues of masculinity. Here the focus was on media exposure and on public interventions, including in universities and on the terrain of research. While many men became involved in this project, Bob Connell and Jeff Weeks were among the major figures to place the spotlight on masculinity and to problematise the concept. The effect of these interventions was to show how masculinity was implicated in gender inequalities and irrevocably to end the idea that there was just one kind of masculinity.

A major focus of profeminist work has been on the issue of violence against women. In a number of countries, including Australia, Britain and the United States, men have come together to publicise the issue and to work with violent men. Perhaps the apogee of this movement was the establishment of an international organisation for men against violence against women. Founded in Canada in 1991, the White Ribbon Campaign was a response to the 1989 killing of 14 women by a single man in a Montreal University. The Campaign is now organising from South Africa to Scandinavia and from the United States to Australia. In South Africa, violence remains a major social problem. The Gender Equity Task Team identified it as the major obstacle to the transformation of the education system in 1997, and in 1999 a variety of government ministries were battling to tackle the very high levels of violence. The Commission on Gender Equality has committed its energies to addressing issues of violence and is beginning to widen its focus from protecting women from men's violence to working with men to understand and prevent violence. This mirrors developments in civil society where a number of organisations like ADAPT in Gauteng, the '5 in 6' Project in the Western Cape, and Masimanyane in the Eastern Cape have been established to work with men around issues of violence.

The South African post-apartheid state has been very active in generating gender policy. Amongst its initiatives was the establishment of the Commission on Gender Equality in 1996. The Commission's brief is to monitor, research, protect and promote gender equality. Significantly, one of its 11 commissioners is a man. This year for the first time it has begun to campaign around issues of men and masculinity.

This book, then, is prompted by two, interrelated concerns: the first intellectual, and the second, political. The first concern is to identify and explore the different forms in which masculinity as a collective social form is expressed in South Africa. Related to this is an investigation of the way in which masculinity is implicated in gender inequalities and of how masculinities are changing. The second concern is to widen debates about gender and to promote a rethinking of masculinity which offers new ways of imagining masculinity and, for men, suggests new ways of being a man.

Inevitably this book has gaps. I am particularly aware of its weakness in focusing on 'black' and white masculinities and its failure to explore ethnicity. This is solely the result of my inability to find scholars in South Africa who are working on this issue. Since beginning this book I have become aware of the work of Goolam Vahed, at the University of Durban-Westville, who is beginning to study Indian, Muslim men.

Nevertheless, this book is the first of its kind to examine South African men and masculinities. It explores the particular conditions under which masculinities are formed, showing that not all men are the same and that masculinities change, particularly when a society is in transition. Different visions of masculinities are emerging in South Africa, and with them the hope of a more peaceful society.

*Robert Morrell*
October 2000

NOTES

1. R.G. Morrell, 'White farmers, Social Institutions and Settler Masculinity in the Natal Midlands, 1880–1920'. Ph.D. thesis, University of Natal, Durban, 1996.
2. A report on the Colloquium was published in 'Masculinity in South African History: Towards a gendered approach to the past'. *South African Historical Journal* 37(1997): 167–77.

# Introduction

# The Times of Change
## Men and Masculinity in South Africa[1]

ROBERT MORRELL

'South Africa is one of the last bastions of chauvinism. Every white and black man in this country should be locked up in a room with five women for a few weeks,' said renowned playwright, Athol Fugard, in 1994 a few months after South Africa's first democratic elections had brought the African National Congress (ANC) to power (*Sunday Times*, 27 November 1994). In 1996 Greig Coetzee a young poet, described South African men as 'fossils' (*Sunday Times*, 14 July 1996). The refrain was taken up in 1998 when a Durban academic was reported as describing South African men as the 'world's biggest pigs' (*Independent on Saturday*, 5 September 1998).

The unflattering view of South African men is a stereotype. Not only does it isolate specific aspects of masculinity and represent these as common and universal, but it fails to capture masculine diversity. What could be more different than the image of a grim-faced, rifle-toting soldier clad in camouflage gear, patrolling the streets of a township and a colourful cross-dresser, strutting his stuff in a gay pride march? The chapters that follow discuss the range of masculinities in South Africa, in the process both undermining the stereotypical view of southern African men and addressing its basic thesis – the reactionary and unreformed character of South Africa's men.

While South Africa's political and economic systems have been changing, there have also been changes in gender relations. Since 1994 government policies have reduced some of the inequalities that separate women from men. Much of the focus of public interest and concern, however, remains fixed on the inferior and subordinate position of women relative to men. Another change in gender relations that has received less attention has been the change in masculinity. In the 1990s men and masculinity internationally have become the object of interested

3

speculation, with the media asking the following questions: Are men in crisis and should they be assisted to recover their masculinity? Are men able to be part of a quest for gender justice? Are men actually just as entitled as ever before and committed to holding onto their privilege at the expense of women? Commentators looking for signs of positive change found it in the emergence of the 'New Man'. This was a term coined to refer to men who did not subscribe to stereotyped ideas such as that all women were nags, that women's place was in the home, or that women should look nice but say little. New men were in favour of women's liberation, looked after the children, supported women in their desire to develop careers, and were sensitive and introspective people. But there were also alarming and reactionary developments by men bent on turning back the feminist tide. Fundamentalist groupings like the Taliban movement in Afghanistan emerged to deny women rights and to drive them back into public invisibility.

The volatility of gender change is important for two reasons. In the first instance it shows that masculinity can and does change and that it is therefore not a fixed, essential identity which all men have. Secondly, gender change reveals that men differ – not all have the same masculinity. Theorists have attempted to elaborate on this observation by talking of a number of masculinities.

In the 1990s, the importance of recognising masculinity as a key aspect of gender and of addressing issues of masculinity has become acknowledged internationally. This has for the most part been the result of an international drive for gender equality that has been going on for over three decades. The Beijing Declaration of Women in 1995 was the culmination of a period of vigorous international action to promote the rights and interests of women. It marked the moment when nations from all over the world committed themselves to accelerating and intensifying efforts to promote women's rights. At the same time, new initiatives were being made to broaden the campaign to realise gender equity. Stemming in part from the intellectual labours of leftist scholars supportive of feminism, a 'new men's movement' had emerged. This was in most instances an organic development in which men came together to discuss gender relations and specifically to discuss the role of men in the exploitation of women. Amongst the most public expressions of this movement was the British publication, *Achilles Heel,* which was founded in the early 1970s and became a forum for the discussion of masculinity and specifically how the private related to the public (Seidler 1992). By the 1990s governments, development agencies and agencies of the United Nations were beginning to include issues of masculinity within the purview of their gender policies. Amongst the most progressive in this regard were the Scandinavian countries.

The Swedish Ministry of Industry, Employment and Communications states its position in the following terms:

> The overriding goal of Swedish equality policy is to ensure that women and men enjoy equal rights, obligations and opportunities in all areas of society. Traditionally, gender equality issues have been the concern of women. Very few men have been involved in work to achieve equality. However, if equality is to become a reality in all areas of society, a genuine desire for change and active participation on the part of both women and men are called for. (1999: 1)

In the developed world, efforts to include men and masculinities in gender work focus on a number of issues: violence, peace, fathering and childcare. Initiatives involve working with men to develop policy on paternity leave and promoting fathers' involvement with childcare, on measures to prevent domestic violence, to work with offenders, and to develop international guidelines to reduce social and political aggression and thus promote peace (Lorentzen and Lokke 1999; Breines 1999).

In the context of the developing world, initiatives have understandably been somewhat different. Population and AIDS are dominant issues in Africa (Parker 1995). Elsewhere, classic development work which aims to promote women's access to resources and more generally to creating harmonious and egalitarian gender relations is slowly becoming infused with issues of masculinity. Exhorting development agencies to move in this direction, Andrea Cornwall observed in 1997 that gender and development work currently offers little scope for men's involvement. 'Old-style feminist theory dealt with them at one stroke: men were classed as the problem, those who stood in the way of positive change' (1997: 10). She argued that people working in the field should move beyond generalisations and work with and from personal experience to open up spaces for change amongst and by men. It is with this call in mind that UNESCO and European agencies have begun to ask questions like 'How can men gain from gender equality?' In this way, an effort is being made to get men involved in striving for gender equality, even though this may mean taking different steps (sensitive to local requirements and attitudes) from those taken in Europe (see Swedish Ministry for Foreign Affairs 1999).

It is, of course, not the case that men are objects of curiosity and constructive work only to those institutions committed to gender equality. The other major development in the 1990s has been the emergence of the Men's Movement often, though not always, in opposition to feminism. Across the world organisations established exclusively for men have flourished. The (mainly white) Promise Keepers and the (black) Million Man March in the United States of America (USA) have been the largest and most influential, but in a range of social locations and with differing agenda, movements have developed to tackle what many men see as a 'crisis of masculinity' (Messner 1997). Two major features of the crisis of masculinity have been that a generation of children has grown up without fathers, and that the rise of women in the workplace has taken jobs from men and eroded their authority. The recommendations of this diverse movement are frequently at odds with those of profeminists. For example, Steve Biddulph, a popular Australian lecturer, tours the world preaching the importance of fathers and calling for the recognition of fathers as indispensable to the well-being of boy children (Biddulph 1994). This is very different from the arguments of profeminists that children can be well brought up by gay parents and that the nuclear family is not essential. In the section of this chapter entitled 'Masculinities in transition' the impact of these two contending global gender trends will be examined in the context of South Africa.

This chapter consists of five sections. The first section explains some of the concepts which have developed in the 15 years from 1985 and which are associated with the field of study now commonly termed Men's Studies or Critical Men's Studies. The second section provides a short history of masculinity in southern Africa. The third section surveys gender power in South Africa showing that while political power has passed to a black majority, gender power remains in the hands of men. The fourth section reviews the contributions to this volume and focuses on the ways in which men and masculinity are changing in a transitional context. The fifth and final section discusses the politics of masculinity: how men have responded to the social, political and economic changes of the 1990s. In this section the continuing importance of race and class are underlined, but evidence of new integrative forces within South African society that are shaping new masculinities is presented.

## The theory of masculinity

The theories and debates which are unfolded here are heavily influenced by the work of Bob Connell, an Australian sociologist. In two seminal books, *Gender and Power: Society, the Person and Sexual Politics* (1987) and *Masculinities* (1995), Connell developed a theory of masculinity which sought to take account of psychological insights and social forces, which attempted to blend personal agency with social structure, and which worked to blend the diverse intellectual influences of materialism, feminism and critical theory.

In his 1987 book, *Gender and Power*, Connell demonstrated how gender was a concept of power. He showed how individual men each enjoyed the 'patriarchal dividend', 'the advantage men in general gain from the overall subordination of women' (Connell 1995: 79). Being a man, Connell argued, conferred power. But not all men shared this power equally and not all were individually exploitative. In his second book in 1995, *Masculinities*, he developed the theme of different masculinities. He showed that while men oppressed women, some men also dominated and subordinated other men. In developing this thesis Connell showed that there was a masculinity that was hegemonic – one that dominated other masculinities and which succeeded in creating prescriptions of masculinity which were binding (or at least partially so), and which created cultural images of what it meant to be a 'real man'. There were also three non-hegemonic categories of masculinity: subordinate, complicit and marginalised. Generally speaking, these were masculinities developed outside the corridors of power. Minorities, defined in terms of race, class, ethnicity or sexual orientation, all characteristically understand what being a man means differently from members of the ruling class or elite and from each other too.

Masculinities are fluid and should not be considered as belonging in a fixed way to any one group of men. They are socially and historically constructed in a process which involves contestation between rival understandings of what being a man should involve. There are, according to anthropologists, a core set of activities or traits which are transculturally associated with men (Gilmore 1990; but see Gutmann 1997). Other theories, however, argue that masculinity is so culturally variable and so context dependent that only its connection to physical possession of male genitalia is uncontestable (but see Butler 1990).

Masculinities are constantly being protected and defended, are constantly breaking down and being recreated. For gender activists this conceptualisation provides space for optimism because it acknowledges the possibility of intervening in the politics of masculinity to promote masculinities that are more peaceful and harmonious. For gender scholars, the challenge is to identify what forces operate to effect change in masculinities, when, where and how such changes occur, and what their effects are. These issues are taken up in various ways in this book.

Masculinity is also a term that refers to a specific gender identity, belonging to a specific male person. While this gender identity is acquired in social contexts and circumstances, it is 'owned' by an individual. It bears the marks and characteristics of the history which formed it – frequently with salient childhood experiences imparting a particular set of prejudices and preferences, joys and terrors. Masculinity viewed in this particular way can be understood as something that can be deployed or used. Individuals can choose to respond to a particular situation in one or another way. While there are criticisms of this conceptualisation as voluntaristic, such a construction allows for the examination of individual masculinities at work. It also promotes the examination of the micro aspects of masculinity, particularly of the body – that major bearer of masculine value and symbolism. In some of the contributions in this book, the authors will examine how masculinity was acquired, how it changed and developed, how it was used, and what the consequences were of particular displays of masculinity.

Masculinity is not inherited nor is it acquired in a one-off way. It is constructed in the context of class, race and other factors which are interpreted through the prism of age. Boys develop a masculine gender identity which is deficient relative to the adult masculinity of men. The stages by which boys become men – manhood – are a source of anxiety and a rite of passage. There is no set or prescribed procedure but the determination to become 'a man' is a powerful feature of masculinity which some of the chapters in this book discuss.

While masculinity is not automatically acquired, it is also true that boys and men are not entirely free to choose those images which please them. Their tastes and their bodies are influenced, some would say shaped, by discourses of gender which they encounter from birth. Debbie Epstein and Richard Johnson offer the following definition:

> Human agents cannot stand outside culture and wield power precisely as they wish. Power is always limited and shaped by systems of knowledge which also shape the subjects and objects of power. . . . power/knowledge position us as subjects of particular kinds. They put pressure on us to adopt particular identities . . . in this particular sense, power and knowledge as discourse 'constructs' social identities. (1998: 15)

The mass media and the people and organisations who use them, institutions like schools and the managers and employees who inhabit them, leisure and work activities and the people who are involved in them – all these media, places and people are involved in the complex process of constructing gendered discourses. The discourses that become dominant tend to illegalise or censure certain gender constructions (for example,

8

being gay) and tend to affirm other gender constructions (for example, being heterosexual) (Buchbinder 1994). At the personal level people are constantly contributing to, undermining, and drawing upon gender discourses. While there is an overall pattern which collectively serves to legitimate forms of gender inequality and power, gender talk is often highly contradictory. While contradictions, according to classic Marxist reasoning, have the capacity to undermine ruling relations, it can be the case, as Jeff Hearn shows, that the capacity of individuals to juggle two sets of opposing views can legitimate and perpetuate gender power. Hearn (1999) shows that men who are violent towards women intimates often use language to normalise the situation while at the same time acknowledging that their actions are 'wrong'.

While the majority of men mostly perpetuate and reproduce dominant gender relations and forms of masculinity, there are some men who either consciously or unconsciously oppose the hegemonic prescriptions of 'exemplary' masculinity. Cultural theorists like Jonathan Dollymore (1991) have located such forms of opposition into two categories of transgressive or transformative behaviour. The categories describe two types of dissident behaviour – one which transgresses but remains beyond or outside societal norms, and another which transgresses *and* forces change in existing norms and perceptions. This book provides a number of examples of men collectively challenging the gender order (a term coined by Connell to define the unequal distribution of gender power in society).

A major debate within critical men's studies concerns hegemony. The term, borrowed by Connell from Gramsci, refers to a particular form of masculinity which is dominant in society, which exercises its power over other, rival masculinities, and which regulates male power over women and distributes this power, differentially, amongst men. Feminists have long argued that men collectively have power over women. The advance of critical men's studies has been to disaggregate this idea and show that not all men have the same amount of power or benefit equally from it, and that power is exercised differently depending on the location and the specific arrangement of relations which are in place. Hegemonic masculinity does not rely on brute force for its efficacy, but on a range of mechanisms which create a gender consensus that legitimates the power of men.

There are two approaches to the issue of hegemony. One approach based on cultural studies and post-structuralism, posits a constantly changing hegemonic masculinity. For example, in specific situations it might be possible to see a constant shifting of hegemony as the complex of power is woven by participating actors, each with agency and capacity

(Cornwall and Lindisfarne 1994). This approach credits every person with some power and is useful in instances of micro analysis. The weakness of this approach is that it can lose sight of the big picture and the universal truth that feminists have noted and fought against for two hundred years – that gender relations are power relations and men have power. A second approach based on a multilayered model of gender power, insists that hegemonic masculinity is a structured relationship in which in highly complex ways power is distributed between men and women in unequal ways. There are objections to the use of the concept of hegemonic masculinity – that it is imprecise and that it is too rigid to capture the complexities of gender power – yet it remains indispensable for the purposes of analysing relations between men, and between men and wider society.

A number of theorists addressing the issue of power, and specifically patriarchal power, have identified social locations where such power is produced and reproduced (Walby 1990). Connell (1987) has theorised three levels of gender power – labour, power (identified as multiple actions which include force and decision by one [male] person over another [female] person) and cathexis (the social structure of sexuality and emotions). In the chapters that follow, the authors examine the ways in which the power of men is produced and exercised in different situations. The authors show how critical other social factors are in understanding masculinity, which serves as a caution against studying gender relations in isolation.

Race and class are of major importance in determining how men understand their masculinity, how they deploy it, and in what form the patriarchal dividend comes to them. In the next section a brief history of South African masculinity will be unfolded in which the salience of these factors will become apparent. For the moment, however, it is necessary to point to existing literature to identify the ways in which the factors of race and class have thus far been treated.

Black masculinity is a significant area of study in the USA. Scholars such as Robert Staples and Marlon Ross have pointed out that blacks are underrepresented when it comes to positions of power and wealth, and are overrepresented in prisons (Ross 1998). Announcing a new aspect of minority politics, Staples calls for special attention to be given to black American men. The success of feminism in focusing attention on the disadvantaged lot of women has had the unintended consequence of making the problems of black men invisible and depriving them of a voice to state their case (Staples 1982: 3). Another approach to race and masculinity comes from Harry Stecopoulos and Michael Uebel (1997) who examine the construction of male subjectivity in the context of race. Their starting point (shared by various contributors in this book) is identity politics and the idea that people have multiple identities. This approach is particularly powerful in dealing with literary and media representations of masculinity. It exposes the racialised nature of representation and maps its effects on the male body and mind. Yet it seldom moves to examine lived reality, life on the street, in the factory, and/or on the sportfield. It is removed from such realities and often lacks a dialogical connection with the material world.

In Britain, black masculinity is also understood as a minority masculinity, reflecting the demographic and social realities of that country. Two scholars who have examined the lives of black men have both sited their studies in the troubled contexts in which many live their lives – schools and the street. Salie Westwood examines racism and the oppositional reflex of young black men to the power of white authority in the street, while Mairtin Mac an Ghaill (1994) takes his investigation into a comprehensive (government) school where he comes to similar findings – of young black men developing counter-cultural expression and a bodily toughness that speaks of resistance to condescension.

The British approach is more helpful for an understanding of race in South Africa because it is more sensitive to the overlap of class and race. Yet its applicability to South Africa is limited because, as with the USA, it handles race as a minority unit of analysis.

There are many studies which have looked at working class masculinity. Most stress the importance of the workplace and wage-earning activities and show the tension between class alienation and gender power. Thomas Dunk's study (1991) of the small Canadian town of Thunder Bay describes a white working class, showing its racism, its liking for sport, popular culture and male pursuits and its exclusionary and dismissive attitude towards women. Cynthia Cockburn (1983) examines British workers in the workplace facing the pressures of mechanisation and the assault on class organisation. Here too she finds a reactive quality in the masculinity of the skilled print craftsmen which expresses itself in their defensive battle against the restructuring of the industry and in their attack on the position and entry of women into the trade. And in Australia, Bob Connell (1991) shows how the process of becoming a working class 'lad' and the absence of clear life opportunities has a dispiriting and dangerous outcome on the way young unemployed whites consider and conduct themselves. All of these studies place conditions of material life, especially the labour market, the workplace and the job, at the centre of their analysis of working class masculinity.

## The history of masculinities in twentieth century southern Africa[2]

Masculinities in southern Africa both reflect the region's turbulent past and have been a cause of that turbulent past. In 1900 the sub-continent was at war. The two Boer republics were on the offensive driving the numerically superior British forces back. Africans, theoretically uninvolved and non-aligned, were engaged in wars of their own, seeking to reclaim lands lost during wars of dispossession in the nineteenth century or attempting to claim a niche in the labour market as well-paid labourers, or forced, in some cases, to serve on one or other side. But the war in the first instance was a reflection of an aggressive masculinity implicit in imperial policy and visible in the person of Lord Alfred Milner, the High Commissioner who precipitated war with the independent Republics. The masculinity of the men of the Boer Republics was complicit too – its 'independence loving' aspect concealed a willingness to resolve disputes by fighting and an unbending resolve to defend 'the Boer way of life'. Amongst the African participants too, a masculinity which held martial achievements to be the highest mark of a man, contributed to the rapid escalation and bloody conclusion of the war. Masculinity and violence have been yoked together in South African history.

North of the Limpopo River, the imperial dreams of Rhodes and his obsession with painting Africa red, of controlling land and people, of realising an ambition with scant regard for the human cost, was generating conflict too. Occupation of parts of 'Rhodesia' soon sparked off a war (1893) and a rebellion (1896–7). Ideas of racist superiority and a willingness to translate these views into inhumane and brutal policies rapidly produced a racial schism in Rhodesia. It was to take a costly guerilla war by the Zimbabwe African National Union (ZANU) and the Zimbabwe African People's Union (ZAPU) in the 1960s and 70s to formally destroy jingoistic white settler rule. But by that time, African patriarchy had blended with the materialist orientations of capitalism, spawning political intolerance and ethnic tensions. A state-sponsored cult of the individual was established. President Robert Mugabe developed a militaristic and homophobic programme safely beyond public criticism. He licensed the deployment of the North Korean trained 5th brigade against 'dissidents' in Matabeleland, the bloody involvement of troops in the war in the Democratic Republic of Congo, and public attacks on the emerging gay movement. The promise of a socialist revolution with an attendant pledge of women's liberation, so fresh in the early 1980s, evaporated into poverty and authoritarianism.

South of the Limpopo River, the end of the war in 1902 left the land basically divided between white commercial landowners and small-plot farmers and African subsistence and peasant farmers. In the case of the African farmers, disintegrative forces within the formerly independent and autonomous polities became exaggerated. A class of black farmer which had emerged in the late nineteenth century sought incorporation into the emerging British colony of the Union of South Africa. Called 'Black Victorians', the men and women of this class modelled themselves on metropolitan images of manhood. Accumulation and prayer, habits of industry and purity were incorporated into the emerging gender identities of the *amakholwa* and the Eastern Cape peasant class. Those less fortunate, or less enamoured with the opportunities of the market economy and more sanguine about being admitted into white society, were corralled in rural areas where traditional forms of authority and justice still held sway. Here the chiefs were men, the warriors were men, and, increasingly, the workers who could not avoid the demand for wage labour were men. The African middle class, relatively prosperous, politically articulate and optimistic at the turn of the century was destined to whither away. In its stead, the major configurations of masculinity which emerged as the twentieth century wore on were shaped by two major experiences and traditions. The first was that of the workplace, primarily the mines. The second was rural life which became increasingly impoverished as more and more people were crammed onto smaller and smaller plots of land. Yet in the rural areas, social hierarchies which had preceded colonialism remained in place. Colonialism may have destroyed the material base of the African economies, but it did not destroy the history which was woven into a myriad of gendered rituals which served to legitimate the sexual division of labour and male power. In the countryside, older men commanded respect. They were part of a gender system which had, at its apex, the chief. He dispensed rights to communal land to men alone. He was a law maker and interpreter, a mediator, a diplomat and later on, a tax collector and co-opted official of the white government. Below him were elders, men with a smaller realm of authority and below them, the adult men and, at the bottom of the male hierarchy, the youth, the uninitiated. Public life by and large was a world that belonged to men. Although the public/private division which is a feature of feminist writings in the developed world can be discerned, the divisions in community life were less rigid. While the rights of women were limited, there was a presumption about the importance of community and the essential role that women played within the household and the larger social units.

During the 1920s and 30s South Africa was becoming an increasingly racially divided society. The possibility of a gradual process of racial integration disappeared. Africans were limited to working class positions in the cities and on white farms or could remain in the rural areas as subsistence farmers. But the low productivity of agricultural land in the African reserves impelled increasing numbers of African men to seek wage labour. The process of proletarianisation was skewed since women were generally unable to get either employment or urban residential rights. For African men in the urban areas life was a grim struggle. These men were subjected to the rigours of industrial labour and a racial hierarchy, paid pitifully low wages, and forced to work under hazardous and demanding conditions. They developed ways of surviving which drew on their understanding of what it meant to be a man in the rural areas but also which adapted to their new conditions.

Ways of surviving involved first and foremost ways of combining – ways of preserving friendship networks which echoed those of the home village, its language, rituals, familiarities. The forms of social organisation which emerged among African workers reflected rural life. The age cohort was one form of organisation, bringing men of similar age together with a common purpose, often of defence but also to find jobs and provide assistance for friends newly arrived in the city. Such organisations frequently included an ethnic dimension, fuelled by the divide and rule logic of mine-owners who placed workers in exclusive ethnic compounds. The result of these developments was that new forms of masculinity emerged amongst African men which included notions of work and ethnicity. A reputation of being the quickest shaft diggers was developed amongst BaSotho workers on the gold mines. This was hard and dangerous work, demanding endurance and physical strength. Miners came to tell a story about themselves which made claims about their masculine capacities. This reflected their subordination in a workplace owned and controlled by white capitalists and supervisors and bore the mark of the demands of the gold mining industry for productivity. The result was a Sotho masculinity which came to include the claim that all BaSotho men were physically tough and strong and able to undertake the most dangerous and arduous mining jobs (Guy and Thabane 1988).

While the masculinities which emerged amongst African men testified to the power of colonialism and capitalism, they also showed that masculinity constructed in sites of apparent servitude could nevertheless both challenge ruling class and race prescriptions and remain the gender property of these men. This complex situation – of formal white control but of agency of black labourers – was violently played out underground by black miners and white supervisors in a struggle to impose themselves. Afrikaans-speaking supervisors used violence to assert themselves, a violence legitimated in racist discourse and taught in schools and families.

Black men resisted and thus validated violence as a way of dealing with power inequalities. It is widely claimed that the goldmines made South Africa politically and economically. In this instance, the many violences of South Africa can be traced back to the gold mines as well (Breckenridge 1998).

During the 1930s, the threat of a white working class uprising which had flared up in the 1922 Rand Rebellion, was dissipated by economic growth and diversification. Work at a 'civilised' wage was found for most formerly unemployed or unprofitable small-holding white farmers. A racial solidarity which had been threatened by the ethnic differences between Afrikaans- and English-speakers became less of an issue and a number of integrative forces (for example, compulsory and free education for whites) promoted racial homogeneity. In this period, metropolitan values of manhood were disseminated through British-controlled commerce, industry, finance and government administration. Some Afrikaans-speaking men were still united by a Republican masculinity (Swart 1998). They yearned for a return to the days of Boer independence when men had more autonomy, were relatively free from a tyrannical state or employer and during which the extended family presided over by a patriarch still existed free from the ravages of urbanisation. Republican masculinity and continuing domination of politics and economy by English-speakers promoted a new Afrikaner nationalism with an attendant, modernised form of ethnic masculinity. The desire for freedom from British influence and superiority over blacks was interpreted into a new masculinity which stressed the importance of independence, resourcefulness, physical and emotional toughness, ability to give and (depending on your position) take orders, of being moral and God-fearing. These values were gendered in the church, the schools, community meetings, on the sportsfields and in the Afrikaans media. English-speaking white men supported the South African Party, the dominant political party, in its policy of developing a national identity. Part of this policy was to reduce ethnic tension. This resulted in the gradual reduction of the jingoistic excesses which were associated with the form of masculinity found in British public schools. Two World Wars had brought the white men of South Africa together. The national obsession with sport ensured that many of the features of masculinity that start wars and make their waging possible – dogmatism, belief in divine support, willingness to take risks, capacity to ignore danger and put up with discomfort, little regard for the rights of others, the worship of the body – were carried through into the 1950s.

The Second World War was a turning-point for much of the world, and the process of decolonisation gathered speed thereafter. The process of decolonisation may well have been partly the product of the changes in masculinity which the devastation of war wrought. The confidence and optimism that took nations to war was replaced by a new caution, a willingness to renounce control, to hand over the instruments of rule to indigenous people. The old model of masculinity was remoulded and reshaped in the next thirty years bringing to the West a major challenge to the *status quo*, offering up new formulations of the meaning of life and of being a man. While much of the world grooved to rock and roll, to the sound of anti-Vietnam war chants and John Lennon's 'Give Peace a Chance', South Africa showed that there was nothing automatic about the direction of change. Far from taking up the flame of counter-culture, South Africa got stuck in a McCarthy-like era. The men who had not fought against Hitler were amongst those who brought the National Party to power in 1948. Borrowing heavily on German iconography and some of the ideas of national socialism, the Afrikaner National Party froze South African society in the 1950s. The apartheid policy was introduced in 1948. Not only was the discourse of the state filled with the language of separation, service, obedience and the communist threat, its apparatus was expanded to throw a highly controlled web of regulations over, particularly, the country's black population.

While elsewhere in the world, indigenous people were experimenting with new-found political rights, and in the First World young people were making love not war, South African men were subject to very different pressures and influences.

Production under apartheid extended the process of ultra-exploitation to the manufacturing industry. Employment levels were high for whites and blacks, but working conditions and remuneration for work were hugely different. Whites remained in supervisory jobs and continued to relate to black employees from a *baasskap* (master or boss) position. With virtually no protection from government or from trade unions (which were banned) the African worker was brutalised. Death in the course of work – either from accidents, diseases, or from punitive and violent forms of labour control – was routine. It was hardly surprising that in the newly created townships for Africans, a violent masculinity took root, particularly among the youth and their gangs. Africans were paid very little, crime became rampant, and both in the execution of crime and in its control (by township residents) violence became common.

The history of masculinity is not made exclusively by men. Women opposed certain aspects of masculinity and supported others. They did so in ways that reflected the class and race forces discussed above. A history

Robert Morrell

of South African femininities has not yet been written, although there are a large number of works on women. For our purposes we need to note that while women operated in oppressive gender contexts, many supported 'their' men. This support ranged from white women sending food parcels to their 'boys on the border' in the 1970s and 80s, to black women like Winnie Madikizela Mandela, advocating the killing of spies and collaborators in the turbulent 1980s. Race and class loyalties and political agendas were often stronger than gender subordination. This should not obscure the fact that the struggle against gender oppression and efforts to live with or to accommodate it is a constant theme in the history of South African women.

An analysis of the state cannot ever be reduced to its gender composition, but it is also not incidental to the state's policies. The South African government was made up of men – Afrikaans-speaking, white men. They espoused an establishment masculinity which was authoritarian, unforgiving and unapologetic. This kind of masculinity was forged in the Afrikaans-medium, all-white schools, and reinforced in such institutions as the *veldskole* (schools for field craft) and in the commandos. After 1961, when the Sharpeville shooting pushed South Africa to become independent and leave the Commonwealth, the military was already an important force within government. By the end of the decade, it was virtually in control of government. A system of commandos bound white men living in the rural areas to active involvement on a yearly basis in the military, while at the end of the 1960s all white men were eligible for conscription into the army, airforce or navy. A passive white population accepted these developments not only because it believed government propaganda about '*swartgevaar*' (the danger posed by blacks) but also because the idea of being a man – being a protector, a wage-earner and knowing the right thing to do – made such steps seem perfectly logical. By 1970 South Africa was a highly militarised state with a panoply of repressive instruments to deal with those who did not agree with the direction of government policy.

The apartheid era was a critical period for black people in South Africa. It created ethnic labels and promoted ethnic identities. Indian, coloured and various 'tribal' African identities were fostered. A hierarchy of races was created by differential state spending which in turn determined that most Africans would be in menial labouring positions, Indians and coloureds in artisanal or protected enclaves of the labour market, and whites in supervisory and professional positions. Race and class were thus manipulated by the state and this affected gender identity. South Africa became atomised. The social distance between people of different races

17

was increased by laws that prevented the sharing of leisure time and facilities such as schools and sports venues, and absolutely prohibited mixed marriages. By contrast, there were activities that dented the totality of the apartheid masterplan. Sport was very popular with black and white men alike. Whites tended to be initiated into sport at an early age as spectators (mainly of rugby, cricket and soccer) and participants (at school where sport was compulsory). Sports facilities at school for Africans, and to a lesser extent coloureds and Indians, were non-existent. Nevertheless, soccer gained a wide following amongst Africans while rugby was played and watched by black people in the western and eastern Cape. As political isolation robbed the country of international competition, provincial competition became all the more fierce. Andre Brink, the South African novelist, described an effect of the obsessive preoccupation with sport: 'On the playing fields themselves, foul play came to elicit admiration. South Africa's greatest rugby heroes tended to be those known to instil terror in their opponents through the violence of their dirty tricks' (*Weekly Mail and Guardian*, 30 June–6 July 1995).

To conclude this historical section it is possible to offer a partial explanation for the observation about the chauvinism of South African men. South Africa, until recently, was a man's country. Power was exercised publicly and politically by men. In families, both black and white, men made decisions, earned the money, and held power. The law (both customary and modern) supported the presumption of male power and authority and discriminated against women. But the country's history also produced brittle masculinities – defensive and prone to violence. For white men, the uneven distribution of power gave them privileges but also made them defensive about challenges (by women, blacks, and/or other men) to that privilege. For black men, the harshness of life on the edge of poverty and the emasculation of political powerlessness gave their masculinity a dangerous edge. Honour and respect were rare, and getting it and retaining it (from white employers, fellow labourers or women) was often a violent process. Men in South Africa were chauvinistic, but this description is too sweeping and loaded to advance analysis or to capture the diversity of their experiences. In the following two sections, the differing positions and responses of men to transition will be discussed.

## South Africa in transition

In 1990 Nelson Mandela was released from prison and a transition period to the first non-racial elections was initiated. From the point of view of masculinity, the heartening thing about this was the evidence that it provided that the content of masculinity was not fixed and unchangeable.

The men who agreed to this landmark shift had earlier been committed to a military defence of white privilege or the armed overthrow of white rule.

In 1994, following the first democratic election, the Government of National Unity was created. Twenty-five per cent of the new parliament were women, including the Speaker of the House and three cabinet ministers. This was in stark contrast to the male-dominated parliaments of previous years. Once in power, the ANC used its parliamentary strength to promote a vigorous gender campaign. This was in good measure the result of a well-organised women's lobby and the work of the Women's National Coalition. In the next few years, the following were established: the Office of the Status of Women in the Deputy President's office, the Special Standing Committee on Women and the Women's Empowerment Unit in parliament, as well as the Commission on Gender Equality.

The second national election in 1999 increased to 30 per cent the number of women in parliament. More significantly, 24 per cent of cabinet ministers were women, and over half of the deputy ministers. The interventionist role taken by the state in reshaping gender relations is significant and will be discussed further below, but understandably the implementation of policy and the actual impact on existing gender relations has been uneven. Views about the progress made (which specifically focus on the improvement in the position of women) range from uneven progress (Sadie and Loots 1998), to the laying of a platform for more thorough gender change in the near future (Hassim and Gouws 1998), to the lament that economic change is very slow and non-existent in some areas (Makgetla 1995; Taylor 1997).

The shape, composition and policies of the state changed dramatically in the 1990s, but the direction of the economy did not. Fears were expressed by economists in the early 1990s that South Africa might opt for a '50% solution' in which white control of the economy would be broken and the middle class would become racially integrated, but the nature of the economy would be left effectively unchanged (Morris 1991). A '100% solution' would involve a commitment to redistribution and redress which would prioritise addressing unemployment and the racially skewed labour market. Critics now suggest that these concerns were warranted (Marais 1998). The number of unemployed people has risen and poverty is widespread (May 1999). As the chapters that follow show, these factors have had important consequences for gender change. High levels of poverty allied with rising expectations have proved a tragic mixture for fostering the growth of violent masculinities.

The 1990s were marked by very high levels of violent crime. Bank robberies, car hijackings, assaults, murders and rapes all reached alarming levels. By 1996, according to figures released by the World Health Organisation, South Africa had the highest rate of violent death in the world. The rate of 57 per 100 000 was down from 64,6/100 000 in 1995, but still eight times higher than in the USA (*Sunday Tribune*, 12 May 1996), and contrasted even further with New Zealand rates of 2,37/100 000 (*Daily News*, 23 September 1999). South Africa has the highest rate of rape in the world with an estimated one million women raped a year (*Weekly Mail and Guardian*, 2–8 July 1999). It is second only to Colombia as the country with the highest number of gun-related homicides. Levels of gun ownership are very high – there are thirteen million firearms in a country of forty million people. Seven hundred people apply for gun licences every day (*Independent on Saturday*, 17 July 1999). South Africa also has one of the highest rates of AIDS infection in the world. According to 1996 figures, 1,8 million people were HIV positive in that year (Leclerc-Madlala 1997: 363). Since then the epidemic has gathered pace, and as a result life expectancy has dropped. It has been predicted that by 2005 only 13 per cent of the population will reach the age of 40 (*Independent on Saturday*, 8 May 1999). Some insight into these trends is provided by Carol Bower, Cape Town Rape Crisis Director: 'There is a high level of tolerance (of rape) in all our communities . . . in general the attitudes that prevail are attitudes that women are under obligation to do what they are told and they deserve what they get' (*Weekly Mail and Guardian*, 2–8 July 1999).

Government intervention and social violence are both predicated upon existing gender relations and constructions of masculinity, and both factors in turn influence such constructions. In the following section, the factors that have affected men will be examined.

## Motors and sites of change

What changes masculinities? It is tempting to answer this question with a decisive flourish, to proclaim a particular agent as the cause of change. In reality, changes in masculinity are highly complex and are better understood as part of society which Mann terms 'a patterned mess' (1993: 1). There is often a gap between intention and effect, though generally speaking it is easier to understand changes in masculinity by examining specific moments, institutions and actors. In the previous section I attempted some generalisations in order to provide some context, to chart some historical themes and to give a sense of the bigger picture.

The state is the most important single agent of change. It is both the result of the political transition and the catalyst and motor of transition.

As Bob Connell (1990) has argued, the state creates gender categories and shapes them. While it is often the primary protector of the gender order it can be a force for change although this is never unambiguous.

In times of transition the state (and its citizenry) becomes involved in issues of masculinity whether it likes it or not. In post-war Germany, for example, the state dealt with a crisis of masculinity and anxieties about national and racial identity, by remasculinising the war-ravaged country (Moeller 1998). This was a project built on the ruins of defeat. It sought to create a new image of the German man which had no link with the disgraced Nazi past. Part of this public campaign also involved cleansing the returning soldiers of their violence. There was a conscious attempt to move German men away from militarism and to locate them in the home and at work (Jefford 1998).

In South Africa, the context is different. The state is a symbol of victory – victory over apartheid. Yet its circumstances have some things in common with the German state of the 1950s. Many of its men have been involved in military actions. Women are more involved and influential in the economy and public life than before. The state is trying to stabilise and unite a country, it is engaged in nation building, and its male citizens are unsettled and unsure of their place in the new order.

Since 1994 the state has been visibly working on principles of gender equality, but the gender work of its predecessors was much less obvious. In many of the chapters in this book the hand of the state is evident without the state itself appearing to be the primary actor. The gender interventions of the state in the 1990s are clearly revealed by Thokozani Xaba. His chapter shows how the changing position of the liberation elite – from 'state in exile' to government – is reflected in changing gender values. Violence in the liberation struggle was noble and necessary. In the new South Africa, it is criminal and destructive. This is not just a case of images, representation and value. As Xaba shows, the changing political landscape has led young African men to choose crime and violence, and they have been transformed in the public mind from heroes to villains.

The post-1994 state is caught up in the contradictions of its own violent past as well as in the legacy inherited from the previous state. Jacklyn Cock's chapter shows that the state has not moved decisively to demilitarise society and its 1999 decision to spend R3 billion on rearming its security forces is testimony to this.

The South African state has always played a major role in the economy and it is in the workplace where specific masculinities are formed and performed. The gold mines have been the backbone of the country's economy for over a century. They have depended upon and institutionalised a male, African, migrant labour source. Catherine Campbell and Dunbar Moodie examine how the dangerous nature of the work and the particular living conditions of the compounds have combined to give expression to particular and, in some cases, dangerous forms of sexuality, and how the emotional bleakness of the compounds has given rise to particular social bonds which replicate family life in the men's rural homes and which provide emotional sustenance. Migrant labour has been a feature of life for African men living in the rural areas for one and a half centuries. Benedict Carton describes the tensions that this form of labour produces in his examination of a rural area in KwaZulu-Natal. The homecoming of young migrants imports rough urban values and unsettles the rule of the rural patriarchs – challenging the generational hierarchy and its associated values of respect and deference.

The apartheid state also played a major role in racialising space in the country. In the black townships boys were brought up in a socially fractured environment with little prospect of well-paid work. Many thus turned to crime. The process of growing up took boys through the stage of being youths. It was (and still is) in this stage that many became acquainted and involved with crime. In the apartheid period, the hopelessness of this situation was temporarily ameliorated by heroic involvement in 'the struggle' (Hemson 1996). But with the ending of the struggle, the youth remained stuck in situations that were often hopeless. As Katharine Wood and Rachel Jewkes show, the unavailability of work, an essential part of working class masculinities around the world, placed greater emphasis on heterosexual activity, which confirmed gender power inequalities, fuelling gender violence as it did so, and confirmed the vulnerability and pain that African township youth experience. The allure of crime is discussed by Xaba and by Sean Field. The latter shows how deeply alienating township life can be. Field's study of two men shows how township life contributed to toughness being revered as an essential part of masculinity. But he also shows that toughness could be used 'respectably' (in sport) or violently as a way of becoming a criminal.

On the other side of the fence, apartheid created white suburbs. These housed men assured of jobs (at least before the mid-1980s), who had family homes, stable environments, status and political influence. Kobus du Pisani shows how in the ethnically defined and contained Afrikaans-speaking community, a hegemonic Afrikaner masculinity developed which identified the following features as desirable elements of masculinity: white, financially independent, Protestant, mature (over 25 years old), and of irreproachable personality. This form of masculinity nestled comfortably in the patriarchal Afrikaner family though it also showed itself adept at responding to change. Media images derived from emergent mass culture in the USA and, later on, the energy of self-made men like Anton Rupert and Jan Marais shifted the centre of hegemonic Afrikaner masculinity so that it was more materialist and competitive, particularly in sport. But it remained in relative terms socially and politically conservative, and it remained hostile to black, English and working class challenges to its prescriptions. The dilution of white privilege by the De Klerk government in the 1980s affected the lower levels of the middle and skilled working classes. In addition, the withdrawal of support from unprofitable white farms threatened the livelihoods of many small farmers. These were mostly Afrikaans-speaking men. Thus it was that a bellicose right-wing movement emerged under the leadership of Eugene Terre Blanche. According to Sandra Swart this movement attempted to keep white supremacy alive. Its methods, born of desperation, were violent and its politics dogmatic. Swart calls the masculinity of this movement 'hard' to distinguish it from the 'soft' masculinity of the government 'doves' who were, at that time, seeking negotiated reform.

Competitive team sports have been important in South Africa for much of the twentieth century. Even when sport was racially segregated men, particularly in urban areas, were obsessed with it. Black and white men, usually in racially separate groups, participated and spectated in large numbers throughout the century. Sport, particularly the major winter sports of soccer and rugby, were woven into hegemonic masculinities. Men required knowledge in order to follow and talk about sport. They needed bodily skills and toughness to participate and compete successfully. While these attributes were generic amongst men, race and class and sport type generated different emphases. Soccer played by black township children and men, for example, developed into a showcase of artistry. Clever feet were the hallmark of the best soccer players. To dribble and show off, to please the crowd was what players aspired to do well. Amongst white rugby players, the emphasis was much more on physical and mental toughness and winning. Skill counted for little unless it could be turned into victory. Rugby stressed physical confrontation, perseverance and skill, and these were equated with white masculinity.

Amongst minor sports like surfing, alternative masculinities failed to emerge. Despite the promise of its 'hippy' origins and its early emphasis on recreation, surfing became highly competitive and commercialised. Glen Thompson argues that surfing was a sport for boys who couldn't play rugby – mostly English-speaking boys and men from the coast. Over time, the leisure orientation which offered some chance of a more tolerant, anti-authoritarian sport, became competitive and commoditised. It developed its own macho orientation. The racist context of the sport (it was for whites only in the 1970s) and the strength of consumerist culture ultimately blunted its transformative capacity.

The beautiful beaches and seas of South Africa were only in the early 1990s made accessible to black South Africans. Until then beaches were racially segregated and there were few opportunities for black people to participate in aquatic sports. Political transformation, however, has given African township youth the opportunity to engage with the sea and realise their bodies in new ways. Crispin Hemson studies the African Zulu-speaking youth of a Durban township, and demonstrates how lifesaving offers a way of escaping poverty and of constructing new forms of masculinity. Township youth generally live dangerous lives on the edges of crime. Their lives are characterised by little life opportunity and a randomness which finds expression in anti-social activity, drug abuse, and a heavy emphasis on heterosexual expressions of masculinity. Lifesaving offers an escape and the opportunity to construct different ways of being. The escape is from the monoracial environment of townships to the multiracial environment of the beaches where the youngsters confront the race hierarchies that are the legacy of apartheid South African. The new masculinities constructed in this environment draw on a traditional Zulu lexicon of masculinity and rough township masculinities which emphasise perseverance and self-confidence respectively. The result, evident in the bodily conscious, confident and resilient lifesavers offers some insights into what a new South African masculinity, freed from the dominating force of poverty, might look like.

South Africa has compulsory education for all and schooling is potentially one of the great integrative social forces of the new South Africa. However, schools are wracked by violence and not many people see them as an avenue to escape poverty. Having a tertiary level education qualification, however, remains a passport into the middle class. In Zimbabwe, Rob Pattman looks at a cohort of students in a Teachers' Training College. Here he sees how the opportunity to enter the middle class by becoming a professional (teacher) is contradictorily associated with misogynistic features of township culture and antagonism towards white privilege and the colonial past. The construction of a post-colonial masculinity involves affirming Zimbabwean nationalism whilst silencing competing masculinities which are emerging amongst less affluent and secure African men and which are more critical of the classed nature of the *status quo*.

Discussions about men in the new South Africa can be understood in terms of the discourses used. Rival interpretations and prescriptions about men coalesce as discourses. So, for example, in the British context concern about the academic achievement of boys is expressed in terms of boys as victims of a girl-centred education system, boys as essentially non-academic, and boys as victims (equally with girls) of poor schools (Epstein, Elwood, Hey and Maw 1998). A similar set of discourses can be discerned in South Africa – men as victims of the advancement of women, men as naturally violent and competitive, and men as victims (equally with women) of policies such as structural adjustment.

In a transitional society such as South Africa, the question of which discourse is hegemonic is a complex one. The pre-existing, formerly hegemonic white masculinity continues to exert influence via media images and through institutions (particularly business) in which such masculinity remains embedded. Since all masculinities influence one another and are never discrete and bounded entities, elements of white masculinity can still be seen in many other masculinities, primarily in the emphasis on achievement and appearance, which are features of a commoditised society. Yet masculinities that formerly were oppositional – urban black and rural African masculinities – are now jostling for ascendancy. The emerging masculinities draw on competing images and legacies. One of the most powerful masculinities centres on Nelson Mandela and has been termed a 'heroic masculinity' by Elaine Unterhalter (1999). Others derive their existence from the egalitarian world of transnational agencies (like the United Nations) which emphasise human rights and gender equity.

Struggles over masculinity are ceaseless. Even before the new state was inaugurated in 1994, political parties were using particular images of masculinity to project their image and gain supporters. Waetjen and Maré argue, in the case of the Inkatha Freedom Party and its rivals the ANC and the Congress of South African Trade Unions (COSATU), that gender values were tied up with ethnic representations and had major implications for the type of utopian society each imagined. Inkatha's Zulu masculinity selectively used aspects of rural African masculinity to contrast itself with the urban-leaning COSATU. Inkatha's model was authoritarian and explicitly patriarchal, invoking values of obedience and responsibility as those central to manhood. In the context of Zimbabwe, the existing gender order was challenged by the installation of a female chief. As Björn Lindgren shows, this challenged the idea about exclusive male power and decision-making. Local support for the female chief was based on kinship. National opposition was framed in the language that still holds the public world to be naturally male-dominated. The tensions between local and national and the way in which such loyalties cut across gender conventions show how volatile gender relations are. In the face of gender challenges, the defenders of hegemonic masculinity are vigilant, guarding male privilege and recreating a gendered discourse for this purpose.

Historically the racial and interventionist nature of the state has profoundly shaped gender relations. It has divided black from white men and it has consigned most black men to servile, labouring conditions or to positions of unemployment. The new state has the capacity to reverse this situation, but it will take a long time and the effects of globalisation will tend to slow down the rate of change.

## Masculinities in transition

No one masculinity or group alone is likely to be the carrier of new values. Gender change is a highly complex process and it occurs within individuals, within groups and within institutions. Yet it is important to look for signs of change, even if these, as Lynn Segal (1990) has observed, tend to occur in slow motion.

The responses of men to changes in South Africa can be grouped into three categories: reactive or defensive, accommodating, and responsive or progressive. These are not watertight categories and there are always areas of overlap and contradiction. For example, the black, urban youth masculinity described by Crispin Hemson still contains a worrying capacity for violence. Yet it also is anti-individualist and communitarian and is engaged in a project of redefinition that is essential for gender change. Consequently, the categories are used here as a way of mapping the field and making sense of a wide range of responses amongst men to the experience of transition.

### Reactive or defensive responses

In the first category, men have attempted to turn back changes in order to reassert their power. This is captured in the amusing bumper sticker, 'Forget about the whale, Rather save the white male.' One of the few explicit organisational manifestations of this is the South African Association of Men (SAAM) which was launched in 1994, shortly before the elections which heralded an end to white minority rule. Primarily a white, middle class organisation, its goal was to fight discrimination against men in order to 'restore the tattered remains of the male image' (quoted in Lemon 1995: 61). It explicitly dedicates itself to challenging modern feminism whose core is said to contain 'an often-vicious loathing of traditional masculinity' (O'Malley 1994: 26). The language of 'crisis' infuses the movement's discourse. It is not coincidental that the movement emerged at a time when white men were facing their greatest challenge. In the political sphere, government was being 'taken over' by blacks; in the business world, affirmative action policies were 'giving jobs to blacks'; and in public spaces, gay men were openly flaunting their sexuality, a clear sign that the homophobic grip of hegemonic masculinity was losing its strength. Since then, a large stratum of white opinion has harped on the 'crisis' in South Africa. Attention has been directed at the failings of the new government, the rising crime rate, the decline in white standards of living, and net (white) emigration. Commenting on these developments, a professor at the Rand Afrikaans University engaged in a study of the psychological effects of car hijackings, delivered the opinion that 'South African society stood a chance of "a total breakdown"' (*Natal Mercury*, 30 October 1995).

Not all masculinist responses have been racially exclusive or middle class. In September 1999 the Promise Keepers was launched in a Pretoria rugby stadium by Dr David Molapo. The gathering, with overt Christian overtones, was attended by thirty thousand men and was dedicated to creating 'good role models' for the country (*Natal Mercury*, 20 September 1999). The initiative received a mixed reception from observers. Men were commended for doing something to 'raise the standard' and take responsibility. The racially integrated nature of the launch and its sheer scale were also impressive. But it was also observed that this was a men's only movement. Women were excluded, thus perpetuating the idea that decision-making and action in the public sphere were the domain of men (*Weekly Mail and Guardian*, 17–22 September 1999).

In the 1990s there was a rise of vigilante movements dedicated to protecting children from drugs, wives and daughters from rape, and society from lawlessness. These movements have a class agenda too – upholding the rights of property owners. But these concerns should not be construed in a narrow way. Security of possession and safety from crime are concerns for a large swathe of black and white people who have some stake in the current *status quo*. Men have presented themselves as protectors and dispensers of justice. In the Northern Province, Gauteng and Mpumalanga, white farmers and black businessmen, township residents and farm labourers have formed an organisation called Mabogo. It is much feared, hunting down criminals and dispensing brutal justice on the spot. A number of those assaulted have died. There is no specific gender message in what Mabogo does, but it is predicated on a reactive agenda of restoring male authority. Another initiative directing itself to the 'protection of male rights' is the movement by fathers to claim paternity rights. In some countries, like Norway and Sweden, this has been a major area of gender equality work, but in South Africa (and in many other countries such as the USA) men have been galvanised *against* women to claim access to children. In Durban, for example, TUFF (The Unmarried Fathers' Fight) has been established as a support group as well as a lobby to contest laws which discriminate against unmarried fathers (*Sunday Tribune,* 22 October 1995).

The appalling rise in incidents of rape in South Africa can also be considered as a masculinist response to transition. Among the most blatant statements in this regard comes from a member of the South African Rapist Association which was formed in a Gauteng township in the early 1990s. Objecting to being politically sidelined by 'senior comrades' in the run-up to the 1994 elections, a member said:

> We rape women who need to be disciplined (those women who behave like snobs), they just do not want to talk to people, they think they know better than most of us and when we struggle, they simply do not want to join us. (Goldblatt and Meintjes 1997: 14)

The feminist view that rape (and other related acts of violence, for example, spousal abuse) is one way of asserting the dominance of men over women is certainly borne out by comparative studies. In Zambia Dalene Rude (1999) has shown how widespread such violence (in this case leading to death) is, and how ineffectual the law has been in protecting women from these vicious attacks.

For African men the last few decades have seen the erosion of their positions in this country and elsewhere in Africa (Silberschmidt 1992). Migrant labour is experienced by many men as reducing their male prerogative:

> The kind of life [in the hostel] was very difficult. Because at home I live with my wife who does everything at home. But now everything changes. Because I left my family I am the only person responsible for cooking, washing my clothes and dishes and cleaning the room. After work, I am tired but I have to cook for my supper. Because I don't want to cook I have to eat bread and tea. (quoted in Von Kotze 1996: 156–7)

In this situation, men long for the rural areas where they were respected and 'treated "like a man"'. Women bore the brunt of these feelings of emasculation and compensatory entitlement. Rural women described the situation as follows: 'the countryside (is) a drunkard's paradise, where men

Robert Morrell

come home to drink and lord it over women, only to leave them again, penniless and pregnant with another child' (Von Kotze 1996: 157). But the situation is changing as women gain independent access to land, income and positions of authority.

In the countryside, laws to give women access to land, to allow them to open bank accounts and generally to free them from dependence have not been welcomed. In 1995 in KwaZulu-Natal, Dr Sibongile Zungu was appointed chief, breaking male monopoly of this position. Opposition was so fierce that she was forced to resign within a few years. The guardians of African patriarchy have not only reacted to the challenge of women. The youth have been shrugging off the power of their fathers and, during the 1980s, challenged that power openly, leading to bloody confrontations (Campbell 1992). Particularly during the 1980s, older black men responded violently to the generational challenge, often forming vigilante groups to 'put young men in their place'.

*Accommodating responses*

Not all men have responded defensively. In the second category of responses, some which are apparently traditionalist and might be considered defensive can in fact be understood as attempts to resuscitate non-violent masculinities. One example is the intiation practices amongst African youth. The practice of circumcision has never been stopped and, if anything, it is currently on the increase in rural and urban areas. Tragically high death rates from botched circumcision operations are one measure of the spread of the practice. Being initiated into manhood has strong ethnic connotations but it also invokes the ideal of manhood which is responsible, respectful and wise. This is distinct from the anti-social masculinities of many of the street youth where the knife, crime, rough behaviour and a loyalty to one's gang and nobody else are more the norm. A different kind of initiation occurs amongst adult men in the Soweto Flying Squad. Here the rituals are new and informal, and the penalty of failing to adhere to them can be death. The members of the Flying Squad create and are united by a masculinity forged in the dangerous world of crime control. Those who fail the initiation are asked to leave the Squad. This masculinity shows similarities with that of adult men in rural Xhosa society in the first half of the twentieth century. Joan Wardrop argues that this masculinity requires level-headedness and restraint. It rests on a capacity to act, and is combined with a self-knowledge that is necessary to judge when to act. Despite the context, it is a masculinity that dampens violence rather than provokes it.

Some theorists argue that crime and the problems of wild youth are the fault of broken families and absent fathers. They imply that only the restoration of the traditional family will solve the problem. Healthier home environments and loving adults (not necessarily biological fathers) are likely to help. But there are other ways of promoting change and there are factors that are already assisting this process. Up until 1996 thirty thousand boys a year received whipping as a result of court sentences (Pinnock 1997). Millions of children received corporal punishment at school each year. The formal end to state violence against children will provide a healthier context for youth work in the future.

For township youth who do not look to 'tradition' for their inspiration, there are other ways of rejecting violent masculinities which attempt to re-establish the power of men. Crispin Hemson shows how young township men have tried to accommodate change, making sense of their masculinity through two diverse sets of symbols – rural and urban. Sean Field similarly shows how men have tried to move with the times, not always giving up their male power, but also not fighting for the restoration of some pre-existing patriarchal order. Yet the subjectivities that are constructed under the new South African conditions still have to negotiate the legacies of race and class inequality. Kopano Ratele talks to some black 'ouens' (men, 'lads'). His informants are young, urban and educated. Their positions in society are changing and their prospects are improving. They are exploring new ways of being, but they still cling to old ways, not least the claim to superior status over women. In time, the increase of women's economic and public power will challenge (and already is challenging) the discourse of male superiority. In the meantime, processes of asserting racial identities are becoming less violent, slowly being disconnected from an oppositional imperative to be assertive and dogmatic.

The horror of the political violence of the 1970s and 80s has affected many men and they have had to confront their masculinity in the process. In the 1980s Mr Mavundla, a chef from Margate, heard that his wife and son had been murdered in the KwaZulu-Natal civil war. 'I discovered that my wife had been abducted, killed, burned and thrown into a toilet pit', he testified to the Truth and Reconciliation Commission (TRC). 'I am no longer a man – no wife, no home, no family' (*Sunday Tribune*, 18 June 1996). In such situations a range of responses has been possible. The TRC has suggested that, for many, acceptance and forgiveness have been incorporated into new self-understandings of what it is to be a man. The tragedy of AIDS is also contributing to gender change. While, on the one hand, the spread of AIDS is promoted by misogynistic and heterosexual masculinity, its consequences, on the other hand, are forcing men to confront death and its attendant emotions. In the same way as the ghastly

Robert Morrell

killing of the First World War opened the minds of a generation to peace, so AIDS appears to be forcing men to contemplate their mortality and vulnerability (Morrell 1999).

The absence of any widespread male opposition to the improvement in women's positions and to the tolerance of gay men is possibly the most impressive testimony to the accommodationist position, although misogyny and homophobia have far from disappeared.

### Responsive or progressive responses

Evidence of the third category of response, emancipatory masculinities, is most obvious in the gay movement. Ronald Louw's extraordinary tale shows how the gay movement existed in a marginal, if tolerated, position in the heydays of apartheid. Since the early 1990s it has been much more public, jostling for public visibility, claiming the right to representation and acceptance. There has been a dramatic increase in gay literature which would have been banned under the censorship laws of the apartheid regime. *Outright*, a gay magazine, has appeared regularly since 1993. In addition, a major collection of gay and lesbian essays was published in 1994 (Gevisser and Cameron). At the end of 1995 and beginning of 1996 a gay and lesbian art exhibition, entitled Gay Rights Rites Re-Writes, toured the country. It was a conscious attempt by gay artists to contribute to the attempt to enshrine the protection of sexual orientation clause in the Bill of Human Rights then under discussion. The National Coalition for Gay and Lesbian Equality has been very active in publicly championing issues including gaining legal recognition for gay marriages and the removal of sodomy as a criminal offence. Its cause has been assisted by the coming out of Edwin Cameron, a Supreme Court Judge.

In organisational terms, there are many examples of men attempting to challenge violent masculinities and, in so doing, developing new models of how to be men. Possibly the most visible of the organisational responses was in the form of the End Conscription Campaign (ECC). Founded in 1983, it was an organisation of young white men opposed to serving in the South African Defence Force (SADF). It challenged the legitimacy of apartheid generally, but specifically opposed military service against fellow (black) citizens (Nathan 1989). In 1985, half the men conscripted failed to report for service. Banned by the state in 1988, the ECC offered a non-violent, anti-authoritarian vision of masculinity for young white men.

A number of organisations currently work in the field of violence, trying to get men to take responsibility for violence, to condemn it and work for more equitable gender relations, domestically and publicly. Initi-

31

atives have been undertaken that cross gender and race barriers in an attempt to combat violent masculinities. The White Ribbon Campaign (against men's violence against women) and Gun Free South Africa (lobbying for stricter gun laws and a small defence budget) are two examples of such initiatives.

Amongst middle class, mostly white, professionals the idea of the 'new man' is widespread. These men may be involved in men's groups engaged in introspection and gender-consciousness-raising, or they may have an equal division of housework with their partners, or they may be heavily involved in childcare. Some black men are also embracing this new masculinity. Pushed in part by the rise of black women into professional positions which has made it difficult for the traditional sexual division of labour in the home to be maintained, young black male professionals have become much more participatory in the home and supportive of their partners' professional goals (Maforah 1993; Madlala 1995).

While change can be viewed sociologically or collectively, it is also important to note that change can (and does) happen individually. In Jonathan Hyslop's chapter, the author traces the historical development of his own masculinity across three generations. The history is one of colonialism, racial privilege and racial prejudice, but it is also about powerful women (and an implicit challenge to hegemonic ideas of the woman's place) about war-time suffering, humour and endurance, love and loyalty. At the end of it, the author comes out as a man highly critical of injustice, militarism and bigotry. This is paralleled in the novel by Harold Strachan (1998), *Way Up Way Out*, where despite growing up in a parochial provincial setting, being dragooned in an authoritarian schooling system and experiencing the brutalisation of war-time military training, the author also ends up as somebody highly critical of the political and gender order.

This raises the question of where – in which class – one is most likely to find progressive gender change. Romanticism about the working class or liberal dreams about the middle class need to be eschewed. In a range of ways, both working and middle class men are changing, responding to the particular challenges of their circumstances in ways which reflect their class position, but are not determined by it. In the case of Protas Madlala, a black professional trying to enter the spirit of the 'new man', it is the conservative weight of working class men that is the problem: 'It would have been impossible for me to live as a feminist in a working-class, high-density settlement. By now I'd be ostracized by the menfolk who'd ridicule me as *umfazi* (a woman)' (1995: 97). On the other hand, amongst the middle class elites, old boys' networks which ensure that men retain power are still much in operation and sideline women (Madonsela 1995: 30).

There has been no single or clear response to gender conditions in the new South Africa. But the diversity of responses and the relative absence of gendered organisation amongst men should not obscure the fact that the gender order is changing. This is as much an effect of an interventionist state committing itself (at least at the level of policy) to gender equity, as of the small moves made, often in contradictory ways, by men themselves. Hegemonic masculinity has shifted and continues to shift.

## Conclusion

This chapter started with a description of South African men as chauvinistic and misogynistic and, to this could be added, homophobic. The chapters in this book show that there is no one, typical, South African man. They show that there are many different masculinities, some of which support violent and exploitative gender relations, others which accept such gender relations, and still others which oppose them. Consistent threads running through the chapters are the categories of race and class which have taken a particular form under apartheid and whose legacies live on in the new South Africa.

A country such as South Africa which is undergoing radical change, forces gender responses. Some of these are exceedingly violent and may be seen as part of a wider social attempt by men to deal with feelings of emasculation or the actual loss of status and power. However, there are also opportunities for realising gender justice. Such change can be quite rapid – as in the case of state interventions which put gender legislation on the statute books and which, more subtly, attempt a project of remasculinisation to present new images of manhood for the new country. But for the most part gender change is slow. South African men have confronted and will continue to confront conditions which undermine their economic condition and which are likely to cause them to question their masculinity. There are important reasons to believe that the social experiments such as the TRC, movements like ADAPT (the Agisanag Domestic Abuse Prevention and Training) founded by young men to combat domestic violence, and discourses of peace will push South African men in the direction of emancipatory masculinity.

Changing Men in S.A.  – D

NOTES

1. I'd like to thank the following for their comments on this chapter: Bob Connell, Fran Fearnley, Georgina Hamilton, Geoff Schreiner and Sandra Swart.
2. Some of these ideas have been explored in R. Morrell (1998), 'Of Men and Boys: Masculinity and Gender in Southern African Studies', *Journal of Southern African Studies* 24(4).

BIBLIOGRAPHY

Biddulph, S. 1994. *Manhood: An Action plan for changing men's lives.* Stroud: Hawthorn Press.

Breckenridge, K. 1998. 'The Allure of Violence: Men, Race and Masculinity on the South African Goldmines, 1900–1950', *Journal of Southern African Studies* 24(4).

Breines, I. (interviewed by O. Holter) 1999. 'Men, Women and a Culture of Peace', *IASOM Newsletter* 6(2).

Buchbinder, D. 1994. *Masculinities and Identities.* Carlton: Melbourne University Press.

Butler, J. 1990. *Gender Trouble: Feminism and the Subversion of Identity.* London: Routledge.

Campbell, C. 1992. 'Learning to Kill: Masculinity, the Family and Violence in Natal', *Journal of Southern African Studies* 18(3).

Cockburn, C. 1983. *Brothers, Male Dominance and Technological Change.* London: Pluto.

Connell, R.W. 1987. *Gender and Power: Society, the Person and Sexual Politics.* Palo Alto, California: University of California Press.

———. 1990. 'The state, gender, and sexual politics', *Theory and Society* 19.

———. 1991. 'Live Fast and Die Young: The Construction of Masculinity among Young Working-class Men on the Margin of the Labour Market', *The Australian and New Zealand Journal of Sociology* 27(2).

———. 1995. *Masculinities.* Cambridge: Polity Press.

Cornwall, A. 1997. 'Men, Masculinity, and "gender in development"', *Gender and Development* 5(2).

Cornwall, A., and N. Lindisfarne, eds. 1994. *Dislocating Masculinity: Comparative Ethnographies.* London: Routledge.

Dollymore, J. 1991. *Sexual Dissidence: Augustine to Wilde, Freud to Foucault.* Oxford: Clarendon Press.

Dunk, T.W. 1991. *It's a Working Man's Town: Male Working-Class Culture.* Montreal/Kingston: McGill/Queens University Presses.

Epstein, D. and R. Johnson. 1998. *Schooling Sexualities.* Buckingham: Open University Press.

Epstein, D., J. Elwood, V. Hey and J. Maw. 1998. *Failing Boys? Issues in Gender and Achievement.* Buckingham: Open University Press.

Gevisser, M. and E. Cameron, eds. 1994. *Defiant Desire: Gay and Lesbian Lives in South Africa.* Johannesburg: Ravan Press.

Gilmore, D.D. 1990. *Manhood in the Making: Cultural Concepts of Masculinity.* New Haven/London: Yale University Press.

Goldblatt, B. and S. Meintjes. 1997. 'Dealing with the Aftermath: sexual violence and the Truth and Reconciliation Commission', *Agenda* 36.

Gutmann, M.C. 1997. 'Trafficking in Men: The Anthropology of Masculinity', *Annual Review of Anthropology* 26.

Hassim, S. and A. Gouws. 1998. 'Redefining the Public Space: Women's Organisations, Gender Consciousness and Civil Society in South Africa', *Politikon* 25(2).

Hearn, J. 1999. *The Violences of Men.* London: Routledge.

Hemson, D. 1996. '"For sure you are going to die?": Political Participation and the Comrade Movement in Inanda, KwaZulu-Natal', *Social Dynamics* 22(2).

Jeffords, S. 1998. 'The "Remasculinization" of Germany in the 1950s: Discussion', *Signs* 24(1).

Leclerc-Madlala, S. 1997. 'Infect One, Infect All: Zulu Youth Response to the AIDS Epidemic in South Africa', *Medical Anthropology* 17.

Lorentzen, J. and P.A. Lokke. 1999. 'Men's Violence Against Women: The Need to Take Responsibility', *IASOM Newsletter* 6(2).

Mac an Ghaill, M. 1994. *The Making of Men – Masculinities, Sexualities and Schooling.* Buckingham: Open University Press.

Madlala, P. 1995. 'Male Feminist Experience', *Agenda* 24.

Maforah, N. 1993. 'Black, Married, Professional and a Woman', *Agenda* 18.

Makgetla, N.S. 1995. 'Women and Economy: Slow Pace of Change', *Agenda* 24.

Mann, M. 1993. *The Sources of Social Power : The Rise of classes and nation-states, 1760–1914*, Volume II. Cambridge/New York: Cambridge University Press.

Madonsela, T. 1995. 'Beyond putting women on the agenda', *Agenda* 24.

Marais, H. 1998. *South Africa, limits to change: The political economy of transformation*. London/Cape Town: Zed/University of Cape Town Press.

May, J., ed. 1999. *Poverty and Inequality in South Africa*. London: Zed.

Messner, M. 1997. *Politics of Masculinities: men in movements*. Thousand Oaks: Sage.

Moeller, R.G. 1998. 'The "Remasculinization" of Germany in the 1950s: Introduction', *Signs* 24(1).

Morrell, R. 1999. 'Boys, Men and Questions of Masculinity in South Africa'. In L. King, ed., *Questions of Intimacy: Rethinking Population Education*. Hamburg: UNESCO.

Morris, M. 1991. 'State, Capital and Growth: the political economy of the national question'. In S. Gelb, ed., *South Africa's Economic Crisis*. Cape Town: David Philip.

Müller, D.K., F. Ringer and B. Simon, eds. 1987. *The Rise of the Modern Educational System: Structural Change and Social Reproduction 1870– 1920*. Cambridge/Paris: Cambridge University Press, Editions de la masion des Sciences de l'homme.

Nathan, L. 1989. '"Marching to a different beat": the history of the End Conscription Campaign'. In J. Cock and L. Nathan, eds., *War and Society: The militarization of South Africa*. Cape Town: David Philip.

Parker, R. 1995. 'Gender, Sexuality and Health: Building a New Agenda for Sexuality Research in Response to Aids and Reproductive Health'. Unpublished mimeo.

Pinnock, D. 1997. *Gangs, Rituals and Rites of Passage*. Cape Town: Africa Sun Press/Institute of Criminology, University of Cape Town.

Ross, M.B. 1998. 'In search of Black Men's Masculinities', *Feminist Studies* 24(3).

Sadie, Y. and E. Loots. 1998. 'Gender Sensitivity in RDP Presidential Lead Projects', *Politikon* 25(2).

Rude, D. 1999. 'Reasonable Men and Provocative Women: An Analysis of Gendered Domestic Homicide in Zambia', *Journal of Southern African Studies* 25(1).

Segal, L. 1990. *Slow Motion: Changing Masculinities, Changing Men*. London: Virago.

Seidler, V.J., ed. 1992. *Men, Sex And Relationships: Writings from Achilles Heel*. London: Routledge.

Silberschmidt, M. 1992. 'Have men become the weaker sex? Changing life situations in the Kisii district, Kenya', *Journal of Modern African Studies* 30(2).

Staples, R. 1982. *Black Masculinity: The Black Male's Role in American Society*. San Francisco: Black Scholar Press.

Stecopoulos, H. and M. Uebel, eds. 1997. *Race and the Subject of Masculinities*. Durham and London: Duke University Press.

Strachan, H. 1998. *Way Up Way Out*. Cape Town: David Philip.

Swart, S. 1998. '"A Boer and his gun and his wife are three things always together" – Republican Masculinity and the 1914 Rebellion', *Journal of Southern African Studies* 24(4).

Swedish Ministry for Foreign Affairs. 1999. *Men's Voices Men's Choices*. Stockholm: Government Printer.

Swedish Ministry of Industry, Employment and Communication. 1999. *Men and Equality*. Stockholm: Government Printer.

Taylor, V. 1997. 'Economic gender injustice: the macro picture', *Agenda* 33.

Unterhalter, E. 1999. 'The work of the nation: Heroic adventures and masculinity in South African autobiographical writing of the anti-apartheid struggle'. Unpublished paper.

Von Kotze, A. 1996. '"The creaking of the word": A feminist model?' In S. Walters and L. Manicom, eds., *Gender in Popular Education Methods for Empowerment*. Cape Town/London and New Jersey: Cace/Zed.

Walby, S. 1990. *Theorizing Patriarchy*. Oxford: Basil Blackwell.

Westwood, S. 1990. 'Racism, black masculinity and the politics of space'. In J. Hearn and D. Morgan, eds., *Men, Masculinities and Social Theory*. London: Unwin Hyman.

# PART ONE

Men's bodies are often represented as powerful, as instruments of force. But men's bodies are not uniform, and they do not have equal power. Inequality and oppression are embodied in men's bodies. Particularly in South Africa, the activities of men's bodies have differed and their potentials have varied according to context. Race has been a powerful determinant of bodily action. Colonial and apartheid policies and legacies have meant that white men have used their bodies in strikingly different ways from black men. Under apartheid white men had power over black men, but this is changing with the country's transition to democracy.

The privileged access of white men to positions of power, jobs, guns and sporting opportunities is on the decline. Some white men have fought to retain their power and have drawn on images of white supremacy to mobilise their claims. But bodies can also be vulnerable and even ridiculous. White supremacist masculinity is no longer hegemonic and imitating the voortrekkers no longer works to garner support.

Technologies of power, such as the gun, are no longer monopolised by one race group. Guns are now easily accessible. They are supplied to the national defence force but private ownership is significant. There are over four million registered firearms in a country with a population of forty million. These guns are used to protect property and for criminal purposes. Eleven thousand people a year die of gun wounds. South Africa is a gun-rich society and masculinities, black and white, worship the gun. Guns have become an extension of the body and a tool for exercising power.

Sport has often been entwined with violent masculinities. In many instances sportsfields have become places where violent conduct is legitimated, but they have seldom been able to contain this violence. Sometimes sport has actually fuelled violent masculinities. In South Africa, sport has been integral to hegemonic masculinity, but as facilities and space have been deracialised, so new masculinities have emerged. Market forces are not neutral in this process. In some cases they encourage competitive masculinities and a consumer culture. In other cases, the opportunity to earn a wage in the process of exercising the body has allowed young African men to develop new forms of self-expression in which the discipline of the body leads them away from the violence-ridden cultures of the townships.

# The Body in Action
## Guns, Sport and Violence

# CHAPTER 1

# Gun Violence and Masculinity in Contemporary South Africa

## JACKLYN COCK

## Introduction

Every day 32 people are murdered with a firearm in South Africa (*Gun Free Newsletter* 1998). The level of violent crime and conflict linked to the proliferation of guns and other small arms is an indicator of a level of social disintegration in South Africa which threatens among other things the consolidation of democracy. Guns are a key feature of hegemonic masculinity. Their ownership and use varies across racial lines and between institutions, but nevertheless is central to the way many men act out their masculinity.

The social legacy of armed conflicts in southern Africa includes antagonistic social identities and an ideology of militarism. Violence is regarded as a legitimate solution to conflict and a crucial means of both obtaining and defending power. The conclusion of the armed struggle was not accompanied by effective disarmament and demobilisation. There are thus a great many small arms in private and public hands. Guns provide the power to express social antagonisms in violent ways.

The research on which much of this chapter is based was conducted in South Africa and Mozambique between 1994 and 1999. Eighty semi-structured, in-depth interviews were conducted with key informants involved in the supply of and demand for small arms in the southern African region. This research strategy was adopted to avoid the tendency of questionnaires to fracture experience when respondents are encouraged to reduce their experiences and understandings to fragments which can be captured in a question-and-answer format. Informants were selected not on the basis of their representivity of any larger universe, but on the basis of their expertise and experience in both supply and demand issues.

Informants included key actors within the gun culture such as organisers of war games and managers of shops selling toy guns. In interviews with gun owners the relation between their understandings of guns as a cause of or a solution to criminal violence was a key theme that was explored.

## Poverty and guns

In contemporary South Africa widespread poverty and a high unemployment rate have contributed to the commoditisation of violence as increasing numbers of citizens have come to rely on criminal violence of various kinds as a means of livelihood.

Two informants with criminal convictions both emphasised that they had been forced into criminal activity for economic reasons. As one said, 'A hungry stomach knows no law' (Interview, Alexandra youth 1998). According to another informant from Soweto, 'Ex-combatants are often used as paid assassins. They will kill for a plate of porridge, R200 and a bottle of brandy' (Interview, Soweto 1998). The interrupted education, lack of marketable skills, training in the means of violence and (frequent) political disillusion, make ex-combatants potentially lethal.

There is no homogeneous social category of gun owners. They include not only criminal networks and political groupings with paramilitary formations, but also sportsmen including hunters, the security forces, citizens, and private security firms. However, it is argued here that small arms are often the basis of a militarised identity that is lethally connected to gender, ethnicity, race, nationality and political affiliation. The militarisation–masculinism nexus is especially powerful.

Particular guns have powerful social meanings. In apartheid South Africa the symbol of masculine, revolutionary resistance was the automatic assault rifle, the AK-47.

## The AK-47: example of contested social meanings and identities

The contested social identities of 'terrorist' or 'revolutionary' are condensed in the image of the automatic assault rifle – the Kalashnikov AK-47.

The AK is not just a gun. It is a legend, a currency, a symbol of liberation and violence. As Chris Smith has written, it is 'the most potent symbol of conflict and violence in the closing years of the 20th century' (1996: 1). It has been described as the most effective assault weapon in the world, and has changed forever the way wars are fought. Since it first went into production in 1947 some seventy million AK assault rifles have been manufactured, and are in use in the armies of 55 nations.

Jacklyn Cock

In February 1997 Russia celebrated the opening of an exhibition to mark the fiftieth anniversary of the production of the Kalashnikov assault rifle. One of the most prominent exhibits was the Kalashnikov assault rifle that a North Vietnamese soldier used to kill 78 Americans in the Vietnam War (*The New York Times*, 13 March 1997).

This is a grisly reminder of how today the AK-47 is invested with powerful symbolic force. It is a contradictory symbol. To some it is a symbol of criminal lawlessness, while to others it is a symbol of revolutionary resistance. Whereas, as Ellis (1975) has argued, the machine gun represented the power of the imperial armies, the AK is an icon of the anti-establishment insurgent.

Particularly during the apartheid era, for many young, black South African men the AK-47 became a mythic icon, a powerful symbol, a 'marker' of group identity. It was a kind of code to assert one's political allegiance that carried great significance for individuals.

At this time the AK-47 was a powerful ingredient in the portrayal of the African National Congress (ANC) as a demonic force. The ANC was portrayed by the South African Broadcasting Corporation 'as folk devils – incarnations of evil and inhumanity' (Tomaselli 1987: 4). Part of this process of demonisation involved stressing the relationship between the ANC and the Union of Soviet Socialist Republics (USSR); and the AK-47 provided the link. The AK-47 was the bearer, the material evidence of the 'communist onslaught'. It was constantly described as 'a Russian made' weapon, and there were frequent references to 'Russian arms and ammunition' in the state-controlled media, as well as in media displays of captured weapons. This was the evidence to support the apartheid regime's assertion that resistance to apartheid was not indigenous but inspired and supplied by the USSR. Thus the identity of this gun marked the identity of the Russian demon-terrorist.

Ironically, supplies of thousands of AK-47s were an important part of the undeclared war of destabilisation that was directed against neighbouring states externally, and against the ANC internally by the apartheid regime. AK-47s were included in weapons which were supplied to the National Union for the Total Independence of Angola (UNITA), and Renamo (the resistance movement in Mozambique) as well as to Inkatha (the predominantly Zulu political grouping within South Africa). For example, almost forty thousand AK-47s were purchased from Poland, Romania, Bulgaria, Yugoslavia, Hungary and China between 1976 and 1986 specifically to be given to UNITA (Cameron Commission 1995).

The AK-47 is attractive for a number of reasons. Firstly, it is relatively cheap. In Namibia, Angola and Mozambique an AK-47, complete with a couple of clips of ammunition, can be bought for less than $15 or for a blanket or a bag of maize or some second-hand clothes. In South Africa the going price can be as high as R1 500 so there are substantial profits to be made (Smith 1996: 43). Secondly, the AK is extremely robust. It has only 16 moving parts, is easy to maintain, durable and rarely breaks down. Lastly, anyone can learn to use it in two or three minutes. It 'can be stripped and reassembled by a child of 10 years' (Louise 1995: 10), which makes it particularly attractive to the increasing numbers of child soldiers in the world.

To many of these young soldiers the AK has an explicit sexual meaning: 'The particular savagery of war in the 1990s taps into . . . . the wild sexuality of the adolescent male. Adolescents are supplying armies with a different kind of soldier – one for whom a weapon is not a thing to be respected or treated with ritual correctness, but instead has an explicit phallic dimension' (Ignatieff 1997: 127). Ignatieff maintains that 'when a war is conducted by adolescent irregulars, savagery becomes one of its regular weapons' (1997: 127).

The reaction to gun violence recorded in these media accounts reflects a number of distortions concerning the AK-47. Despite the commonsense view, the AK is not the most commonly used weapon in violent crime compared to pistols and revolvers. For instance, in 1995 high calibre automatic weapons, such as AKs were used in only 6 per cent of the 7 169 murders reported in South Africa in that year. Admittedly this represents an increase from 1992 when less than 3 per cent of all murders were perpetrated with automatic assault rifles. However, these figures would suggest that the obsessional focus on AK-47s in the contemporary South African media is an ideological hangover from the demonisation of *Umkonto we Sizwe* (MK) guerrillas during the apartheid era. While this demonisation is shifting, the link between AK-47s and other types of guns and masculinity is deeply embedded in the social order.

## Gun violence and masculinity

Men, as William Beinart has written, are 'the primary agents of violence in most societies' (1992: 473). A number of attempts to analyse the complexity of modern masculinity explain this violence in terms of the 'new biology'. For example, Fukuyama advises us to accept male violence as part of 'biologically grounded nature' and 'seek to constrain it through institutions, laws and norms' (1998: 40). Other commentators have emphasised the sexual nature of gun violence with guns representing phalluses and bullets representing 'genital fluid' (Theweleit 1989: 31). The approach in this chapter is that the 'gender identities of men are socially constructed, changeable and often contradictory. It follows that there are many masculinities' (Morrell 1998: 8). However, this chapter argues that violence is bound up with male identity in many different cultural contexts in contemporary South Africa. Guns are common to both white and black masculinities. They are a transracial integrative force which contributes to the maintenance of a violent hegemonic masculinity.

Guns are part of the dominant masculine code in many diverse cultural groupings in South Africa. For example: the white *Afrikaner Weerstandsbeweging* (AWB) leader Eugene Terre Blanche instructed his followers to 'buy weapons, collect weapons and clean your weapons. The Boer and his gun are inseparable' (cited in *The Star*, 14 May 1990). In another time and place, a young black man from Soweto insisted, '. . . for you to prove your manhood these days, you've got to own a gun' (Interview, Soweto 1998).

To a diverse number of young South African men guns are a marker of status, and signal a particular style. For example, to many members of organised crime syndicates in Soweto ostentatiously displayed firearms indicate the status of being a 'big man' (Wardrop 1996: 8). For several black Sowetan informants guns were a marker of power and of a strong, 'notorious' identity. 'For me being a man, it [a gun] has been something that we intend to use in order to make a fast kill or to prove your existence, you know – how notorious you are' (Interview, Soweto 1998).

A number of Sowetan male informants emphasised that guns invested the bearer with power: 'People are arrogant because they know you won't do anything to them while they are carrying a gun . . . . if he's carrying a gun he's big . . . . he must be feared, he knows he is carrying a thing which is powerful' (Interview by Gift Motaung, Soweto 1997).

The majority of young black men interviewed thought that guns 'ought to be the preserve of men . . . . a gun for a woman is only suitable if she is a police officer' (Interview, Soweto 1998). However, a number of informants expressed concern about increasing gun violence in the townships: 'We are killing each other, us black men. We just kill randomly. Whites possess these things, but they don't just kill . . . . in the townships they just shoot anyhow, anytime, anywhere' (Interview by Gift Motaung, Soweto 1997).

The style that guns signal is not restricted to political allegiance or criminal defiance. Guns are also a form of social display which can signal male affluence as well. As an informant from the Indian community of Lenasia (near Johannesburg) expressed it, 'If you have a BMW, a cell phone and a glamorous woman you've got a lot; if you've got a gun as well, you've got everything.' According to another informant, guns have even penetrated the Johannesburg white, middle class clubbing scene (Kimon Webster quoted in Coetzer 1997: 10). For many young South African youths of all races guns are associated with a glamorous lifestyle together with fast cars and flashy clothes.

The notion that guns are an effective and necessary form of protection is an important source of legitimation of private gun ownership. The gun combines two contradictory images: it is a means of both order and of violence; and paradoxically it is believed to provide protection from violence through the potential threat of violence. Since the 1980s there has been a privatisation of security as increasing numbers of citizens have lost confidence in the capacity of the state to protect them, and have come to rely on individual gun ownership and private security arrangements.

A common theme articulated by many informants who had purchased guns for self-protection was a sense of being powerless; of being victims of social forces beyond their control. But the psychodynamic power of the gun as protection is largely illusionary since legally owned weapons contribute to the problem of violent crime.

The great majority of crimes committed with firearms are committed with either legally owned weapons used for an illicit purpose, or weapons that have been stolen from their legal owners. It follows that the distinction between legal and illegal weapons is a dubious one: guns are long-life commodities and their change of legal status does not affect their lethal power. The legal supply of small arms is generally the seedbed of illegal flows.

There are 4,2 million licensed firearms in South Africa. Many of these are landing up in criminal possession. In 1997 17 600 of these firearms fell into criminal hands, dramatising the dangerously self-contradictory potential of guns as a means of individual protection.

There is reliable evidence – ironically from the United States of America (USA) – that people are safer without guns. Epidemiological research there has established that a gun in the home is 43 times more likely to kill a member of the household than to kill an intruder (Kellerman and Reay 1986: 1 560).

In relation to the USA, the sociologist James Gibson (1994) has identified a highly energised, new paramilitary culture in contemporary America which he relates to a crisis of identity among American men. He maintains that this culture offers men an escape from the social, political and economic confusions which were provoked by the withdrawal of American forces from Vietnam.

There are similar confusions among some white South African men regarding the ending of armed conflict in southern Africa, particularly

Jacklyn Cock

among those who fought in the South African Defence Force (SADF). In South Africa many white male informants articulated a lack of confidence in the government and the economy, and seemed uncertain of their future in relation to political change generally and affirmative action policies specifically. Both white and black male informants are also troubled by changing gender relations. In South African society there has been a reconfiguration of the discourse on gender since 1990, and women are presenting a challenge to customary male behaviour (Cock 1997). Among diverse categories of men there seems to be different versions of a 'crisis of masculinity' which reflects a social dislocation and confusion about their gender identity. The gun is a convenient peg on which to hang traditional notions of masculine power. Increases in violent crime, gun ownership and a growing gun culture partly reflect these social tensions.

Exploring the connections between these social tensions, the construction of masculinities, and gun violence involves more than exploring individual biographies, motives and meanings. It also involves examining the diverse social organisations, cultural frameworks, social practices, group attachments, and institutions built up around guns. Collectively these constitute a robust 'gun culture' in contemporary South Africa within which a militarist masculinity is an important (but not the only) theme.

## The South African gun culture

This gun culture is not a fixed, ahistorical, essentialist entity, but a set of highly heterogeneous resources which are used selectively by members of different collectivities. Overall this culture operates to provide a social sanction to the possession of guns, and much gun violence follows culturally defined repertoires of behaviour.

The values, social practices and institutions which together constitute this gun culture involve the normalisation, legitimation – and even glorification – of war, weaponry, military force and violence through television, films, books, songs, dances, toys, games, and sports.

Toy guns are a significant component of this culture – a total of 48 different varieties were on offer at a Johannesburg shop in December 1996. For R120 you could buy a model of the American automatic assault rifle, the M-16. Significantly for the argument about difference and identity, this toy was advertised as an 'alien buster'. All of these cultural forms constitute a kind of 'banal militarism' which operates near the surface of social life. Banal militarism is embedded in everyday activities: it works through prosaic routines and rituals to make war, weaponry and violence appear natural and inevitable.

Such banal militarism is exemplified in war games such as paintball,

49

which has become increasingly popular among young, white South African men since 1985. At its core paintball simulates the sequence of killing.

One Johannesburg informant involved in this 'gun culture' spent much of his leisure time playing paintball, practising at shooting ranges, and cleaning and 'stroking' the 12 guns which he owned. This behaviour is chillingly reminiscent of that of the killer responsible for Britain's worst mass murder, the Dunblane school shooting of 16 children and their teacher in 1997.

Gun culture not only operates to glamorise war and weaponry, but also to 'normalise' these social arrangements. Part of this 'normalisation' is the notion that private gun ownership is legitimate and a right rather than a privilege.

It is a 'right' which is frequently harnessed to nationalism and which strengthens the connection between masculinity and militarism. Popular images of nationalist struggles against colonial rule have typically been male. The popular image of the Zulu nationalist is of a man carrying 'traditional weapons': a rawhide shield, knobkerrie and spear. The Zulu King told a mass rally in Soweto that 'the call to ban the bearing of cultural weapons is an insult to my manhood. It is an insult to the manhood of every Zulu man' (cited in Interview, Soweto 1995). A number of Zulu men living in Soweto emphasised that this was a deeply felt connection, 'A man without a traditional weapon is like a Christian without a bible or a soldier without arms' (Interview, Soweto 1995).

Under apartheid, both white and black youths were socialised into a militarist masculinity which was reinforced by a gender-defined sense of social solidarity, a brotherhood of combatants. One such a brotherhood was described in the South African press as 'Apartheid's killers: the braaivleis, brandy and death brigade'. The article began 'Many were loving fathers, caring husbands and seemingly average South African macho men who liked rugby and a few beers. *But* their chosen careers involved wielding extreme violence against enemies of the state and celebrating afterwards' (*The Star*, 24 November 1997, emphasis added). What the article ignores is how such violence is legitimated by shared assumptions and rituals of masculinity.

These rituals of masculinity were central to the socialisation experiences of many white South African men through their experiences at school through cadet programmes preparing them for military service in the SADF, and in the SADF itself. The SADF was a crucial source of ideas about what behavior was appropriate for white South African men. A number of SADF conscripts have emphasised that the core of military training was to inculcate aggressiveness and equate it with masculinity (Cock 1991). Many white South African conscripts came out of their period of military service as 'haters of war'. However, others have been damaged and brutalised by their experiences of violence and drew from them a sense of savage superiority to women and those who had not fought, as well as a hatred for a demonised enemy (Cock 1991).

The journalist, Jacques Pauw, who was one of the first to investigate apartheid death squads, maintained that what linked killers such as Eugene de Kock, Ferdi Barnard and Paul van Vuuren, was 'that they were abused as children' (cited in *The Star*, 24 November 1997). While Pauw was referring to physical abuse it is also clear that as children they were also all socialised into a particularly brutalised mix of racial, ethnic and masculine identities. Often hunting from an early age was a formative ritual. Asked by Pauw, 'How does it feel to shoot a human being?', Paul van Vuuren replied, 'To shoot a human being and a buck are basically the same' (cited in *The Mail and Guardian*, 28 November 1997).

The report of the Truth and Reconciliation Commission (TRC) points to how masculinity is salient to understanding the perpetrators of gross human rights abuses. They write, 'A threatened sense of masculinity is interwoven with a racialised identity and militarism to effect a volatile mixture' (TRC 1998: 12). However, the authors emphasised that

> it is not merely a single identity form that leads to violence. Multiple social identities such as masculinity and racial, militarist and national patriotism combine with religious, ethnic and political identities to render people quite willingly capable of murderous deeds in the play of egotism and pride.   (TRC 1998: 12)

Part of the challenge facing contemporary South Africa is to rework these 'multiple social identities'.

## Conclusion: uncoupling militarism and masculinity

South Africa's transition from authoritarian rule has created a deep well of social anxiety as the familiar social identities and traditional values and practices have been disrupted and breached. One consequence of this social anxiety is the 'emergence of a predisposition to the use of "scapegoats" into which all the disturbing experiences are condensed' (Hall et al. 1978: 157). There are two categories of scapegoats in our context – the ex-combatant and the illegal immigrant – the latter reflecting a hostility to outsiders, as occurred in Britain in the 1970s. Much press coverage of gun violence reflects a sense of blame and indignation towards these social identities. In the vocabulary of social anxiety, ex-combatants and illegal immigrants are easy symbols of menace, social dislocation and threat.

A black, working class youth, an ex-Self Defence Unit member points us to a crucial aspect of the solution to gun violence in South Africa – the creation of new, demilitarised social identities that are sources of affirmation. Now part of the Daveyton Peace Corps this young man commented, 'I was really disappointed at not getting a gun when I first joined the Peace Corps in 1994.' He went on to say, 'after a while I realised that I did not need a gun . . . I now know that the community needs us and values us' (cited by Kirsten, in Cock and McKenzie 1998: 28).

These new social identities involve uncoupling militarism from masculinity. However, the existing militarised masculinity evokes an ambiguous response from both black and white women. In South Africa increasing numbers of women are purchasing guns which could indicate that a male style is being homogenised and spread more widely.

This is part of a global trend. The growing power of women within the USA gun lobby was illustrated in 1996 with the election of a woman, Marion Hammer, as the National Rifle Associations' first female president. She has a solution to gun violence: 'Instead of getting rid of all firearms . . . why not just get rid of all liberals?' (who moan about gun violence) (cited in *The New York Times*, 14 April 1996).

To some informants, gun ownership among women represents an assertion of a feminist identity. A South African woman firearm trainer argues that 'we have come through the sexual revolution to be regarded as equals. We have lost the male protector. Women have to take responsibility for their own protection' (cited in *The Saturday Star*, 2 November 1996). She further advises on how 'women can carry guns for self defence and still look feminine, sexy and demure'.

A Sowetan woman informant maintained that guns were essential even through they meant adopting a masculine identity. 'We are people of Johannesburg too. We must use guns too . . . we must think we are men because as men we can fight back. If we women arm ourselves we will have the power to stop the killing' (Interview, Soweto 1997).

A black working class woman who lived with her mother and sister in Soweto maintained that she had to have a gun (which cost over R1 000) because 'we don't have a father. I am the one who has to make sure that everything is all right at home' (Interview, Soweto 1997). This is partly an expression of the disorganisation of African family life inflicted by apartheid and the rise of precarious and vulnerable female-headed households. But it is a response which is not restricted to such households.

Jacklyn Cock

A white, middle class woman informant linked gun ownership directly to her feminist identity as an independent woman. She maintained that owning a gun (which she wore tucked into the back of her jeans) made her feel powerful, self-reliant and independent.

This kind of thinking is partly a response to an increasing trend for women – in both the USA and South Africa – to be the victims of gun violence. Increasing numbers of the 36 000 rapes reported in 1997, as well as domestic violence generally, involved firearms (interview with the Director of the SAPS [South African Police Services] Crime Management Information System, January 1997).

Change is needed not only at the level of gender identities but to dislodge militarised conceptions of citizenship. A militarised form of citizenship characterised the apartheid era in that political citizenship involved compulsory national military service for white males only. In addition to their exclusion from military service, black South Africans were also denied access to firearms. This prohibition on arms was understood to involve a denial of African manhood as well as citizenship (Hellman 1943: 45). The outcome of this historical legacy is a militarised citizenship and a militarised masculinism. This has devastating social consequences and will be very difficult to dislodge. In most contemporary societies guns and armies are highly gendered. A distinctive feature of South Africa is that in this context guns are also highly racialised and linked to militarised conceptions of citizenship. Among many black South Africans there is now a widespread understanding that access to all levels of the South African National Defence Force as well as access to legal gun ownership are markers of manliness, of liberation, and of full citizenship in the post-apartheid state. A number of black informants emphasised that gun ownership signals citizenship in a post-apartheid society:

> Under apartheid many whites bought guns because us blacks, during those times of apartheid, we resembled flies, we were nothing. The law stood for whites. Now it is painful for whites to see blacks owning guns . . . But maybe when whites see that a black person can also carry a gun maybe they will respect us.   (Interview, Soweto 1999)

Confronting this understanding must come from an indigenous, mass-based demilitarisation movement. This exists in embryonic form in organisations such as Gun Free South Africa and Ceasefire. However, the movement is marked by a social shallowness, being extremely small, fragmented, and mainly white and middle class. Both Gun Free and

Ceasefire are attempting to stigmatise firearms and shift the ideology of militarism which regards violence as a legitimate form of obtaining and defending power. Within both organisations there is some emphasis on alternative gender discourses. This challenge to hegemonic conceptions of masculinity has provoked hostility. Women members of both organisations have been subjected to suspicion, abuse and threats of violence that involve graphic sexual imagery. The latter response underlines the importance of delinking guns and masculinity, a challenge posed thirty years ago by Virginia Woolf when she asked, 'How can we alter the crest and spur of the fighting cock?'

To do so we have to create new gender identities. This cannot be achieved through equal rights feminism – a stunted feminism which focuses on specific issues such as women's access to armies and combat roles. Nor can it be achieved through a radical feminism which focuses narrowly on domestic violence against women. Nor can it be achieved by women acting alone: 'Men need to critique practices and policies which fuel or flow from violent masculinities' (Morrell 1998: 11). Morrell cites militarisation and the ownership and use of guns as examples of such issues. Men need to get involved as pro-feminists acting collectively with women in a transformative feminism which confronts the connections between private and public spheres, questions the understanding of 'difference', and challenges the relation of gender identities to violence and power.

BIBLIOGRAPHY

Beinart, W. 1992. 'Political and Collective Violence in Southern African Historiography', *Journal of Southern African Studies* 18(3).

Billig, M. 1995. *Banal Nationalism*. London: Sage.

Cock, J. 1991. *Women and War in South Africa*. Ohio: Pilgrim Press.

————. 1992. 'The dynamics of transforming South Africa's defense forces'. In S. Stedman, ed., *South Africa. The political economy of transformation*. Boulder: Lynne Rienner Publishers.

Cock, J. and L. Nathan, eds. 1989. *Society at War. The militarisation of South Africa*. New York: St. Martins Press.

Cameron Commission of Inquiry into Alleged Arms Transactions between Armscor and one Eli Wazan and other related matters. First Report. Johannesburg: 15 June 1995.

Coetzer, J. 1997. 'Jacknife hurtle down the freeway of fame', *Music Africa* 2(5).

Ellis, J. 1975. *The Social History of the Machine Gun.* Baltimore: John Hopkins Press.

Fukuyama, F. 1998. 'Women and the Evolution of World Politics', *Foreign Affairs* 77(5).

Gibson, J. 1994. *Warrior Dreams, Violence and Manhood in Post-Vietnam America.* New York: Hill and Wang.

*Gun Free Newsletter.* December 1998 2(4).

Hall, S. and T. Jefferson. 1978. *Policing the Crisis, Mugging the state and law and order.* London: Macmillan.

Hellman, E. 1943. 'Non-Europeans in the Army', *Race Relations* x(2).

Ignatieff, M. 1994. *Blood and Belonging. Journeys into the New Nationalism.* London: Vintage.

———. 1997. *The Warriors Honour.* Oxford: Blackwell.

Kellerman, D. and D. Reay. 1986. 'Protection or Peril? An analysis of firearm related deaths in the home', *New England Journal of Medicine* 24(314).

Morrell, R. 1998. 'The New Man', *Agenda* 37.

Motaung, G. 1998. 'A study of gun violence in Soweto'. Unpublished report.

Pauw, J. 1997. *Into the Heart of Darkness: Confessions of apartheid's assassins.* Johannesburg: Jonathan Ball.

Roth, M. 1983. '"If you give us rights we will fight": black involvement in the Second World War', *South African Historical Journal* 15.

Scott, J. 1996. *Only Paradoxes to Offer.* New York: Routledge.

Smith, C. 1996. 'Light weapons and the international arms trade'. In United Nations Institute for Disarmament Research, *Small Arms Management and Peacekeeping in Southern Africa.* Geneva: United Nations.

South African Police. 1994. *Annual Report of the Commissioner of the South African Police.* RP 58\1994. Pretoria: South African Police.

*Truth and Reconciliation Commission Special Report*, vol. 4. Published in *The Star*, 5 November 1998.

Theweleit, K. 1989, 1996. *Male Fantasies*, vol. 2. Minneapolis: University of Minnesota Press.

Tomaselli, R. 1987. 'Social construction of the "enemy": SABC and the demonisation of the anti-terrorist'. Unpublished paper.

Wardrop, J. 1996. 'Policing the Cities: Soweto, Syndicates and "Doing Business"'. Paper presented to the South African Institute of Race Relations (SAIRR) conference, Johannesburg.

# CHAPTER 2

# *Ukubekezela* or *Ukuzithemba*
## African Lifesavers in Durban

CRISPIN HEMSON

## Introduction

African lifesavers in Durban are relatively recent entrants into a profession that seems to epitomise male physicality. Their presence on all but one of the beaches of this city, the largest port in Africa and a popular tourist destination for visitors from Europe, goes back barely ten years. Lifesaving is a community service, a sport, and an occupation, and it thus readily attracts young males, for whom it provides its own rites of passage – tests at different levels, seasonal work and, finally, entry into full-time employment.

This chapter examines the gendered self-definition of young African men who have lived their lives in Durban's working class townships. As Zulu-speakers they have been encouraged to celebrate the militaristic tradition espoused by Zulu traditional leaders. Conversely, they have grown up in a political climate where the traditional values championed by the Zulu nationalist Inkatha Freedom Party have been rejected, and the physical intrusions of this party's supporters and the forces of the apartheid state violently resisted.

As working class youths the males are inescapably exposed to violence and potentially caught up in it. In addition, when not in their home area they are confronted by active hostility – from other men and from figures of authority. Their lives are subject to extreme risk: young men die in physical attacks, in motor vehicle accidents and, increasingly, of AIDS in a region with very high rates of HIV infection.

The young men who have joined the Thekwini (the Zulu name for Durban) Surf Lifesaving Club (Thekwini SLC) are in many ways representative of African township youth. The context of lifesaving has provided them with a space in which to develop a masculine identity away from the dangerous life of the township streets.

This chapter explores the way the lifesavers act and speak about their masculinity in a discourse which draws on elements of three masculinities. The first is the masculinity of the traditional African gender order, with its values of physical prowess, courage and endurance. In the Zulu rural context, becoming a stick fighter was an important rite of passage into manhood which replaced the circumcision practised in other groups. While the lifesavers in this study grow up in an urban context, they often have close family ties to rural areas in which this masculinity is dominant.

The second masculinity is that of the *amaKholwa*, the converts to Christianity, which emphasises piety, education and familial respectability. While not central in the lives of these young men, it has influenced the way many township people value education and intellect.

The third masculinity has its origins in the emergence of a black, urban working class in the townships constructed under apartheid. This 'black masculinity' (Morrell 1998) is characterised by its oppositional character and violent assertion. It is in tension with both traditional rural and Christian masculinities.

In the discourse of the male lifesavers, the dominant themes – *Ukubekezela* (to be patient, forbearing, long-suffering) and *Ukuzithemba* (to have trust in yourself, self-confidence) – emphasise some elements of all these masculinities, but not others. Their discourse brings them into tension with black masculinity. This tension is illustrated by the gap between discourse and the lived experience, particularly of the adolescent lifesavers who are moving towards employment.

## The club's space

The Thekwini SLC is the home of African lifesaving and the only club with significant African membership in Durban. It was started in the mid-1970s by the first professional African lifesavers, and now has about one hundred members, of whom three are not African. The Thekwini SLC operates on the most northern beach on the Durban beachfront.

Lifesavers perform a key function on Durban's beaches. The beaches are frequented by tourists and many Durban residents who are not familiar with the sea. They can easily get into difficulty and drown. It is the lifesavers, professional and voluntary, who are responsible for preventing this from happening. Their duties also include supervising and patrolling the beaches.

A typical Sunday has voluntary lifesavers joining the professional lifesavers on duty – there are two of the latter on duty daily. Members have

*Members of the Thekwini SLC on a Sunday morning*

the most modern clubhouse of the Durban clubs as their base. This replaced the dreary hut of the apartheid era. Typically there will be about 12 senior male lifesavers, (aged from 18 to 25), a couple of whom will arrive with perhaps 20 young 'nippers' (young trainee lifesavers), more male than female (aged from 8 to 14). About 20 teenage males and a separate group of young women will arrive on foot from the taxi ranks about three kilometres away.

Two of the senior lifesavers will organise training. By 11h00 this will be finished and there will be youngsters on bodyboards in the surf and a soccer game on the beach, while a few of the more experienced members use surf-craft. There are no parents present, and almost no club member is older than 25 years.[1] The small children will be directed and supervised by the Nipper Officer, when they are not playing fairly chaotically. One group of adolescents will be writing responses to test questions read out by an employed lifesaver who is helping them to pass their next Award.

The use of the beach varies substantially according to changes in the season, the weather, surf conditions and time of day. It may have very few people, a few bathers and sunbathers, or it may have a couple of thousand Zionists gathered for a baptism in the surf, with a brass band blasting out religious tunes. There will be a clutch of surfers and bodyboarders, mainly white.

*Members of the Thekwini SLC, aged 17, taking the Surf Proficiency Award test*

These patterns are not long entrenched. The growth in the number of African lifesavers is recent, and follows a rapid increase in the number of African people visiting the beaches in Durban. The clubhouse was completed in 1997 and creates opportunities for more sheltered and comfortable activities. The club has itself grown rapidly in membership in the last two years.

The scenes described do not suggest tension, but the difficulties in achieving a masculine identity appropriate to the club are considerable, and need to be explained.

## Lifesavers on their home ground

Lamontville, 15 kilometres away, is home to most of the lifesavers. It was built in the 1930s as a township for the 'better class native' (Torr 1987). However, the distance from central Durban and the resulting cost of transport made the township an unattractive place to live. Far from being a middle class suburb, it has been a place of the working class, with a large criminal element present as well. It developed a tradition of resistance to the apartheid state, providing, for example, guerrilla fighters for the liberation movement in exile and energetic support for internal opposition to apartheid through the United Democratic Front in the 1980s. Residents of Lamontville know one another well partly because it is one of the

Crispin Hemson

oldest townships and partly because it is small compared to other Durban townships. By the small shopping centre you will find some of the males talking in groups, leaning against the wall, or playing streetball round the corner, while female members will walk past from time to time.

Generally, the lifesavers are also involved in other sports. A focal point is the local swimming pool, previously out of commission much of the year and grey and murky the rest, but now cleaner and clearer, as the new city administration releases funds into African areas. Most of the best swimmers are also lifesavers, and the Lamontville Swimming Club provides members to Thekwini SLC. Without the pool and the club, few young people would begin to swim. Schools in the area have very limited sporting facilities, and there are no privately owned pools.

The schools are not academically successful, and few students progress to passing Grade 12 (the old matriculation examination). Even for those who do pass, job opportunities are very limited, particularly with the decline in the neighbouring manufacturing industries. A small percentage of local residents have moved into middle class jobs, and then tended to leave the area.

The lifesavers seldom join the gatherings of young men who stand smoking cigarettes or *dagga* (marijuana) or drinking, by the side of the road, though friendship and kinship often straddle the divide. The divide occurs in a context of great local violence. Despite the lifesavers' apparent confidence, life is insecure, and witchcraft is practised, or thought to be practised, against people who demonstrate success in life.

The vulnerability of the young lifesavers both to violence and the appeal of violence is illustrated by a particular incident. In 1998, a year after the interviews reported here, the youngest respondent, the popular leader of the younger lifesavers, was murdered in a drunken and apparently random attack by a young man who himself claimed to be a club member. The funeral was highly emotional, with boys sobbing at the coffin, and clinging to each other, while mothers agitatedly tried to silence them.

The death seemed to set off a series of incidents of criminal behaviour, often in some group context – a rape by a club member, a series of thefts by members, the near-fatal stabbing by a local criminal of one member, an assault by two members on another and, finally, a rape case involving two women and seven club members. When the police were involved assaults on the youths were commonplace.

There was some talk that this group was forming into the kind of criminal, drug-dealing gang described in Cape Town by Pinnock (1982). But subsequent disciplinary measures by the Thekwini SLC and perhaps also seasonal employment seemed to succeed in curtailing the behaviour, and no case ended in the conviction of club members. I would contend that various factors in the local community act to limit gang formation. In addition, the opportunities that lifesaving provides for achievement, for physical involvement and especially employment together form a suffi-cient attraction to draw the young men away from criminal behaviour, and into the definition of masculinity embraced by the older lifesavers.

One of the features of the community is that most young males are not isolated from their families, although there is a persistent lack of fathers, or fathers who play a significant role in family life. While mothers express anxiety and concern about their sons, there is also much evidence of closeness and mutual support. When the young lifesaver mentioned above was killed, his friends involved themselves in cleaning his mother's yard, repainting her house, and participating in the customary night vigil as well as the grave-digging.

Furthermore, these are young men who have given time and effort to performing a community service long before they are able to gain employ-ment from it. The local attitude is thus rather that these incidents are aberrations – 'bad behaviour' – rather than an attack on the rest of the community.

Some involvement in violent or illegal action is not necessarily con-demned as it might be elsewhere. The community context is one in which institutions of authority are distrusted. Many young lifesavers have friends or family in prison. More immediately, one club member was recently charged with the murder of a young man who had raped his mother. There is a widespread lack of confidence that the police – who under apartheid were explicitly seen as 'the enemy – have succeeded in trans-forming themselves into instruments of justice. In the absence of impartial authority, it is possible to understand how male assertion moves swiftly to violence. It also indicates how difficult it may be for young males to balance closeness to the violent forces at work around them with a com-mitment to a masculinity which emphasises notions of respectability and forbearance.

## How African lifesaving developed

South Africa's coastline is subject to heavy wave activity and conditions are often dangerous for bathing. South Africans seldom learn to swim in seawater, and there is a lack of calm inland waters. People need pools to learn, yet these amenities were not available to African people under apartheid. The first African lifesavers in the 1970s were from Malawi, where they probably learnt to swim in Lake Malawi (personal communication, Elias Sekgobela). Apart from active exclusion under apartheid, amongst Africans the sea was seen both as purifying and as threatening and dangerous.

From early in the twentieth century, Durban provided seawater pools and later freshwater pools for its white population. Surf lifesaving clubs for whites were formed from the 1920s onwards, and provided training opportunities, with the employment of lifesavers on the beaches beginning in the 1930s. Whites grew up with access to both freshwater and seawater, learning the physical skills and the understanding of surf conditions essential for effective lifesaving. The growth of a beach culture, with its own fashions and jargon, fostered the growth of competitive surfing and lifesaving amongst whites, and the creation of a particular form of white masculinity (Thompson 2000).

In contrast, beach segregation limited the opportunities for Africans by reserving all but the most remote parts of the beachfront for whites. Under apartheid only one beach provided opportunities for African lifesavers, who were paid on lower pay scales.

The end of beach segregation in the 1980s, and the rapid growth in the number of African beachgoers, have made the employment of African lifesavers a necessity. Other lifesavers have had difficulty in communicating with beach users, and cases of racial polarisation in situations of crowd control have spurred on the employment of Africans. In addition, the shortage of lifesavers in places as varied as the United States of America and Dubai have lured the more mobile white lifesavers away to higher-paying jobs. Of the present complement of about 60 lifesavers, some 18 are African, and most of these are members of Thekwini. Many members are seasonal employees who are well-placed to become full-time lifesavers when vacancies occur. Lifesavers have to meet some very specific, easily assessed requirements, such as swimming endurance and physical fitness, and many Thekwini members can meet these.

## Exploring the discourse: the interviews

In 1997 I conducted interviews with eleven African lifesavers. All of them were members of Thekwini SLC, and eight of them were professional lifeguards employed by the city. Two others were Thekwini SLC leaders, and the third was a 14-year-old nipper. The interviews focused mainly on what they see as masculine qualities, on manhood, on their attitudes to other men – in the workplace and beyond – and on their attitudes towards women. The interviews were initially conducted with individuals. English was used, but the lifesavers would turn to Zulu for certain expressions. The most frequently used expressions were subsequently tested in group interviews. These expressions are listed in the table below, and the two most frequently volunteered by the lifesavers are explored in greater depth.

It is important to acknowledge that I have privileged access as a club member – although potentially my age and racial background could skew responses. Consequently, it has been essential to balance the data gathered from the interviews with ongoing observation.

*Valued qualities of men – Zulu terms volunteered by respondents*

| Zulu term | English translation |
|---|---|
| *ukubekezela* | to be patient, forbearing, long-suffering |
| *ukuzithemba* | to have trust in yourself, self-confidence |
| *indoda eqotho* | a genuine, sincere man |
| *ubukhuni ukuba indoda* | it's hard to be a man |
| *amandla endoda amapheli* | a man's struggle never ends |
| *ukuzi nakekela* | to take care of yourself |
| *umzimba* | the body |
| *ukuziqhenya* | to be proud, feel superior to others |

The Zulu terms volunteered by the lifesavers being interviewed referred specifically to conceptions of *adult* masculinity, and even the youngest respondents did not refer specifically to issues of childhood or youth masculinity. On their own there is nothing to locate their discourse within any one of the three masculinities discussed above rather than any other. However, as one explores how these terms are used and related to the context of lifesaving certain sharper distinctions emerge.

Some of the themes that emerged in the interviews are explored to elaborate various aspects of this discourse.

### Ukubekezela

The respondent who first volunteered *ukubekezela*, expressed it as 'grasping the pot even though you can see it is hot'. It is a quality of staying the course, of enduring, and when necessary, accepting pain: 'You tend to persevere and go on till you get [where] you need to get to.'

It relates to two other expressions which were volunteered once only, *ubukhuni ukuba indoda* (it's hard to be a man) and *amandla endoda amapheli* (a man's struggle never ends). The phrase is commonly used in situations where people endure hardship.

Lifesaving provides many such demands. Although much of the time is inevitably spent observing the beach and passing time if the beach is

Crispin Hemson

empty, it does require times of commitment, physical exertion, discipline, and pain. The lifesaver has to maintain a regime of training to keep to performance criteria, while rescues may require exposure to danger. In addition, the transition to employment as a lifesaver may require a change in diet, changes in habits of time, etc., to enable the person to cope with the demands of the work:

> Africans are battling to catch up, because when it comes to doing the job we do it using what we have learnt, nothing else, despite the lack of personal experience.

> Learning to come early, being punctual. It can apply in any other job. Not taking chances – they can trust me. You're like a police-man, for example if a child is lost or a woman raped.

Discipline is essential. The municipality cannot afford to have beaches unguarded by lifesavers, even if in part they are required to deal with monotony, because bad weather may mean deserted beaches.

African people have had to endure great hardships, not least under apartheid, and the concept of *ukubekezela* has encouraged men to feats of endurance. The issue is whether endurance takes place without the ques-tioning and challenge that is possible and necessary in a democratic context. There continue to be situations in which lifesavers must rely on their commitment and endurance, as well as situations where men need instead to be critical and assert their intelligence – such as when faced with racism, inefficiency or criminal violence against them. The concept of *ukubekezela* contrasts with the more hopeful notion of *ukuzithemba* in the emerging masculinity of the lifesavers.

### Ukuzithemba

*Themba* means to 'trust in', 'hope', 'have faith in', 'rely upon', and the lifesavers identify with the full term as meaning 'self-confidence', 'relying on oneself'. It connotes positive self-regard, and could apply to women as well as to men. It is a recurrent concept in the way the lifesavers spoke of their masculinity. Some of the other terms relating to respect and pride speak of a more conservative masculinity that commands respect, but this term does not imply masculine exclusivity.

Amongst the interviewees there were many statements that expressed these notions of self-esteem:

> [I'm proud] that I've made it half-way in life, I've got a house, earn a good salary, and I've got a child. At least I understand other

people and they understand me, I don't get a problem with other people, and I've got a girlfriend. I've still got my mother.

You must be proud – get a good education, a good job. Support your family, respect other people – managers and workers.

Everyone must respect another man.

You have to learn to respect the public, whether they are male or female, and you have to learn how to deal with the public wherever you are, and respect other race groups as well.

In this area there is an implicit rejection of the us-and-them spirit of black masculinity, and an echo of the values of *ubuntu*, a more inclusive notion of mutual respect.

In the professional world participants are expected to acquit themselves with confidence, as in the social environment. A real man (*indoda eqotho*) deserves respect because he achieves what a man must achieve. In this context, manhood is related closely to formal marriage and becoming not just a father but the head of a household. While many young men have children, stable employment enables the father to regularise his relationship with the mother through marriage. In a context of high unemployment a job as a lifesaver provides the secure employment of municipal service as well as benefits such as a housing subsidy.

Another related term is *ukuziqhenya* (to be proud). Lifesaving provides opportunities for these men to claim respect:

. . . in 1995, December a 15-year-old boy was shot and we had to do a CPR procedure on him, and we were able to revive him.

You've got the power to do mass rescues, to rescue more than one person from drowning. That shows that you are a man, because you have saved so many lives.

There is also the notion of independence: '*Ukuzi nakekela* [to take care of yourself] – like when the snakes give birth to the young [that is, snakes are independent from birth].'

The stability, even respectability, implied in these comments differs from the image of lifesavers held by other residents of Durban. Most white people, for example, would probably see lifesaving as a temporary and not particularly desirable occupation.

The two concepts, *ukubekezela* and *ukuzithemba,* are central to the masculinity of which the lifesavers speak, and bring together themes of endurance and assertion. As this masculinity becomes more confident and established, there may well be some questioning of the need to *bekezela*, and perhaps a more explicit distinction between the times it is needed and the times it is not. As the political and institutional context continues to transform, the opportunities for lifesavers to assert themselves in relation to both the employer and their peers may shift the discourse towards *ukuzithemba*.

## The body and physical prowess

In the context of rural migrants who worked on the Durban docks early in the century, Ramsay reports: 'The evidence would suggest that the name "*Ozinyathi*" [men like buffaloes] was linked to the concepts of *ubudoda* [masculinity] and *ubunkunzi* [bull-ness], and seems to have informed and nurtured the spirit of defiance and sense of confidence displayed by those employed in *togt* labour at this time' (1997: 13–4).

How is physical prowess in a very different context treated in the discourse of the lifesavers?

> If you are a small and thin person, if you have everything in your mind, then you are a man. You are using your mind, the most important thing, to be a real man. If you don't use your mind, you are lost, you could be crippled. A real man is one who is using your head. You don't have to use your strength.

> You can have a big *umzimba* [body], but it does not mean that you have the quality of a man.

> Sifiso [a lifesaver present with the respondent] is not masculine, but his mentality fits – within the club there are men who are masculine [presumably in the sense of physically powerful] but who didn't make the time on the swimming test. The mental part of it, the spiritual and emotional part of it, is what matters.

For an occupation that seems to celebrate physical prowess, this language is a striking rejection of force in favour of sharpness, intellect and commitment. *Ozinyathi* now has a pejorative sense (personal communication, David Hemson), and the reason may well be that it denies the intellectual qualities valued both in the context of struggle and in the masculinity of the *amaKholwa*.

## Transitions to manhood

Younger lifesavers move through formal stages before they become adult lifesavers. The progression involves Basic, Intermediate and Advanced Awards for the nippers, the Surf Proficiency Award, and then seasonal and, finally, full-time employment. Achieving these goals builds self-confidence, but staying the course demands *ukubekezela*, and the competing pressures of the surrounding township masculinity intrude, and sometimes succeed in deflecting the adolescents from completing the course.

One respondent explicitly related this process to the Xhosa (not Zulu) custom of initiation schools for young men, which involve circumcision and feats of endurance, a ceremony he had himself gone through:

> You are tensing, you are in pain, there are no women there, you carry on pushing even though you are in pain, you push until you get through, the same as a lifesaver, putting you through the tests until you are there. But you can get shot in the street, or starve, and that's suffering, and what do you have to show for it?

> In our culture, you have to do circumcision, there are different kinds of customs you do in the bush. Those pains are getting you to be a man, and stop being a boy. You can't feel the pain any more. You are a man. This is where we are separated from ladies. A man in our culture must have cows, and a big house. For me, to be a man, you don't have to have any cows to go [to] the bush ... You could go to hospital and do the same thing. For me, you are not forced to go there, you could do your circumcision and say you are a man now ...

In themselves the lifesaving awards are less about the need to accept pain, and more directed to specific competencies, but the speaker sees them and a traditional rite of passage through the same lens. Unlike others, though, he questions whether suffering is an essential element of this process.

There is a similar need to explore the masculinity of the lifesavers not only through the lens of the Zulu terms that were volunteered and that draw on older traditions. The interviews also explored other issues to do with the work and relationships.

### Relating to women

Respondents have doubts about the physical abilities and stamina of the (very few) women lifesavers, but more emphasis falls on their alleged lack of *ukubekezela* (this was completely disputed by young women lifesavers consulted). Women are seen as lacking the ability to handle difficult situations:

Crispin Hemson

*Linda Ndlovu and Xolani Ngidi, two leading members
of the Thekwini SLC*

You get some women lifesavers who are stronger than some of the
male lifesavers. But there are differences when it comes to *ukubekezela.*

For now, girls are not as tough as men, they are meant to be soft
and gentle. They are trying to be hard, to prove they can do what
we do. But when we are in the water, we are all the same. If she can
take the pain, she's equal. She's at your level if she's passed all the
tests.

They don't have patience, and can't cope under pressure. If they
must move some people to the bathing area, they give up trying.

However, there was also recognition of the social origins of limitations on female lifesavers:

> If you are a man, on the busy days at the beach, people won't take advantage of you, not listening to you for example, as they would to a female lifesaver – they would think, it's a female, why should we listen to her. . . . Sometimes male lifesavers will have to deal with drunk people themselves because basically they never listen to a woman in general, mostly blacks in our culture they don't want to be controlled by women.

Otherwise, the attitudes towards women which emerged in the interviews are stereotyped – they are mothers, people to advise them and to tend to their feelings. In addition, there are some ambivalent feelings about violence against women: 'I get cross when we men abuse our physical power over women – sometimes it feels wrong. But sometimes it is necessary, when you're being insulted.'

Negative comments concerned the untrustworthiness of women, or blamed some women because they turn to prostitution:

> Trust a man better – you trust a stone. If you trust a woman, you can trust a snake – her nature is to change all the time.

> Like the women who hang around street corners and sell their bodies. There are a lot of things that they can do besides doing that job, and some women are very young, they can still go to school or they can find another job.

Being a male lifesaver is recognised as rendering one attractive to women: 'In this job it keeps you fit, there's good money, you have a chance to see all the women on the beach. Ja, it is a romantic occupation, if you are into women. Women are more attracted to lifesavers.'

The way women members of Thekwini SLC are handled is somewhat equivocal. Efforts are made to promote their involvement, for example, by freeing them from paying membership fees (which other members tend never to pay anyway), and by issuing them uniforms. But few have qualified fully for employment, and unwanted pregnancies have blocked some careers. Casual interaction between males and females is relaxed and friendly, and membership of the club probably largely protects the women from the harassment they would otherwise be subjected to.

Crispin Hemson

## Relating to other men

A central question must be how male lifesavers with this emerging gender identity relate to each other. As in the township masculinity, peer groups are very powerful. Men, like women, can help you by giving advice, but there is a sense that they might 'undermine' you:

> You get advice from them, and you don't change too much [i.e. having to adjust to women] . . .

> [Things we don't like about other men are] gossiping, undermining and being moody.

> Being able to challenge one another with different things, gaining of lot of knowledge. When men are together, a lot of competition.

> They help create a very important bond in your life, which is friendship. It creates a space to relate your problems and share your problems with your friends. A sense of belonging – knowing you belong to certain friends.

There is constant group interaction – the adolescents in particular can spend hours talking and joking with each other – and also great ease of physical closeness amongst members of the club. It is not so much that men in the club try to be close to each other, so much as that they are relaxed about it. At a meeting there is no reticence about putting an arm around another male, while teenagers may groom each other's hair or draw pictures on their friend's skin. In contrast to comments in Western cultures about masculine isolation (Messner 1987: 56), the lifesavers are constrained little by fear of physical closeness, but emotional intimacy is different: 'I can't allow my friend to know too much about me, because one day he may use it against me.'

## Racism

> The way we are treated is not the same. You can see the expression in your face, they look at you as if you are not a lifeguard, as if you are a small guy. . . . People look at you, 'Oh a black lifeguard' . . . Although I have a qualification, I can't do it [the job], because the situation there is pushing you out, I need to relax my mind a bit.

> If you are black you are the first suspect if something is missing.

> There are very few white lifesavers who have very good attitudes towards us, we have good communication with them, for example,

who like working with different races. Otherwise the rest of them I don't think they deserve to stay on the beach because of their attitudes towards us – black or Indians.

A senior asks you lots of questions to test your knowledge – he doesn't ask white juniors.

Racism undermines a professional identity, and perhaps strengthens the lifesavers' identities as black people rather than as lifesavers. In reality, most lifesavers questioned seem to learn to accommodate racism rather than challenge it, and to put up with it – to *bekezela*.

## Forging a new identity

There is not yet much critical debate on the limits to *ukubekezela*, perhaps in part because the task of establishing a common masculine identity is not secure, and there are constant pressures to pull young men in other directions. The discipline of the job and the financial and social rewards of employment work to secure allegiance to the new masculinity, but the allegiance is hard-won.

Despite the obstacles, the young African men of Thekwini SLC are generating a new masculinity which in significant ways diverges from the black oppositional masculinity of their township peers but which inescapably still draws in some elements of that masculinity, as it does elements of the other two masculinities identified earlier in the chapter.

The emerging masculinity draws its strength from two changing contexts: a political context in which black people now have a stake, and a material context in which career progression and financial security are now possible. These changes create the possibility for men to explore a sense of masculine dignity and autonomy and to break away from what they now experience as the constraints of township masculinity. In doing so they still draw on tropes from earlier masculinities, *ukubekezela* and *ukuzithemba*, which affirm both the tradition of endurance and the impulse to self-affirmation, and which are now brought into the service of a redefined gender identity.

NOTES

1. The author is one of two white members of the Thekwini SLC, and the oldest member.

Crispin Hemson

## BIBLIOGRAPHY

Messner, M. 1987. 'Reformulating the Male Role'. In M. Kimmel, *Changing Men*. Newbury Park: Sage.

Morrell, R. 1998. 'Of Boys and Men: Masculinity and Gender in Southern African Studies'. *Journal of Southern African Studies* 24(4).

Pinnock, D. 1982. *The Brotherhoods: street gangs and state control in Cape Town*. Cape Town: David Philip.

Ramsay, S. 1996. 'Ubudoda and Ubunkunzi: African masculinity and working life in Durban, 1900–1907', unpublished paper.

Thompson, G.L. 2000. 'Making Waves, Making Men: The Emergence of a Professional Surfing Masculinity in South Africa During the Late 1970s'. In R. Morrell, ed., *Changing Men in Southern Africa*. Pietermaritzburg: University of Natal Press.

Torr, L. 1997. 'Lamontville: A History, 1930–1960'. In P. Maylam and I. Edwards, *The People's City*. Durban: Heinemann/University of Natal Press.

# CHAPTER 3

# 'Man, Gun and Horse'
## Hard Right Afrikaner Masculine Identity in Post-Apartheid South Africa

SANDRA SWART

There is a popular joke still to be heard in the bars of South Africa: 'What has four legs and a prick that falls off? . . . Eugene Terre Blanche's horse'. This refers to the now-famous incident of the Afrikaner[1] paramilitary leader Eugene Terre Blanche taking an ignominious tumble from his horse as he sat at the head of an armed, mounted commando of the Afrikaner Weerstandsbeweging (AWB), protesting government iniquity in the early 1990s.[2] The image of this self-styled super-Afrikaner is of an armed khaki-clad horseman followed by a commando of men loyal to him. His assumed role and the gendered identity of his followers have a history.

Terre Blanche established the AWB with six friends in his garage in 1973. Eugene Ney (after Napoleon's Marshall Ney) Terre Blanche ('White Earth') was born in 1941 in the western Transvaal where he still owns a family farm with his wife, Martie, and an adopted daughter. His AWB appellation is 'General', but his legitimate rank is lance corporal in the South African citizen forces. At high school he was captain of the first rugby team and chairperson of the debating club. He joined the South African Police, rising to the rank of warrant-officer and becoming chairperson of the police's cultural group. He was also the one-time bodyguard of Prime Minister John Vorster. It was after becoming disillusioned with Vorster's 'liberal views', that Terre Blanche started the AWB.

The crumbling of apartheid exposed the differences in the supposed homogeneity of Afrikaners and, simultaneously, caused Afrikaners as a whole to suffer a crisis of identity (De Klerk 1984). Afrikaners responded to the changes in various ways. Some embraced the new democratic order while others rejected it. Among those who rejected it, many followed the party-political route but others, like Terre Blanche, adopted an extra-parliamentary approach that only bordered on the legitimate.

From the late 1970s onwards the AWB gained members and popularity. It attracted support from those conservative Afrikaners whom the apartheid state had served; providing jobs, education, security, political power and social status for this group. The label 'Afrikaner male' was synonymous with status, and first place in the power hierarchy was axiomatic. The rapid transition following the transformist endeavours initiated by the ruling National Party (NP) from the 1970s gradually dented the life prospects of some Afrikaners. Things got worse with the unbanning of the African National Congress (ANC) and the progress towards a non-racial democratic dispensation in 1994. The apartheid state was forced to the negotiating table. While senior members of the civil and military bureaucracy were protected under a series of agreements, those Afrikaners on the periphery – policemen, soldiers, owners of smallholdings and minor clerks – were unprotected, and it is from these ranks that the AWB drew its support. These were largely politically conservative lower middle class men, first- or second-generation in the city, but often with connections back to the family farm. In 1990 there were 57 paramilitary groups, and by 1993 there were 200, with a total of about 18 000 members (Seegers 1996: 188). The epitome of these vigilante hard right factions was the AWB. The organisation often maintains that it does not give out membership numbers for 'strategic reasons', but has posted a figure of seventy thousand on its web-site.[3] It is probably about fifteen thousand strong (up from a possible five thousand to nine thousand in 1988) (*Sunday Times*, 25 April 1993).

This chapter explores the reaction of this particular sector of Afrikaner society, which, after forty years of a life-style and status secured by the state, has had to face a multiracial, non-sexist dispensation. While many whites, English- and Afrikaans-speaking, accommodated themselves to the new situation, some rejected, and continue to reject, it. Amongst this grouping, a hard right masculinity is striking. In using the term 'hard', I borrow from Van Rooyen's discussion of the AWB (1994) to evoke a sense of political conservativism and a rigid belief system wrapped up in a militarised, 'hyper'-masculine identity. The organisation in which hard right masculinity is most evident is the AWB. Although the AWB is based in Gauteng, it has support in other provinces, indicating a broad racial and ethnic reaction amongst Afrikaans- and English-speaking whites to the state's 'handover' of power to the black majority.

In South Africa there are multiple definitions of masculinity – with dynamic hierarchies of identity. Different masculinities do not earn equal

Sandra Swart

social respect. Some are actively dishonoured (like homosexuality), some are exemplary (like sporting heroes), and some are socially marginalised (as in the case of certain ethnic groups) (Connell 1996: 209). From the consolidation of Afrikaner dominion in 1948, it may be argued that Afrikaner masculinity assumed a hegemonic form, being culturally dominant, reflecting authority and leadership, not only over other masculinities, but over the gender order as a whole (Morrell 1998).

Hard right Afrikaner masculinity has moved over the short space of a decade from a hegemonic, indeed an exemplary, identity to a socially marginalised and, in many sectors, an actively dishonoured identity. At the time of political transitions group identities are most volatile and fragile (Munro 1995). The AWB was essentially a body created by political and social transition where class positions were inverted. In the process, cultural ideals concerning manhood were challenged. It is in this context that I'd like to pose the question, 'How does a once hegemonic man cope with a fall from his horse?'

## Losing the reins of power

The AWB was born out of the material decline of Afrikaner men whose upward class mobility had been facilitated by apartheid. The deepening of class divisions and loss of faith in the old ideology of unity, led to an alienated sector of society. On 16 December 1988 Terre Blanche noted: 'Our government is creating a new poor white class, and we must rise as a nation out of this' (Hochschild 1991: 254). The rise of the hard right has been couched in terms of an inherent bigotry, but the rise of the AWB cannot be attributed to a latent fascism in the Afrikaner. The key lies in the collapse of Grand Apartheid and the failure of the NP to forge a political settlement accepted by all its followers. On the political level, the deviation from exclusive white privilege alarmed those at the bottom of the hierarchy. The AWB have been likened to the Ku Klux Klan (Sparks 1990: 324) and the National Front (Harrison 1981: 271), both drawn from alienated sectors of society who fear that their governments have sold out the white lower middle class to other ethnic or class groups. As cultural identity and political power remain inextricably linked in the experience of the Afrikaner (Van Niekerk 1987), political shifts have been interpreted as cultural betrayal (Munro 1995).

For decades, being a white male meant being kept from poverty, with jobs in the traditional Afrikaner preserves like the mines, railways, the police, and the civil service being handed down 'from father to son' (Hochschild 1991: 189). Now the fathers are retrenched and the sons face competition from blacks in the workplace. Jobs are disappearing with the recession and automation in industry. The NP has become increasingly the dominion of the upper class Afrikaners who can afford increased 'generosity' to the black majority. Poorer Afrikaners suffer black competition for jobs and feel sold-out by the upper middle class Afrikaner. On their web-site the AWB contends, 'The Boer nation is currently governed by uncivilized, inexperienced gluttons because of shrewd planning and betrayal from within its own ranks.' The AWB attracted and continues to attract whites who feel threatened socio-economically by more upwardly mobile blacks on the shop floor.

During the late 1970s and early 80s, the NP government increasingly turned a blind eye to infringements of the Group Areas Act which led to race-mixing in the lower income bracket areas. The relaxation of the industrial colour bar caused the number of registered black apprentices to increase eightfold between 1981 and 1985. The position of blue-collar workers was further jeopardised by automation in industry. The early 1980s witnessed the worst economic recession for whites since the 1930s. Between 1981 and 1986, the figure for registered white unemployed increased from 6 000 to 32 000 (Leach 1989: 108). The AWB promised a return to the sanctuary of white male privilege. While it provided an attraction for bigoted fanatics, ordinary blue-collar workers, minor civil servants, and debt-ridden farmers were also drawn to it. The AWB also ran a welfare programme, the *Volkshulpskeme*, donating food, shoes and old clothing to poor whites. In Pretoria, unemployed AWB members were used as strike-breakers or to replace black workers who were trying to unionise (Hochschild 1991: 212).

As the underlying material or structural bases of gender relations shift, the meaning of masculinity is contested and, sometimes, redefined (Kimmel 1987a: 134). Changes in masculinity result from struggles for hegemony (Connell 1996: 210).[4] For some Afrikaner men the loss of hegemony meant re-inventing themselves to adapt. For the hard right it meant re-entrenching. Like vigilante groups in the United States of America, the AWB has formed a militia which propagates a particular 'hard' kind of masculine identity. Two very different images of the hard right exist: one of a bombastic but essentially impotent blue-collar clique, and the other of a powerful body of men capable of violent acts to restore the old order.

The former views the conservative Afrikaner with derision: 'What's the definition of an Afrikaner? . . . Someone who's always tinkering with his brake linings.'[5] After work you can find him in the all-male bar, drinking brandy and coke, still in his blue overalls. He will probably have strong opinions about rugby and have engine-oil under his finger-nails. He may have a fibre-glass Kudu in his garden.[6] As the self-styled Afrikaner dissident Rian Malan noted: 'Out in the plots a Boer too poor to afford a real farm, can plant mealies and own a cow and some sheep and live out his fantasies' (1990: 94).

The latter image of the hard right is the view, projected by the AWB, that its members are heroic family men struggling for the *volk* (Afrikaner people) to govern themselves in an all-white state based on the old republics of the Transvaal and Orange Free State. According to the AWB web-site the 'need exists for the Boer nation to have a free Sovereign Republic . . . where murderers, criminals and the ignorant can no longer rule over its free spirited citizens'. Internationally, this call is couched in the increasingly sophisticated language of the self-determination of ethnic minorities (*Vrye Weekblad*, 21 September 1990). The AWB asserts that it is a '. . . freedom movement whose highest priority is to gain [its] own Sovereign Republic'. As the Boer nation descends from the 'best nations of old Europe, the UK, Americas, the antipodean countries and Russia', the organisation is not limited to Afrikaans-speakers, but also welcomes English-, French- and German-speakers. On this basis, the AWB also solicits donations in dollars, pounds, marks, roubles or rands. This identity is an amalgam of republican ideology, racism, militarism, and history, both remembered and misremembered.

## Horse and gun

The paramilitary commandos of the AWB are based on the historical republican model (Swart 1998). For many, Afrikaner masculinity has come to be encoded and institutionalised in the republican commando system, a loose form of Afrikaner military organisation which originated in the nineteenth century. As armed mounted combat groups, commandos functioned as a practical and symbolic mode of masculinity. The commando system historically extended into politics, culture and social mythology (Frankel 1984). Under apartheid, the army was divided up into permanent members and so-called 'citizen force' commandos. This commando system entailed the division of the country up into a number of geographically defined regions, which then fell under the military control of a local commander. The members of these commandos were all adult white males living in the area who were of a military age and who had already completed their compulsory call-up period of national service. Such men were liable for call-up periods of one month per year with their local commando. Although the ANC government has dispensed with this system, there still remains a large reservoir of white males who have had extensive military training. The commandos are part of the social machinery in the construction of Afrikaner manhood. AWB rhetoric draws on Afrikaans oral tradition, which maintains that every Boer male is a born fighter, inheriting ancestral shooting and equestrian skills (Kemp 1941: 165, 173). There is a romantic tradition that no military training was necessary: that the Boer life-style would suffice in teaching him equestrian skills, riflery, scouting and combat ability. This was a mythic image: 'Man. Horse and gun' meant military preparedness (Van der Merwe 1987: 7). The image of the Boer warrior as *volksheld* (people's hero) was important amongst the array of images used to bolster Afrikaner nationalism.[7] A useful way to create a common Afrikaner cause out of the several factions which made up the AWB and to create a shared ideal (and help to support AWB claims to speak for all Afrikaners), was to exploit the unifying potential inherent in the image of the heroic Boer in his commando.

The AWB explicitly denied women a role from the outset, on the grounds of the biblical injunction that women may not have authority over men – a principle written into the AWB programme. Section 6 states that 'women can serve with full voting rights in the *burgerrade*' (citizens' committees). However, no woman may serve in a position of authority over any male: 'As wives and mothers, women serve in an auxiliary capacity as caterers and providers of hospitality.'[8] They also serve a rhetorical function – used as metonyms to represent white Afrikaner civilisation. Women are the symbol of that which the AWB seeks to protect. The white Afrikaans-speaking heterosexual family unit is seen as the minima of civilisation. The closely-affiliated all-woman 'Kappie Kommando' provides organisational space for hard right women. This group, whose symbol is the old Voortrekker bonnet, serves as a pressure group committed to traditional values: urging their men 'Get rid of the *Hensoppers* and the *Joiners* [the 'handsuppers' – the Boers who surrendered to British forces during the Anglo-Boer War – and the 'sellouts'] and we women will honour you' (Harrison 1981: 271).

Much rhetoric surrounds the possession of weapons. Like right wing vigilante groups in America, the AWB invokes a call to arms in defence of republican freedom. Terre Blanche's cry, guaranteed to draw applause, 'We will not give up our guns. We will make war!' is similar to the American militia motto: 'Livefree or die'. Terre Blanche responds violently to government vacillations in gun-ownership legislation and members or allies of the organisation have been linked to weapons theft. The English-speakers who can escape on dual-citizenship passports, are dubbed *soutpiels* (salt penises), as with one foot in Africa and one in Europe, their genitalia are left hanging in the sea. The Afrikaner, however, the AWB argues, is destined to stay in South Africa and thus has to prepare for war. In 1990 Terre Blanche remarked: 'I will personally expel any member of the AWB who hands in his weapon. An unarmed White Man in Africa is a dead White Man.'[9]

Attired in their trademark khaki uniforms, AWB commandos have actively asserted their masculinity through violent acts.[10] One of the first acts of the group was to tar and feather a professor of history. In 1979 during a lecture at the University of South Africa, Professor Floors Van Jaarsveld suggested the de-sanctification of the Day of the Covenant, the quasi-mythical pact with God some early Afrikaans settlers made in order to defeat a Zulu army. An AWB sortie burst in, with Terre Blanche carrying a small horse-whip, disrupting the assembly and assaulting the speaker. He defended himself in court on the grounds that he was protecting a sacred day on behalf of the Boer people, and was fined R600 for *crimen injuria* (a fine paid for by public subscription).

The group subsequently announced several intended acts of terror: plans to infest the multiracial holiday resort Sun City with syphilis germs and to blow-up non-racial hotels in the early 1980s (Kemp 1990: 47). Their vaulting ambition often led to absurdity: as in May 1993, when the AWB publicly revealed their Underwater Commando Unit: two frogmen in full wet suits and flippers managing to march abreast. The AWB's dramatic, televised incursion into Bophuthatswana in 1994 to buttress the black homeland government ended in tragic farce when three 'advance guard' AWB members were gunned to death by a black soldier as they tried to surrender next to their old Mercedes Benz sedan.

In the early 1990s the AWB engaged in a systematic terror campaign. In 1990 extremist white groups perpetrated 50 counts of political violence, 15 per cent of all such acts nation-wide (*Vrye Weekblad*, 14 December 1990). The focus later moved to public demonstrations – occasionally culminating in violence, like the 1993 occupation of the World Trade Centre, seat of multiparty negotiations. The group has fascist overtones, with a swastika-like flag, a proclivity for loud German marching music, and a weakness for BMWs (Kemp 1990: 4). But the historical roots lie firmly with a quest for the lost rural Utopias of the old Boer republics. Their anthem '*Kent Gij dat Volk?*' ('Do you know the people?'), is the melancholy national anthem of the old Transvaal Boer Republic. Terre Blanche invokes '*die trane van gister*' ('the tears of yesterday'), and makes much rhetorical capital of the Boer's history of suffering. The appellation 'Boer' is favoured over 'Afrikaner' in order to indicate a distance between the sell-out Afrikaners of the former governing National Party and to invoke the republican understanding of Boer manhood inextricably linked to the commando system. The group subscribes to the apartheid myths of total onslaught, communist danger, and even fears of the Illuminati or international monetary conspiracy. Demagogues thrive on enemies and the AWB offers the blacks, the Jews, the *hendsoppers*, the British-Jewish parliamentary system, foreign investors and the government as enemies.

Although Terre Blanche's powerful, charismatic personality permeates outsiders' understanding of the AWB, ordinary men in lesser leadership roles adopt the Boer patriarchal mantle with equal dedication. In April 1994, for example, an AWB commando awaited the democratic elections on a farm in the Magaliesberg mountains of the north-western Transvaal. The camp was established on the farm of an AWB leader, Manie Maritz – named after his father Salomon Gerhardus 'Manie' Maritz, a rebel leader in 1914. Maritz provided a haven from the 'New South Africa', awaiting the instructions from AWB high command. Limping from a horse-riding accident, he patrolled the farm and fed fifty Afrikaners, of both genders and all ages, three meals a day, because 'He had no choice. He was a Boer . . .' (Boynton 1997: 23). He identified strongly with Afrikaner heroes of the past, particularly the quixotic martyrs who tried to restore a Boer republic in 1914. Like the rebels, he was part of a patriarchal power structure based on the commando system, impelled by the cult of the male father figure-hero personality, supported by a base of loyal women. Like his role models, he and his refugees suffered fear of black peril, loss of jobs, loss of civic privileges, loss of hegemonic language and loss of control over the transmission of their culture. When asked about the presence of skinheads and foreign mercenaries on his farm, he answered that, after all, French volunteers had helped the Boers in the South African war. He played down the importance of class, emphasising that it was Afrikaner culture he hoped to preserve. He appealed to the disempowered, the peripheral, the poor and the bitter – offering a rebel manhood that was once again rough-hewn from past rhetoric. Maritz is yet another horseman with a gun and a sense of history, trying to hold on to what it means to be a Boer, and therefore, a man.

### An end to *baasskap*

The men who support the AWB relied on *baasskap* ('being the boss' or exercising hegemony) over the black majority. As apartheid dissolved, they dedicated themselves to reasserting white *baasskap*. A demonstration in 1989, for example, included the placards: 'Go Away Baboons' and 'Let the Kaffirs Kill themselves' (*Sunday Star*, 24 September 1989). They have organised a youth wing, *Stormvalke*, and commando, *Brandwag*, to quell potential black uprisings. The changing racial order overturned the old hierarchies, challenging the identity of white men – particularly in spheres which had come to rely on everyday assertions of white superiority over black. The AWB drew a great deal of support, for this reason, from the police force. Brigadier Theuns Swanepoel, who formed the bodyguard 'Aquila' for Terre Blanche and is notorious for being the officer who ordered his men to open fire in Soweto in 1976, estimated that in the late 1980s 70 per cent of white police officers belonged to the far right. Under apartheid, the predominately Afrikaans police force was seen as the front-line in a war of national survival (although officially police officers are not allowed to join the AWB). Brutalising peer group pressure and everyday experiences of extreme inter-racial violence coupled with a low-paying, low-status job create a disaffected brotherhood. As journalist and political commentator, Allister Sparks noted: 'Put him [the Afrikaner] in a uni-form, give him a baton and a gun, and you give him a licence also to go about affirming his manhood and his whiteness by beating up blacks' (1990: 343).

In 1988 Barend Strydom, an AWB member and a former policeman, randomly opened fire on the black people in Strijdom Square, Pretoria, killing seven and wounding twenty-two of them. On his arrest, an AWB spokesperson noted: 'There is support, or rather sympathy, for Mr. Strydom. We do not say what he did was a good thing. But we understand and we are sympathetic . . . the AWB is not to blame, the government is to blame for what happened' (Hochschild 1991: 216). Terre Blanche blamed the removal of influx control and curbs on police powers for Strydom's actions, and at his trial Strydom said, 'Each black person threatens the continued existence of whites . . .'.

Astonishingly, racial distance and enmity has occasionally been over-come by a common paternal, militaristic masculinity. In November 1993, for example, the AWB and Inkatha Freedom Party (IFP) held a joint march in which Zulu warriors shouted 'Viva AWB!' and the AWB has admitted to training IFP cadres (*Rapport*, 20 November 1993). Similarly, the AWB attempted to aid the black homeland government of Bophutha-tswana (BOP). In March 1994 when the civil servants went on strike and riots ensued, the BOP Minister of Defence asked the white right but centrist Volksfront for help (Seegers 1996: 282). It was the AWB, how-ever, which responded to buttress Lucas Mangope's government, but they had to be ignominiously rescued by the South African Defence Force.

## The ride and fall of Terre Blanche

As precipitous as the fall from his horse was, was Terre Blanche's 1990 fall from power. Terre Blanche ran the AWB along patriarchal lines with himself as the elected father figure in charge of the paramilitary commandos. The source of the articulation and promotion of gendered rhetoric is the demagogic oratory of the AWB leadership, predominately that of Terre Blanche, in a series of 'meetings' to recruit for the commandos. As a charismatic paternal figure, Terre Blanche ran the AWB with his cult of the personality. His famously off the cuff speeches were made from key words jotted onto the back of a cigarette packet – which were then auctioned at the end of the meeting to raise funds. Pupils who read the set books by E.N. Terre Blanche seldom attribute them to him, but Terre Blanche has won three awards from the Afrikaanse *Taal en Kultuur-vereeniging*, and has released two poetry CDs.

In 1988 Jani Allan, a blonde English-speaking gossip writer for a liberal newspaper, interviewed Terre Blanche. She was attracted by his hyper-masculinity, labelling him 'RamBoer'. Rumours circulated after Allan's rapturous column, in which she sighed: 'I'm impaled on the blue-flame of his blow-torch eyes.' A British court revealed in 1992 that she had been impaled on a good deal more than that. The affair became international gossip after a libel case between Allan and Channel 4, which further embarrassed Terre Blanche. Dubbed 'a pig in a safari suit' by Allan, he was reduced to the status of a womanising, alcoholic buffoon (UK *Sunday Times*, 9 August 1992). In an interview published in the *Fair Lady* magazine in December 1989, Allan said she had once hit Terre Blanche with a horse-whip in front of his wife after he had started 'blubbering and bawling' in her flat the night after revelations of his affair became public. She also dismissed allegations of a sexual relationship with Terre Blanche as absurd, adding insult to injury by calling him 'fat'. There were intra-organisational calls for his dismissal as the heroic image of the *volksheld* (people's hero) had been fractured. The masculine code, which insisted on moral rectitude backed up by biblical injuncture, had been broken. The very symbol of that which the AWB seeks to protect – the Afrikaans family unit – had been violated. Today, Terre Blanche serves a six-year sentence in the Ventersdorp jail; imprisoned not for his public right wing political actions, but for his assault of a black employee (*Mail and Guardian*, 17 June 1997).

The cartoon opposite illustrates the dangers of creating an exemplary, flawless masculinity and then elevating it to hyperbolic proportions. It becomes a caricature and a parody. Terre Blanche and his men, by adopting a hyper-masculinity rendered it a burlesque. They became like bodybuilders who try to extend one understanding of masculinity to its limits and end up on the competitive weight lifting circuit screeching,

Sandra Swart

dripping orange-brown competition dye, wearing diapers and eating baby food (Fussell 1992). In this way, the masculine identity becomes not threatening, but ludicrous.

## Gender anxiety

There is widespread media concern today over a 'crisis' in masculinity, particularly a crisis presented by the challenge of feminism. The theorist Harry Brod has shown that the white Western middle class man casts a nostalgic eye back towards the 1950s – ostensibly the last moment of fixed masculine practices. Brod quickly subverts this happy picture: showing the pervasive male fear of being robotised by industrial corporations, becoming merely men in 'grey flannel suits'.[11] Similarly, the gender anxiety of the hard right Afrikaner in a time of socio-political transition is revealing of the way formerly hegemonic masculinity roles are re-fashioned or re-entrenched. Analysing modes of masculinity at crisis points, as done in this chapter, also helps to dispel the myth that today's world is uniquely threatening to the male ego – that we are not facing a singular crisis of masculinity today, but that masculinities confront continual crises arising from transforming socio-political contexts (Brod 1987: 46). Nostalgia for a 'stable' past justifies intransigence and legitimises conservatism. Exposing the historical construction of past identities can free men to adopt new identities.

## Conclusion

Even with Terre Blanche in gaol, the AWB limps along. As their leader contends: 'The Boers haven't finished trekking. They are just next to the road resting their oxen and planning the political trip ahead' (*Mail and Guardian*, 6 March 1998). Modern hard right Afrikaners are the products of the intolerable pressures of a transforming South Africa, marooned by the demise of the apartheid state. Unseated by a democratic dispensation, they are attracted by the AWB in that its ideology caters for the gender anxiety generated in a time of transition when group identities are most fragile. The AWB members' masculine identity is not challenged by Afrikaner women. It has, however, lost its hegemony. It is no longer exemplary and has become socially marginalised and actively dishonoured by the state. The AWB supporters are able to cling to a known gender role. In addition, the organisation promises to restore the lost security and status once the automatic due of an Afrikaner male. Paternal leadership figures serve to replicate patriarchal society in a new constitutionally non-sexist environment.

The AWB draws on a re-fashioned image of Boer male identity to validate and articulate its position. In the inextricable mixing of gender and ethnic identity, the right wing Afrikaner male seeks his race in his manhood. A composite of bravery and bravado, the men of the AWB make their plans and hold their meetings and recruit other men lost in the New South Africa.

## NOTES

1. In this chapter, 'Afrikaners' will refer to white, Afrikaans-speaking people. Afrikaans is the home language of many black people, but historically, especially under apartheid, they were socially, politically and economically excluded from membership of the racially exclusive group which gave support to the governing National Party.

2. For a discussion of the AWB and its dimensions see, for example, Johann van Rooyen (1994), *Hard Right – the New White Power in South Africa*; A. Kemp (1990), *Victory or Violence: The Story of the AWB*; and P. Kotze and C. Beyers (1988), *Opmars van die AWB*.

3. The AWB web-site can be found at http://www.lantic.co.za/~awb/

4. For the ways masculinities are structured and change historically see: Robert Nye (1993), *Masculinity and Male Codes of Honour in Modern France*; and Michael Kimmel (1996), *Manhood in America: A Cultural History*.

5. Overheard in a bar in Malvern, an Afrikaans working class suburb in KwaZulu-Natal.

6. Indeed, the AWB commando leader Maritz does. See the documentary 'Horseman Manie Rides to Defeat' (Johannesburg: Free Film Makers, 1992). The large antelope, the kudu, makes a popular shooting trophy and its meat is dried for biltong. A fibre-glass copy of the kudu fulfils the same role as the planting of a symbolic crop of mealies in an urban garden: it serves as a reminder of the Afrikaner male heritage as farmer and hunter.

7. For an analysis of the creation of this identity in the South African war, see, for example, Kobus du Pisani and Louis Grundlingh (1998), '"*Volkshelde*": Afrikaner nationalist mobilisation and representations of the Boer warrior'.

8. Women do undergo weapons training in self-defence.

9. In a speech given on 14 March 1990 in Klerksdorp.

10. This is ironic given that in the Anglo-Boer War the name adopted for an English soldier was a 'khaki' and an Afrikaner would be shot for wearing it.

11. Michael S. Kimmel has also shown that 'crises' have afflicted an orthodox sense of masculinity throughout history, citing examples from seventeenth century England and nineteenth century America. See M. Kimmel (1987b), 'The Contemporary "Crisis" of Masculinity'; and E. Pleck and J. Pleck (1980), *The American Man*.

BIBLIOGRAPHY

Boynton, G. 1997. *Last Days in Cloud Cuckooland – Dispatches from White Africa*. Johannesburg: Jonathan Ball.

Brod, H., ed. 1987. *The Making of Masculinities: The New Men's Studies*. Boston: Allen and Unwin.

Connell, R.W. 1996. 'Teaching the Boys: New Research on Masculinity, and Gender Strategies for Schools', *Teachers College Record* 98(2).

De Klerk, W. 1984. *The Second (R)evolution – Afrikanderdom and the Crisis of Identity*. Johannesburg: Jonathan Ball.

Du Pisani, K. and L. Grundlingh. 1998. '"Volkshelde": Afrikaner nationalist mobilisation and representations of the Boer warrior'. Rethinking the South African War, Unisa Library Conference.

Frankel, P.H. 1984. *Pretoria's Praetorians: Civil-Military Relations in South Africa*. Cambridge: Cambridge University Press.

Fuessell, S.W. 1992. *Muscle: Confessions of an Unlikely Bodybuilder*. London: Scribners.

Harrison, D. 1981, 1985. *The White Tribe of Africa*. London: Ariel.

Hochschild, A. 1991. *The Mirror at Midnight*. London: Collins.

Kemp, A. 1990. *Victory or Violence: The Story of the AWB*. Pretoria: Forma Publishers.

Kemp, J.C.G. 1941. *Vir Vryheid en vir Reg*. Cape Town: Nasionale Pers.

Kimmel, M. 1987a. *Changing Men*. California: Sage.

———. 1987b. 'The Contemporary "Crisis" of Masculinity'. In H. Brod, ed., *The Making of Masculinities: The New Men's Studies*. Boston: Allen and Unwin.

———. 1996. *Manhood in America: A Cultural History*. New York: Free Press.

Kotze, P. and C. Beyers. 1988. *Opmars van die AWB*. Morgenzon: Oranjewerkers Promosies.

Sandra Swart

Leach, G. 1989. *The Afrikaners*. London: Macmillan.

Malan, R. 1990. *My Traitor's Heart*. London: Bodley Head.

Morrell, R. 1998. 'Of Men and Boys: Masculinity and Gender in Southern African Studies', *Journal of Southern African Studies* 24(4).

Munro, W.A. 1995. 'Revisiting Tradition, Reconstructing Identity? Afrikaner Nationalism and Political Transition in South Africa', *Politikon* 22(2).

Nye, R. 1993. *Masculinity and Male Codes of Honour in Modern France*. New York: Oxford University Press.

Pleck, E. and J. Pleck. 1980. *The American Man*. Englewood Cliffs: Prentice-Hall.

Seegers, A. 1996. *The Military in the Making of Modern South Africa*. London: I.B. Tauris.

Sparks, A. 1990. *The Mind of South Africa*. London: Heinemann.

Swart, S. 1998. '"A Boer and his Gun and his Wife are Three Things Always Together": Republican Masculinity and the 1914 Rebellion', *Journal of Southern African Studies* 24(4).

Van der Merwe, P. 1987. 'Die Militere Geskiedenis van die Oranje-Vrystaat, 1910–1920'. MA degree. Bloemfontein: University of the Orange Free State.

Van Niekerk, P. 1987. 'Paradigmaverkuiwing in Afrikanerdenke', *Politikon* 14(1).

Van Rooyen, J. 1994. *Hard Right – the New White Power in South Africa*. London: I.B. Tauris.

# CHAPTER 4

# Making Waves, Making Men
## The Emergence of a Professional Surfing Masculinity in South Africa during the Late 1970s

GLEN THOMPSON

It's a man's world and never more so than in the water.
(*Down The Line*, 5 September 1977: 14)

## Introduction

The history of surfing in South Africa is about expressions of masculinity and the lure of the ocean waves. It has been a white, largely English-speaking and middle class adventure/extreme sport, upholding a hegemonic white masculinity privileged in terms of class, race/ethnicity, language and social differences between women and blacks (Epstein 1998: 50–1). Yet, surfing receives far less attention than rugby and cricket from white South Africa's sporting culture because the surfing population is smaller, has a counter-cultural reputation, and is confined to the coast. Surfing began among Durban's lifesavers in the late 1940s and spread down the coastline to the Cape (Jury 1989: 11). Since those early days the sport has gained momentum among the youth and became institutionalised in competitive surfing. Its 'alternative' image has also been commercialised into a fashion industry. Durban, or 'Surf City' as it is more popularly known, has remained the country's surfing capital through the years.

This chapter aims to explore the relations of culture and masculinity in South African surfing. Specifically, the making of a professional surfing masculinity in the years 1976 to 1979 is contextualised. In 1976 South African security forces were in Angola. In that year black students in Soweto began a protest that rocked the country, an event that can be seen as the start of the end of apartheid. The Soweto student uprising resulted from the crisis within African schooling and alerted a cocooned white society to the vulnerability of their 'whiteness'. The edifice of apartheid laws, state coercion, the socio-economic planning of South African's working and leisure lives, and Cold War geo-politics, which stalled decolonisation in southern Africa and attempted to contain the Namibian conflict, did not automatically secure white privilege in the face of black resistance (Beinart 1994: 227). The post-Sowetan political climate shaped the anxiety of a white social consciousness.

*Free Ride*, a popular surfing movie featuring the South African professional surfer Shaun Tomson, epitomised the 1970s spirit of riding waves on either single or twin-fin surfboards. While the introduction of tri-fin surfboards in the 1980s ended this era of surfing, the professional male surfer birthed in the late 1970s remained surf culture's ideal. These years which preceded my beginnings as a 13-year-old Durban 'grommet' (young novice surfer) in 1983 left traces which were influential in shaping my own white masculinity.

Surfing in South Africa emerged in the post-World War II era and then saw the 'golden age of longboards' (mid-1960s) displaced by the 'shortboard revolution' and an Aquarian hippie culture in the early 1970s (Dell 1992; Jury 1989). Barnett's surfology, *Hitting the Lip: Surfing in South Africa* (1974), documented this history along with the ocean lore, popular surf spots, advances in surfboard design, and the voices of South Africa's 'great men' of surfing. It was also a social text of how male surfers interacted with their context. Barnett described surfing as 'an ideal South African sport. It raises those involved in it above the mundane levels normally prescribed by our social environment' (30). Yet Barnett did not explore the 'mundane levels' of social life: beach apartheid remained hidden. The encoding of leisure space, beach useage and 'inter-racial' sporting activities in apartheid legislation disallowed blacks access to white beaches and consequently white beach culture. But even the differentiation on the beach of an up-country ('Vaalie') holidaymaker from local beachgoers was marked in both attitude and dress. Barnett's book implicitly recalls a world of gender and racial identities silenced in a celebration of South African surfing and echoes the themes found in later literature, such as in the surfing magazine, *Zigzag*.

This chapter examines the historical specificity of the making of a South African professional surfing masculinity during the late 1970s and is primarily based on an analysis of the themes, issues and images that appeared in *Zigzag*, supplemented by personal memory, interviews and other sources. Unless otherwise noted, all quotations are from various issues of *Zigzag*. The title of the magazine will not be repeated each time, only the details of the issue and the relevant page number.

*Zigzag* published its twenty-third edition in January/February 1999. It began as a newsprint tabloid in December 1976. The name of the magazine was located in the heart of surfing culture – the action of riding waves. Notwithstanding the cultural imperialism of the long-standing Californian magazines *Surfer* and *Surfing*, the only South African competition this magazine has faced was from the short-lived *Down The Line* (late 1970s) and *African Soul Surfer* (mid-1990s). *Zigzag*'s survival has been dependent on an unqualified leaning toward the documentation of competitive surfing and the promotion of surfing culture. The commercialisation of surf culture and the rise of professional surfing in the late 1970s created a context in which the editorial team chose to highlight the activities of a select group of competitive male surfers and subordinate the representation of recreational surfers – male, female and black. It was within that discursive and material process that a professional surfing masculinity was constructed as the dominant masculinity in South African surfing culture.

*The author at Victoria Bay, southern Cape, in 1984*

## 'Hawaiian winters': cultural imperialism

Since the 1960s, Hawaii has been mythologised by South African surfers. Surfing's Hawaiian roots led (male) surfers to see Hawaii both as a site to prove their manhood and as a form of social escapism. It was the received 'Hawaii' constructed through the American surf films, such as *The Endless Summer*, and magazines that promoted the Californian dream (Crawford 1997). This American cultural imperialism was further encouraged by the globalisation of the surfing industry and the commodification of Hawaii as the competitive arena for professional surfing in the late 1970s. In so doing, Cape Town and Durban became identified less with the English colonial heritage and more allied with the Californian image of a privileged and middle class leisure culture. It was this cultural imperialism which located 'Hawaii' for the South African surfer in *Zigzag*, an important site for the production and dissemination of local and international surfing knowledge and masculinities (cf. Connell 1997).

Surfing discourse in *Zigzag* gained its meaning through comparison and contrast to the Hawaiian surfing experience. 'Hawaii' was paradoxical at times. It was a palm tree 'paradise' worthy of 'pilgrimage'. It was also a 'battle', a 'testing ground', 'intimidating' in its assertion of a 'macho image' in the crowded winter waves which 'break you in' (March/May 1977: 9). Yet, the huge Hawaiian waves had a humbling effect on a surfer, displacing aggression with fear: 'Hawaii . . . unzips your soul, spreads your wares out like an elaborate psychic buffet' (Dec 1978/Feb 1979: 12). Surviving those waves engendered a status based on physical prowess and an induction into the surfing 'brotherhood'. *Zigzag* was therefore a site in which the gender relations ordering, and reflecting, the masculinist perceptions of men who surfed were configured by representations of a 'Hawaii' both as personal paradise and purgatory.

Encouraged by *Zigzag's* representations of 'Hawaii' was a discourse elevating the status of professional surfers: 'Surfers everywhere talk of having "made it" once they've surfed Hawaii. They talk of it as a sort of final experience – something one must do at some point in one's career' (Dec 1978/Feb 1979: 12). The link between 'Hawaii' and South African competitive surfing became crucial to *Zigzag* from 1977 onwards. Alongside this, the growth of the surf industry fixed its commercial gaze on the professional contest arena of the Hawaiian winters of December/January each year. It was not surprising to see a picture of the 'Bay boy', Shaun Tomson, surfing Hawaiian winter waves on the June/August 1977 magazine's cover. By focusing attention overseas, 'Hawaii' was a form of evasion from the political while perpetuating the male dominance of surf culture.

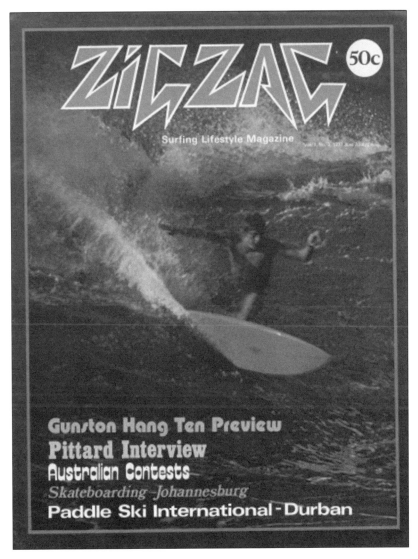

*Shaun Tomson on the cover of* Zigzag, *June/August 1977*

'Hawaii' was an important trope to Durban's 'Bay boys', the Bay of Plenty beach surfers who had become the pre-eminent surfing community in South Africa at the time. These surfers were indicative of Durban's growing surfing industry. *Zigzag* was able to tap into the commercial and cultural orientation towards the Bay of Plenty by featuring many of the 'Bay boys', of whom Shaun Tomson was the most visible. On the Bay's shoreline, the Dante's tearoom verandah was the social arena. It was here that stories of 'surfaris', the wave of the day, and sexual prowess were told and the future of South African professional surfing decided. More than food and drinks, Dante's provided a context for male bonding and an affirmation of heterosexual gender/sex relations (cf. Messner 1992).

But it was in *Zigzag* that the cultural ideal of the white South African professional surfer emerged. In writing of these representations of men, I do not assume unproblematically the association of maleness with masculinity. Recently scholars have come to see that masculinity has 'multiple and ambiguous meanings which alter according to context and over time' (Cornwall and Lindisfarne 1994: 12). Yet in *Zigzag*, masculinity was identified with men: essentialised as assertive in their bodily performance on waves and their dominance over women.

## Institutionalising the professional surfer

*Zigzag*'s dissemination of the cultural ideal aided the institutionalisation of professionalism in surfing. The formation of the South African Professional Surfing Association (SAPSA) occurred after the Hawaiian winter of 1977/78 (March/May 1978: 38) and formalised links with the newly formed International Surfing Professionals (ISP). SAPSA drew clear lines between professional and amateur surfing. One of the attempts at categorising professional surfers was the use of a contest ranking system similar to that of the world tour. The system attempted to lend financial stability to a struggling local contest circuit (March/May 1978: 28). It was the sense of status associated with sporting prowess and financial gain that the SAPSA system facilitated. The institutionalisation of a masculine competitive ethos centred on men who made surfing their business. The surf industry's increased sponsorship supported these men over amateur surfers.

The ability of professional surfing to monopolise the masculine identification in and with the surf industry enabled the creation of a specific materialist configuration of masculinity: the surfing hero who attained higher cultural value than amateur surfers did – in both the media and the surfing community. It was a representation of masculinity based upon financial stability, surfing prowess and the romanticisation of the surfing

Glen Thompson

lifestyle. In effect, the young, middle class surfing businessman became a cultural icon, a configuration not isolated from the dissemination of representations of professional surfers on the world tour. In South Africa the ultimate endorsement of a surf product was its usage by the 1977 world professional surfing champion, Shaun Tomson.

Through the press and surfing magazines, the professional surfer, amid a wider surge of professionalism in other sports elsewhere in the 1970s

*Shaun Tomson as cultural icon (first printed in the 1970s, reprinted in* Zigzag, *Sept/Oct 1993: 39)*

(Messner and Sabo 1990; Connell 1995) became the ideal representation of a surfer. This was in contrast to the dissenting masculine image of the long-blonde-haired, tanned beach bum (Pearson 1982). The possibility of this latter masculinity subverting the hegemonic configuration was clearly recognised within the surfing community, yet only muffled responses were heard in *Zigzag* (Dec 1979/Feb 1980: 4). SAPSA aimed to promote surfing to the general public as 'clean cut'. The mobilisation of Shaun Tomson in the press had a specific goal for surfing, namely, to help South African surfing re-orientate itself away from the early 1970s image of 'drug addicts, lay-abouts and beach bums' (Stander 1986: 50–1). SAPSA's representation of 'the surfer' was new and symptomatic of an emerging surf fashion industry – in which Tomson had direct commercial interests through the company Shaun Tomson Surfboards. These images flew in the face of earlier portrayals of surfers as resistant to any work ethic. The marginalisation of the leisure surfer and the amateur surfer by the rise of professionalism paved the way for a specific class-bound, and market-orientated, surfing masculinity. It was based upon the competitive sporting ethos of macho masculine values like physical strength, agility and prowess on the waves. At the same time, professional surfing formalised the 'man-on-man' contest system in 1977, emphasising surfers who 'literally do battle against one another' in a fraternal spirit (Sept/Nov 1977: 12). It was these aggressive psychic and physical masculine attributes that brought financial reward and status to surfing's cultural icons. The source of this masculine aggression was located in either the object of that aggression – the waves – or in the ethos of competitive surfing – the satisfaction of defeating one's peers. This behaviour asserted the masculinist tendency within surf culture and closed off representations of not only recreational and amateur male surfers but also women.

## Surfers and women

The professional surfer did not challenge the gender order in South Africa. The making of a professional surfing masculinity was based directly on the sexual division of leisure time between male surfers and women – as girlfriends, sisters or wives who sat on the beach. Women who participated in this beach culture reflected by a returned gaze the dominant and subordinated surfing masculine identities constructed by men, though not always without contestation.

*Zigzag* gave women little voice, except in the letters section. 'Noelene' came to the defence of a male surfer when a teenager complained of their continual conversations about waves (Dec 1978/Feb 1979: 4), and *Zigzag* used the teenager's letter to perpetuate a male surfing image, albeit in its more stereotypical form (March/May 1979: 4). Male surfers asserting their masculinity by emphasising their shared experience of wave-riding also replied to the teenager's letter: 'Surfers can only talk about waves because we are into our sport. We keep the memory of that insane tube ride, that radical re-entry, etc. fresh in our minds until the next time' (March/May 1979: 4). Notwithstanding some bruised male egos, the letters section of *Zigzag* pointed to male surfers' location within a male-dominated sporting culture.

The male-dominated gender order can clearly be seen in the language used in *Zigzag*, particularly in the slippage between 'boards' and 'broads' (March/May 1978: 23). Sexuality was referred to metonymically in describing Tomson's 1977 fifth consecutive win of the prestigious Gunston 500. Started in 1969, the Gunston 500 was South Africa's first internationally recognised annual professional surfing event. In *Zigzag* the Gunston 500 contest and the ocean were given feminine qualities while Tomson's surfboard, 'that there phallic symbol tube machine', drew on images of male power. The waves of the Bay of Plenty were likened to 'a blushing bride' that became 'moody', 'broody', 'full of womanly wiles', or 'coy and shy'. The contest suggested male sexual virility as Shaun Tomson was seen as the 'favourite to take her again', yet there was also a hint of incest, in Tomson's 'surfing the woman he's grown up with . . .' (June/Aug 1977: 7).

Tomson's competitive/sexual prowess was asserted most fully as a professional surfing masculinity (June/Aug 1977: 7). Linking the emerging masculine identity of the professional surfer to male sexual, social and cultural power was, therefore, explicit in *Zigzag*.

Women surfers received no mentioned in the early issues of *Zigzag*. The suppression of women's surfing experience had much to do with the assertion of the masculine identity of physical prowess. The opposition to women surfers, and masculinity over femininity, by male surfers was more generally part of the social dynamics of beach culture. Tanning, a white, middle class leisure activity, positioned women in beach culture as passive objects (Fiske 1989). This reflected negatively on those women who competed in the male domain of surfing. The women who participated in the professional surfing circuit did so with fewer contests and little financial reward. They also dealt with sexism in the water from their male counterparts (*The Daily News*, 13 July 1977). In perpetuating a dominant masculine surfing identity, the subordination of women enabled the promotion of male professional surfers at a time when the surf industry was in its infancy and lacking large amounts of capital to invest in the sport. This was a bias common to the gender order of the late 1970s.

## Surfing and the political

*Zigzag* produced and disseminated the social experience of surfers and reflected the everyday lived reality of white society. By turning my attention to how the post-Sowetan political context was viewed in the pages of *Zigzag*, I focus on those representations that examine the relationship of surfers to the 'crisis in confidence in white society' (Manzo 1992: 206).[1] The crisis was exacerbated by increasing international isolation, a repressive state, economic recession, and by an emerging popular black political assertiveness that was echoed in resistance poetry: 'The ocean waves echo with screams of bereaved parents . . .' (Mtshali 1986: 42–3).

A patterned response of evasion by surfers towards social change is found in the pages of *Zigzag*. Surfers evaded social discipline and ideological control rather than overtly resisting forms of domination. The politics of everyday life were rather directed towards the bodily pleasures of riding waves. This surfing mentality[2] re-orientated life away from the shore, so that the meaning constructed through surfing by surfers was a form of the denial of South Africa's social reality. This was evident in the Hawaiian Dave Ahrens's welcome at the Durban airport: 'You've come at a good time,' said his South African host (June/Aug 1977: 26). It was the quality of the waves breaking along the Durban beachfront, and not the political crisis of civil unrest in the townships, that was being commented on. Similarly, Mike Ginsburg's escapist sentiment that 'surfing was the only sane thing left in a world gone mad . . .' negated the existence of a world beyond the beach (March/May 1978: 10). This surfer's escape into the waves attempted to evade the everyday anxiety of a privileged life within white society.

Serving in the South African Defence Force (as all 18-year-old white South African males were required by law to do) was specifically seen to close off the surfer's world. For example, Peter Rademeyer expressed a sense of regained freedom on leaving the army (March/May 1978: 34). However, the political resignation of these young men at having to undergo national service was also evident. This provides evidence of white society as 'people who are privileged by that power and, paradoxically, in their privilege victims of it' (Crapanzano 1985: ix). The militarisation of society was also seen as a direct threat to competitive surfing, causing much resentment among surfers – even though the machoistic qualities of assertiveness, bravery and enduring pain promoted in conscription were echoed in the surf. As one surfer, Anthony Brodowicz, commented in *Zigzag*: 'The army put a real dent in my career. It really screwed everything up in my surfing. I lost a year in the water, missed two Gunstons and two national championships' (Sept/Nov 1978: 15).

On the one hand, surfers' desires to evade conscription were essentially self-indulgent and therefore only posed a feeble challenge to the state's ideology, especially as the evasion of military service was a criminal act for white men. On the other hand, surfing was not readily available to the state for the hegemonic mobilisation of a white, national South African masculinity (Morrell 1997: 175). The mobilisation of this hegemonic masculinity is much more effectively seen in a sport such as rugby (Bonnin et al. 1998; Grundlingh et al. 1995).

## Surfing and race

*Zigzag* upheld white privilege when commenting on 'race'. *Zigzag*'s norm was to report on tanned bodies in the surf. Yet, the presence of various Hawaiians at the 1977 Gunston 500 emphasised 'racial' difference (Sept/Nov 1977: 21). This ambivalence to 'race' was evident in *Zigzag*'s treatment of Dane Kealoha, a Hawaiian competitor at the 1979 Gunston 500. His 'race' was marked out by probing his parents' descent and his 'dusky brown' back. One racist incident was given attention. In a visit to South Africa in 1976, Kealoha was denied service at an East London restaurant. On Kealoha's winning of the Gunston 500 in 1979, the magazine openly condemned the restaurateur's racism and idealised the new champion. Therefore, while the roots of racism on dry land were not challenged, the contest in the waves offered a refuge from which the 'issue of equality' could be seemingly both evaded and broached (Sept/Nov 1979: 6–8).

This ambivalence was also evident in the donation of surfboards to the Indian lifesavers at a Durban club. The expressed desire to stimulate 'the keenness the Indians are showing in surfing' illustrated that access to wealth excluded many black South Africans from the sport. The small black surfing communities in Isipingo beach, south of Durban, and in the Western Cape went virtually unnoticed, except in the December 1977/February 1978 issue. This media exclusion reflected the constraints on black participation effected by apartheid. As a result 'the best and most beautiful stretches [of beachfront] have been reserved for white use, whilst those furthest away, least attractive and, above all, most dangerous have been set aside for the black majority' (Archer and Bouillon 1982: 167). By representing surfing as the sole sporting preserve of white society, *Zigzag* confirmed the existence of pervasive racial discrimination and inequality.

The world did not stand idly by as apartheid developed. The anti-apartheid movement mobilised world opinion and the imposition of a sports boycott was a direct result. This was keenly felt by white society (Beinart 1994: 215) and 'politics' finally impinged upon the sport of surfing. In 1978, the Australian surfing team did not participate in the

1978 World Amateur Championships held in East London as 'certain political considerations' led the Australian government to pressurise the Australian Surfing Association to stay away from South Africa (Sept/Nov 1978: 13). Similarly, Shaun Tomson was banned from surfing in a Brazilian professional contest in 1978, hampering the defence of his world title. In that context, and in the bid to gain recognition for the fledgeling professional sport, Shaun Tomson's win of the 1977 world professional championship was shown as asserting a national 'pride' in the sport (March/May 1978: 16). Surfing thus gained national recognition and became part of a campaign to overcome the country's political isolation (Dec 1979/Feb 1980).

## Conclusion

In this chapter, the forging of the professional surfing masculine identity in South Africa during the late 1970s has been contextualised by means of a cultural materialist analysis of the surfing magazine *Zigzag*. I have argued that the representation by *Zigzag* of 'Hawaii', overshadowing the 'Bay boys', affirmed a professional surfing masculinity and the material demands of the surf industry. Within this material context, a professional surfing masculinity became culturally dominant over recreational and amateur male surfers, women and blacks. South African professional surfers were firmly located within a male dominated gender order, and were keenly aware of the negative effects of conscription and the international sports boycott on their sport. On the one hand, the power of apartheid in late twentieth-century South Africa ultimately did not allow white male professional surfers to retreat out into the ocean waves. On the other hand, the small numbers of surfers and the marginal position of surfing as a sport meant that any possible challenge it could mount against hegemonic representations of masculinity failed to materialise. A history of surfing provides insight into how masculinities are contextually and culturally bound. This is especially true for the South African professional surfers who were making waves locally and globally during the late 1970s.

NOTES

1. Differences of language, class, politics and culture made for a 'fragile unity' in white society – upheld by the state's normalisation of racial

capitalism, the exclusion of persons by means of 'arbitrary constituted races', and an entrapment within a psychological apartness ordered by their social and political experience.

2. Crispin Hemson (2000) demonstrates how class and race forces operated distinctively to shape masculinities amongst African lifesavers which were quite different from the masculinities of the white surfers.

BIBLIOGRAPHY

Archer, R. and A. Bouillon. 1982. *The South African Game: Sport and Racism*. London: Zed.

Barnett, C. 1974. *Hitting the Lip: Surfing in South Africa*. Johannesburg: Macmillan.

Beinart, W. 1994. *Twentieth-Century South Africa*. Oxford: Oxford University Press.

Bonnin, D., R. Deacon, R. Morrell and J. Robinson. 1998. 'Identity and the Changing Politics of Gender in South Africa'. In D. Howarth and A. Noval, eds., *South Africa in Transition: New Theoretical Perspectives*. London: Macmillan.

Connell, R.W. 1995. *Masculinities*. Cambridge: Polity Press.

———. 1997. 'Men in the World: Masculinities and Globalisation'. Unpublished paper for the Colloquium, 'Masculinities in Southern Africa'. Durban: University of Natal.

Cornwall, A. and N. Lindisfarne. 1994. 'Dislocating masculinity: Gender, power and anthropology'. In A. Cornwall and N. Lindisfarne, eds., *Dislocating Masculinity: Comparative Ethnographies*. London: Routledge.

Crapanzano, V. 1985. *Waiting: The Whites of South Africa*. London: Granada.

Crawford, C. 1997. 'Waves of Transformation: California Surf Culture since World War II'. Unpublished paper for the First International and Eleventh National MELUS Conference: Honolulu, Hawaii.

*The Daily News*, 13 July 1977.

Dell, A. 1992. 'The History of Surfing'. Unpublished History 3 long-essay, University of Natal, Durban.

*Down The Line*, 5 September 1977.

Epstein, D. 1998. 'Marked men: whiteness and masculinity', *Agenda* 37.

Fiske, J. 1989. *Reading Popular Culture*. London: Routledge.

Grundlingh, A., A. Odendaal and B. Spies. 1995. *Beyond the Try-line: Rugby and South African Society*. Johannesburg: Ravan Press.

Hemson, C. 2000. '*Ukubekezela* or *Ukuzithemba*: African Lifesavers in Durban'. In R. Morrell, ed., *Changing Men in Southern Africa*. Pietermaritzburg: University of Natal Press.

Jury, M. 1989. *Surfing in Southern Africa including Mauritius and Reunion*. Cape Town: Struik.

Manzo, K. 1992. *Domination, Resistance, and Social Change in South Africa: The Local Effects of Global Power*. Westport: Praeger.

Messner, M. and D. Sabo, eds. 1990. *Sport, Men and the Gender Order: Critical Feminist Perspectives*. Champaign: Human Kinetic Books.

Messner, M. 1992. *Power at Play: Sports and the Problem of Masculinity*. Boston: Beacon Press.

Morrell, R. 1997. 'Masculinities in South African History', *South African Historical Journal* 36.

Mtshali, M. 1986. 'Hector Peterson – The Young Martyr'. In S. Ndaba, ed., *One Day in June: Poetry and prose from troubled times*. Parklands: AD Donker.

Pearson, K. 1982. 'Conflict, Stereotypes and Masculinity in Australian and New Zealand Surfing', *Australian and New Zealand Journal of Sociology* 18(2).

Stander Snr, B. 1986. 'Natal Surfriders Association'. In South African Surfriders Association, *Moments*. Durban: South African Surfriders Association.

*Zigzag* December 1976/February 1977 to December 1979/February 1980.

# CHAPTER 5

# Masculinity and its Malcontents
## The Confrontation between 'Struggle Masculinity' and 'Post-Struggle Masculinity' (1990–1997)

THOKOZANI XABA

I nearly did not recognise the tall young man who almost obsequiously greeted me in August 1993 in Kwamashu (near Durban in KwaZulu-Natal). I had last seen him ten years previously when he was only 11 years old. His father had been a friend whom I treated as an elder brother before his untimely death when this young man was too young to know him.

'Fernando!' I exclaimed.

'Uncle! You recognise me. I was afraid that you were not going to recognise me.'

'I was unsure at first, but then I could not miss the resemblance between you and your father.' I should not have said that. The mention of his father made Fernando react as though something had hit him in the middle of the chest.

'You should tell me about my old man sometime,' he said sadly.

When we parted, I could not help noticing the number of people who had stopped what they were doing and were unobtrusively looking our way. I was to discover later that Fernando was one of the 'exiles'.[1] I was to learn that the gunfire which rang out almost every night came from his place; he and the 'comrades'[2] tested their guns under the cover of the night. The reason people had been looking our way, was that I was the first 'non-guerrilla' and 'non-comrade' person with whom they had seen Fernando talking. Some told me later that they thought that he was holding me up.

In the following year, I met Fernando about ten times. During most of those times we only greeted each other and went our way. However, on one occasion I came across him walking to the store with three children. I was carrying a plastic bag containing fruit. As I was offering the fruit to the three children, he asked me to lend him R2,00. Since I did not have any money on me, I asked him to walk with me to the house to fetch it. On our way, I asked him if he had found employment. 'I can't, I do not have an ID,' he said, lowering his voice.

'Why don't you get one?', I enquired.

'I have tried – two times – and have not had any response.'

'Do you want me to help you try again?' I asked, opening the gate to our yard.

'No. The police are looking for me,' he said matter-of-factly. When we got to the house, I gave him R5,00 since I did not have a R2,00 coin.

'I shall repay you as soon as I can,' he promised.

'Don't worry about it,' I said.

I moved to another area and months went by. One day I visited Kwamashu and heard people singing 'freedom songs' which were periodically broken by the sound of a 'pump shotgun'. 'Fernando is dead,' said the man I was visiting. I enquired about the circumstances of Fernando's death but he did not have the details.

As the days went by, from talking to people here and there, the story which emerged was that Fernando was killed by the police who had been looking for him for some time. Reportedly, the police found Fernando with two or three friends in an outside building of what Fernando and his friends considered to be their 'safe house'. They told Fernando's friends 'Get up, you are arrested!' When Fernando also tried to get up, he was told not to bother himself. A gunshot rang out and a bullet went through his forehead and took the back of his head with it. Another went through his cheekbone and took out what remained of his brains after the first shot. Reportedly, seven bullets found their way into and through his body. Where Fernando and his friends had been hiding, the police found a cache of arms – some of which had belonged to members of the police who had been robbed and killed.

The story which came together was that Fernando (a former guerrilla) had returned to South Africa and found it difficult to get employment. At the time of his return, his contemporaries who were in 'people's courts' were contemplating their future since the political leadership was distancing themselves from their practices and functions. While their functions were nullified, attacks against them by the police had not ceased. According to the youth, such attacks, indeed, seemed to be intensifying. Fernando's function then was to train these men to defend themselves. What seems to have been the proof of the success of such training was that in many shoot-outs against the police none of the men were either injured or arrested.

As time went on, some of the former 'comrades' who did not work, and could not get IDs and, therefore, could not find employment, found ways of using their guns to earn money. Some used their guns to rob banks and others used them in contract murders. They reportedly replenished their stock of arms by attacking police and taking their firearms. One thing they did not do was hold up their neighbours. In fact, they are reported to have 'cleaned the area' (that is, searched for and killed those who preyed on the 'community'). One man captured the feelings of many when he mourned Fernando's passing by saying, 'We have lost a hero . . . .'.

⟫◆⟪

## Introduction

This chapter is about the struggle heroes of yesteryear who have become the villains and felons of today. The African township youth, the 'young lions' or 'the footsoldiers of the revolution', have become marginalised and some have become full-time gangsters. The journey from fame to notoriety was associated with changes in the culturally projected ideals of masculinity and in the socio-political conditions of post-apartheid South Africa. The transformation of masculinity is shown by presenting what happened to young men trained in the use of military weapons who found themselves without any means to support themselves or to get the lavish consumer items they believed they deserved. The shift corresponded to the emergence of a new set of gender norms which supplanted many of the old 'struggle' norms. This chapter addresses the preoccupations of former 'exiles' and 'comrades' who were not assimilated into the official defence forces of the new South Africa, who cannot return to school, and who are perennially unemployed. They find themselves in a system which they consider to have rewarded those who did not 'put their bodies on the line'.

Fernando's[3] story is not unique: neither in the way he lived his young life nor in the manner in which that life was prematurely and violently ended. His story represents a direct confrontation between 'struggle masculinity' and 'post-apartheid masculinity'. Like Fernando, numerous former 'exiles' arrived in the early 1990s with the hope of contributing to the development of the communities they were trained to defend. They were, however, rapidly drawn into the socio-economic struggles (such as rent and service boycotts, stayaways, etc.) in which 'comrades' and their communities were engaged. Many initially began by participating in 'defence committees' which protected communities from vigilantes and the state. But the nature of their battles against the state coupled with the methods they employed in fighting the state, progressively isolated them socially, economically and even politically. They began turning against the communities for whose defence they had been prepared to lose their lives barely five years earlier.

The concept of masculinity is often used in a manner that implies homogeneity among men. Connell (1995) corrects this by recognising a multiplicity of masculinities. In his typology of *hegemonic, subordinate, complicit* and *marginalised* masculinities, he describes the characteristics of each type – including their fluidity – while stressing the importance of investigating the relations between the different types. He maintains that hegemonic masculinity 'occupies the hegemonic position in a given pattern of gender relations, a position always contestable' (77). However, when the given pattern of relations changes, 'the bases for the dominance of a particular masculinity are eroded' (77).

Challenges and changes to hegemonic structures are often considered to originate from and to be affected by the *subaltern*. But the experiences of a few countries – Russia and South Africa, for example – have shown that such changes can also be effected from above (by the elite or the state). In these cases, the question is how those affected respond to such changes. If, as Cornwall and Lindisfarne emphasise, the control of one form of masculinity is 'never totally comprehensive' nor does it 'ever completely control subordinates' (1994: 5), how do subordinate masculinities respond to changes that occur when political and social power change hands and new gender prescriptions result? This chapter examines such a contest between 'struggle masculinity' and 'post-struggle masculinity' during South Africa's transition from apartheid to democracy and beyond.

In this chapter, 'struggle masculinity' refers to the type of masculinity which became dominant among young, urban Africans during the days of the struggle against apartheid (in the 1980s). It is a socially constructed, collective gender identity. Its main characteristics were opposition to

108

Thokozani Xaba

the apartheid system (which included Bantu Education, exploitation of workers and communities, high rents and rates, and suppression of protest) and political militancy. Because many older African people (particularly men) were perceived to be complicit with apartheid, such opposition assumed a posture which was anti-authority. Since 'struggle masculinity' existed side-by-side with *street masculinity*[4] which was disparaging towards women, 'struggle masculinity' was tainted by some of the negative attitudes and behaviours towards women. 'Post-struggle masculinity' is the masculinity which seeks to supplant 'struggle masculinity' in post-apartheid South Africa. Its main characteristics are respect for 'law and order', the restoration of 'public order', the resumption of paying for services, respect for state institutions, co-operation with police, and fighting crime.

Before we discuss these two masculinities any further, we need to take a few steps back.

## 'Liberation now, education later'

Like Fernando, the youth who became 'comrades' or 'skipped the country' for military training were responding to a call to overthrow apartheid domination. They were recruited into political organisations in the 1970s and 80s during the intensification of the resistance campaigns spearheaded by the internal anti-apartheid organisation, the United Democratic Front (UDF) (founded in 1983) and the exiled African National Congress (ANC). Understanding the price of activism and seeing the costs borne by friends, relatives and associates, the youth nonetheless joined in numbers and remained members of both legal and underground organisations. For many, this meant that their education was interrupted as slogans such as 'liberation now, education later' resonated with their feelings. For the most part, theirs was an existence of daily confrontation with the police, the army and vigilantes. The objectives of 'the struggle' as well as songs such as '*Qiniselani nina maqhawe*' ('Hold on you heroes'), '*Siyaya ePitoli*' ('We are going to Pretoria'), and '*Singamasotsha kaTambo*' ('We are Tambo's soldiers'), together with slogans such as '*Niyabesaba yini na*'? ('Are you afraid of them?')[5] and *Dlala AK-47*' ('Play AK-47'),[6] spurred them on.

In townships, 'comrades' took it upon themselves to organise 'defence committees' whose responsibilities included protecting communities from the state and the 'third force' (clandestine forces either armed and controlled by the state or operating with its tacit consent), as well as 'weeding out' state informants. Some townships were effectively 'freed' from direct state repression through such measures as chasing state officials away and replacing them with popular institutions such as 'people's courts', as well as barricading the entrances and exits to the townships with burning tyres so that the police and army had difficulty in moving around.

Numerous factors conspired to produce 'struggle masculinity'. The upbringing of youth in poor households of impoverished and poorly serviced townships, coupled with the relations they had with state institutions, engendered opposition to the state. The apparently symbiotic relationship between capitalism and apartheid produced antipathy to capitalism. 'Comrades' were impatient with the elders who either seemed to be tolerating or accommodating of apartheid and this created tensions between the young and the old.[7] The demands to intensify the struggle by boycotting white shops and staying away from work exacerbated conflict as elders went to war against the youth whom they saw as preventing them from earning a living which would enable them to support their families. The young men were seen as the 'warriors' of their areas who stood with the community while the older men were seen as 'vigilantes' who served the interests of the state. All parties to the conflict were able to retrieve images from the past which suited and supported their position in the conflict.[8]

During those days, being a 'comrade' endowed a young man with social respect and status within his community. Being referred to as a 'young lion' and a 'liberator' was an intoxicating and psychologically satiating accolade. This was especially so to young men who were members of a group with low social status and who came from families where accolades of any kind were hard to come by. The accolades would have given any young man an idea of himself which was disproportionate to reality. Such accolades also came along with the kind of power and respect which attracted women to men. As such, 'young lions', especially those who were in leadership positions, were coveted by women. In fact, some tended to have access to more than one woman at a time, either as girlfriends or sleeping partners. Indeed, the more status a man had, the more women there were to whom he had access.

For some 'comrades', the daily hide-and-seek with vigilantes and police as well as reliance on home-made weaponry quickly became insufficient responses against a force bent on repression. Formal military training was the next logical step to take. Between the mid-1970s and the late 1980s, large numbers of 'comrades' opted to join the liberation forces in exile.

## Masculinity and a new gender order: transforming masculinity

What seems to have contributed greatly to the ostracisation of 'comrades' and 'exiles' was the series of events which unfolded immediately after the 1990 unbanning of political parties and the freeing and return of their

Thokozani Xaba

*Toy soldier: A younger young lion at the launch of the ANC's Youth League*

leadership. The UDF was absorbed into the ANC and many of its hundreds of affiliates were disbanded or just faded away. For the 'comrades', former members of these organisations, their dissolution left them without a political parent. Initially this did not create difficulties since they considered the ANC and the South African Communist Party (SACP) as their primary political homes.

In 1994, the main liberation organisations (the ANC, SACP and the Congress of South African Trade Unions) became part of a Government of National Unity having gained a majority of votes in the first democratic election in South Africa. The task of building a new society began in earnest. As the government, the former liberation organisations assumed the responsibility for maintaining 'law and order' as well as protecting property and lives. As such, they had to instil a new culture of paying for services and respect for state institutions.

The political transition that brought the ANC into government was accompanied by changes in the gender order. ANC leaders were compelled by their office to create new norms of gender behaviour. This process fed into the construction of human rights discourse but it was also skewed by the gender politics of the ANC which stressed gender equality and women's rights. These values are a world away from struggle masculinity. As the content of the gender order changed, the comrades were forced to make choices. Some 'comrades' and 'exiles' joined the national armed and police forces where their skills were put to use. But others, like Yasmina,[9] for one reason or another, either did not qualify or were 'demobilised'. These 'comrades' and 'exiles' who had been recruited and trained to undermine and fight state institutions and personnel now found themselves on the other side of the social, economic and political fence. Without much formal education, they could not find reasonably remunerative employment. Without employment, they could not legitimately get money to buy what they considered to be 'the best things in life' – expensive cars, clothes and jewellery (for their girlfriends).

## Masculinities of survival

Former 'liberation soldiers' sought but did not find confirmation of their masculinity from the new society where a new hegemonic form of masculinity had been installed. The masculine characteristics they possessed were inappropriate for the new South Africa. They resorted to finding affirmation and confirmation from each other and no longer looked to the liberation movement for endorsement or approval. The type of masculinity they recognised was a masculinity born out of the harsh environment in which they live. In that environment, they learned to rely on one another both for support and for company. They depended on one another for shelter, food, and protection. In this regard, the former comrades essentially operated like a close-knit and supportive family.

The comfort provided by such a 'family' came with obligations. The primary obligation was to do for other members of the 'family' as was done for you. Since survival depended on the survival of the 'family', a person was obliged to 'stand by' the 'family' whatever the consequences. The mark of 'a real man', in the eyes of the 'family', was the extent to which a man 'stood by' the 'family' and its members.[10] In an environment where he was a social, economic and political outsider, such a stand was taken in the context of defiance against authority and its organisations. Defiance against authority manifested itself both in a disregard for authority and in open confrontation with it and its institutions. Often, confrontation with authority involved violence. The survivors of such encounters received accolades from their friends for being 'mamba',[11] and 'bhoza',[12] that is, 'real men'. Quite often, the successes of 'comrades' and 'exiles' in such confrontations made young acolytes aspiring to be 'real men' emulate them.

The 'families' laid down codes which were not written down anywhere but were understood by all.[13] Among these codes was the demand and maintenance of a person's respect and honour. As economic, political and social outsiders, former 'comrades' and 'exiles' did not have access to the trappings of general respect and honour. Respect and honour among them rested on their ability to dictate terms and procedures within the areas they considered to be their domains. Those who violated such terms and procedures were often violently reprimanded. The vigorous and virulent enforcement of the group's codes contributed to the notoriety of some 'comrades' and 'exiles' for their hair-trigger irritability and the 'unnecessary' violence in their communities.

## Displaced masculinity

Former 'comrades' and 'exiles' formed survivalist groups[14] during the days of confrontation with the police and these exist to the present day. In the current conjuncture these groups, in David Hemson's words, face 'marginalisation, dispossession, and powerlessness' (1997). Among these groups, in the new era, are different gradations of criminality. Some are composed only of former 'exiles' and 'comrades', others incorporate members of purely criminal gangs, and still others are completely criminal gangs. Some of the groups have various women who are associated with them as either girlfriends or as people called upon to assist in petty crimes. The crimes are designed for accumulation – robbery and car hijackings are therefore common. The levels of violence that accompany these crimes range from assault to rape and murder. These activities were sometimes condoned in a previous era and context, but the new era rejects both their motivations and activities.

When the gender norms of a society change, boys who modelled themselves in terms of an earlier, 'struggle' version of masculinity may grow up to become unhappy men. Those who cannot change together with the society or who do not possess the skills to make it in the new social environment find themselves strangers in their own country. If the new values are totally opposed to the former expressions of masculinity and manliness, boys find themselves, later in life, ostracised and, sometimes, outside the law. What was normal and acceptable behaviour suddenly becomes inappropriate and, often, criminal. What made some people heroes within their communities in the old order, may be the exact reason for their ostracism and punishment in the new order. Transitional societies tend to make the heroes of the past the villains of the present.

Fernando's case and the cases that follow are a few examples of how the old forms of masculinity have been expressed in the new order. They reveal the types of activities in which the former 'comrades' have engaged in in order to acquire what they could not get by other means. The violent form of such actions is not accidental but derives from the socialisation (in families, schools and the violent 1980s) to which former 'comrades' and 'exiles' were exposed. The cases also reveal what happens to those who express their masculinity in ways which are neither supported by the state nor by communities. Once the expression of such masculinity has ceased to be legitimate, 'comrades' and 'exiles' become 'fair game'.

The five cases which follow were part of a larger study of informal forms of justice conducted in African urban areas around Durban. The people interviewed for the study of informal forms of justice were residents of six townships around Durban, namely, Chesterville, Clermont, Kwamashu, Lamontville, Ntuzuma and Umlazi. The rest of the evidence is drawn from interaction and interviews with members of youth groups, former 'comrades' and former 'exiles'. Except for those incidents that also appeared in newspapers, fictitious names are given to former 'comrades' and 'exiles'.

### Confiscating property at gunpoint

Kwamashu, C- and D-Sections (August 1993)

On Saturday 28th August 1993, three 'exiles' were killed at D-Section while trying to rob a shack-store owner. They – together with some of their friends who escaped – were notorious for preying on their neighbours. They were reported to have held-up residents and then taken TVs, VCRs and the like. In some cases, they raped old and young women and even children.

On Monday 30th August 1993, two more 'exiles' who, reportedly, had been among those who escaped on Saturday, were killed near the Kwamashu train station. They were reported to have been killed by being tied to a minibus and then dragged along at high speeds. For more impact, the minibus would make abrupt stops and starts as well as sharp swerves to the left and right. Before very long, the minibus returned dragging their bruised lifeless bodies drenched in muddied blood.

On Thursday 2nd September 1993, three more 'exiles' from the original group were shot dead with high calibre bullets at point-blank range while still inside a minibus taxi. (*Ilanga*, 6–8 September 1993)

'Comrades' and 'exiles' who did not have legitimate means to procure the 'good things' in life used their guns to frighten and to overcome those who attempted to prevent them from obtaining such 'good things'. They thus turned their weapons against the people they had been trained to protect. They used guns to have their way with those people's property, as well as their wives, mothers, sisters and daughters.

### The gang-rape and murder of a local woman

Chesterville (December 1994)
Early in January 1995, a group of young men were stoned to death – in full view of the public – because they, reportedly, had raped and killed a young local woman.

The story which came together was that Nomusa, who was a Christian and 'a good person', was coming from church when a gang of about six boys, notorious for disporting themselves by raping women, approached her. She may have first thought of running away but the fact that she recognised some of them may have influenced her fatal decision not to flee.

After forcibly bringing her to the ground, the boys raped her in turns and, when they were finished, began assaulting her. It is during this time that high-pitched screams – of the names of the boys that she recognised – were heard. People who were still out then heard the names of people Nomusa shouted but did not venture to assist her, fearing for their own lives.

It was only when the sun came out the following morning that the residents of Chesterville could find out what had happened to Nomusa. She was found raped, stabbed and stoned to death, and the Bible she had been carrying had been placed on her chest. The residents who gathered around her body – most of whom were women – were incensed. They wanted to lay their hands on the people who had committed such a crime.

The boys whose names Nomusa had shouted were found first. They were taken to a field where they were asked about the incident. They confessed to having raped and killed the woman, giving, as an extenuating circumstance, the fact that they had been taking mandrax. They named their accomplices and were then sentenced to 'suffer as she had suffered'. They were stoned to death in broad daylight – by mostly women and children. The same fate befell the other boys except for one who was later shot in the back of the head at point-blank range.

Community disgust towards the boys was such that hardly anyone other than the members of their families attended their wakes (an event normally attended by most people who had been familiar with the deceased and his or her relatives). Over and above this, initially, their parents and relatives were told not to bury them in the community cemetery. One woman is reported to have said emphatically – to which others assented – 'Those dogs should not be buried here!' However, after some entreaties from other concerned people who pointed out that the decision to prohibit the burials was affecting innocent people, that is, parents and relatives, the parents and relatives were allowed to bury the boys in the community cemetery. But they could only do so if they were to be earlier than usual, that is, so that they would leave the cemetery before the arrival of Nomusa's funeral procession.   (*Ilanga*, 8 December 1994)

'Struggle masculinity' considered women to be fair game. The current high incidence of women who are kidnapped and kept for days while being raped repeatedly by any number of the members of a group underscores the prevailing attitude towards women.[15] Killing the victim in these cases is a way of ensuring that there are no witnesses to the crime.

### Killing the killers

The former 'comrades' often demarcate the areas under their control (Glaser 1998). Within such areas their word is law. Failure to heed their commands and demands is heavily punished. Since their unofficial power

Thokozani Xaba

is not overwhelming, former 'comrades' and 'exiles' almost always eventually lose the territorial battles to the numerically superior residents of the area. The following case shows how this competition resulted in the death of a policeman and the death of several former 'comrades'.

Ntuzuma (June 1995)
A group of teenage boys who had been terrifying the Ntuzuma community for more than a year had their days numbered when they raised the stakes of crossing their path. First, they banned police from their area. Within days of that decision, they captured a policeman – who lived in the area – while he was waiting for public transport, killed him and took away his service weapon. A few days thereafter, two of the boys disappeared and were later found dead with bullet wounds. While no one could claim to have seen or heard anything, it was openly discussed that they had been killed by the police in revenge for the policeman who had been killed by the same boys. This was further affirmed by the fact that the mother of one of the boys threatened to take legal steps against the police, for the death of her son.

Later that month, the surviving members of the gang – who were resorting to extorting money from taxi drivers – were abducted by 'unknown men' and were later found shot dead in one of the community sports fields. Again, while no one claimed to have seen or heard anything, the story which went around was so clear that either the people telling the story had first-hand knowledge of events or the person who told it initially had an extremely vivid recollection of the unfolding of events that day. The story was that taxi drivers abducted the boys from their homes, bundled them into two minibuses and drove them to the sportsfield where they were summarily shot dead as they were pleading for their lives.

It was unclear who notified the police of the incident and the bodies since few people – among those who would discuss the event – did so without displaying a sense of relief at the death of the young men. (*Ilanga*, 29 June to 1 July 1995)

### Protecting the community from its former protectors
Kwamashu, L-Section (July 1995)
In Kwamashu's L-Section, 'the cleaners', a group of 'comrades' who were fed-up with 'the dirties', a group of 'exiles' who had been terrorising the area, resolved to end the problem once and for all. Daily, they set about looking for 'the dirties', where they were

known to live and where they were known to 'hang out'. Whenever a member of 'the dirties' was found, summary justice of 'a hole in the head' was administered.

Sensing their impending demise, 'the dirties' chose to go down fighting. They embarked on counter-attacks on 'the cleaners' and their neighbours. From there, the violence degenerated into conflict between the two L-Section communities. On some occasions, the neighbours of 'the dirties' were also attacked since, it was claimed, they provided 'cover' for 'the dirties'. In the ensuing battle of mutual decimation, the argument that the neighbours of 'the dirties' had no choice but to do as 'the dirties' said or else, could not receive much favour. The violence became a 'war' between people who lived in two different parts of L-Section.[16] At least one person was hospitalized or buried every week between the end of June 1995 and February 1996.

The violence spread outward from L-Section and affected life in other parts of Kwamashu. One such example was the murder of a teacher in one of the schools in Kwamashu, which resulted in teachers downing chalk and the disruption of education (*Ilanga*, 28–30 March 1996). Conditions got so bad that a group of women from L-Section marched to the ANC offices in Durban to seek the intervention of the ANC (*The Natal Mercury*, 29 January 1996).

This case is one example of how the old and new masculinities are shaping up in the new era. Those who have been left behind socially, politically and economically create spheres within which their word is law. They confiscate property at will and rape young and old women as they please. Those who are part of the new dispensation take it upon themselves to 'protect the community' from those who terrorise them. The clash of these two masculinities results in violence, as was the case in Kwamashu's L-Section between 1995 and 1996. The conflict in L-Section continued well into 1997.

### Stoning the former liberators

At a community meeting to address incidents of rape and housebreaking in Madiba Valley (Marianhill), two young men, Sibusiso Shabalala (22) and Mzi Sibisi (23) were stoned by members of the Marianhill community. Sibusiso died during the attack and Mzi, a former MK commander, managed to escape with his life. The two men were accused by a group of women of causing 'trouble' in the area. (*The Natal Mercury*, 24 March 1997)

Township struggles were not fought by men alone. In this case, the participation of women in violence is evident. Little research has been conducted on violent femininities in South Africa, although Clive Glaser (1992) has revealed the existence of ruthless female gang leaders on the Witwatersrand in the 1950s. This case likewise alerts us to the error of assuming that femininity is synonymous with passivity and nurturing. Struggle masculinities will only be fully understood when we know more about struggle femininities.

## Conclusion

This chapter has argued that particular configurations of masculinity forged in one historical moment can become obsolete and dangerous in another. This is particularly true in transitional societies. The young African males who became 'exiles' and 'comrades' in the 1980s sacrificed their formal education in the process. Furthermore, in training to become soldiers, they failed to acquire skills marketable in the workplace. Their situation became desperate in the 1990s when they failed to obtain the documents needed for seeking employment. This led them to lives of crime. It has been further argued that the particular socialisation of former 'comrades' coupled with their social circumstances led them to violent crime. Their situation in the 1990s made it possible for former 'exiles' and 'comrades' to commit violent crimes, as well as display a dangerous and deadly bravado, for which they were notorious. The daring escapades in which they engaged were those which resonated with their own conceptions of masculinity.

For the few 'exiles' and 'comrades' living lives of crime, it is no secret that the knife-edge life of violent crime is eminently more remunerative than the palliatives offered by the Adult Basic Education and Life Skills Programmes in which former 'comrades' and 'exiles' are expected to enrol. It is almost impossible to encourage anyone to exchange a life, however dangerous it may be, in which there is a possibility of driving a C220 Mercedes Benz for a life in which he will be a carpenter, electrician or painter or, more likely, unemployed. To attain such luxuries a person has to be more daring and brutal and, consequently, is also more likely to be killed. For many, however, such risks seem worth taking and seem eminently better than any benefits promised by any of the 'programmes' offered to them.

The risks that 'comrades' and 'exiles' take have led to the confrontation between them and the post-apartheid state. Such confrontation has led not only to an excoriation of former 'comrades' and 'exiles' but also to a celebration of pictures of the lifeless bodies of alleged 'hijackers' or 'robbers' which are periodically presented in the media. While such pictures satiate the hunger for revenge, they declare emphatically to the repudiated young men that it is 'open season' on them. 'Struggle masculinity' may, in time, disappear as the numbers of former comrades decline and the social and economic landscape changes. But the likelihood exists that African township youth who continue to have limited opportunity for upward social mobility will develop oppositional forms of masculinity. These forms are likely to contain violent elements drawn from the repertoire developed and utilised by the comrades and their apartheid state opponents. And so long as these young African men are also the recipients of violence (by members of the police and community), they will have great difficulty developing more peaceful, non-violent masculinities.

NOTES

1. 'Exiles' is a term reserved for those who left South Africa and joined the liberation forces in exile. These former guerrillas returned to South Africa from various military bases in the early 1990s.
2. 'Comrades' refers to the youth who fought against apartheid within South Africa and did not leave the country for military training.
3. Not his real name. In fact, except where the names originate from another source, I use fictitious names to protect the identity of participants in this study.
4. This refers to the masculinity represented by the '*tsotsis*' or youth gangs. For an example, see Clive Glaser (1997).
5. To which the crowd responds, 'No we are not afraid, we want them!'
6. This slogan was accompanied by verbal imitation of an AK-47 sound.
7. In order to curb incidents of crime prevalent in urban areas, older men established disciplinary systems that echoed those of rural areas. According to older men, such systems sought to maintain order that seemed to be dissipating in urban areas. Because such structures performed the function of the police, because some people within them were either policemen or police reservists, and because they often used excessive violence, they were slowly seen as instruments of state oppression. Young men who opposed them were seen as serving the interests of the people.
8. Inkatha, in particular, was able to use Zulu mythology to mobilise its supporters (see Waetjen and Maré in this volume).

9. Yasmina is an unemployed former Umkonto we Sizwe (MK) guerrilla who discovered that, despite repeated attempts to register as a former guerrilla, her name was not in the Central Personnel Register which was used by the South African National Defence Force (SANDF) to recruit former guerrillas (*Weekly Mail and Guardian*, 9 February 1996).

10. Protecting one another from physical harm, economic hardship, social ostracism, and helping maintain one another's psychological stability was a mark of most close-knit communities forced to respond to external pressures. Sitas, discussing similar circumstances for hostel dwellers in the East Rand, refers to that complex of relations as 'defensive combinations' (1996: 237).

11. The mamba is considered to be one of the most fearless and fearsome snakes.

12. Bhoza is a derivative from 'boss'. But the sense given to it in this regard is that of having power and ability to do what you want.

13. Among the codes they use is that a 'real man' survives any confrontation. Such confrontations include confrontation that the former comrade himself may initiate. In many such instances, winning sometimes means killing the opponent. Another code is that a person has to prohibit others from making him feel less than a man. This compels former 'comrades' to respond violently to those who 'insult' or 'disrespect' them. Insults include remarks made against a member of the group, stepping on someone's shoes, moving into their area (especially if a person engages in activities which compete with those the group engages in), and flirting with their girlfriends as well as refusing to do as he is told.

14. This study refers only to groups of former 'exiles' and 'comrades' and not to the numerous, amorphous criminal gangs. While, for the most part, there were less than ten groups operating at one time in each of the townships around Durban, it was difficult to estimate the numbers of people involved, at each point in time, in each group. For most groups, there was a core of about ten people who converged around a distinct leader. Closely associated with the core were other more numerous younger people who moved in and out of the group. Some of these younger people were later incorporated into the group and others moved on to other engagements. While the groups were relatively small, their actions made people in their neighbourhoods feel besieged. The frequency and brutality of some of their actions and the seeming inability of the police to either curb them or to effectively deal with them fuelled the perception that there were more groups

than the number that existed, and that they had boundless capabilities.

15. Three schoolboys who had raped two girls were seen pointing and laughing at the girls they had raped. The schoolmates of the raped girls declared war on the rapists and their school because 'It was time for us to exercise our manhood and attack first.' From the ensuing knife and panga battles, at least one boy was stabbed in the back and many others were seriously injured (*Sunday Times City Metro*, 28 February 1999).

16. When one of the prominent members of one group was arrested, the 'community' is reported to have raised funds to bail him out since, they claimed, they felt unsafe without him.

BIBLIOGRAPHY

Beinart, W. 1997. 'Men, Science, Travel and Nature in the Eighteenth and Nineteenth Century Cape', *Journal of Southern African Studies* 24(4).

Berger, P.L. 1966. *The Social Construction of Reality*. London: Penguin Books.

Breckenridge, K. 1998. 'The Allure of Violence: Men, Race and Masculinity on the South African Goldmines, 1900–1950', *Journal of Southern African Studies* 24(4).

Burns, C. 1997. '"A Man is a Clumsy Thing Who does not Know How to Handle a Sick Person": Aspects of the History of Masculinity and Race in the Shaping of Male Nursing in South Africa, 1900–1950', *Journal of Southern African Studies* 24(4).

Campbell, C. 1991. 'Learning to kill? Masculinity, the family and violence in Natal', *Journal of Southern African Studies* 18(3).

———. 1992. 'Identity and gender in a changing society: the social identity of South African township youth'. Ph.D. thesis: University of Bristol.

Cock, J. 1980. *Maids and Madams*. Johannesburg: Ravan Press.

Connell, R.W. 1987. *Gender and Power*. Stanford: Stanford University Press.

———. 1995. *Masculinities*. Cambridge: Polity Press.

Cornwall, A. and N. Lindisfarne, eds. 1994. *Dislocating Masculinities: Comparative Enthnographies*. London: Routledge.

Corrigan, P. 1990. *Social Forms/Human Capacities: Essays on Authority and Difference*. London: Routledge.

Du Pisani, K. 1997. 'Perceptions of masculinity in the Afrikaans community 1935, 1965, and 1995: a tentative comparison'. Paper presented at the Colloquium, 'Masculinities in Southern Africa'. Durban: University of Natal.

Epprecht, M. 1997. 'The Unsaying of Indigenous Homosexuality in Zimbabwe: Mapping a Blindspot in an African Masculinity', *Journal of Southern African Studies* 24(4).

Erikson, E. 1950. *Childhood and Society*. New York: Norton.

Everatt, D. and E. Sisulu, eds. 1992. *Black Youth in Crisis: Facing the Future*. Johannesburg: Ravan Press.

Everatt, D., ed. 1994. *Creating a Future: Youth Policy for South Africa*. Johannesburg: Ravan Press.

Glaser, C. 1992. 'The mark of Zorro: Sexuality and Gender Relations in the Tsotsi Sub-Culture on the Witwatersrand, 1940–60', *African Studies* 51(1).

———. 1998. 'Swines, Hazels and the Dirty Dozen: Masculinity, Territoriality and the Youth Gangs of Soweto 1960–1976', *Journal of Southern African Studies* 24(4).

Hearn, J. 1997. 'Searching for the Centre of Men and Men's Power'. Paper presented at the Colloquium, 'Masculinities in Southern Africa'. Durban: University of Natal.

Hemson, D. 1997. 'The embrace of comradeship: masculinity and resistance in KwaZulu-Natal'. Paper presented at the Colloquium, 'Masculinities in Southern Africa'. Durban: University of Natal.

Hirschowitz, R., S. Milner and D. Everatt. 1994. 'Growing up in a violent society'. In D. Everatt, ed., *Creating a Future: Youth Policy for South Africa*. Johannesburg: Ravan Press.

Hyslop, J. 1997. 'Jandamarra, My Great-Grandfather and the British Empire: Reflections on Colonial War, Family History and the Making of Men and Women'. Paper presented at the Colloquium, 'Masculinities in Southern Africa'. Durban: University of Natal.

'Invisible Man'. 8 April 1996. Episode of the SABC 3 programme *Chronicles of Change*.

Jourard, S. 1971. 'Some lethal aspects of the male sex role'. In S. Jourard, ed., *The Transparent Self*. New York: D. Van Nostrand Company.

Kimmel, M. 1996. *Manhood in America*. New York: Free Press.

Mager, A. 1997. 'Youth Organisation and the Construction of Masculine Identities in the Ciskei and Transkei, 1945–1960', *Journal of Southern African Studies* 24(4).

Marks, S. 1994. *Divided Sisterhood: Race, Class and Gender in the South African Nursing Profession*. New York: St. Martin's Press.

Merton, R.K. 1938. 'Social Structure and Anomie', *American Sociological Review* 3.

Mokwena, S. 1992. 'Living on the Wrong Side of the Law'. In Everatt and Sisulu, eds., *Black Youth in Crisis*, 30–51.

Nichols, J. 1975. *Men's Liberation: A new definition of masculinity*. New York: Penguin Books.

Ramphele, M. 1992. 'Social Disintegration of the Black Community'. In Everatt and Sisulu, eds., *Black Youth in Crisis*, 10–29.

Seekings, J. 1993. *Heroes or Villains?: Youth Politics in the 1980s*. Johannesburg: Ravan Press.

Sinha, M. 1995. *Colonial Masculinity: The 'Manly Englishmen' and the 'Effeminate Bengali' in the Nineteenth Century*. Manchester: Manchester University Press.

Sitas, A. 1996. 'The New Tribalism: Hostels and Violence', *Journal of Southern African Studies* 22(2).

Stavrou, V. 1992. 'The Alexandra Community Crime Survey'. Project for the Study of Violence.

Straker, G. 1992. *Faces in the Revolution: The Psychological Effects of Violence on Township Youth in South Africa*. Cape Town: David Philip.

Swart, S. 1997. '"A Boer and his Gun and his Wife are Three Things always Together": Republican Masculinity and the 1914 Rebellion', *Journal of Southern African Studies* 24(4).

Sykes, G.M. and D. Matza. 1957. 'Techniques of Neutralization: A theory of Delinquency', *American Sociological Review* 22.

Walker, C. 1990. *Women and Gender in Southern Africa to 1945*. Cape Town: David Philip.

# PART TWO

This section explores one central question: How do men operate in defined social circumstances and institutions where they have authority? This question addresses a major theme in feminist literature – the way in which men, individually and collectively, exercise their authority over women, other men, and children. This theme remains central in the critical study of men and masculinity but it now also includes considerations of identity. Men can be fathers, family members and heads of extended families. These institutional locations are not simply occupied by men – they are the places where men reflectively and reflexively act out their masculinity.

For rural African men location within a family, homestead and kinship groups has generally been associated with occupying a position of power with respect to women, children and younger men. Manly status has been derived from having many wives and children, from receiving respect, and from taking decisions. Authority emanating from familial positions is always contested and challenged and therefore has constantly to be defended and re-asserted. This is done by developing masculinist discourses which define these positions as the exclusive domain of men by rejecting alternative (potentially egalitarian) understandings of masculinity.

For white men the identity of the father figure has been understood in ethnically specific ways. For English-speaking, urban men the nuclear family has been the extent of their 'kingdom', though since the 1980s this kingdom has been buffeted by democratic forces and demands that they share responsibility for child-rearing and give up some of their traditional decision-making powers. For Afrikaans-speaking men the family remains a power base though its shape has been changed by nationalist and economic forces and the extent of their domestic powers has been diluted. These broad generalisations should not obscure the importance of women in families nor their role in shaping masculinity. Men are not only related to women in oppositional and hierarchical terms. Men also live with women, are influenced by them, love them and narrate their own personal histories with reference to the different women in their lives.

# Fathers, Families and Kinship

# CHAPTER 6

# Locusts Fall from the Sky
## Manhood and Migrancy in KwaZulu

BENEDICT CARTON

A week before Christmas in 1992 locusts fell from the sky. It had been a bright morning until they dropped through ribbons of dust above the Thukela River valley. Recent cloudbursts had relieved a drought in this arid region of KwaZulu, a homeland for Africans classified as Zulu under the apartheid regime. The bulbous swarm descended on fresh tracts of green that streaked the ridges, but posed no threat to eroded fields long since devoid of minerals.

The locusts appeared as an omen to some people in the homesteads that are devoid of young men. With the advent of gold mining on the Witwatersrand in the late nineteenth century, Thukela valley residents had grown accustomed to the return of male migrants on holiday leave from work in distant industrial centres. Poverty and joblessness in contemporary KwaZulu – a geographically fragmented, barren territory in the Natal province (KwaZulu-Natal after 1994) – continued to drive many young African men to cities such as Durban and Johannesburg, where they sought employment and lived for almost fifty weeks of the year. During the extended Christmas season the centrifugal movement was reversed, with labour migrants streaming home. As the cloud of locusts flew toward more verdant hills, an initial wave of minibus taxis carrying migrants navigated the tortuous promontory road that led to the Thukela River.

The arriving men, most between twenty and forty years old, would soon launch themselves into week-long festivities. Emboldened by urban life far from the constraints of homestead patriarchy, they exuded a bravado that fuelled raucous beer parties and stick fighting competitions. Such unbridled behaviour at these homecomings would expose the uneasy balance between renewing bonds of masculinity and upholding customs that called for *gravitas* and public order. The swarm of locusts not only

129

foreshadowed the coming of migrant labourers; it also heralded the resurgence of power struggles between aged fathers and their adult sons. The late-nineteenth-century shift in the Thukela valley from subsistence production to labour migrancy had stirred bitter conflicts between homestead heads (patriarchs) and wage-earning young men. This past turmoil resonated in the late-twentieth-century tensions kindled by labour migrants who, during brief stays at home, asserted their masculinity over existing patriarchal expectations of customary respect.

When older Africans aired their grievances in archival court records, they often spoke wistfully of a nostalgic alternative to their fallen state, a glorified past devoid of disobedience at home. Such testimony, peppered with barbs about rambunctious juniors and overbearing colonists, showed how African patriarchs saw the array of hostile forces. They not only chafed at white intrusion but also lamented the greater individual mobility of juniors. What sparked my interest as I examined the historical record was how strongly it echoed the contemporary concerns of the Thukela valley elders.

In various interviews that I conducted with the older men of the valley during my fieldwork they described their struggle to uphold their power against the challenges of migrant workers whose return spawned turbulence.[1] Their testimony revealed that a number of rival interpretations of manhood existed in the valley. These competing expressions of masculinity threatened to undermine the customary authority of the resident patriarchs.

## Context: historiography and autobiography

Current historiography of the 'creation of tribalism' in industrialising South Africa links social conflicts, labour migrancy, and community politics in homelands like KwaZulu. A prevailing interpretation contends that rural African men, defending traditional patriarchy, used militant ethnic nationalism as a rampart against encroaching modernity and radical political ideologies. As migrant labourers in cities, they toiled to maintain their 'tribal' identity, sending remittances to dependants and visiting their homes in the countryside, thereby reaffirming their position as husbands and fathers. Recent studies of 'masculinity' delve into violent urban clashes (over male authority) between male migrants and black township men, but leave for future analysis the rivalries between rural African men.[2]

My formative perceptions of rural Zulu masculinity and the generational obligations underpinning patriarchy were drawn from disparate personal experiences: my first encounters with Zulu cultural nationalists,

Benedict Carton

memories of my youth in Manhattan, New York, and my father's stories of childhood in Russia in the years immediately following the Bolshevik revolution in 1917. These impressions inspired my investigation of young African men coming of age in KwaZulu, a region buffeted by tumultuous political strife from the 1980s onwards. My research focused on a violent rebellion of young Zulu-speaking African men – against the constraints of colonial law and African patriarchs – in the first decade of the twentieth century as white rule was being consolidated in the subcontinent.

Before beginning fieldwork, I studied the *isiZulu* language in an American graduate school with a young male teacher from KwaZulu who championed Zulu ethnic pride. He insisted that I learn both the 'proper' *isiZulu* spoken in the countryside – shunning any urban slang – and the customs that upheld the social hierarchies of homesteads. On my first trip to collect oral history in KwaZulu, I met the patriarch who was to become my long-term host in the Thukela valley, a polygynous homestead head with five wives and more than twenty children.

The power relationships in the Thukela valley struck me as remarkably similar in many ways to my own upbringing. Some valley youths, for example, clubbed together in age regiments to test their mettle in turf battles, but concealed their bluster around elders, especially their patriarch who was to be honoured for his lore. I grew up in New York City with a similar band of male friends who journeyed with me through adolescence. We had our own unwritten code of loyalty when we cavorted on sidewalks and played sports against rival neighbourhood groups. We tried to look as if we could strut through any hostile territory. But my father's strict discipline tempered my fantasies of street toughness. When I was a boy my father was in his late-middle-age, 35 years older than my mother. He was the youngest son of Jewish peasants living in a Russian *shtetl* (a hamlet), and was not yet ten years old when the Bolshevik revolution hurtled into his life. My father regaled me with tales of his exodus in the early 1920s from the Ukraine to Romania and then to America, a flight propelled by pro-tsarist forces who unleashed pogroms, massacres of Jews and Bolshevik sympathisers. He described leading his family, including his father, to safety through the counter-revolutionary attacks in the Ukranian countryside. This was a period of both fear and emancipation for my father. The collapse of Jewish patriarchy in the Ukraine and the family's relocation to America placed him in a generation of young immigrant men who were able to realise destinies different from those of their fathers. At later Passover seders in Philadelphia, my grandfather would extol his youngest son's feat of conducting the family from peril, a sentiment echoed in the following passage by African patriarchs in

Natal who saw themselves as overrun by vast transformations of the early twentieth century.

### 'We were saved by our sons'

> The past dry and rainless years, coupled with the fact that Europeans . . . have forced us to use the poor waste lands . . . has resulted in a yearly failure of our crops. Famine threatened us, but we were saved by our sons. [T]heir hard earned money . . . enabled us to buy . . . imported mealies and other overseas foodstuffs, we should not have deigned to touch in former years, to keep ourselves, our wives and families alive. (Statement of Chiefs, Headmen, Official Witnesses and Kraal-heads, 7 October 1905)

Since at least the late 1800s, African subsistence in the Thukela valley had been in varying states of crisis. The grip of environmental pressures – tightened in the 1890s by droughts, locust plagues, a rinderpest epidemic among cattle, and mounting colonial land appropriations – suffocated agricultural production. With the 'yearly failure' of crops, homestead heads now regularly needed to purchase food in addition to securing the cash to pay annual taxes levied by the Natal colony. From the early 1900s onwards, patriarchs' access to money depended primarily on the remittances of unmarried sons, whose increasing departure to work in white-owned mines and on commercial farms undermined the capacity of

*Staged photo of young men in martial regalia c.1900*

132

Benedict Carton

*Photo of mock stick (faction) fight between young men c.1900*

patriarchs to command labour and loyalty in their own homesteads. Wages paid by colonial employers enabled a young male migrant to buy his own cattle and thus gain the means to marry, eroding his father's authority to allocate bridewealth cattle from the homestead herd. A man's prestige was measured to a large extent by the number of kin, wives, and children he supported.[3]

At the start of the twentieth century when labour migrants went home for short visits, resident patriarchs complained of blatant youthful defiance, particularly at public celebrations where the migrants controlled the flow of alcohol and rituals of mock warfare. The homestead heads who tried to contain assertive younger men were sometimes overwhelmed by insubordination. Aggressive displays of manhood, in effect, positioned migrants against older, established patriarchs.

As in the early 1900s, today many male youths in the Thukela valley seek greater social autonomy from their elders. Although boys typically labour for their patriarch, for example, as herders of his cattle, with greater access to primary education in poorly-equipped schools, they also use the classroom as an escape hatch from household responsibilities. Male teenagers also have many more opportunities for part-time employment close to home. Since the 1980s, for example, they have worked for minibus taxi drivers, collecting fares from passengers, and have cultivated small patches of *dagga* or *insangu* (marijuana) for street dealers in Durban. Nonetheless, familial loyalty still determines to a large extent when boys, in the eyes of their elders, can become adolescents and, later, young men, a climb in status that hastens their movement into labour migrancy. With full-time employment, usually secured with the help of an older relative or neighbour, and the acquisition of valuable property like furnishings and bridewealth cattle, young men can show the trappings of manhood. But it is only by taking a wife, having children, and building a homestead that men can begin to assume the privileges and responsibilities of a homestead head.

## An echo of the past

> If there is an assembly ... women would go on the left and men on the right. ... Beer was said to belong [to] the older [men]. ... A headringed man [homestead head] was always shown respect (*hlonitshwa'd*). ... The juniors drink and pass it on to the others without setting it down, but when the olders get it they may set it down, seeing it is theirs. (Ndukwana, Homestead Head, 3 September 1903, in Webb and Wright [1986])

The night before the locusts fell I attended a beer party that eerily fitted Ndukwana's century-old description. My host had arranged the first evening 'assembly' of December in his homestead. He presided in a hut. A row of older male guests sat on little wooden benches to the right of the doorway, while four of the host's wives sat on mats to the left. A clay pot of *amabele* (sorghum beer) was ready to be passed along the right side of the hut. According to convention, the women could not drink and I, the youngest man, would only be permitted to sip the beer after the patriarchs tasted some first. To an observer familiar with local social hierarchies, my host was a champion of *amasiko* (traditional customs). He was also a rarity: an international musician wealthy enough to live elsewhere who chose to settle in the Thukela valley (where his father was born), use his royalties to sustain a large homestead, and rekindle patriarchal rites. When my host was hailed, he was called by his 'praise' name, Macingwane, after the Chunu chief who in the early nineteenth century refused to submit to Shaka, the founder of the Zulu kingdom.

The revellers were neighbours, former migrant labourers, ranging from fifty- to seventy-years-old, who spent their earnings and now their pensions to maintain their standing as homestead heads. Like my host, each supported more than one wife and provided in-laws with bridewealth cattle. Polygyny more than age, they said, ensured their seniority, and the worship of *amadlozi* (ancestral spirits) inspired them to be strong husbands in old age. Ancestral spirits were said to enter men and enhance masculine qualities such as wisdom. To act like a man, *ukudoda*, meant to do something worthy of praise. Before we started to drink my host invoked the *amadlozi* to stamp out the petty jealousies that threatened *ukuhlonipha*, customs of avoidance and deference that reflected gender and generational divisions. The gathering murmured in agreement, several patriarchs affirming the appeal by inhaling snuff, a granular mix of charred tobacco and aloe flakes. *Ukuhlonipha* rituals expressly circumscribed the public conduct of women and youths. My host's wives and children had greeted the arriving homestead heads by kneeling, gazing downward, and speaking in hushed tones. His teenage sons clustered in the dark outside the party hut and watched their father, observing an *ukuhlonipha* code, learning to emulate the *isithombe sikababa*, the 'image' (masculine bearing) or 'alter ego' of their father.

Not all manifestations of my host's patriarchal power, I learned, emerged from such august origins. Two months before the December beer party, I saw what I believed was a divine token of ancestral worship. One morning I passed a blue glass bottle dangling from a tree near my host's cattle enclosure. Thinking it was an invocation of his *amadlozi* spirits, I gave it a wide berth, whereupon my host asked me why I avoided his rubbish. I explained how in Louisiana and Mississippi trees adorned with blue bottles may have reflected a rite of Kongo slaves who worshipped their ancestors in America. Having misinterpreted my halting *isiZulu*, he chuckled at the idea that Kongo people imported a custom of throwing garbage into trees. Over time, I came to understand that an idealised facade of patriarchy contradicts actual expressions of African masculinity.

The homestead heads who were defenders of generational privilege spurned *izimanje zentsha*, the 'customs of now, customs of modern youth', which they saw as a menace, but they also recognised the futility in containing rowdy, younger wage-earning migrants. This Faustian bargain intrigued my host. One of his favourite monologues pondered the declining state of *ukuhlonipha* and urged its defenders to halt the slide. At the December beer party, guests joined my host in an hour-long requiem on the loss of deference. They lamented the muffled voice of the KwaZulu homeland leadership in negotiations between the African National Congress (ANC) and the white National Party, although they did not advocate the politically combative version of rural tradition devised by the Zulu nationalist Inkatha Freedom Party (IFP). The anti-government protests by township youths upset some revellers who feared that the rebellion of young activists would further corrode family life. The masculinity of urban youths, they implied, was volatile, devoid of 'respect' for patriarchal authority. They recited stories from Radio Zulu news programmes of how

ANC boys and young men, 'the comrades' or *amaqabane*, prevented older men from going to their jobs during worker 'stayaways' and attacked the homes of KwaZulu homeland officials.[4] A spectre of murderous factionalism between supporters of the IFP and the ANC haunted the valley. Few men at the beer party took part in political struggles or embraced Inkatha's call to defend, by force if necessary, independent homeland status for KwaZulu. Most were unnerved by the spectacular transformations in South Africa since Nelson Mandela's release from prison in February 1990. Near dawn, the talk of civil conflict gave way to a more pressing worry: how to manage the youthful labour migrants and the binges that would follow during Christmas week. There were no resolutions and we soon drifted off to our beds.

## He had 'conquered, conquered, conquered'

Early the next morning, minibuses snaked along the flatland abutting the Thukela River, stopping every few hundred metres to discharge returning migrants. Some of these young men seemed tense. Toting parcels and crates of beer, they hurried up footpaths to their homesteads. The anticipation of Christmas, in this area a secular rather than religious observance, collided with another pervasive feeling, the nearness of death. In the late 1980s a local war had erupted over the killing of the district chief by his own brother. The successor chief would rule over 150 homesteads scattered across approximately 32 square kilometres. He would receive a salary from the KwaZulu homeland government, itself funded by the white regime in Pretoria, and tribute from his followers, usually in the form of livestock. In return, he would allocate meagre retirement pensions to resident patriarchs (who once were migrants) and land on which to build new homesteads. The 'faction fight', as valley residents called the feud, preserving the terminology of white Natal colonists, grew fierce when labour migrants came home to bolster the two opposing groups, one comprised of supporters of the slain chief, the other group of his brother's allies. A series of *ukuphindisela* (revenge attacks) ended only when the chief's brother's followers bought several AK-47 assault rifles in Johannesburg and shot more than a dozen adversaries in a week. While the fighting subsided, survivors nevertheless harboured vendettas. Some valley residents feared that a cycle of *ukuphindisela* could erupt again since blood vengeance, they said, was a 'Zulu' reaction to internal political strife.[5]

Just as the locusts began dropping, my host and I drove to a beer festival that was to carry on for several days. The party was being thrown by a cousin of the slain district chief. Although not quite noon, drunken migrants, holding luggage and packages, stumbled about. My host and I found the chief's cousin in a quiet corner of the compound sitting under a tree. We exchanged lengthy formal greetings and then began to eat from a wooden tray lined with strips of roasted meat. A boy crouched by the tray and offered me thin pieces of the goat's leg, which I dipped into a mound of salt and chased with beer. Afterwards, I wanted to stroll and take in the spectacle, but the chief's cousin warned that I, *umlungu*, (whiteman), was not known by the revellers in his compound and ought not to wander far. I had yet to feel personal or racial hostility in the valley, but now I did in overlooking my host's caution. After walking around and being on the receiving end of what I interpreted as unfriendly stares, I came back to the chief's cousin. Hours of drinking passed until the shadow of the ridge reached our tree, announcing the end of the afternoon. The chief's cousin eyed the dimming horizon and shouted for his friends to organise the next event: a tournament of stick fighting. The homestead was now crammed with labour migrants, carrying wooden sticks and tough cowhide shields.

The place of combat was two hundred metres away, at a gently sloped clearing amid the thorn scrub. The rough ground had to be smoothed, so the revellers commanded a group of boys to collect and heave fist-sized rocks into the surrounding bush. Meanwhile, labour migrants paired off and sparred; others deflected imaginary blows and moved their arms like pendulums. More and more boisterous labour migrants streamed to the pitch and folded into a semicircle. Several of the valley's homestead heads observed from a discreet distance, but most were absent. The older men's role as mere onlookers laid bare the dichotomy between the vision of dignified manhood that they sought to maintain and that of the returned migrants spoiling for a fight.

After the migrants formed a full circle, the local schoolmaster, a man in his thirties, strolled into the makeshift ring, clutching a white hand towel and his weapons. In a teacher's blue slacks and white shirt, the 'Professor', as he was widely known, assumed command. He barked '*wadla, wadla, wadla*', proclaiming he had 'eaten, eaten, eaten; conquered, conquered, conquered'. The crowd hooted approvingly. One labour migrant then bounded into the ring, wearing a cowskin apron, sneakers, no shirt, and a holstered pistol on his hip, a mix of traditional and contemporary garb. Two valley homestead heads sought to referee the bouts, but were nudged aside by the man with the holstered pistol who appointed two labour migrants to umpire. Victory, it was decided, would be awarded after one fighter landed a flurry of blows. I had been told that stick fighters revelled in the threat of injury because scars and per-

*A mix of traditional and contemporary garb: a migrant
labourer with skins, sneakers, and holstered pistol*

manent lumps were badges of manly prowess. Like boxing, stick fighting
oscillated between coiled restraint and bursting lunges.

With no other challengers, the Professor and the man with the holstered pistol turned on each other. The Professor crumpled quickly, dropped
by a surprise strike to the head. Bleeding from the scalp line, he picked
himself up, pressed his towel against the wound, and groped his way
through the spectators. Two more migrants sauntered into the ring, almost masking their inebriation, and launched into a furious thrust and
parry. They were remarkably adept at defence, prompting the crowd to
call for them to close in. After several minutes of scuffling one tripped and
fell backwards, breaking his stick against the ground and ending the bout.
With this finish, many spectators glanced skywards, recognised the onset
of twilight, and moved away. Nightfall beckoned the migrants to resume

Benedict Carton

drinking. Over the next week, they would turn the valley into an orgy of beer parties and stick fighting.

On 2 January 1993 the whine of straining transmissions shook me from morning sleep. I went to a hut window in my host's homestead and glimpsed a line of taxis climbing the promontory road. The migrants were returning to the cities. Within a few days the valley settled into an eerie hush. The remaining older patriarchs reclaimed the mantle of subdued patriarchy which they would hold until the Easter holidays in April when the migrants would come back to the valley and revive the generational struggles over rowdy public masculinity.

## NOTES

1. My fieldwork in rural KwaZulu spanned the 1990s.
2. Selected scholarship on the 'creation of tribalism', militant ethnic nationalism, violent conflict, and labour migrancy: L. Vail (1989); S. Marks and S. Trapido (1987); P. Bonner, et al. (1989); B. Bozzoli (1987); and W. Beinart (1992). For discussion of labour migrants in a world of urban masculinity: R. Morrell (1998); and K. Breckenridge (1998).
3. For an extensive analysis of this generational conflict, see B. Carton (2000).
4. For a study of fears among older patriarchs in Natal townships, see C. Campbell (1992).
5. For a study of faction fighting and codes of revenge, see J. Clegg (1981).

## BIBLIOGRAPHY

Beinart, W. 1992. 'Political and Collective Violence in Southern African Historiography', *Journal of Southern African Studies* 18(3).

Bonner, P., I. Hofmeyr, D. James and T. Lodge, eds. 1989. *Holding Their Ground*. Johannesburg: Ravan Press.

Bozzoli, B., ed. 1987. *Class Community and Conflict: South African Perspectives.* Johannesburg: Ravan Press.

Breckenridge, K. 1998. '"We Must Speak for Ourselves": The Rise and Fall of a Public Sphere on the South African Gold Mines, 1920 to 1931', *Comparative Studies in Society and History* 40(1).

Campbell, C. 1992. 'Learning to Kill? Masculinity, the Family and Violence in Natal', *Journal of Southern African Studies* 18(3).

Carton, B. 2000. *Blood from Your Children: The Colonial Origins of Generational Conflict in South Africa.* Charlottesville/London/Pietermaritzburg: University Press of Virginia/University of Natal Press.

Clegg, J. 1981. '"*Ukubuyisa Isidumbi* – Bringing Back the Body": An Examination of the Ideology of Vengeance in the Msinga and Mpofana Rural Locations, 1822–1944'. In P. Bonner, ed., *Working Papers in Southern African Studies*, vol. 2. Johannesburg: Ravan Press.

Marks, S. and S. Trapido, eds. 1987. *The Politics of Race, Class, and Nationalism in Twentieth Century South Africa.* London: Longman.

Morrell, R. 1998. 'Of Boys and Men: Masculinity and Gender in Southern African Studies', *Journal of Southern African Studies* 24(4).

'Statement of Chiefs, Headmen, Official Witnesses and Kraal-heads', 7 October 1905, 1/SNA 1/1/328 2833/1905. Minutes, Secretary for Native Affairs. Pietermaritzburg: Natal Archives.

Vail, L., ed. 1989. *The Creation of Tribalism in Southern Africa.* Berkeley: University of California Press.

Webb, C. and J. Wright, eds. 1986. *The James Stuart Archive*, vol. 4. Pietermaritzburg: University of Natal Press.

# CHAPTER 7

# Jandamarra, My Great-Grandfather and the British Empire
## Reflections on Family History, Colonial War, and the Making of Men and Women

JONATHAN HYSLOP

In October 1995, I sat in the Battye Library in Perth, Western Australia, and ran my fingers over the discoloured inks and faded pencil marks of messages sent and received by my great-grandfather, John Mitchell Cadden, a hundred years before. Those messages were written in little police posts in the Kimberley, the far north of Western Australia, where Cadden was stationed as a non-commissioned officer in the mounted police. There he was involved in a war of colonial conquest, pursuing an Aboriginal band of men, led by a man called Jandamarra, who were resisting white pastoralists' incursions into their lands. With Cadden in the Kimberley was his family, including his daughter, my grandmother Pearl Beatrice Cadden. A continent and seventy years away, in the Johannesburg of the 1960s, Pearl was going to be the dominant figure in my childhood. She was a person with many admirable qualities, but underlying this was a strange obsessionality. At Pearl's core was a deep fearfulness, which she transmitted to me. Pearl had a complex relation to men and ideas of masculinity; and it was she who most shaped the childhood formation of my identity. Looking at the telegrams, letters and reports in the Battye Library file, the question of the connectedness of family history was inescapable. Was there a link between the kind of man John Cadden was and the person I became? Did his involvement in a violent colonial war shape Pearl's childhood? Were there aspects of myself which were a long-term historical inheritance from those times in the Kimberley?

It is these issues that this chapter seeks to unravel. There are three aspects of the way in which I do this that I would like to highlight. Firstly, in my handling of the theme of the formation of masculine identity I focus on the role of a woman, my grandmother. Much discussion of male childhood becomes fixed on the relationship with the father. Even when the father is absent it seems to be assumed that his role in male socialisation is all-important. But conceptions of masculinity carried by women can be decisive for the social shaping of the boys they rear (Lewis 1991). Secondly, the chapter suggests that the violence of colonial conquest, the hardships of early colonist life and colonial involvement in imperial wars were, for several generations of settler society, factors which corroded personal and familial relations. In colonial patriarchies, fearful men produced fearful families. Finally, I want to argue that the specific traumas of the settler colonial experience had effects which were transmitted to subsequent generations. The patterns set up by the colonisation process were not contained within their own time and place, but poisoned the dynamics of families and were thus transmitted forward.

## John Cadden's daughter and the sacrifices of Empire

John Cadden[1] was born in Brisbane in about 1861. In the early 1890s Cadden was a miner in Glen Innes, New South Wales. In 1885, he married Annie Pearce, whose Irish parents had come to the country in the famine-propelled migration of the mid-century. Two sons were born to

*Annie Pearce Cadden and John Mitchell Cadden – Perth 1911*

Jonathan Hyslop

Annie and John; then in November 1891, my grandmother. Over the next few years four sisters followed, of whom three survived.

In 1892 Cadden appears in the West Australian Gold Rush which had erupted shortly before. Coming at the time of the major economic depression of the early 1890s, the gold discoveries in Coolgardie and later Kalgoorlie drew a massive movement of people from the Eastern states to the thinly populated West. But if Cadden was in search of gold, he failed to prosper. He joined the police and was soon posted to the Kimberley, taking his family with him.

My grandmother told me only four things about this part of her childhood. The family had gone to 'the North' when she was small. A baby sister had died there. Pearl remembered her father driving her in a horse-drawn trap through a bush fire. And she spoke of the Aboriginals. She called them 'terrible people'.

In 1896, Cadden was transferred to Perth and soon left the police force. He acquired two horse-drawn cabs, and became a cab driver. The family lived in the working class suburb of Victoria Park, in the south of the city. Cadden's trade was fairly good until the motor car began to sideline the horse, and he then retired, living in Victoria Park until his death in 1954.

The children were raised in what seems to have been an atmosphere of fervent British patriotism. John Cadden seems to have had a strong strain of deference toward the upper classes. His proudest boast was that Sir John Forrest, Western Australia's dominant political figure, insisted that Cadden and no one else, drive him from Government House to Parliament House. The Cadden children were brought up in the Wesleyan Church, which was pugnaciously pro-Empire. The family were part of the world described by historian Bobbie Oliver who writes that in pre-World War One Western Australia, through the churches (especially the Protestant denominations) and the education system:

> . . . the ideology of Empire dominated the culture and learning experiences of the people and two . . . ideologies . . . related to Imperialism – renewed militarism and devotion to royalty – were spread with considerable efficiency.   (1995: 34)

This account is borne out by the fact that in the war-time referenda on military conscription in 1916 and 1917, Western Australia returned large majorities in favour of compulsory service, whereas the proposals were defeated in the nation as a whole.

One can see the coming of war in a photo album which Pearl left behind. It starts with holiday snaps of the years 1912, 1913, 1914: picnics, people wearing straw boaters and sun hats boarding a launch. Then suddenly, war: the Australian Imperial Force with their digger hats and horses parading through Perth. And Jack and Billy, Pearl's brothers, in uniform. They go off to war, and life in Victoria Park continues. There are pictures of Pearl training as a nurse. There are pictures from the brothers in Egypt and in England. But Jack didn't come back. After miraculously surviving the Western Front, in 1918, he contracted influenza in London. Billy arrived at the hospital in London to be told that Jack had just died. Another young man did not return from the war, of whom Pearl said little; but it seems that she had hoped to marry him.

It may have been this loss that propelled her, in 1922, into marrying my grandfather, Bert Oates. It was far from a happy marriage, but the decision transformed her life. Bert had been born in Farrell's Flat, a tiny town in South Australia. His father, Philip Oates was a boundary rider on one of the vast pastoralist estates. Shortly after Bert's birth they joined the exodus to Western Australia. In Perth, disaster, in the form of typhoid, struck the family. Philip died, leaving Bert's mother, Mary Nicholls, to bring up four children. This she did through great hardship, working as a laundress and midwife. Bert started working at the age of 12, but studied in night school, showing a phenomenal mathematical skill which he was to retain throughout his life, and learning book-keeping. In the First World War he survived the holocaust of the Western Front, probably because he was recruited into the Artillery rather than the Infantry. Jokes about the benefits of being a gunner were practically the only thing he ever said about his war service.

At the end of the war, Bert and his brother Len came up against the grim economic reality of inter-war Western Australia. The Western Australian economy entered a recession so deep that the 1913 per capita level of income was not regained until the 1950s (Oliver 1995: 34). But an opportunity arose for the brothers. Shortly after returning from the war, Bert and Len were offered jobs by an Australian called Atkinson, who was living in Bloemfontein. Atkinson had apparently gone to South Africa as part of the Australian contingent in the Boer War and stayed on. He had started a blacksmith's business which was now expanding. The firm re-tailed Model T Fords and needed book-keepers. Len and Bert proved to be far more than this. They rapidly took the lead in the business, which became 'Atkinson-Oates'. This was the launching pad for a career in which Len and Bert were to become central figures in the South African motor car industry.

In 1922 Bert returned to Perth to marry my grandmother, and brought her to Bloemfontein. Pearl was rocketed from working class Victoria Park to wealth in South Africa. After a few years in Bloemfontein, at the beginning of the 1930s, the Oateses moved their business to Johannesburg. Pearl found herself living at the centre of South Africa's new bourgeoisie in a mansion in Houghton, Johannesburg. The house was named Burra-Burra. It was only recently that I realised it was named after a fabulously successful mine near Bert's birthplace. Bert was descended from the Cornish miners, who had fled the declining mines of their county and sought wealth in the mineral fields of Australia. He seemed to be saying, in naming his South African house, that he had gained there what his kin had mostly failed to find in Australia.

Pearl and Bert had three children: a son, John, my mother and my aunt. But wealth was no protection against tragedy and the Empire continued to demand its sacrifices. At the outbreak of the Second World War John (concealing that he was under-age) joined the South African Air Force, and trained as a fighter pilot. After flying in the North African campaign, he was sent on to Italy. John's Spitfire was shot down in combat and his body was not found.

## On the making of men and women

These were the experiences which shaped Pearl. What did they make of her, and of her understanding of men and women? And how did that in turn affect me?

Pearl had a deeply ambiguous attitude to militarism, which was crucial to my future. There was in Pearl's personality, a strange interweaving of her devotion to the martial virtues of the British Empire with a sense of the personal tragedies inherent in that involvement. In one corner of the entrance to Pearl's house was a virtual shrine to her political hero, Jan Christiaan Smuts. There, a group of portraits showed Smuts in the uniform of a Field Marshall of the British Empire. It was less any specific political doctrine of Smuts that appealed to Pearl than his role as a decisive uniformed male military figure in the service of Britain. Around the corner, in the living room, the pictures of Smuts were echoed by a portrait of Pearl's lost son, John. In the painting, John wore the uniform of a South African Air Force officer, the khaki colour and the cut of his uniform echoing Smuts's appearance in the next room. The aura was one of commemoration of a lost race of military giants whose valour made them mythical.

Throughout the period of her life from her childhood to when South Africa left the Commonwealth in the early 1960s, Pearl's symbolic identification with the Empire, its leaders, victories and sacrifices, seems to have been a constant theme in her life. But there was a complication. Pearl was enormously fearful for those she loved in a way which contradicted her abstract worship of military heroism. Certainly by the time I was born in 1954, this fear ruled Pearl's life. In my childhood Pearl's constant theme was 'be careful', 'look out', 'something might go wrong'. There was a perverse gap between Pearl's idealisation of dead uniformed heroes and her constant strictures against exploration, risk and daring. It was as if an image of masculine heroics was being set up and subtly undermined at the same time. When I think of my childhood this was manifested in the way in which my brother and I endlessly dressed up and acted out episodes of derring-do as commandos, knights, cowboys and so on. Yet outside the realm of fantasy I was an exceedingly frightened and nervous child. The ideal I was imbibing and the emotions being created in me did not link up.

Pearl's lifetime experience of male death was surely crucial in creating this ambiguity. Having lost her boyfriend, brother and son to war, she was certainly worried it would happen again. John, in the years before he died, gave up using his baptismal name and adopted the name Jonathan. When I was born and given this chosen name in his memory, Pearl I think came to feel that I was his replacement, and that somehow by protecting me she could prevent his tragedy from reoccurring. Of course it was a stifling sort of protection. The message was that a realm of danger lay beyond the fence of Pearl's house.

This unhelpful socialisation was paradoxically useful when it came to my own minor confrontation with military power. At 16, like other white South African boys of my generation, I had to register for service with the South African Defence Force (SADF). Of course many things made me resistant to the idea of the call-up I could expect at 17 – exposure to anti-apartheid political ideas; reaction against my authoritarian schooling, of which the army sounded like a continuation; admiration for American counter-culture and anti-war movements; horror stories from conscripts about their persecution by sadistic non-commissioned officers; and my intuition that as a poor athlete I would not do well under the rigours of basic training. But I think that there was also a sense that my childhood militarism, learned largely from Pearl, operated at such a level of abstraction and fantasy that I had not really internalised it as a guide to daily life. My desire for personal autonomy and self-preservation was much stronger, and was decisive in my determination not to go into the military. It was not combat dangers that were at issue as at that time (the very early 1970s) there was little military combat involving the SADF, and in any case I could almost certainly have fixed a sedentary job in the army on health grounds. Rather, it was the need for personal freedom which made the thought of military service unbearable. And in a certain sense Pearl created that need and legitimised it at the same time. I wanted to get out of the claustrophobic world she created and also did not want another kind of personal subordination. And yet there was also an underlying sense that Pearl had created in me, that it was legitimate to fear and resist external forces that might destroy me.

The second aspect of Pearl's personality which I think shaped me was her hostile relationship to the kind of model of masculinity represented by Bert and his brother Len. To comprehend this, one needs to understand the difference between the ways in which Pearl reacted to her new social fate, and the way the brothers did to theirs. On the one hand, Pearl was, I think, disconcerted by her meteoric upward social mobility. Despite forming a number of good friendships in Johannesburg, she found herself uncomfortable in the city's upper class milieu. She talked disparagingly of 'social people', by which she meant socialites. She enjoyed certain pleasures of wealth – travel, cultivating a magnificent garden, accumulating books and pictures. But her pursuit of these activities was in part a shield against a social environment in which she did not enjoy participating. In some ways her persona adapted to the norms of smart Johannesburg society – her accent became less noticeably Australian than that of her sisters who remained at home and she moved from the Wesleyan to the more socially prestigious Anglican church. But one had the impression that she found difficulty in adapting to her new environment. She retained an egalitarian touch in her ability to form warm acquaintances with the shop assistants, postmen and gardeners whom she encountered. One felt that she enjoyed these contacts more than her relations with the despised 'social people'.

Len and Bert, on the other hand, comfortably conquered the world of the Johannesburg bourgeoisie on their own terms, keeping their unabashedly Australian working class identities apparently intact. They radiated a masculinity that was loud, outgoing and hedonistic. Theirs was a world of club bars and card schools where they held forth in the most strident of Australian accents. They enjoyed their wealth thoroughly, and their particular enthusiasm was that quintessential Australian working class preoccupation, horse racing. They became kingpins in the racing world of Johannesburg.

There was something of what Australians call the 'larrikin' about the brothers. The larrikin is the turn of the century urban Australian male self-image of the smooth-talking, rule-defying, gambling, loveable rogue (Glynn 1996: 230–1). Len and Bert's characters made them extremely popular, but took them well beyond the bounds of strict business rationality. They were extraordinarily generous, constantly giving large handouts to family, friends and charitable causes. Their business deals were not cautious, producing both resounding successes and near disasters (from which they always bounced back).

Pearl must have come into conflict with this wheeling-dealing, bar room masculinity at an early stage of their marriage. By the time I first remember her, she was massively censorious of every aspect of Bert's life. She criticised all his personal habits bitingly to his face, when he was at home, embarrassed by his lack of gentility. But she also seemed to resent the time he spent at clubs, cards, racing and golfing. She derided each of these pursuits with jokes about their futility. Pearl was also very hostile to the world of business, which she talked of in disparaging terms. However, Pearl's complaints were clearly a metaphor for the breakdown of her relationship with Bert. She was excluded from the masculine world of Bert and Len and the resulting hostility produced a downward spiral of mutual resentment.

Pearl's hostility to Bert cut me off from some of the things I might have learned from him. Because of Pearl's emotional hold on me, I largely accepted her hostile vision of Bert. I absorbed her stigmatisation in Bert of many features which I would now consider in a much more positive way: his practical engagement in the world, his sociability, his capacity to adapt and innovate. Much later in life these were all things which I wished I had in greater measure. I had been cut off from a model which, for all its negative features, could have taught me much that was helpful.

Thirdly, Pearl gave me a sense of the world as a threatening place. Pearl always seemed to be searching for explanations. Although she had very limited formal education she read voraciously: newspapers, books on current events, middlebrow novels. There was a sense of intellectual search about her. But Pearl's attempts to make sense of things pulled her toward extreme doctrines, perhaps because, for much of her life, she found what was happening to her and her world so frightening as to be inexplicable in conventional ways. Not surprisingly, given the contexts of her life, two particular themes wove through her thinking. The loss of loved ones produced a search for spiritual reassurance. And a life in two societies embodying severe forms of racial domination – turn of the century Australia and mid-century South Africa – produced an attraction toward the weird intricacies of racial political ideologies.

In the period of my childhood Pearl's beliefs became increasingly focused on questions of politics. As South Africa left the Commonwealth at the beginning of the 1960s, the certainties of imperial loyalty in which

Jonathan Hyslop

Pearl had been raised started to disintegrate. Moreover, she felt directly threatened by anti-colonial revolt in Africa, and the rise of opposition in South Africa. As Richard Hofstadter (1979) says in his classic study of political paranoia, such paranoia is most likely to be evoked by a fear of catastrophe, and a feeling that there is a confrontation of irreconcilable interests at work. For Pearl in the context of the 1960s, both factors applied. The possibility of a catastrophe seemed real. This was the era when pictures of Belgians fleeing rebels in the Congo appeared in the press, and one million French departed from Algeria. White South Africans feared that their world would be swept away at a stroke. And for Pearl the conflict was certainly irreconcilable. Pearl was a paternalistically kindly employer of gardeners, servants and drivers, of some of whom she seemed fond. But she had a visceral, readily proclaimed hostility to black people as a whole, which even as a child I found striking. Pearl could not conceive of the possibility of compromise in racial politics. It was for her a conflict of absolutes.

The political consequences of this were farcically grim. In the late 1960s a black-bordered photograph of the assassinated Verwoerd appeared in her hallway, glowering across at Jannie Smuts on the other side. This embarrassed most of Pearl's friends and family, who although far from liberal, were certainly not National Party supporters. Pearl became a subscriber to a journal called the *South African Observer*, edited by a Mr S.E.D. Brown. Brown believed that John Vorster was in the process of selling out true apartheid policy as conceived by Verwoerd. Verwoerd's killing, Brown suspected, was a plot by agents of the Kremlin (or the CIA; it came to much the same thing in Brown's world) to destroy the white man in southern Africa. It got worse. Pearl subscribed to an American publication called *Common Sense*, edited by one Conde McGinley, whose picture subsequently appeared in the house. Conde McGinley believed that Henry Ford of Dearborn had been right about The Jewish Conspiracy. He was a great admirer of the man whose name he wrote as 'The late Senator Joe McCarthy (Patriot)'. McGinley believed that water fluoridation and gun control were part of a Jewish-Communist plot to ensure that patriotic Americans were drugged and disarmed when the Red hordes arrived. Pearl's imperial loyalty had transmuted into sympathy for neo-fascists.

While never quite declaring for Brown and McGinley's ideas, Pearl connsistently pronounced them 'interesting'. Behind her attraction to conspiracy theories lurked her fear. It was not so much that the particular ideas of extreme rightists attracted her intellectually, as that their paranoid politics accorded with her feeling that she was under constant external threat. For Pearl life as a whole felt cataclysmic. Political ideologists like Brown and McGinley reassured her by telling her that her feelings were a realistic representation of a world controlled by conspiracy. These figures of male authority assured her that there were politically occult explanations for apparent chaos.

Whilst I was never really influenced by Pearl's political ideas, evolving in a very different, leftward, direction in my teenage years, I did imbibe from her a sense of a pervasively threatening world.

## Drawing some conclusions

What was the story behind Pearl's adult behaviour? What happened to the Cadden family in the Kimberley of the 1890s? Does it provide a key to what took place later? I do not pretend to have the answers. I know too little about Cadden's experience of the war against Jandamarra, too little of his relations with his family to make very confident assertions.[2] Even if I were better informed, family history can never really provide the level of explanation and identification one seeks. Ultimately, I have to be content with telling the stories of the past. But curiosity spurs one to speculate. And the Jandamarra story (Pedersen and Woorunmurra 1995) at least provides a context for doing so.

In the Kimberley of the 1880s and 90s a small war broke out between the settlers and the local hunter-gatherers, the Bunuba, who regarded the settlers' livestock as they did any other animal and were soon killing them on a large scale. Violent, armed clashes between the two sides escalated in intensity and frequency. Jandamarra was a Bunuba who worked as a tracker for the police. However, when he was involved in the capture of Ellemarra, a Bunuba leader, Jandamarra turned on Constable Richardson, whom he was accompanying, and killed him. Jandamarra freed Ellemarra, joined his rebel band and became their leader. Cadden was amongst the policemen who were sent in unsuccessful pursuit of Jandamarra. In the following months several bloody clashes occurred, including instances when the police launched surprise attacks on Aboriginal bands, killing at random. Through a series of resignations, and his promotion to sergeant, Cadden was left in charge of the local police. Although it seems that he tried to avoid violence as far as possible,[3] he was presiding over an operation which had taken on a genocidal character. Finally, in March 1897 Jandamarra was killed, and his head hacked off as a trophy by two policemen who arrived on the scene. The dispossession of the Bunuba could now take place unimpeded.

What are some of the conclusions that we can draw from the above story and other evidence? Let's start with the image of the uniformed man, represented in Pearl's house by the nook dedicated to Smuts. The story suggests that Pearl's first images of men would have been of John Cadden and his police colleagues. Photographs (Pedersen and Woorunmurra 1995) show the mounted police of the 1890s in their uniforms, which are of a military cut; forage caps, tunics and boots. So it would not have been surprising if the uniform and masculinity had become closely linked in Pearl's mind. John Cadden would most likely have been her first image of a uniformed man; but this was followed by others. Her photo albums were full of pictures of young men about to go off to the First World War. By now the uniforms were not the dark shades of the police, but the various khakis of the twentieth century British imperial forces. The colours of those uniforms were similar to those which Smuts and John would wear in the pictures in Pearl's house.

Those portraits at Burra-Burra were, I think, about two aspects of Pearl's relation to men; the ambiguous security of male authority figures represented by Smuts, and the tragedy of male sacrifice represented by John. Pearl had identified with the Empire for most of her life. It gave her a security based on its definition of how the world should be, a security guaranteed by uniformed authority figures from Sergeant Cadden to General Smuts, who apparently mastered the chaos of the world. But it also took away those closest to her. For the first part of her life the reassurance may have seemed to justify the personal price, maintaining her mental map of the world in a kind of balance. But in the end that balance broke down. Like other Anglo-South Africans, she felt betrayed and confused by the disintegration of the British Empire. She was propelled into a search for new authority figures from Verwoerd to Conde McGinley. She no longer had the faith which had enabled her to see her young male friends, her brothers and John go off to war, and became focused on evading threats and dangers to members of her family.

The story of Jandamarra also helps to make some sense of Pearl's fundamental fearfulness and her racism. In her early childhood, the family was living in a situation of war. Accounts of the Kimberley settlers' responses to the Jandamarra episode suggest that they were in a state of collective psychosis. Their sense of threat was overwhelming, and so was their desire for retribution. So a belief in a very direct and immediate threat from black people must have pervaded Pearl's early life. Hence, surely, her description of Aboriginals as 'terrible people', and the way she transposed a kind of rage against black people to her new life in South Africa. Her encounters with Aboriginals in the North are likely to have been such as to reinforce this hostile image, for she probably encountered the Bunuba and others in conditions which degraded and dehumanised them. Photographs in the Pedersen and Woorunmurra book show Aboriginals in the Kimberley, chained and manacled as they were brought in by mounted policemen, or in the ill-fitting uniforms of prisoners, working at arduous manual labour; 'terrible' images indeed. And let us remember the extent to which John Cadden was implicated in all of this. Even if Pedersen is right in his estimate that Cadden was not a man who sought out violence, he was inevitably involved in a world of extraordinary destructiveness. Cadden was present at the pursuit of Jandamarra's band; he was in command of men who were sadistic and eager to kill. He worked with men who found it appropriate to cut off their enemy's head and display it as a trophy. This was the world in which my grandmother grew up, and in which her ideas of men and her ideas of race developed.

But just as it is necessary to highlight what the colonists did, it is also necessary in order to comprehend this to understand what drove them, and the tragedy of their own lives. The extraordinary hardships experienced by the nineteenth century British colonials often led to men initially channelling their frustrations into violence, authoritarianism and exploitation against their own families. The nightmare of colonisation for the colonised contained within it what was often a nightmare life for the colonial family. For every Randlord or rich New South Wales squatter, there were thousands of dirt-scrabbling prospectors and small farmers, drifting day labourers and phthisis-wracked miners. These men experienced a daily struggle for survival: and it was a battle which encouraged them to treat their families harshly. The Australian writer Merv Lilley captures this aspect of the colonial experience in these words:

> . . . facing the high mortality rate of the underfed, diseased, in a land without facilities or compassion where the children were defenceless victims of slave labour in the struggle to succeed, to rise above all that had been the lot of working men and women. . . . The Irishmen and Englishmen built railways by hand, hated each other or married each other's women, still in hatred, reproducing the new Australian who neither hated nor loved the children, but flogged them, tied them to trees while they grubbed the land, leaving them to battle with the ants for many hours at a time. (1994: 140)

The impossible problems that the colonists faced fostered in the men a brutality toward their families. And it was also the desperation of these men that made them available for mobilisation against indigenous people. John Cadden came out of the world that Lilley describes. He passed though the harsh world of New South Wales mining, and of the Western Australian goldfields, where food shortages and typhoid epidemics reigned. This was the experience that mobilised him into becoming a foot soldier for the Empire. If as one of his police colleagues thought (Pilmer 1927), Cadden was not equipped for the frontier battle, this might have been just one more felt humiliation, given the world in which they lived. Even if Cadden was not a brutal man by the standards of his day, there must surely have been a streak of anger there, affecting every aspect of his life.

What did John Cadden's own traumas do to him, and how was that reflected back on to his family? Pearl seems to have been very fond of her father and spoke of life in Perth as happy. Yet there clearly was a domestically tyrannical aspect to Cadden. Pearl talked of covering her ears to shut out the sound of John Cadden beating her brothers. He bitterly resisted Pearl's desire to become a nurse, an issue over which they waged a protracted struggle.

Perhaps for Pearl there was unconsciously something very frightening about the form John Cadden's masculinity took that re-emerged in her conflicted relationship with Bert. Perhaps beneath the 'happy' surface of the family life Pearl remembered a level of fear. Was there a sense of slippage between apparent and underlying feelings that fed into her attraction toward conspiracy theory with its idea of a 'deeper' reality?

Certainly something must have frightened Pearl. Looking at pictures of her with her sisters in their youth, the others look cheerful, lively, open-

*Pearl (extreme left) and her younger sisters – Perth 1912*

faced; Pearl seems remote, abstracted, enclosed. Was it the memory of the Kimberley? Pearl was old enough to remember that time, which her sisters were not. Or was it some kind of abuse, abuse by fear, by insecurity, by empathy with the suffering of others? Pearl had been exposed in her most formative years to colonial war, and to the emotions of her father, a man participating in that war.

NOTES

1. Information about the Caddens and the Oateses in this chapter derives from John V. Kinsella, unpublished manuscript, Geraldton, no date, in the possession of the author; birth and marriage certificates of P.B. Cadden and H.G. Oates, in the possession of the author; numerous interviews with family members; and correspondence with various local history bodies, genealogical associations and libraries in Australia.

2. The events in which Cadden was involved were given a superb record in 1995. An Australian historian, Howard Pedersen, working with Banjo Woorunmurra, a custodian of the oral tradition of Jandamarra, produced a blending of documentary and oral sources in a fine book. This work, *Jandamarra and the Bunuba Resistance*, (Pedersen and Woorunmurra 1995) provides a richly detailed narrative of the Jandamarra episode.

3. Personal communication from Howard Pedersen, 1997.

BIBLIOGRAPHY

Glynn, S. 1996. 'Urbanisation in Australian History'. In G. Whitlock and D. Carter, *Images of Australia: An Introductory Reader in Australian Studies*. St Lucia: University of Queensland Press.

Hofstadter, R. 1979. *The Paranoid Style in American Politics and Other Essays*. Chicago: University of Chicago Press.

Lewis, P. 1991. 'Mummy, Matrons and Maids: feminine presence and absence in male institutions, 1934–63'. In M. Roper and J. Tosh, eds., *Manful Assertions: Masculinities in Britain since 1808*. London: Routledge.

Lilley, M. 1994. *Gatton Man*. Ringwood: McPhee Gribble.

Oliver, B. 1995. *War and Peace in Western Australia: The Social and Political Impact of the Great War 1914–1926*. Perth: University of Western Australia Press.

Pedersen, H. and B. Woorunmurra. 1995. *Jandamarra and the Bunuba Resistance*. Broome: Magabala Books.

Pilmer, R.H. 1927. 'Men's Work: An Australian Saga'. Manuscript in the Derby Public Library, Western Australia.

# CHAPTER 8

# Puritanism Transformed
## Afrikaner Masculinities in the Apartheid and Post-Apartheid Period

KOBUS DU PISANI

In 1948 the National Party (NP) unexpectedly won the general election. For the next forty years, this party would govern South Africa, creating and instituting the apartheid system. In the process, Afrikaner nationalism would become a racist, militaristic and authoritarian force. Behind and within Afrikaner nationalism were prescriptions for correct male behaviour which were woven into hegemonic Afrikaner masculinity.

In this chapter the hegemonic form of Afrikaner masculinity is analysed in its historical context. The forces and agents which shaped and transformed it, its role in apartheid society, and its response to societal change are discussed. These aspects are clarified by tracing how the primary symbols of Afrikaner masculinity have been modified over the years. The focus is on changes in symbols/metaphors of Afrikaner masculinity, not because they in themselves constitute hegemonic masculinity, but because they operate within the setting of gendered social relations and are easily identifiable expressions of the main trends in hegemonic Afrikaner masculinity at particular stages of Afrikaner nationalist development.

The emergence of a hegemonic Afrikaner masculinity marginalised alternative masculinities by silencing or stigmatising them. Hegemonic Afrikaner masculinity was intricately bound up with social and political power in Afrikaner society and hence with Afrikaner nationalism. It changed over the fifty year period under review by accommodating and absorbing social change and gender challenge, which came from sources such as the youth, women, global culture and class transformation. Although hegemonic Afrikaner masculinity changed over time it did not lose its essential puritan character. The question at the end of the twentieth century and against the background of a process of rapid and unpredictable change in Afrikaner society after the demise of apartheid, is whether coherent gender configurations still exist within Afrikanerdom? Has hegemonic Afrikaner masculinity reached the end of the road?

## The puritan nature of Afrikaner hegemonic masculinity

Hegemonic Afrikaner masculinity was essentially puritan in nature.[1] It took an unyielding Protestant view based on 'pure' New Testament principles, and rigid austerity and strictness in conduct and morals. The puritan basis of Afrikaner masculine ideals stemmed from the strong influence of religion in Afrikaner society and the close synergy between religious, political and cultural leadership in Afrikanerdom. In the pre-apartheid period church leaders played an important role in the establishment and moral foundations of the Afrikaner-Broederbond and in the launching of Christian-National Education (Morrell 1998). Throughout the apartheid era Afrikaans churches remained the leading institutions in Afrikaner society in terms of opinion-making in the realm of morality (Du Preez 1983).

Initially the puritan ideal of Afrikaner masculinity was expressed in the image of the simple, honest, steadfast, religious and hard-working *boer* (farmer): the personification of puritan moral values and work ethics. For many years after the majority of Afrikaans men had ceased to be farmers this remained the dominant representation of Afrikaner masculinity. In due course, this rural-based primary symbol of masculinity was modified and supplemented by other symbols in the process of societal change wrought by urbanisation and modernisation. Rural traditionalism and urban modernism were merged into a modified puritan ideal of masculinity by incorporating elements of the urban lifestyle into traditional perceptions of masculinity. The process of modernisation of the Afrikaner culture was ameliorated by shrouding it in traditionalism (O'Meara 1983: 165–6).

Afrikaner nationalist mobilisation led to conformity within the organised Afrikaner establishment and in expressions of masculinity. An indication of the core values of Afrikaner hegemonic masculinity at the start of the apartheid era can be found in the membership requirements of the Afrikaner-Broederbond. White, financially independent, Afrikaans-speaking, Protestant men (by implication adherents to the Calvinist version of Christianity and members of any of the three big Afrikaans churches: the Nederduitse Gereformeerde Kerk [NGK or DRC], the Gereformeerde Kerk [Dopper Church], or the Nederduitsch Hervormde Kerk) over the

Kobus du Pisani

age of 25 could become members if their proposers could confirm their irreproachable character and their commitment to their fatherland, language and culture (Du Pisani 1998). Combined with other elements of Afrikaner masculine identity, such as heterosexuality and political conservatism, these requirements represented the ideal of Afrikaner hegemonic masculinity. It was a construct of that emergent middle class version of Afrikaner intellectualism known as Christian-Nationalism and expressed the ideal, but in many cases not the reality, of what Afrikaner masculinity entailed.

With an Afrikaner government in power after the 1948 election Afrikaner nationalist men – politicians, senior civil servants, church leaders, academics, educationalists, journalists and businessmen – occupied the most influential and powerful positions in South Africa. The male-dominated network of Afrikaner organisations, which had come into existence during Afrikanerdom's struggle for political power, was used by the National Party leadership to consolidate that power. Women did not fill leadership positions in the power centres of Afrikaner society. In the 1950s traditional conservatism in Afrikaner society held steady and the hegemony of the puritan ideal of Afrikaner masculinity was consolidated.

## Men of the world: the forces of globalisation

As in other modernising cultures, there was consistent interaction between nationalising and globalising forces in Afrikaner society when Afrikaner urbanisation gained momentum in the twentieth century. Urban dynamics were bound to modify Afrikaner world-views in the long run. Despite strict control of the mass media by the government globalising influences infiltrated Afrikaner society through literature, films and other media, music and business contacts, and started broadening Afrikaner ideas about masculinity.

Afrikaans literature introduced European ideas to Afrikanerdom. A trend in Afrikaner masculinity, which had started in the 1930s, was its increasing sophistication. Because of rising levels of education a more intellectual approach with a European flavour became apparent. Increased awareness of aesthetics and an appreciation for the arts took root in the Afrikaner urban middle class culture. Through their exquisite poetry the so-called *Dertigers* (Generation of Thirty), who dominated Afrikaans literature for some decades, elevated the image of Afrikaner masculinity to a higher plane of cultivation than before. These poets were also the most prominent source of *lojale verset* (loyal resistance) against Afrikaner nationalist conformism (Van Wyk Louw 1939, 1958). However, at that stage narrow-minded Calvinist *dominees* (ministers of religion),

Christian-National school teachers and right-wing NP politicians were dominant in Afrikaner society. When conservatism started losing its grip on Afrikaner thinking the next important Afrikaans literary movement, the *Sestigers* (Generation of Sixty), heralded greater open-mindedness among Afrikaners (Antonissen 1960).

Due to the popularity of the cinema as a form of urban entertainment Hollywood films were a major source of American cultural influence. Movie stars became role models in the Afrikaner urban community and the image of the Hollywood actor was extensively used in advertising in Afrikaans magazines and newspapers. This non-traditional image was not narrow-mindedly puritan and often focused on the 'good life', where men indulged in the pleasures of modern urban society by enjoying the best in clothing, food, drink and various types of luxuries. Advertisements depicted the increasing affluence of urban middle class Afrikaners and were far removed from the notions of the nobility of poverty and hard work, which had been dominant in the time of poor whiteism. The Hollywood style was emulated by the masculine heroes in Afrikaans popular literature and Afrikaner urbanites identified with Hollywood exponents of masculinity such as James Bond, even though they were often playboy types deviating from the puritan ideal of masculinity.[2] When television was introduced in South Africa in the mid-1970s, after it had been resisted successfully for many years by conservative Afrikaner nationalists, Hollywood's influence on Afrikaner values was strengthened by the inclusion of a large proportion of American programmes in South African television schedules. Television heroes became the new role models of masculinity (Van Vuuren 1983; Maré 1985).

Globalising influences also entered the Afrikaner culture via the youth through music and fashion. From the late 1950s pop music gained tremendous popularity among the Afrikaner youth. Pop singers were the idols of the young generation. The hippy counter-culture of the late 1960s did not catch on in the Afrikaner culture to the same extent that it did among young English-speaking South Africans. Many young Afrikaners remained respectfully conformist in the suburban framework. However, in increasing numbers others started expressing their protest against the conservative establishment in their taste in music, dress and lifestyle. In due course their outlook would impact upon hegemonic Afrikaner masculinity.

Increasing links with the international business world during the emergence of Afrikaner capitalism provided the major globalising impetus in Afrikaner society in the early apartheid period. Increasingly Afrikaans men became business executives: well-dressed men who had business

lunches in fancy restaurants and played golf. Young Afrikaans businessmen such as Anton Rupert and Jan S. Marais established links with the
capitalist world. Rupert expressed the outlook of the 'new men' as follows:
'I am a man with a Christian conscience, child of Christian civilization. I
am Afrikaner-born. I am a South African. I belong to the Western world. I
am a world citizen' (De Klerk 1975: 294). In learning the art of making
money the 'new men' acquired international manners, thought-patterns,
attitudes and styles typical of modern capitalists. Afrikaner capitalism had
taken a turn away from the vision of a *volk* (people) saving itself from
poverty.

By the 1960s fewer than 10 per cent of Afrikaners still lived on farms.
Afrikaans literature portrayed the Afrikaners' experience of the industrial
world (Antonissen 1960). In a series of *Huisgenoot* articles Wim Hartman
depicted 'the new Afrikaner' as a city dweller, used to the bustle of the city
and no longer bound to the *platteland* (countryside), although some
nostalgia regarding rural life remained. The Afrikaner urban culture began
to take the form of a mass culture. The new monied classes were 'conditioned by a thousand subtle hidden influences in their daily routines,
from suburb to office, factory, classroom, drive-in, the seaside and back
again to their homes' (De Klerk 1975: 300).

Economic prosperity had a decisive impact on the lifestyle, orientation
and moral values of the Afrikaner community. Average Afrikaners were
much more well-to-do and their world-view more materialistically in-
clined than before. In middle class society the focus was on success.
Competitiveness and awareness of achievement increased. The ideas of
upward mobility, power and status featured prominently in advertising.
Competition and a faster pace of living brought pain and pleasure. On the
one hand, social problems such as debt, alcoholism and suicide entered
the profile of Afrikaner masculinity. The negative impact of the lifestyle in
the cities on men's health was reflected in many advertisements for remed-
ies for stress and exhaustion. On the other hand, with more money in
circulation, middle class urban Afrikaners were transformed into modern
pursuers of pleasure. Prosperity went hand-in-hand with new status symbols such as motor cars and luxury holidays. Beaches and game reserves
became the means of escaping the rigours, tensions and pressures of city
life. Recreational activities were associated with male social status. Advertising slogans such as 'Enjoy a lager and be happy' and 'Braaivleis, rugby,
sunny skies and Chevrolet' suggested that the successful man was entitled
to some pleasure of the type that might not be approved by the more
pietistic Afrikaners.

Feminism never really gained a foothold in Afrikaner society because of the strong grip of patriarchy, puritanism and authoritarianism. The isolated voices of Afrikaner feminists were largely smothered by anti-feminist indoctrination although some feminist ideas filtered indirectly through to Afrikaner society via Afrikaner women in academic circles, anti-sexist journalists, and more enlightened male church leaders. However, the majority of Afrikaner women supported rather than challenged patriarchy.

The puritan orientation of the majority of Afrikaners caused many qualms in the process of adaptation to the modern urban world. Afrikaans churches and Christian-National educators, grappling with the implications of growing prosperity, warned about the dangers of materialism. However, the Nederduitse Gereformeerde Kerk (Dutch Reformed Church) and other Afrikaans churches were cautious not to alienate the Afrikaner businesspeople and affluent middle class Afrikaners among their members. In popular literature materialism was often denounced as negative and associated with banality, dishonesty, immorality and abuse of power.[3] However, puritanism was a contested concept, and while it did not preclude the enjoyment of material possessions, wealthy Afrikaners could easily rationalise their indulgence in material security and worldly pleasures.

From the late 1960s changes in Afrikaner moral values became increasingly visible. Religious fundamentalism and pietism still prevailed in the Afrikaans churches, but in the urban environment churches did not have the same grip on their members as in rural communities. Among urban Afrikaners the strictly puritan moral codes of the past were gradually relaxed. Casinos in neighbouring black states supplied the demand for X-rated entertainment. Afrikaans jokes in circulation increasingly alluded to drunkenness or sex. The best example of the new morals prevailing in Afrikaner society was to be found in the Afrikaans Sunday newspapers such as *Dagbreek*, *Die Beeld* and later *Rapport*. These papers built up their circulation through sensational and controversial reporting, scandals, gossip and daring sexual undertones.

*Sedebewakers* (supporters of traditional moral values) resisted tendencies which they regarded as signs of moral decay. Fundamentalist *dominees* sounded warnings against secularisation and permissiveness, and the Afrikaans churches for many years took a strong stand against Sunday newspapers. A letter-writer objected to the 'erosion of sound hero-worship' caused by the hero of a serial story in *Die Huisgenoot*, whom he regarded as a *dopsteker* (drunkard) and a *meisieverleier* (seducer).[4] A popular point of dispute in the mid-1960s was the impact of the popularity of the Beatles among the youth. Old-fashioned Afrikaner patriarchy

Kobus du Pisani

with its predilection for militaristic discipline at home and in the schools could not stand the Beatles' licentiousness and their long hair, which was regarded as a sign of effeminacy.

The overall impression of perceptions of masculinity among Afrikaners in the 1950s and 60s is one of a modernising phase in which the *verligte* (enlightened) section among Afrikaner men was slowly breaking free from the inhibitions of traditional conservatism. By the early 1970s money, the Beatles and James Bond had started transforming the puritan ideal of masculinity. With the generation gap in Afrikaner society that opened up in the 1960s between the older and younger generations hegemonic masculinity became more contested than ever before.

The impact of globalising influences was restricted by South Africa's growing isolation in the international community during the 1970s and 80s, but since the advent of the 'new' South Africa in 1990 the country has more than ever been opened up to globalising influences.

## The family man: upholding patriarchy

Long before the advent of apartheid the power of patriarchy in Afrikaner social life had been consolidated and firmly entrenched in gender relation patterns on a conservative religious basis. Patriarchy, the rule of the father, was justified in all spheres of society in terms of biblical texts. Symbols of masculinity and femininity were manipulated to uphold patriarchy. Through their endorsement of the principle of patriarchal authority Afrikaans churches and schools influenced the majority of Afrikaner men and women to accept patriarchy as 'natural' and 'normal'. Where conservatism and Christian-Nationalism prevailed, family life was dominated by the patriarchal head of the family; a division of labour along gender lines was strictly adhered to; the wife and mother was restricted to a domestic role; men enjoyed better access to education; political leadership was the exclusive domain of men; and in the Afrikaans churches women were barred from the special offices (Cloete 1992; Ackerman 1994; Du Pisani 1996).

Puritan Afrikaners viewed the male-headed family as the cornerstone of a healthy society. The image of the male head of the family was cast in the mould of the 'good provider', that is, the homely and reliable family man and the caring head of the household (Bernard 1995; Collier 1995). The image of successful fatherhood has been associated in advertisements of, amongst others, insurance companies, banks and correspondence colleges, with career success and the acquisition of material assets, which would enable the father to take proper care of his family. The Afrikaans churches have held the view that the male head of the family should fulfil a priestly function, by not only providing his family with material things, but also looking after their spiritual well-being.

In the height of apartheid male domination at home was hardly questioned. Most Afrikaner women resigned themselves to patriarchal authority and a domestic role (Landman 1994). Many Afrikaner fathers stoically maintained an affective distance between themselves and their children, and corporal punishment was the accepted method of disciplining children.

Theoretically male power in the family was reduced by radical changes in South African marriage law after 1980. But the practice and the old-fashioned ideal of the happy marriage survived. The traditional notion was that a man should fully accept his responsibilities as spouse and father when he entered into marriage and that gadding ways, infidelity and divorce should be condemned. In the 1990s in much of the Afrikaner community the basic idea that a man and woman can only find complete fulfilment in a heterosexual love relationship in an atmosphere of domestic stability and security is still upheld. Some Afrikaner men, however, have joined the ranks of the so-called 'new men', who accept changing gender roles and strive to be non-sexist, non-autocratic, more involved in domestic responsibilities, emotionally more responsive and more willing to criticise their own position and practices. Although the 'new men' probably constitute a relatively small minority in Afrikaner society, traditional notions about marriage and the family have gradually changed in favour of more equality between partners in love and marriage.

The ideal of fatherhood may not have changed too dramatically in Afrikaner culture, but the gap between the ideal and reality has become more evident. Up to the 1960s taboos prevented public discussions of domestic violence and 'deviant' sexual behaviour. An image of the family and home as a safe haven prevailed. Since the 1970s the veil of secrecy over the reality of domestic violence has been lifted in the media and the reality of unhappy marriages and domestic violence has been exposed. The ideal of a family life of stability, security and emotional fulfilment, is overshadowed by the evidence in many letters to popular magazines of unhappiness and unfaithfulness within marriage. An even more negative picture of the family man emerges from dozens of letters by women who are the victims of male violence at home and daughters who are sexually abused by their fathers. The traditional image of the 'good father' who protects his womenfolk within the family from external threats is brought into question as the extent of domestic violence, often perpetrated by seemingly 'normal' men, unfolds. Violence by men within the family is a major social problem in Afrikaner society.

Kobus du Pisani

## Warriors and sportsmen: Afrikaner images of heroism

Authoritarianism and militarism have been consistent features of conservative Afrikaner masculinity. Authoritarian tendencies among Afrikaners are attributed to religious views based on Calvinist Protestantism, which endorse the principles of the sovereignty of God and predestination, and start from the premise that there is only one correct way of thinking and behaving. Many men are guilt-driven to obey higher authority. There is a high level of respect for leaders and authority, the adherence to rules, the self-image of moral superiority and the tendency to place people in separate compartments by classifying them as 'different' or 'other'. In the apartheid era Afrikaner authoritarianism stemmed from identification with a group whose identity was intertwined with the social and economic benefits deriving from political dominance. Because of the strong ethnic identification among Afrikaners individual critical thinking was not welcomed and both personal needs and group values were subjected to the cohesion of the group and its members (Korf 1998).

Conservative Afrikaners in particular have always regarded themselves as a people with a proud military tradition. Military victories (for example, Blood River, Amajuba, Spioenkop, and Magersfontein) were celebrated in Afrikaner nationalist historiography and Christian-National school history textbooks. The heroic warrior (with General Christiaan de Wet as the supreme example) was a prominent metaphor of Afrikaner masculinity. In times of war, for example, the South African War, the First World War and the Second World War, the warrior image was prominent.

From the 1970s, against the background of the deteriorating security situation of the apartheid state vis-à-vis the black liberation struggle, the so-called securocrats in command of the armed forces became a dominant force in South Africa. The idea that communists, with the aid of 'terrorists', the antitheses of 'real' Afrikaner masculinity, were launching a 'total onslaught' on the country, gained ground in government circles as the so-called bush war on the border between South West Africa and Angola dragged on. Militarisation in the 1970s and 80s impacted upon the lives of young male Afrikaners. Compulsory military service for all young, physically fit, white South African men was introduced. This brought the soldier image to the fore. For one to two years the lives of 18-year-olds were largely controlled by corporals and sergeant-majors, many of whom were tough and crude professional soldiers. After their initial military training national servicemen were regularly called up for military service. Afrikaans schools and churches participated in pro-government indoctrination. The puritan sense of duty was invoked to mobilise and motivate young men for military service. They were told that they had to fight for the survival of Western civilisation and Christianity in southern Africa. The military successes of the South African Defence Force (SADF) in the bush war were publicised in such a way that the image of the South African warrior hero was revived (Du Toit Spies 1989; Steenkamp 1989).

A large majority of young Afrikaners were induced by government propaganda and a youthful desire for adventure to participate enthusiast-ically in military service, which assumed the status of an initiation process into manhood. However, dissatisfaction with and resistance to military service grew with time. Conscientious objectors agitated against conscrip-tion, and some young men left the country to escape military service. In novels and plays young Afrikaans writers questioned the underlying ideo-logical motivation for the bush war and portrayed its negative impact on young men (Van Heerden 1983, 1984; Opperman 1986; Behr 1993). Next to the positive view of soldiers as heroes who sacrificed their lives for *volk en vaderland* (people and fatherland), the negative image of men who were psychologically destroyed during the bush war and became misfits in civil life emerged, revealing how expressions of masculinity were distorted in the context of guerrilla warfare.

Sportsmen were often idolised in a similar way to war heroes. In the apartheid era the physical prowess and moral strength of sporting heroes were celebrated and highlighted as examples for the youth of puritan masculinity, conveying the message that through dedication, self-application, discipline and hard work one could succeed in life.

Rugby, with its macho image, was regarded by Afrikaner males as the 'king' of sports. The Springboks (South African rugby players) occupied a special position as national heroes and their matches were given extensive coverage in the Afrikaans media. Rugby became an important vent for male aggression, not only for the players but also for the spectators. Almost like the old *krygshelde* (military heroes) the national rugby team had to defend the honour of the nation. A defeat in a test series amounted almost to a national disaster (Grundlingh, Odendaal and Spies 1995).

When the Afrikaners lost their political power in the 1990s sport, and particularly rugby, became even more important in Afrikaner society. It seemed as if Afrikaner men tried to compensate for their loss of political power by focusing their attention on sport. Much of the effort that previously went into the political struggle was now focused on support for provincial and national sports teams. The 1995 Rugby World Cup victory of the Springboks was a moment of special pride. It was interpreted as proof of the physical superiority of Afrikaner men. The Springboks were trained as 'perfect machines' built up to a 'super race'.[5]

Today Super 12 and rugby test matches are advertised in the media as

Kobus du Pisani

battles in a war between nations. Sporting heroes are still being idolised and rugby heroes seem to overshadow all other Afrikaner heroes. More Afrikaners than before are now selected for the national cricket team (the Proteas), and cricket has become the second most popular spectator sport among Afrikaners. As Afrikaner interest in general news coverage wanes, watching sport on television is becoming one of the primary forms of weekend entertainment.

## Dealing with 'deviance' among Afrikaner men

Potential external threats to hegemonic masculinity, for example, Anglicisation in the early twentieth century and miscegenation in the urban context, were easier for Afrikaner masculinity to counter than 'deviance' from within. In the pre-apartheid period 'deviant' expressions of Afrikaner masculinity were effectively neutralised by incorporating them into mainstream Afrikaner nationalism. The danger of moral decay among poor white Afrikaners fighting for material survival manifested itself in, amongst others, indifference to the church, broken families, domestic violence, alcoholism, sexual promiscuity and crime. This was actively countered by the Afrikaans churches and Christian-National schools. In order not to alienate poor whites from the *volk* the idea of the nobility of poverty was advanced and promoted. In the cities the labour movement posed another threat to Afrikaner hegemonic masculinity. Class divisions could dilute Afrikaner ethnic identity. Consequently, Afrikaans urban working class men were deliberately incorporated in the nationalist movement by re-affirming the value of manual labour as *volksdiens* (service to the nation) and by setting up an alternative Afrikaner nationalist trade union movement (Schumann 1940; Naude 1969; O'Meara 1983).

Liberalism and homosexuality were two primary manifestations of masculine 'deviance' in Afrikaner society during the apartheid years. Strategies to counter them within hegemonic masculinity differed and led to quite different results.

In the first twenty years of the apartheid period conservatism was the trademark of the National Party. Less conservative Afrikaans men were excluded from the Afrikaner establishment. They were marginalised in Afrikaner organisations and often joined the ranks of opposition parties. Liberalism among Afrikaners was then regarded as *volksverraad* (treason). Liberals were branded as lackeys of the communists, the arch-enemies of Afrikaner nationalism. The anti-liberal and anti-communist witch-hunt against dissidents in Afrikaner ranks reached a peak in the early 1960s (Du Pisani 1986).

The 1960s brought triumph for Afrikanerdom with the establishment of the Republic of South Africa in 1961, but these years also heralded a period of growing division among Afrikaners. A section of Afrikanerdom started moving away from old-fashioned conservatism, and a process of gradual liberalisation was set in motion. Polarisation between two factions in Afrikanerdom culminated in an all-out battle for supremacy in all spheres of Afrikaner society between *verkramptes* (arch-conservatives) and *verligtes* (enlightened or open-minded ones) in the late 1960s.

The changes occurring in Afrikaner society were slow to be reflected in hegemonic masculinity. The conservative Afrikaner elite, who had their roots in the era of struggle in the 1930s and 40s, were still at the helm. In the mid-1960s the hegemonic ideal of Afrikaner masculinity which had come into its own with the assumption of power by the National Party in 1948 was intact. The Afrikaner elite in the NP, the Broederbond and the Afrikaans churches still endorsed the conservative, puritan image of the Afrikaner man. Portrayals of the Afrikaner male achiever in the Afrikaans media emphasised puritan qualities such as diligence, self-discipline and strong principles.

B.J. Vorster (Prime Minister of South Africa from 1966 to 1978) reflected many of the typical characteristics of the middle-aged Afrikaner man of the 1960s and 70s. He was a deeply religious family man with conservative values, but he was not as rigidly fundamentalist as the former generation of Afrikaner politicians. He loved hunting and sport and he had a pragmatic attitude towards politics. His successor, P.W. Botha (1978 to 1989), continued the pragmatic and reformist or, as he called it, 'adapt or die' style of policy-making. Pragmatism and reformism ran counter to conservative tendencies and by the early 1980s *verligtheid* had attained hegemonic status in Afrikaner nationalist ranks. The conservative leadership had been replaced in all spheres of Afrikaner society (the National Party, the Afrikaner-Broederbond, cultural organisations, churches, universities, schools, newspapers and business enterprises) by more liberally-minded male leaders whose perceptions of masculinity gained social dominance.

F.W. de Klerk (President of South Africa from 1989 to 1994) is the man recorded in history as the Afrikaner leader who launched the 'new' South Africa. He personifies the transitions that took place in Afrikanerdom during the final phases of apartheid. He started out as a conservative National Party politician, continued in the reformist style of his predecessors, and was swept along by the South African realities in a process over which he eventually had little control.

Liberalism was gradually accepted by Afrikaners. In the mid-1990s Afrikaners began to abandon their traditional home in the NP and transferred their allegiance to the Democratic Party, formerly a bastion of liberalism. This trend cannot be interpreted purely as the liberalisation of Afrikanerdom because the Democratic Party has become more conservative, and based its 1999 election campaign on resisting the black-dominated African National Congress (ANC). Afrikaners are pragmatically adapting themselves to the new situation without attaching themselves to rigid ideological positions.

In contrast to liberalism, attitudes towards homosexuality have not changed much amongst Afrikaners. Homosexuality was considered to be sinful, unnatural and abnormal, and not even talked about in 'decent' circles. Homosexuals would have been faced with social ostracism if they had dared to come out. Thus homosexuality was suppressed as an alternative expression of masculinity through isolation and a conspiracy of silence.

In the apartheid state heterosexuality was imposed by criminalising homosexuality in terms of common law plus sections of the Immorality Amendment Act (1969). Legislation was primarily aimed at regulating homosexual activity between white men to curb the perceived threat of an emerging urban gay subculture. According to Elder (1999) the objective of the strict measures against homosexuality was to show that the NP government was protecting the culture and morality of Afrikanerdom. Homosexuality was thought of as 'a bodily transgression against natural encodings of the body'. Elder's conclusion is that white male homosexuality threatened 'a patriarchal and racial order that shaped interlocking structures that provided many white Afrikaner males access to power in South Africa during apartheid'.

From the late 1960s, when the gay rights movement was gaining momentum in the United States and Europe, homosexuality started featuring as a topic of public discussion in Afrikaner circles (Du Pisani 1999). The church which might have intervened to stifle the development of this discourse, side-stepped the issue and it was left to individual church leaders to pronounce upon the matter.

In the 1970s, following the ideological shift towards *verligtheid* in Afrikanerdom, a theological shift occurred in the Afrikaans churches. The younger generation of church leaders emphasised that the Bible should be interpreted critically as a text from a specific cultural background and should be made relevant to the needs of contemporary society by each generation. Individual Christians should take a larger measure of responsibility for their own decisions. The Afrikaans churches' view of homosexuality softened without changing fundamentally. Homosexuality was still regarded as in conflict with the biblical doctrine, but pleas were made that homosexuals should be accepted as church members in a spirit

169

of Christian love. Church members should be tolerant and assist homosexuals to be 'healed' by the grace of God.

In the 1980s anti-homosexual legislation was seldom applied, gay couples openly lived together, the Gay Association of South Africa was established (1982), and the first National Gay Convention was held (1985). Homosexuality featured more prominently in Afrikaans literature, when novelists and poets such as Koos Prinsloo and Johann de Lange started exploring this topic. Performing artists such as Pieter-Dirk Uys and Nataniël also played a role in changing perceptions of homosexuality. Conversely, the AIDS scare emphasised the dangers of promiscuity and lifestyles contrary to societal mores, resurrected homophobia, and seemed to harden the attitudes of those with an anti-homosexual stance.

The 1990s brought a turning-point for gay rights in South Africa when discrimination on the grounds of sexual orientation was outlawed by the new constitution and homosexuals obtained theoretical equality before the law. In the new psychological climate an increasing number of homosexuals felt free to 'come out'. The first gay protest marches were organised in 1990. Even gay theological students and ministers of religion came out. Hendrik Pretorius (*Om gay te wees: straf of seën?* 1990) and Pieter Cilliers (*'n Kas is vir klere* 1997) published books about their experience as gay Christians. They accused the churches of a cold, dogmatic and hypocritical approach to homosexuality, which did not reflect the mercy of God and alienated homosexual members. To them the 'turn or burn' attitude of the churches was unacceptable. Some Afrikaans churches, at first slow to respond, have started taking a more open-minded view. At its 1995 General Synod the Dutch Reformed Church commissioned a new study on homosexuality to determine how the church should handle practical situations. That this investigation has taken place in consultation with gays represents progress, because the church is at last talking *with* gays, and not only about them.

Today homosexuals are more readily accepted in Afrikaner society, particularly among the higher social classes. If still not acceptable among the majority of Afrikaners, homosexuality has at least become accepted as part of social reality. Nevertheless, prejudice persists and in practice the discrimination against and the marginalisation of the gay community continues in most spheres of society. The majority of Afrikaans homosexuals have not come out because they still fear condemnation by society, rejection by their families, and victimisation in the workplace.

## Afrikaner masculinities in the aftermath of apartheid

With the transition to the 'new' South Africa the 1990s have been an age

Kobus du Pisani

of major change in the country. The Afrikaners have lost their political power and WAMs (White Afrikaans Males) have felt threatened by affirmative action and gender equality campaigns. Truth and Reconciliation Commission (TRC) revelations about atrocities perpetrated by people such as Eugene de Kock have helped to demythologise apartheid in Afrikaner ranks. Moderate Afrikaners have denounced apartheid. The Dutch Reformed Church confessed its guilt with regard to its support for apartheid and asked for forgiveness. That Afrikaner men are trying to free themselves from the legacy of apartheid can be seen in the texts of recently published novels and autobiographies (Malan 1990; Coetzee 1998). The influence of racism on the majority of Afrikaner men has not been eradicated, but there is at least a pragmatic acceptance of the irrevocable demise of apartheid within Afrikaner society, with the exception of a small right-wing fringe.

Today many diverse images and expressions of masculinity coexist in Afrikaner society. Many Afrikaners left the National Party (which became the New National Party) and joined other parties so that Afrikaners have become spread over almost the entire political spectrum. The range of political views in contemporary Afrikanerdom is exemplified by the ultranationalist Eugene Terre Blanche on the right, and the ANC's Carl Niehaus and Dirk du Toit on the left. Some Afrikaner male achievers are still constituted in conventional, essentially conservative terms. Christo Wiese, head of a large business empire and one of the richest men in the country, is described as '*die kaalvoetseun van Upington wat die suksesleer in die sakewêreld tot bo geklim het*' ('the barefoot boy from Upington who climbed to the top of the ladder of success in the business world'). Through hard work, dedication and sacrifice – in other words, puritan qualities – he reached the top.[6] Many yuppie Afrikaners desire to break free from conventionalism and like to project the impression of individualism. The epitome of non-conservative Afrikaner masculinity is Max du Preez, former editor of *Vrye Weekblad* and television presenter, and now editor of *De Kat*. He projects an image that is arrogant, spiteful, shows no respect and loves controversy. He finds it hard to submit to authority and discipline. He is divorced and not a family man. However, despite his unorthodox tendencies something in him reminds one of puritanism. He admits that he comes from a conservative Afrikaner family and that he is a Calvinist in his heart of hearts. Afrikaans men such as Du Preez strive for independence and individualism. To break away from the stereotypes, to do their 'own thing', to be involved in unorthodox activities in a creative and adventurous way – that is the ideal of Du Preez's generation. The desire to break free from existing stereotypes about the Afrikaner has been exemplified by trends in Afrikaans rock music and the emergence of groups such as the *Jong Afrikaner Anargiste* (Young Afrikaans Anarchists).

Afrikaner cultural identity and hegemonic masculinity have come through various phases in the twentieth century: from rural traditionalism at the beginning of the century to urban modernism in the middle of the century, to the postmodern world of technology and globalisation. In the process, perceptions and metaphors of masculinity have been transformed as expressions of masculinity and lifestyles have diversified. Strict puritan morals have been relaxed. Patriarchy has been challenged, but not toppled. It is not easy to determine the exact nature of contemporary Afrikaner hegemonic masculinity and its direction. Trends in Afrikaner culture have followed general Western trends, but globalising influences have not led to the wholesale abandonment of former racial, religious and class distinctions underlying Afrikaner ethnic and masculine identities.

The core of Afrikaner hegemonic masculinity remained relatively intact throughout the apartheid period, despite a process of gradual change in gendered social relations. But relinquishing political power in 1994 signified a major break with the past for Afrikanerdom. The number of Afrikaner men in positions of public power is declining and men are not as dominant in the domestic sphere as before. Afrikaner masculinity no longer prescribes ideals of masculinity to South African society at large, to white men in general, or even to Afrikaans-speaking, white men. It is thus difficult both to conceive of or detect a hegemonic Afrikaner masculinity. Understandably, elements of the former puritan hegemonic masculinity are still present, but with the end of apartheid and the decline of Afrikaner nationalism there is no longer the political or economic support necessary for one version of Afrikaner masculinity to assert its hegemony as before. But Afrikaner nationalism has not disappeared, and given its record of pragmatic adaptation to circumstances it is conceivable that a new hegemonic Afrikaner masculinity may in due course emerge.

NOTES

1. The Afrikaans author W.A. de Klerk called the Afrikaners 'the Puritans in Africa' and various other studies have emphasised the puritan nature of Afrikaner nationalism. The 'Puritan' is regarded by Paul Hoch (1979: 118) as one of two dominant expressions of masculinity in the Western cultural tradition.

2. See *Die Huisgenoot*, 7 May 1965: 42–3.
3. See, for example, Julie Espach, 'Goud en silwer het ek lief', *Die Huis-genoot*, 9 October 1959: 24; and Kas van den Bergh, 'Dood begin by 40', *Die Huisgenoot*, 8 January 1965: 50.
4. *Die Huisgenoot*, 15 January 1965: 6. See also *Die Kerkbode*, 7 December 1966: 817; 11 November 1970: 684–5; Treurnicht 1975: 81.
5. *Die Huisgenoot*, 25 May 1995: 12–3. See also *Die Huisgenoot*, 6 July 1995: special World Cup supplement.
6. *Die Huisgenoot*, 16 February 1995: 20, 21, 23.

BIBLIOGRAPHY

Ackermann, D. 1994. 'Context, challenge and change: perspectives on women in South Africa'. In Institute for Reformational Studies, *Women in Africa*. Potchefstroom: IRS.

Antonissen, R. 1960. 'Die Afrikaanse letterkunde in die twintigste eeu'. In P.J. Nienaber, ed., *Perspektief en profiel: 'n Geskiedenis van die Afrikaanse letterkunde*. Johannesburg: Afrikaanse-Persboekhandel.

Behr, M. 1993. *Die reuk van appels*. Somerset-West: Queillerie.

Bernard, J. 1995. 'The good-provider role: its rise and fall'. In M.S. Kimmel and M.A. Messner, eds., *Men's Lives* (3rd edition). Boston: Allyn and Bacon.

Cloete, E. 1992. 'Afrikaner identity: culture, tradition and gender', *Agenda* 13.

Coetzee, C. 1998. *Op soek na Generaal Mannetjies Mentz*. Cape Town: Queillerie.

Collier, R. 1995. *Masculinity, law and the family*. London: Routledge.

De Klerk, W.A. 1975. *The Puritans in Africa*. Harmondsworth: Penguin.

Du Pisani, J.A. 1986. *John Vorster en die verlig/verkrampstryd. 'n Studie van die politieke verdeeldheid in Afrikanergeledere, 1966–1970*. Bloemfontein: INEG.

———. 1996. 'Die Afrikaanse vrou se posisie in kerk en samelewing: evolusie van die Nederduitse Gereformeerde Kerk se standpunt', *Koers* 61(3).

———. 1998. 'From puritanism to postmodernity – changing perceptions of masculinity in the Afrikaner culture'. Paper, Crossroads in Cultural Studies Conference, Tampere, Finland.

———. 1999. 'The "good old days" when there were no homosexuals and sexual perverts among Afrikaans men'. Paper, South African Historical Society conference, University of the Western Cape, Bellville.

Du Plessis, A. 1997. 'Searching in an "empty closet": a history of homosexuality in South Africa', *Historia*.

Du Preez, J.M. 1983. *Africana Afrikaner: meestersimbole in Suid-Afrikaanse skoolhandboeke*. Alberton: Librarians.

Du Toit Spies, F.J. 1989. *Operasie Savannah: Angola, 1975–1976*. Pretoria: SAW.

Elder, G.S. 1999. 'The South African body politic: space, race, and heterosexuality'. Paper, Japanese Association for African Studies Annual Conference.

Grundlingh, A., A. Odendaal and B. Spies. 1995. *Beyond the Tryline, Rugby and South African Society*. Johannesburg: Ravan Press.

Hoch, P. 1979. *White hero, black beast: racism, sexism and the mask of masculinity*. London: Pluto Press.

Korf, L. 1998. 'Die sosiale identiteit van 'n groep stedelike Afrikaanssprekendes in die postapartheid Suid-Afrika'. Ph.D. thesis, Potchefstroom University.

Landman, C. 1994. *The piety of Afrikaans women*. Pretoria: Unisa.

Malan, R. 1990. *My traitor's heart. Blood and bad dreams: a South African explores the madness in his country, his tribe and himself*. London: Vintage.

Maré, L.S. 1985. *Die verband tussen televisie en die waarde-oriëntasies van volwasse blankes en kleurlinge: resultate van navorsing wat van 1972 tot 1985 onderneem is*. Pretoria: RGN.

Morrell, R. 1998. 'Of Boys and Men: Masculinities and Gender in Southern African Studies', *Journal of Southern African Studies* 24(4).

Naudé, L. 1969. *Dr. A. Hertzog, die Nasionale Party en die mynwerker*. Pretoria: Nasionale Raad van Trustees.

O'Meara, D. 1983. *Volkskapitalisme. Class, capital and ideology in the development of Afrikaner nationalism, 1934–1948*. Cambridge: Cambridge University Press.

Opperman, D. 1986. *Môre is 'n lang dag*. Cape Town: Tafelberg.

Schumann, C.G.W. 1940. *Die ekonomiese posisie van die Afrikaner*. Bloemfontein: Nasionale Pers.

Steenkamp, W. 1989. *South Africa's border war, 1966–1989*. Johannesburg: Ashanti.

Treurnicht, A.P. 1975. *Credo van 'n Afrikaner*. Cape Town: Tafelberg.

Van Heerden, E. 1983. *My Kubaan*. Cape Town: Tafelberg.

———. 1984. *Om te awol*. Cape Town: Tafelberg.

Van Vuuren, D.P. 1983. *Navorsing oor die effek van televisie in Suid-Afrika*.

Kobus du Pisani

*Resultate uit ondersoeke wat gedurende die tydperk 1972–1982 onderneem is*. Pretoria: RGN.

Van Wyk Louw, N.P. 1939. *Lojale verset*. Cape Town: Tafelberg.

———. 1939. *Berigte te velde*. Pretoria: Van Schaik.

———. 1958. *Liberale nasionalisme*. Johannesburg: Nasionale Boek-handel.

# CHAPTER 9

# Men Rule, but Blood Speaks
## Gender, Identity, and Kinship at the Installation of a Female Chief in Matabeleland, Zimbabwe

BJÖRN LINDGREN

## Introduction

In December 1996, Miss Sinqobile Mabhena was installed as the first female Ndebele chief in Zimbabwe, to rule over the Nswazi area in the Umzingwane district, situated in Matabeleland South. She had been appointed chief by President Robert Mugabe a year earlier, but the installation had been postponed because of protests from other chiefs in Matabeleland. When the installation finally took place it caused an outcry among many Ndebele. This was publicly vented in the newspapers *The Chronicle* and *The Sunday News*, based in the city of Bulawayo. The critics argued that to have a woman as chief was both against Ndebele culture and tradition. It was unheard of having a woman to rule men.

While some of the critics blamed the Mabhena family for choosing a woman as chief, others blamed the government for imposing a female chief upon them. Miss Mabhena, the eldest of four sisters, was moreover young. She was 23 years old when she replaced her late father. Apart from the Sotho chief Ketso Mathe (towards the border of South Africa) no one had ever heard of a female chief in Matabeleland. However, most of the critics whose opinions appeared in *The Chronicle* and *The Sunday News* were not from Nswazi themselves. They were chiefs from other chieftaincies and intellectuals from Bulawayo. They were men and they were outsiders. In contrast, many people from Nswazi supported their new chief.

The reasons why the installation of Sinqobile Mabhena created such a

177

debate both in the media and amongst locals are manifold. They could be described in terms of how various identities related to ethnicity and locality were used and ascribed to people for political ends (Lindgren 1998a). However, in this chapter I focus on identity in relation to 'gender' and kinship. In general, Ndebele categorise human beings into men and women as two different sexual types. The distinction is centrally determined by the genitals of a person but also includes appropriate forms of behaviour.

The installation of Sinqobile Mabhena as a female chief challenged the gender order in Matabeleland generally. More specifically, it challenged the gender regime within traditional leadership, in that power relations, 'marriage' customs, and the division of labour were reversed. As a result, the installation threatened a dominant form of male identity by questioning a hegemonic masculinity connected to the system of patrilineality, patrilocality, and *lobola*[1] (bridewealth). While critics essentialised male and female identities in this process by emphasising sex as genitals, supporters reconstructed these identities by emphasising behaviour and capabilities. With the installation, the 'traditional' succession principle 'from father to eldest son', which takes into account both sex and kinship, was divided into two principles stressing either sex or 'blood'.

## The Ndebele: a conglomerate of people with roots in Zululand

The Ndebele in south-west Zimbabwe are categorised by linguists and anthropologists as a Southern Bantu people in contrast to the Shona-speaking peoples in the country, that is the Zezuru, Korekore, Manyika, Ndau, Karanga and Kalanga (for example, Bourdillon 1991: 16ff.; Von Sicard 1975; Murdock 1959). The Ndebele number over one and a half million while the Shona peoples together consist of about eight and a half million, in a total population of ten and a half million (Census 1992a). Like the Ndebele, the Shona practise a patrilineal principle regarding the succession of chiefs, that is, a chief should be a man. However, unlike the Ndebele, the Shona also practice a collateral principle where, ideally, the position as chief should circulate in one generation between different houses before being passed on to the next generation (Bourdillon 1991: 106; cf. Jacobson-Widding forthcoming: Ch. 1).[2]

Most scholars divide the Southern Bantu peoples into four different groups primarily on linguistic grounds: the Nguni, the Sotho-Tswana, the Venda and the Tsonga. The Nguni, in turn, is divided into four sub-groups: the Xhosa, the Swazi, the transvaal Ndebele and the Zulu. The latter includes the three Nguni off-shoots: the Ngono, the Shangana and

Björn Lindgren

the Ndebele (for example, Kuper 1982: 5ff.; Breutz 1975; N.J. van Warmelo 1974; but see Murdock 1959).

The Ndebele with whom I am concerned, were the last of these off-shoots to leave what became Zululand in South Africa. As such, the Ndebele have much in common with the Zulu regarding language and culture, including succession rules of male chiefs and the practice of patrilineality, patrilocality and *lobola* (cf. Carton 1998, 2000; Gluckman 1940, 1950; Vilakazi 1962; Berglund 1976).

The migration from Zululand to today's Zimbabwe is well documented (Cobbing 1976; Rasmussen 1978), although Ndebele and British historians differ in their representations of the Ndebele past (Lindgren forthcoming). In short, Mzilikazi Khumalo left Shaka's Zulu kingdom with an Nguni following in about 1820 and ended up in what is today Matabeleland in Zimbabwe in 1840. These people probably got their name during this migration north by Sotho-Tswana people who called them Matebele (Hughes and Van Velsen 1954), and they should not be confused with the transvaal Ndebele who have a completely different history and who have lived in South Africa since the seventeenth century (Breutz 1975). In 1870, Mzilikazi was succeeded by his son Lobengula, who reigned over the Ndebele until the British took over in 1893.

When Mzilikazi and his Nguni followers had left Shaka, their numbers were reinforced during their way north by, among others, Sothos and Tswanas in South Africa and Botswana, and by Shonas (notably Kalangas and Karangas) in today's Zimbabwe. In effect, the Ndebele today consist of people from many different origins. The most obvious way to tell if an Ndebele is of, for example, Nguni, Sotho, or Shona origin, is by his or her *isibongo* (pl. *izibongo*). This is variously translated as 'totem name', 'clan name', 'praise name', and 'surname'. However, the *isibongo* is not an infallible guide to a person's origin, since people may change their name or use other strategies for conveying their past (Lindgren 1998b).

## Chief Mabhena and the Nswazi chieftaincy in Umzingwane

Sinqobile Mabhena, her family, and the people living within her chieftaincy, Nswazi, are firmly linked to the Ndebele past. Like most chiefs in Matabeleland, Sinqobile Mabhena and her relatives are of Nguni origin.[3] The Mabhenas settled at Umzingwane river together with one of Mzilikazi's regiments, the amatshetshe regiment. This regiment (*ibutho*) was led by the Masukus. However, the area in which the amatshetshe regiment settled became too vast to rule. In 1910, Ndamoya Mabhena was asked to take over the Nswazi part of it as the first Mabhena chief.[4] Although

Umzingwane and Nswazi belonged to the Ndebele 'inner state' rather than the 'tributary state' (Cobbing 1976, 1977), its inhabitants were of various origins. While some were Nguni and some Sotho, many were Shona who had inhabited the land long before the Ndebele arrived.

Today, Umzingwane is a district in Matabeleland South, one of Zimbabwe's eight provinces. The district has a population of 65 000 inhabitants, including the Mabhena chieftaincy, Nswazi, which contains 10 000 people (Census 1992b). The district is administratively divided into 18 wards which, in turn, are divided into a number of villages. These villages consist of up to a hundred homesteads (*imizi,* sing. *umuzi*) spread over large areas with maize fields, bushveld and small mountains inbetween. Nswazi follows the borders of wards six and seven which contain five and four villages respectively. Since her installation, Sinqobile Mabhena is seen by many as *the* head of this area, despite the existence of two elected councillors at a ward level with whom she also works.

Like her male colleagues, Sinqobile Mabhena holds meetings and courts where she informs Nswazi people about political decisions and tries to solve disputes. Apart from a headman and several kraal heads, she has five advisors who help her. The headman often tries to solve disputes

*The Nswazi chieftaincy is situated at the eastern fringe of the Matopos hills, inhabited by some 10 000 people*

himself before the matter reaches the chief. The subjects of these disputes include, for example, divorces, ownership of cattle, and land conflicts. While the headman is authorised to fine people up to Z$500, the chief may fine people up to Z$1 000. Apart from this, the chief is also represented in the district council, otherwise made up of the councillors. In total, ten chiefs are represented in parliament. For their work the chiefs get a small allowance from the state.

According to law, the chief should above all be responsible for 'traditional' matters, while elected politicians should deal with development. However, this has never worked in practice and chiefs and other traditional leaders are also involved in the development of dams, roads and schools. As a consequence, a new act has given traditional leaders more political power than before (Traditional Leaders Act 1998, implemented 1 January 2000). One of the key issues in this act concerns the right to distribute land. Hitherto, it was the councillors who have been responsible for the allocation of land, but due to corruption and other problems chiefs and other traditional leaders have now taken over this task. The position as chief, already an important political post, has thus been vested with more power.

## Challenging the gender order: the *indunakazi* as an anomaly

Robert Connell (1987: 119ff., 1996) has suggested that society-wide gender relations are patterned in terms of a gender order, whereas in the case of social institutions such as traditional leadership, gender regimes exist. The installation of Sinqobile Mabhena as chief did *not* follow the established gender order in Matabeleland, and it did *not* accord with the gender regime surrounding traditional leadership. Indeed, power relations, marriage customs, and the division of labour were reversed.

'Marriage' was at the centre of the debate about Sinqobile Mabhena as chief. The Ndebele practise a heterosexual marriage built on monogamy or polygamy and they follow a patrilineal principle regarding descent, succession and inheritance, where the *isibongo* (the totem or clan name), social positions, and property are inherited through the *male* line. In general, they also follow a patrilocal principle regarding residence, where a new couple move to stay with the husband's father or to the husband's father's area of living. These two principles support each other in that goods inherited from father to son include cattle, which together with money is used for *lobola* in exchange for one or several wives and the children they bear.[5]

As in many other rural areas in Matabeleland, the homestead in Nswazi is related to the traditional leadership structure with the man positioned above the woman. There is a saying in Ndebele that men rule: *Indoda yinhloko yomuzi* (literally: 'the man is the head of the household'). These words are sometimes used by a man when he wants to finish a quarrel with his wife as a reminder that she should respect him. In the same way as a wife should respect her husband, the head of a homestead should respect the *usobhuko* (the kraal head), who in turn should respect the *umlisa* (the headman), who in turn should respect the *induna* (the chief). An *induna*, as the term implies, is the most respected *man* within the traditional leadership structure, and now the *induna* is a woman.[6]

Linguistically, the term *induna* is connected to maleness in itself. The adjective *-duna* means male, while the prefix *in-* turns it to the noun 'chief, officer, captain' (cf. Pelling 1971). When discussing the matter with some Nswazi people, they suggested that the dictionaries should be re-written to take account of the installation of Sinqobile Mabhena. A new word with the feminine suffix *-kazi* should be added: *indunakazi*, meaning female chief.[7]

Now, how should a man behave towards this *indunakazi*? As towards a chief or as towards a woman? Should he greet her as a superior or as an inferior? Should he eat together with her, normally a great honour if the chief is a man, or should he refuse, since men normally do not eat together with women, at least not in public settings. In meetings, should he talk

*Chief Mabhena and her advisors*

Björn Lindgren

after her as her subject, or should he talk before her as a man? And what happens if she marries? Is she superior or inferior to her husband? And who will succeed her? The installation of Sinqobile Mabhena as chief caused a lot of anxieties. It challenged the established gender order in Matabeleland, as well as a gender regime within the traditional leadership structure totally controlled by men, and it brought deeply held values about a dominant form of Ndebele male identity to the fore.

## Threatening male identity: questioning hegemonic masculinity

The choice and subsequent appointment and installation of Sinqobile Mabhena as chief in Nswazi has been publicly discussed since her father, Howard, died in September 1993. Howard Mabhena, the former chief, had four daughters but no son. At his burial, Sinqobile stood for him at his grave as his first born. To stand for one's father (*ukuma ubaba wakhe*) is normally done by the eldest son. That is, the son stands at the head of the deceased with his father's knobkerrie (cane) and possible other regalia to show that he is now the head of the family. Thus, when Sinqobile stood for her father this was a clear indication that the Mabhena family had her in mind as Howard's successor, instead of, as was done in the past, either choosing the late chief's half-brother, another close male relative, or to revive the late chief's lineage by arranging the birth of a son after his death (cf. Hughes and Van Velsen 1954: 92; Gluckman 1950: 182–3; Vilakazi 1962: 4).

Originally, Sinqobile was supposed to have been installed as chief in November 1995, but due to protests from other chiefs the installation was postponed for over a year. Sinqobile was finally installed on 21 December 1996, after several meetings with the Mabhena family, chiefs, and administrators. At this point some thought the public debate had come to an end. However, the discussions were intensified with chiefs and intellectuals protesting louder than ever, especially in the daily press.[8]

Chief Khayisa Ndiweni, the most senior chief in Matabeleland, and chiefs Nyangazonke Ndiweni and Veza Maduna stood by their earlier critique that it is against 'Ndebele culture and tradition' to have a woman as chief by not attending the installation ceremony (*The Chronicle*, 27 December 1996; *The Sunday News*, 22 December 1996).[9] Governor Welshman Mabhena of Matabeleland North argued that the case might be taken to the High Court, adding that: 'As Ndebeles we are not going to allow our culture to be abused by anyone. Whatever has so far taken place is a mockery of our culture, which we will fight to the bitter end' (*The Sunday News*, 19 January 1997).[10] And secretary-general Agrippa Ngwenya of the Vukani Mahlabezulu Cultural Society wanted to nullify the installation since it was carried out despite objections by 'Ndebele traditional leaders' (*The Sunday News*, 26 January 1997).[11]

These and similar statements uphold something akin to Robert Connell's (1987: 183, 1996) 'hegemonic masculinity', defined with reference to 'Western' societies as a stylised ideal masculinity which often is made public in the media and does not necessarily correspond to the majority of men. According to Connell, hegemonic masculinity is based on heterosexuality in connection with the institution of marriage. It is always constructed in contrast to subordinated femininities as well as various subordinated masculinities, such as homosexuality. The most common femininity worldwide Connell terms 'emphasised femininity' – a femininity which adapts to men's power and is organised around compliance rather than resistance. As such, and as I interpret the terms here, hegemonic masculinity and emphasised femininity are what many people in different ways support ideologically, but are not necessarily what they represent themselves.[12]

With minor alterations, these concepts make sense in relation to the chiefs' and intellectuals' reactions to the installation of a woman as chief. I suggest that the dominant form of Ndebele male identity is, on the one hand, built on social interaction (structured by power relations, marriage customs, and the division of labour) and, on the other hand, on ideology (in the form of hegemonic masculinity). This masculinity is based on the idea of a heterosexual 'marriage', but in this case following the principles of patrilineality, patrilocality and *lobola*. As in Connell's work, hegemonic masculinity is constructed in contrast to subordinated femininities, notably 'emphasised femininity', as well as in contrast to subordinated masculinities (related to, for instance, male homosexuality).[13]

When chiefs and intellectuals say that the installation of Sinqobile Mabhena is against Ndebele culture and tradition, that they will fight it to the bitter end, and that they want to nullify it, they are essentialising this particular male identity by invoking the 'gender order' in Matabeleland and the 'gender regime' within traditional leadership (that is, established patterns of power relations, marriage customs, and division of labour), and by reproducing hegemonic masculinity. Likewise, they are essentialising a subordinated form of female identity built on the same gender order and gender regime, on the one hand, and 'emphasised femininity', on the other hand, by trying to exclude women from posts within a specific 'male' profession because of their genitals.

## 'A chief begets a chief . . . . The second wife is just a girlfriend'

Although many chiefs and intellectuals were critical of the installation of Sinqobile Mabhena as chief, many of the people in Nswazi, both men and women, supported Sinqobile. This was indicated as early as June 1994, when the Mabhena family publicly announced their choice of successor. Sinqobile was accepted as the rightful heir of Howard at a meeting where she was paraded in front of headman Absalom Ndlovu, 17 kraal heads, and 256 registered subjects.[14] The reasons Nswazi people gave for their support were many, dealing with culture and tradition, equal rights, and the capabilities of a chief.

*The succession order of the Mabhena chiefs in Nswazi*

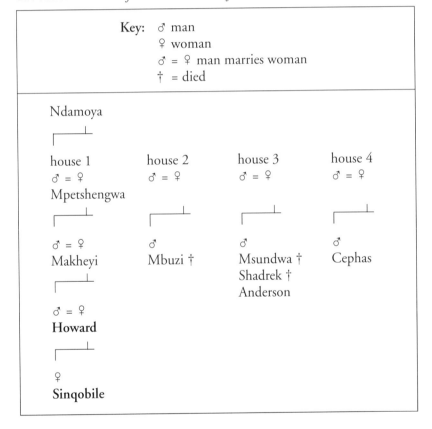

Nswazi people argued that culture had indeed been followed by pointing out that a chief begets a chief (*induna izala induna*) and that Sinqobile Mabhena like her predecessors is the first born within the great, or the first, house (*indlu endala*). 'It's obvious according to Ndebele culture that the heir should come from the first house,' said Mrs Sibanda, a farmer in her fifties. 'The second wife is just a girlfriend,' she added with reference to Sinqobile's grandfather's half-brothers Anderson and Cephas, who the chiefs had proposed as the correct candidates and who come from a second and a third house.[15]

Others legitimised Sinqobile Mabhena as chief, not by arguing that culture had been followed, but by arguing that culture changes, sometimes by comparing her with other female leaders in Zimbabwe. 'There is nothing wrong with her as chief,' Mr Jacob Ndlovu, a young carpenter, said. 'You find women in parliament. I like to see that change and see what women can do. Perhaps they can improve our situation.'[16] Mrs Hadebe, an elderly woman with beer brewing as a speciality likewise held: 'Those who are complaining, they don't know. These days we are living in a changing world. We have headmasters, MPs and governors who are women. There is no problem having a woman chief.'[17]

Some people also referred to equal rights between men and women as a means to legitimise their new chief. 'I think Khayisa Ndiweni tried to discriminate [against] her', said Kem Ndlovu, an elderly kraal head. 'In our country there are women who are capable of being chiefs, even more capable than men.'[18]

And Mrs Vainah Ndlovu, a farmer and former teacher in her forties, said:

> As far as I am concerned, I am supporting Sinqobile. There is always men, men, men. We women are downtrodden. Since she is a woman, maybe some of our things will be taken into consideration. . . . Men says chiefs are for men. I don't understand why they stick to it. Is it my being a man or a woman? Is it not a question of intelligence, the way I am, the way I listen to people? . . . A human being is a human being. It's not a matter of if its a man or a woman.[19]

Instead of essentialising the female identity based on 'emphasised femininity' and disqualifying Sinqobile Mabhena as chief because of her genitals, Nswazi people, as well as some people outside the chieftaincy, reconstructed this identity by claiming that a 'human being is a human being' and that a woman can do what a man can do. As a consequence, they also challenged hegemonic notions of masculinity by placing the emphasis on capability not on genitals. This alternative reading of gender had not only to do with Sinqobile Mabhena as chief, but with people's own identities as men and women.

As understood by the critics' argument that 'men rule' and the supporters counter argument that 'blood speaks', the installation of Sinqobile Mabhena also became a debate about rules of succession. With the proposal of Sinqobile Mabhena as chief, the principle stating that the eldest son takes over after his father was split into two principles. The 'traditional' principle states that a chief must both be a man and descend from the great house. People were now confronted with either following the principle that a chief must be a man, and pick a man from a lesser house (that is, Anderson or Cephas), or the principle that a chief must descend from the great house, and settle for a woman (that is, Sinqobile Mabhena). While the critics opted for the first principle, again stressing sex as genitals as the most important criterion, supporters opted for the second principle, stressing kinship, or blood, as the most important criterion.

## Essentialisation and reconstruction as processes of change

Robert Morrell (1998) has proposed that scholars dealing with South Africa not only should deal with the taken-for-granted 'white' hegemonic masculinity but with other hegemonic masculinities such as 'African' and 'black' masculinities. Aware that colonialism changed the conditions in South Africa, he asks: 'Did indigenous gender regimes continue to exist and, if so, what implications does this have for an understanding of masculinity, and particularly, hegemonic masculinity?' (614). In Matabeleland, the gender regime of traditional leadership has continued to exist, albeit in a transformed way, and it reflects the hegemonic masculinity of the gender order.

In this chapter I have suggested that the installation of Sinqobile Mabhena as a female chief challenged the gender order in Matabeleland as well as the gender regime of traditional leadership, that is, social relations between men and women structured by power relations, marriage customs, and the division of labour. I have also suggested that it threatened a dominant form of male identity built, on the one hand, on social relations and, on the other hand, on cultural values as ideology. And I have suggested that it questioned a hegemonic masculinity built on the idea of heterosexual 'marriage', as Robert Connell (1987: 186) proposes, but in connection to patrilineality, patrilocality, and *lobola*.

In this process of change, opponents and critics of Sinqobile Mabhena essentialised male and female identities by emphasising sex, and held Sinqobile could not be chief because of her genitals. By contrast, Sinqobile's supporters in Nswazi proposed a gender-free reading, saying she should be chief because of her blood connection (kinship) and her capabilities.

There are several reasons why people in Nswazi supported Sinqobile Mabhena as chief. The core of the Mabhena family wished Sinqobile to take over after her late father, and many people in Nswazi respected the chiefly family's choice. The critique from 'outsiders' also irritated many

Nswazis, leading them to defend their 'own' decision. However, the decision to install a female chief and the support this was given would not have been possible without a changed attitude towards women more generally. There is always a dialectic relationship between social relations and cultural values. In this case, a change in values towards women preceded an actual change in social relations among traditional leaders. As Mrs Hadebe (quoted earlier) said, 'We have headmasters, MPs, and governors who are women,' but traditional leadership was, and still to a large degree is, something for men.

The relations between men and women in Zimbabwe are 'unequal', if by this we mean that men in general dominate women in areas such as marriage and labour. Indeed, the Zimbabwean state as such has been described as producing a singular nationality based on patrilineal descent (Cheater 1998). In this context, the single installation of a female chief may not change much. However, the essentialisation and reconstruction of male and female identities was not only about Sinqobile Mabhena. It was also a question of people's own male and female identities. What this means to people in the long term remains to be seen. Perhaps in the future Sinqobile Mabhena will be replaced by a male and her period as chief set in parenthesis. Or, perhaps the installation of her as chief marks a change which will open up traditional leadership to women.

Who is going to succeed Sinqobile Mabhena is still an open question. In October 1997, Sinqobile Mabhena married a teacher in Nswazi, Regiment Sibanda, and in January 1998 she gave birth to their first child – a daughter named Nobulelo. From their perspective, Nobulelo could very well take over after her mother as chief. She would simply be referred to as Chief Mabhena when acting as such, although carrying her father's *isibongo* Sibanda.[20] However, others are more sceptical of such a solution. '[The] chieftainship was given to a family, the Mabhena family, by the Masukus, and not a Sibanda family', local historian Pathisa Nyathi says. 'She [Sinqobile] is the last Mabhena person, and therefore will be the last chief. . . . It won't be easy at all for her off-spring, any of them, to claim it. They have no basis at all, unless we change the laws, the rules, the traditions.'[21]

NOTES

1. I follow the English use of the term *lobola* both as a verb and a noun. In its strict meaning in *isiNdebele* and *isiZulu*, *lobola* is translated as a

verb, to give *lobolo* (bridewealth), while *lobolo* (*ilobolo*) is translated as a noun, the bridewealth itself (Pelling 1971; Doke et al. 1990; cf. Carton 1998: 33 fn).

2. As in the case of Sinqobile Mabhena, there are exceptions to this patrilineal principle regarding succession. Michael Bourdillon (1991: 55; personal communication) reports, for instance, of a Shona female chief in the Mutoko district. Moreover, in Manicaland the daughters of the Manyika paramount chief may function as his headmen. These daughters may have 'lovers' and children, but may not be married with *roora*, that is, bridewealth (Bourdillon 1991: 54–5; Jacobson-Widding forthcoming: Ch. 3).

3. Most chiefs in Matabeleland are of Nguni origin due to Mzilikazi Khumalo's migration from today's Zululand and the British colonial practice of installing chiefs of Nguni descent (cf. Hughes 1956: 56). In contrast to the chiefs, many headmen and kraal heads are not of Nguni descent. In Nswazi chieftaincy, the headman Absalom Ndlovu is of Sotho origin while the many kraal heads are of varying descent, including Nguni, Sotho and Shona origin. However, Chief Ketso Mathe in the Gwanda district is Sotho. In contrast to the Nguni who practice exogamy, the Sotho allow endogamy (see, for example, Kuper 1982). A Mabhena may thus not marry a Mabhena, but a Mathe (or Nyathi to which the Mathe belongs) may marry a Mathe (or Nyathi). In the former case, the chieftaincy may move into another family or clan at marriage since the heir of a Nguni female chief inherits his (or her) father's *isibongo*. In the latter case, the chieftaincy remains within the family or clan since the heir belongs to the same family as both his parents.

4. Personal File 5, Sinqobile Mabhena, Umzingwane district's administrative archive. Julian Cobbing (1976: 70–1, 1974) has briefly described the Masukus' and the *amatshetshe* regiment's settlement in Umzingwane, and refers to *amatshetshe* as one of the older regiments that originated from Zululand. Robert Morrell (1998: 621) has suggested that such regiments, different as they were in comparison to European military organisations, produced a distinct form of 'African' masculinity.

5. The system of patrilineality, patrilocality and *lobola* has changed over time, both regarding the extent of its usage and in content. However, generally the system is much the same as that described by Max Gluckman (1940, 1950) and Vilakazi (1962) regarding the Zulu in the 1940s and 50s, and as described by Hughes, and Hughes and Van Velsen (1954, 1956) regarding the Ndebele in the 1950s. Although

*lobola* (or *lobolo*, if using the noun) often is translated as '*bridewealth*', many Ndebele emphasise that *lobola* is not a gift in exchange for a wife but for the children she bears. Often *lobola* is paid not after a couple has moved together, but after they have got children (cf. Hughes and Van Velsen 1954: 99). The children then belong to the husband's family, also in the case of divorce (although a dispute would arise if a mother claims guardianship of a minor child according to Zimbabwean law).

6. The *induna* (pl. *izinduna*), *umlisa* (pl. *abalisa*), and *usobhuko* (pl. *osobhuko*) are today all regarded as traditional leaders. However, while the position of *induna* and *umlisa* existed before the Ndebele settled in Matabeleland, the position of *usobhuko* was created during colonialism as a means to collect tax (Hughes and Van Velsen 1954: 71; Hughes 1956: 31; Cobbing 1976). The *usobhuko* (from the Ndebele term *ibhuko*, derived from the English word 'book'; cf. Pelling 1971) handled the tax book.

7. Interview in English with Phineas, Jairos and Lavert Dube, Nswazi, 27 February 1997.

8. *The Chronicle* 27 December 1996, 21 January, 6 February, 1 March, 5 March, 12 March 1997; *The Sunday News* 22 December 1996, 19 January, 26 January, 2 February 1997.

9. See *The Chronicle* 16 May, 18 May, 24 May 1996, and *The Sunday News* 30 June 1996 for reports on the chiefs' critique. The English terms 'culture' and 'tradition' are used as synonyms in these articles. In Nswazi, people used the Ndebele term *isiko* (pl. *amasiko*) for both culture and tradition, explaining that it embraces both.

10. Welshman Mabhena is a cousin of Sinqobile's grandfather, Makheyi. The latter lost the chieftaincy after misappropriation of public funds before independence. Makheyi is still alive. He refuses to be chief again, even if a retrial of his crime should allow him to, and strongly supports his granddaughter as chief. (Interview with Makheyi Mabhena in *isiNdebele* 2 February 1997. Philip Moyo and Absalom Ndlovu interpreted.)

11. The Vukani Mahlabezulu Cultural Society is based in Bulawayo and has as its general purpose the promotion of Ndebele culture. The society was formed in 1991 and had about 500 members in 1997. 'Vukani Mahlabezulu' is roughly translated as 'Wake up people', with reference to the Ndebele (originally the Zulu) as the people.

12. Connell is not always clear whether he uses hegemonic masculinity as a description of cultural values or social relations, or both. Personally I prefer to separate the two and mainly refer to hegemonic masculinity

as values, here termed 'ideology', because of its hegemonic form. Connell seems to put a stronger emphasis on hegemonic masculinity as cultural values in *Gender and Power* (1987: 183ff.), where he describes it as an ideal masculinity often made public in the media, and in 'New Directions in Gender Theory' (1996: 163–4), where he refers to it as 'substantially a social construction' and a culturally authoritative pattern. In *Masculinities* (1995: 67ff.), however, Connell uses a much wider definition of hegemonic masculinity, relating the concept to cultural values as well as social relations, among other things.

13. Homosexuality is prohibited by law in Zimbabwe. In January 1999, former president Canaan Banana was sentenced to ten years imprisonment (nine suspended) for homosexual offences. Earlier, in 1995 and 1996, President Robert Mugabe and the government of Zimbabwe banned homosexuals from participating in the Zimbabwe International Book Fair, in 1995 paradoxically on the theme 'Human rights and justice' (Dunton and Palmberg 1996). See also Marc Epprecht (1998) on male homosexuality in Zimbabwe.

14. Personal File 5, Sinqobile Mabhena, Umzingwane district's administrative archive.

15. Interview in *isiNdebele* with Mrs Sibanda, Nswazi, 21 March 1997. Philip Moyo interpreted.

16. Interview in English with Jacob Ndlovu from Nswazi, Umzingwane district, 2 April 1997.

17. Interview in *isiNdebele* with Mrs Hadebe, Nswazi, 14 February 1997. Absalom Ndlovu interpreted.

18. Interview in *isiNdebele* with Kem Ndlovu, Nswazi, 27 February 1997. Absalom Ndlovu interpreted.

19. Interview in English with Vainah Ndlovu, Nswazi, 13 February 1997.

20. Interview in English with Sinqobile Mabhena and Regiment Sibanda, 7 March 2000.

21. Interview in English with Pathisa Nyathi, Bulawayo, 15 March 2000.

**BIBLIOGRAPHY**

Beach, D. 1986 (1994). *War and Politics in Zimbabwe 1840–1900*. Gweru: Mambo Press.

Berglund, A. 1976. *Zulu Thought-Patterns and Symbolism*. London: Hurst and Company.

Bourdillon, M. 1991 (1976). *The Shona Peoples*. Gweru: Mambo Press.

Breutz, P.L. 1975. 'Die Südost-Bantu'. In H. Baumann, ed., *Die Völker Afrikas und Ihre Traditionellen Kulturen*. Vol.1. Wiesbaden: Franz Steiner Verlag.

Butler, J. 1990. *Gender Trouble: Feminism and the Subversion of Identity*. London: Routledge.

Carton, B. 1998. '"The New Generation . . . Jeer at Me, Saying We are all Equal Now": Impotent African Patriarchs, Unruly African Sons in Colonial South Africa'. In M.I. Aguilar, ed., *The Politics of Age and Gerontocracy in Africa*. Trenton, N.J.: Africa World Press.

———. 2000. *Blood from Your Children: African Generational Conflict in South Africa*. Charlottesville/Pietermaritzburg: University Press of Virginia/University of Natal Press.

Census. 1992a. Zimbabwe National Report. Harare. (Published in 1994.)

Census. 1992b. Provincial Profile Matabeleland South. Harare. (Published in 1994.)

Cheater, A.P. 1998. 'Transcending the state? Gender and borderline constructions of citizenship in Zimbabwe'. In T.M. Wilson and H. Donnan, eds., *Border identities: Nation and state as international frontiers*. Cambridge: Cambridge University Press.

Cobbing, J. 1974. 'The Evolution of Ndebele Amabutho', *Journal of African History* 15.

———. 1976. 'The Ndebele under the Khumalos 1820–1896'. Ph.D. thesis. University of Lancaster.

———. 1977. 'The Absent Priesthood: Another look at the Rhodesian Risings of 1896–7', *Journal of African History* 28.

Connell, R. 1987. *Gender and Power: Society, the Person and Sexual Politics*. Palo Alto, California: California University Press.

———. 1995. *Masculinities*. Cambridge: Polity Press.

———. 1996. 'New directions in gender theory, masculinity research, and gender politics', *Ethnos* 61.

Doke, C.M., B.W. Vilakazi, D. McK. Malcolm and J.M.A. Sikakana. 1990. *English-Zulu Zulu-English Dictionary*. Johannesburg: Witwatersrand University Press.

Dunton, C. and M. Palmberg. 1996. *Human Rights and Homosexuality in Southern Africa*. Second edition. Uppsala: The Nordic Africa Institute.

Epprecht, M. 1998. 'The 'Unsaying of Indigenous Homosexualities in Zimbabwe: Mapping a Blindspot in an African Masculinity', *Journal of Southern African Studies* 24(4).

Errington, S. 1990. 'Recasting Sex, Gender and Power: a theoretical overview'. In J. Monning Atkinson and S. Errington, eds., *Power and Difference in Island Southeast Asia*. Stanford: Stanford University Press.

Gluckman, M. 1940 (1987). 'The Kingdom of the Zulu of South Africa'. In M. Fortes and E.E. Evans-Pritchard, *African Political Systems*. London: International Africa Institute/Kegan Paul International.

———. 1950 (1975). 'Kinship and Marriage among the Lozi of Northern Rhodesia and the Zulu of Natal'. In A.R. Radcliffe-Brown and D. Forde, eds., *African Systems of Kinship and Marriage*. Oxford: Oxford University Press.

Hawkesworth, M. 1998. 'Confounding Gender', *Signs: Journal of Women in Culture and Society* 22(3).

Hughes, A.J.B. 1956. *Kin, Caste and Nation among the Rhodesian Ndebele*. Lusaka. (Rhodes-Livingstone Papers 25.)

Hughes, A.J.B. and J. van Velsen. 1954. 'The Ndebele'. In H. Kuper, A.J.B. Hughes and J. van Velsen, eds., *The Shona and Ndebele in Southern Rhodesia*. London: International Africa Institute. (Ethnographic Survey of Africa. Southern Africa 4.)

Jacobson-Widding, A. Forthcoming. *Chapungu: The Bird that Never Drops a Feather. Male and Female Identities in an African Society*. Department of Cultural Anthropology and Ethnology. Uppsala University.

Kuper, A. 1982. *Wives for Cattle*. London: Routledge and Kegan Paul.

Leornado, di M. 1991. 'Introduction: Gender, Culture, and Political Economy: Feminist Anthropology in Historical Perspective'. In M. di Leornado, ed., *Gender at the Crossroads of Knowledge*. Berkeley: University of California Press.

Lindgren, B. 1998a. 'The Politics of Identity and the Rhetoric of Culture: Situational analyses of the installation of a female chief in Zimbabwe'. Paper presented at the European Association of Social Anthropology's (EASA's) conference in Frankfurt.

———. 1998b. 'Ndebele Identity as a Practice of Naming: Negotiation of Social Position in Umzingwane, Zimbabwe'. In T. Andersson, E. Brylla and A. Jacobson-Widding, eds., *Personnamn och social identitet*. Stockholm: Almqvist & Wiksell.

———. Forthcoming. 'Representing the Past in the Present: Memorytexts and Ndebele Identity'. In M. Palmberg, ed., *Encounter Images in the Meetings between Africa and Europe*. Uppsala: The Nordic Africa Institute.

Moore, H. 1994. 'Understanding Sex and Gender'. In T. Ingold, ed., *Companion Encyclopedia of Anthropology: Humanity, Culture, and Social Life*. London: Routledge.

Morrell, R. 1998. 'Of Boys and Men: Masculinity and Gender in Southern African Studies', *Journal of Southern African Studies* 24(4).

Murdock, G.P. 1959. *Africa: Its Peoples and Their Cultural History.* New York: McGraw-Hill.

Nyathi, P. 1996. 'Chieftainship row side-tracks reality', *The Chronicle* 30(6).

Pelling, J.N. 1971. *A Practical Ndebele Dictionary.* Harare: Longman.

Rasmussen, K. 1978. *Migrant Kingdom: Mzilikazi's Ndebele in South Africa.* London: Collings.

Sicard, von H. 1975. 'Das Gebeit Zwischen Sambesi und Limpopo'. In H. Baumann, ed., *Die Völker Africas und Ihre Traditionellen Kulturen.* Vol. I. Wiesbaden: Franz Steiner Verlag.

Vilakazi, A. 1962. *Zulu Transformations: A study of the dynamics of social change.* Pietermaritzburg: University of Natal Press.

Warmelo, van N.J. 1974. 'The Classification of Cultural Groups'. In W.D. Hammond-Toke, ed., *The Bantu-Speaking Peoples of Southern Africa.* London: Routledge and Kegan Paul.

Worthman, C. 1995. 'Hormones, Sex, and Gender', *Annual Review of Anthropology* 24.

Yanagisako, S. and J. Collier. 1987. 'Toward a Unified Analysis of Gender and Kinship'. In J. Collier and S. Yanagisako, eds., *Gender and Kinship: essays towards a unified analysis.* Stanford: Stanford University Press.

———. 1994. 'Gender and Kinship Reconsidered: Toward a Unified Analysis'. In R. Borofsky, ed., *Assessing Cultural Anthropology.* New York: McGraw-Hill.

Zimbabwe Government. 1998. Traditional Leaders Act.

# CHAPTER 10

# 'Men amongst Men'
## Masculinity and Zulu Nationalism in the 1980s

THEMBISA WAETJEN and GERHARD MARÉ

The issue of manhood was a visible component in the political violence that emerged in Natal and the bantustan ('homeland') of KwaZulu between supporters of Inkatha and the African National Congress (ANC) during the early 1980s. The conflict, in which more than fifteen thousand people were killed and countless more displaced, continued through South Africa's political transition and has left deeply entrenched rivalries. After five years of sharing offices in the new, legitimate government, these tensions continue to shape South Africa's political landscape.

This chapter examines how the ethnic politics of the Zulu nationalist Inkatha movement shaped and gave meaning to the political practices of its male constituents. Inkatha's emphatic concern with defining and deploying an expressly *Zulu* masculinity was a keystone of its broader mobilisation tactics. Inkatha's primary spokesperson and founder, Chief Mangosuthu Buthelezi, used his public platform effectively for prescribing how Zulu men behaved: politically, in the workplace, in the homestead, and in the struggle against apartheid. Moreover, Inkatha's representations of Zulu masculinity were reinforced by predominating photo-journalistic images of the conflict which featured men adorned with traditional garments and 'cultural' weapons (for example, sticks and spears) at festivals or engaged in vigilante activities.

Our examination of the discourse of Zulu masculinity in Inkatha's mobilisation strategies is based on content analysis of Buthelezi's public speeches over a period from 1975 to 1992. As an aspect of local campaigning, speeches delivered by Buthelezi were the most important vehicle of political mobilisation. While it is difficult, for qualitative and quantitative reasons, to attribute either specific types of masculinist behaviour or increased membership unproblematically to the discourse employed (see, for example, Southall 1986, on Inkatha membership), visible patterns of leadership-approved and ethnically 'correct' behaviour, appropriate to Zulu men, were regularly in evidence. In addition, during the first democratic elections in 1994, while Inkatha gained only 10,5 per cent of the national vote, 90 per cent of this support came from KwaZulu-Natal. As the conveyor of an (ethnic) nationalist vision, Buthelezi's celebrity, charisma and centrality to the ethnic project can scarcely be overemphasised. As a politician, his importance can be gauged from the number of speeches he delivered and the diverse social terrain he covered (Maré and Hamilton 1987:173–4).

Inkatha, an organisation promoted by a conservative bantustan ('homeland') elite to secure its claims in regional capitalist development and local political authority, was considered expressly counter-revolutionary by urban-based liberation organisations like the ANC and the Congress of South African Trade Unions. Yet there is little doubt that Inkatha's appeal spoke to the situations of a vast number of the region's most marginalised and powerless citizens. Inkatha had its most pronounced successes mobilising rural women through a discourse, in large part, of modernisation and development (Hassim 1993; Waetjen 1999). By contrast, Zulu-speaking men were recruited through the language of cultural history and tradition, through appeals to their duties as breadwinners and obedient industrial workers, and through definitions of an ideal manhood that were juxtaposed against those attributed to men loyal to Inkatha's political rivals.

## A brief history of Inkatha

Inkatha, which styled itself as a National Cultural Liberation Movement, was formed in 1975. Its base was the bantustan of KwaZulu, made up of numerous, scattered and fragmented pieces of territory which were meant to be the political and spatial home to the Zulu 'nation'. Chief Mangosuthu Buthelezi, who had been head of the government of Kwa-Zulu since 1970, wished to subvert apartheid's envisaged destiny for each of the ten 'homelands' by refusing to take independence, but at the same time to use the bantustan structures to organise against apartheid.

Inkatha deliberately started as an ethnic organisation, seeing Zulu-speakers as the constituency to which it was entitled and which it represented in every way. However, Buthelezi also had visions of uniting all black people within Inkatha or in affiliated organisations, a vision that had much to do with his own membership of the ANC in the late 1950s

Thembisa Waetjen and Gerhard Maré

and his presentation of Inkatha as the continuation of the 'true' ANC. The history of Inkatha could be drawn through its relationship with South African black nationalism (the 'ANC' strand) and its relationship to Zulu ethnicity (the Inkatha strand). This relationship went from ANC approval for the formation of the Inkatha movement, to outright war between the two in the 1980s and 90s.

Inkatha's founder and central spokesperson, Chief Mangosuthu Buthelezi, emerged during the 1970s as an internationally known figure, representing a capitalist-friendly and conservative platform that – in addition to its opposition to the ANC – ensured Inkatha's reputation in progressive circles as the purveyor of a dubious politics of liberation. His personal status as educated chief and confrontational politician, his previous membership of the ANC, and his stand against puppet statehood drew extensive rural as well as urban support in the region now known as the province of KwaZulu-Natal. He was clearly not to be cast in the same mould as the other bantustan leaders.

There were unforeseen complexities that emerged as the climate and structure of the liberation struggle was transformed in the late 1970s and early 80s. A crucial problem centred on the fact that Inkatha was, almost from the start, institutionally linked to the governmental structures of the KwaZulu 'homeland'. As the KwaZulu government structures gained new entitlements from Pretoria – for example, control over education and its own police force – Inkatha came to be viewed more and more as wedded to the political machinery of apartheid. The KwaZulu Legislative Assembly (KLA) became a recruiting and disciplining apparatus for Inkatha leadership and a means by which its political strategy could be conceived and enforced. Inkatha possessed and effectively utilised the monetary, propagandistic, and policing resources of the bantustan government. Although Buthelezi insisted that he was corroding apartheid from within, Inkatha's critics saw it both as political collaboration and as evidence of Buthelezi's determination to satisfy his own personal 'appetite for power' by means readily available (Maré and Hamilton 1987; Mzala 1988).

The rift that subsequently developed between Inkatha and the ANC was compounded by another important development within the resistance movement – the growing importance of *youth*, as a social and political group, in pushing forward and, finally, leading the efforts to apply pressure on the apartheid state. The massacre of school children in Soweto in June 1976 solidified the determination of anti-apartheid activists and awakened young people in very large numbers to the cause of the liberation struggle. Buthelezi had warned against the policies that led to the 1976 uprising. While he expressed support for the protests and welcomed

197

students to KwaZulu schools, he took an official stance against the protests, cajoling parents to discipline their children and send them back to school, especially in KwaZulu. This position drove a wedge between Inkatha and the urban township youth that would in time become irreconcilable.

In consolidating its support, Inkatha's politics revolved around, on the one hand, its self-representation and, on the other hand, its claim to be the rightful heir of the original, pre-exile ANC. This position was rapidly eroded during the 1980s with the formation of mass-based organisations within South Africa, such as the United Democratic Front, which associated themselves openly with the ANC. Inkatha centred on being the voice and head of a culturally and historically discrete Zulu nation, founded by legendary king and military genius, Shaka. Zulu tradition (Zuluness) – with Inkatha being its modern political expression – was mapped out through the relentless efforts of Buthelezi (Inkatha's most important and almost cultist leader) in symbolic tandem in the 1980s and early 90s with reigning Zulu king Goodwill Zwelithini KaBekhezulu. Through school curricula, newspapers, magazines, and radio productions, as well as through cultural celebrations and speeches, Inkatha promoted a vision of cultural tradition and Zuluness that rested firmly on patriarchal privilege. The blood and stock of kings, chiefs and warriors, of men, was seen to infuse the Zulu nation with genetic continuity and cultural traits that ordained loyalty to the contemporary strategies of Buthelezi's Inkatha (Maré 1993; Golan 1995; Waetjen 1999).

## The political concern with manhood

In the spheres of the workplace and street, city and 'homeland', the struggles over political ideals, strategy, and agency also involved struggle over the meanings of manhood. The definition of what it meant to be involved in the fight for liberation as a radical, a militant, a freedom fighter, a comrade – and conversely, what it meant to be a traitor or a 'collaborator' – was significantly bound up in what it meant to be a man. The use of violence, the display of weapons, the wearing of uniforms, the defence of ideals, as well as the various notions of what constituted loyalty and betrayal, wisdom and foolhardiness, opportunity and defeat, were contested in gendered grammar and practices. The workplace and the street, as well as the valleys and hills of rural Natal and KwaZulu, constituted forums in which the gender identities (or masculinities) of men could be tested, and either established or subverted.

Cynthia Enloe says that 'nationalism has typically sprung from masculinized memory, masculinized humiliation, and masculinized hope'

Thembisa Waetjen and Gerhard Maré

(1989: 44). Masculine identity is obviously formed on a number of fronts. Collective action is a powerful mechanism for defining the content, and for determining the criteria for the distribution of that identity. At a psychological level, manliness may be 'confirmed' within a group through acts of collective violence against other men, through the destruction of other men's property, or through the rape of women, who frequently are viewed either as 'belonging' to enemy males or as 'vessels' of enemy regeneration. While such activities may or may not represent the officially prescribed strategy of a movement's leaders, they are common expressions of the gendered nature of political violence. When the issue of masculinity is raised in the discourses of political leaders, it necessarily interacts with the contexts of individual and group action. It is therefore necessary to stress that the analysis of political discourse in the speeches of political leaders offers a limited, if important, means of understanding how masculinity informs activity at the grassroots level.

Feminist theory has rightly insisted that critical understandings of political processes require sensitivity to the way gender shapes configurations of power as well as the identities and agencies of subjects (Jayawardena 1986; Enloe 1989; Anthias and Yuval-Davis 1989). Until recently, gender has been theorised in political processes almost exclusively in terms of its impact on women. Yet, men are also impacted by gender. Ideals of masculinity infuse the tasks and obligations ascribed to male-bodied citizens by national leaders. In that sense, ideologies of masculinity do political 'work', both in defining the (normative) political agency of men, and as a complex of incentives for men to view political agency as a means by which their manhood may be confirmed. From the perspective of a given movement recruiting membership, the traits and roles that define manhood are an important and powerful resource (Waetjen and Maré 1999). Nationalist narratives are significant in shaping ideals of citizenship as they pertain differently to women and men. While the impact of these discourses at the grassroots level cannot be viewed simplistically, they reveal the official concerns and strategies of a movement's political leadership.

Inkatha's geographically immediate constituency was largely rural, and – according to its own official census – was comprised mainly of members from its youth and women's brigades. Male migrant workers resided further from Inkatha's realm of influence, and were also 'available' for mobilisation by trade unions and other political organisations which emphasised solidarities based on identities of race (as black people) and class (as workers). Inkatha's express concern with recruiting adult men was evident in speeches and public appeals to workers and audiences in the urban townships, as well as to general gatherings at special festivals and rallies organised by Inkatha and the KwaZulu government. From the outset, soon after its formation in 1975, Buthelezi declared Inkatha a movement in which masculine virtue was a central concern, and where '(t)he mobilization of every black man into a cohesive force through Inkatha for our liberation, is something which no black man should be weak-kneed about except for those who are tied down by a slave mentality' (13 July 1975, at Ezakheni).

The available range of identifiably Zulu symbols, histories, and practices that Inkatha was able to draw upon and claim should not obscure the discursive work that had to be undertaken to mobilise Inkatha's potential male constituencies. It is critical, therefore, to observe that Buthelezi's task was complex in that it had to situate ideas about Zulu masculinity (which had an international currency) within the ideological requirements of the contemporary ethos of anti-apartheid politics and his promotion of capitalist development.

The task of cultivating loyalty among Zulu-speaking, wage-earning, urban-dwelling men posed the greatest challenge. Trade unions, organised from the late 1970s first in the Federation of South African Trade Unions (FOSATU) and then, from 1985, through the Congress of South African Trade Unions (COSATU), spoke a political language of class, race and universal democratic reforms, and supported the ANC position. Inkatha, with its rather narrow ethnic appeal, spoke to men whose affiliations to organised labour were weak, and whose interests as a marginalised, migrant class, were not obviously represented by the trade union politics of COSATU. These were men whose home life was firmly situated in the rural areas of the KwaZulu 'homeland', and who straddled a dual existence between urban and rural spheres, with their different principles of political authority and citizenship.

Buthelezi confronted this structural dualism by addressing these men as both 'workers' and as 'warriors'. As workers, men were entreated to be a regiment of disciplined labourers and responsible breadwinners. As warriors, they were offered the privileges of Zulu patriarchal tradition through invocations of the valour, pride, and glory of their renowned forebears. Worker identity spoke to the contemporary concerns of men in the language of modernity. Warrior identity offered a blood brotherhood and worthy heritage that could ease the anonymity and alienation that constituted migrant working life. The ideal Zulu worker sought only a guarantee of employment and advancement within the framework of industrial capitalism. The Zulu warrior promised loyalty to tradition and the authority of the king and his great men. Paired within the framework of

Thembisa Waetjen and Gerhard Maré

Buthelezi's mobilisation discourse, the identities of worker and warrior were constructed as complementary and essential aspects of Zulu masculinity. As the two faces of ethnic manhood, they discursively reconciled the transitory social location of the male migrant labourer.

## Two faces of Zulu masculinity

The narratives of masculinity invoked in Buthelezi's mobilisation speeches were organised around a central assertion: that masculine virtue was contingent upon loyalty to cultural traditions and, by extension, to Inkatha. Being an ideal man meant deriving one's masculinity from the dictates of ethnic heritage. In Inkatha's discourse, the promise of Zuluness to Zulu-speaking men was the refurbishing of nothing less than their manhood.

The conditions of exploitation, poverty, and humiliation that African men were subjected to daily in the *present* (the era of apartheid) were conceptualised in Buthelezi's speeches as representing a loss of a particular kind of *past*. The golden age that was described was an era during which Zulu men could claim a privileged position in relation to other men, as well as enjoy the patriarchal hierarchies that placed them as heads of their households. Buthelezi declared:

> We are a proud people . . . It is important for us to walk tall – to be men amongst men. We Zulus are a courteous and gentle people. We would live in peace with every man and be men amongst men. [But] when our manhood is subverted, when our dignity is sullied, when our courtesy is despised, mistakes are made which are costly . . . We have shown our bravery in the past. We can show it again. (29 May 1979, at Ulundi)

Famous chiefs, heroes, and kings were invoked as definitive models of Zulu manhood. Shaka, the first king and crafter of the Zulu state in the 1820s, is also the original Zulu man, whose special qualities demonstrated the ideal Zulu masculinity. First and foremost, Shaka was a military leader *par excellence* and his genius in this capacity was claimed as an ethnic characteristic. 'We Zulus come from a warrior nation who know what valour and bravery is all about,' asserted Buthelezi (18 January 1992, at Isandlwana). However, he was careful to refute the accusation that these qualities translated into raw violence. Rather, as 'brothers born of warrior stock', Zulu-speaking men were entreated to 'use power and courage to uphold the supremacy of peace over violence and negotiations over revolution' (26 May 1991, at Johannesburg). Zulu might was constructed as a contained power deriving from ethnic affiliation.

Zulu tradition was shown to fit neatly with modern liberal politics. For example, the age of Shaka was described as a time when patriarchy merged easily with democratic values. 'The chieftainship is a people's institution . . . It has always been an instrument in the hands of the people. It has always been a democratic institution' (18 February 1984, at KwaNtabamhlope). By extension, the qualities attributed to Zuluness were deemed advantageous weapons in the struggle against apartheid:

> Our Zuluness is an instrument for liberation and whether the world likes it or not, our Zuluness has been employed and will continue to be employed in the black struggle of liberation because that is what our long line of illustrious kings and marching columns of martyrs and heroes long since departed demand that we do . . . My message to you is to spurn anything and everything which usurps the power of the Zulu input into the black struggle for liberation. We must play our role and we must play our role standing shoulder to shoulder finding the comradeship and brotherhood which is ours.   (25 September 1989, at Stanger)

As a forum of political struggle, the workplace was an embattled terrain. One of the most controversial claims by the capitalist-friendly Inkatha was that it represented working class interests (although Buthelezi's vision was one where responsible capitalism was given a bad name by exploitative capitalism). 'The vast majority of Inkatha's members are workers', Buthelezi announced in one of several appeals to sugar mill workers, 'They labour in apartheid factories and by the sweat of their brow they earn their pittances . . . I speak with the voice of the workers' (13 May 1984, at Ezikhaweni).

In his efforts to present Zulu workers as disciplined, loyal and seasoned by traditional values, Buthelezi's overarching concern was in promoting worker identity among Zulu men. Zulu valour was linked to hard work and the earning of wages. The mettle of manhood was pitted against the exploitation of capitalism through assertions such as: 'I believe that black workers are man enough to take the sting out of capitalism' (13 August 1987, at Ulundi). The manliness of workers was a theme that was employed to discredit the political strategies of trade unions affiliated with the ANC. Worker actions that threatened to disrupt the workplace were rejected on the grounds that they undermined men's ability to successfully fulfil their roles as men. Contesting the strategy of economic disinvestment, for example, Buthelezi invoked two images of masculinity: 'I have stated very often that we here are the descendants of brave war-

Thembisa Waetjen and Gerhard Maré

riors, and that the blood of warriors flows in our veins and that we would not mind suffering or dying if that were to result in our liberation' (1 May 1986, at Durban).

While Zulu men were pronounced fearless, as breadwinners they were encouraged to exercise responsible caution:

> I say only a father who wants to destroy the humanity of his wife and children wants to make them starve because the External Mission (of the ANC) wants them to starve. Only a man who has abandoned all decency will destroy the factory where he works to earn money to buy the food and clothing, and to provide shelter for his family.   (28 September 1985, at Ulundi)

The problem with wage-work under apartheid was conceptualised by Buthelezi as emasculation and not as primarily economic exploitation. When he spoke of the humiliations of the workplace, he spoke of the experiences of men and the indignities they suffered as 'boys' and 'kaffirs' under white management. Men, Buthelezi repeated on numerous occasions, had become 'drawers of water and hewers of wood', a biblical allusion to forced servitude that may have had additional gendered content in a society where these tasks are expressly feminine.

## The 'other' warriors: manhood and the vilification of the ANC

In Buthelezi's conception, the loss of a golden Zulu past was the eroding of its patriarchal privilege. Such erosion was, in large part, associated with urbanisation; and erosion of what Morrell (1998) has called 'African [rural] masculinity' in favour of 'urban, black masculinity'. Morrell (1998: 622) correctly draws attention to continuities, but does not mention organisations and institutions, such as Inkatha, that tried to *mediate* the 'two worlds' of migrant life. The undermining of Zulu patriarchal order was blamed not only on 150 years of colonisation, apartheid and urbanisation, but also on the ANC. The ANC 'Mission in Exile', which was the particular way in which Buthelezi referred to the ANC from 1960 to 1990 in order to posit Inkatha's claim to being the 'true' ANC, was cast as the invention of an expatriate black elite cynically exploiting wayward youth – that is, the new 'breeds' of urban radical masculinity.

Inkatha's politics, with its prescriptions for masculine behaviour (loyalty to Zuluness and obedient wage work) was wrought against a conception of those of the ANC. Speaking to the labour recruiting arm of the mining industry, The Employment Bureau of Africa (TEBA), Buthelezi recalled a recent visit underground. In relating his experience he commented:

It struck me then, and repeatedly I have thought it, that such work situations with their heavy demands on discipline and endurance are far better training ground than any of the so-called guerrilla camps outside the country in making us men among men . . . It is this concern with our involvement in the struggle . . . that leads me to endorse the actions of anyone who goes into the mining industry.   (reported in *Teba Times*, 1982)

The ongoing reference to ANC politics was important to Inkatha's construction of masculinity in at least two ways. Firstly, Inkatha's ideal of political manhood was set against its political 'other' to clarify the moral superiority of its own construction; and secondly, Inkatha's leadership was compared favourably to ANC leadership in terms of the masculine dignity it bestowed to rank and file male supporters. 'All too often', claimed Buthelezi, 'black political organizations have simply made use of trade unionists as their fetch and carry boys to do their dirty work. This is not Inkatha's approach' (13 May 1984, at Ezikhaweni).

'Black bosses' who 'sit drinking whiskey in safe places in the capitals of the world' was how Buthelezi frequently described the ANC. In contrast:

King Shaka participated in all the battles which makes him one of the greatest heroes of our history . . . [The ANC] think the majority of blacks are convenient tools that must serve their own interests, whether this be on the factory floors of our industries or in the bushes where our guerrillas are shaped into cannon fodder . . . In our struggle for liberation we have enemies we have to deal with, from within and without. With this brand of elitist leadership exercised by remote control as friends, who needs enemies?   (24 September 1981, at Stanger)

The menace of the ANC was represented as most insidiously having an impact on the youth, who were the most outspoken against Inkatha and who formed the greatest threat to Inkatha's recruitment efforts in the townships. Alternative views of militancy and what it meant to be a radical were proposed, each of which implicitly drew out a view of young manhood. The ANC was cast as threatening to turn the youth who had rejected the disciplinary voices of their elders into 'cannon fodder' – a frightening image for parents:

I can think of nothing quite so tragic in all mankind's experience as being affronted by apartheid, responding to it as a human being,

Thembisa Waetjen and Gerhard Maré

responding at first with strength and determination, and then losing hope with a starry-eyed commitment to becoming a freedom fighter, leaving the land of your birth, crossing borders, being recruited for training in external military camps, being trained and, once more, losing hope, losing faith in the armed struggle, then becoming an animal to creep back into South Africa to help blacks kill blacks and in the end, to have made no contribution to the freedom of this country and in the end when our country is free, to be an outcast in the midst of the people from whom you came. (19 October 1985, at Ulundi)

Against this image was Inkatha's conception of radical politics. At a 1980 meeting of the Inkatha Youth Brigade Buthelezi told his young supporters:

A radical is he who poses a threat to the *status quo* because he has his feet on the ground and strikes where strokes can be struck, and grasps that which can be grasped, and subdues that which can be subdued and crushes that which can be crushed. There is nothing namby-pamby about being a realist and committed to that which can be done effectively today. There is a great weight behind the argument that it is cowards who opt out of the hard work of the struggle to seek easy solutions in utopian formulas which will never work. . . . Every bit of tradition and every bit of history in our blood will be called upon as we translate our ideas into practice. (23 November 1980, at Ulundi)

As represented in these narratives, the political options for men were narrow. Young men could become soldiers in the struggle as 'cannon fodder' or by becoming the vanguard of modern progress. Older men could become destroyers of family through disrupting their place of work or they could be responsible breadwinners whose stamina would prepare them for a post-apartheid future. These words were spoken against a background of bloodshed and controversy, fuelled from the mid-1980s by the state's military fortification of Inkatha's vigilante regiments. The appeal to men was crucial if Inkatha was to have representation in South Africa's urban industrial centres, most of which were staunchly supportive of the ANC. The image of the proud Zulu warrior was important as a trope which could appeal to men searching for dignity within the context of their continual subjugation. Yet, that militant image had to be effectively merged with other masculine ideals so as to promote Inkatha's politics as a non-violent, and pro-capitalist organisation. Thus, Buthelezi negotiated a complex and sometimes contradictory image of Zulu manhood that allowed for a flexible and contextually relevant politics.

**BIBLIOGRAPHY**

Anthias, F. and N. Yuval-Davis. 1989. *Woman-Nation-State*. New York: St. Martin's Press.

Enloe, C. 1989. *Bananas, Beaches, and Bases*. Berkeley: University of California Press.

Golan, D. 1995. *Inventing Shaka: Using History in the Construction of Zulu Nationalism*. Boulder: Lynne Reinner Publishers.

Hassim, S. 1993. 'Family, Motherhood, and Zulu Nationalism', *Feminist Review* Spring.

Jayawardena, K. 1986. *Feminism and Nationalism in the Third World*. London: Zed.

Jeffery, A. 1997. *The Natal Story: 16 Years of Conflict*. Johannesburg: South African Institute of Race Relations.

Maré, G. 1993. *Ethnicity and Politics in South Africa*. London: Zed.

Maré, G. and G. Hamilton. 1987. *An Appetite for Power: Buthelezi's Inkatha and South Africa*. Bloomington: Indiana University Press.

Morrell, R. 1998. 'Of Boys and Men: Masculinity and Gender in Southern African Studies', *Journal of Southern African Studies* 24(4).

Mzala. 1988. *Gatsha Buthelezi: Chief with a Double Agenda*. London: Zed.

Southall, R. 1986. 'A Note on Inkatha's Membership', *African Affairs* 85(341).

Waetjen, T. 1999. 'The "Home" in Homeland: Gender, National Space, and Inkatha's Politics of Ethnicity', *Ethnic and Racial Studies* 22(4).

Waetjen, T. and G. Maré. 1999. 'Workers and Warriors: Inkatha's Politics of Masculinity in the 1980s', *Journal of Contemporary African Studies* 17(2).

# PART THREE

Masculinity is not something that is purely instinctive or 'natural'. It is also not something that is determined by social norms and acted out according to a prescribed gender role. Rather, masculinity is a gender identity that is constructed by a number of complex processes. These include historical influences – the process of growing up and interacting with other people in specific settings which are themselves gendered. The notion of performing masculinity conveys the idea of agency. It also is able to capture the reflective ways in which men act. Men are conscious of their masculinity and they deploy it in various ways – sometimes instrumentally in order to achieve a particular objective. Mostly, however, men are not conscious in this introspective way, and they 'perform' masculinity in terms of a set of gendered ideas, norms and values which have been fashioned to constitute their own gendered identity. Men may have multiple ways of behaving but the performance of masculinity is ultimately located within gender power structures which locate and place limits on their particular performance. Performing masculinity, therefore, is about men making and remaking masculinity, about challenging hegemonic masculinity and reconstituting it.

Race and class are critical forces in determining the life experiences of men. They do not bear down in a uniform way on all men, and their effects can be very complex. Frequently the burdens of race and class reinforce one another. In South Africa, being black was historically (and unfortunately largely remains) synonymous with being poor. Nevertheless, life circumstances gave men choices even if these were limited by the apartheid context. These choices ranged from how to relate to other men (how to position one's self in relation to other men), how to relate to other classes (for example, whether one should assume the identity and life trajectory of a lumpen or a worker), and how to relate to women. The choices that men make in relation to these questions implicitly affirm a particular masculine style while also negating or rejecting other ways of performing masculinity.

# Performing Masculinity

# CHAPTER 11

# Disappointed Men
## Masculine Myths and Hybrid Identities in Windermere[1]

SEAN FIELD

Masculine myths expose men to the possibility of 'failure' and feelings of disappointment.[2] This chapter explores the significance of masculine myths in the memories of two men from the Windermere community.[3] These life stories are drawn from 54 life story interviews which I conducted in the course of my Ph.D. research (Field 1996). Windermere was a part-brick, part-iron shanty community on the urban periphery of Cape Town. This culturally mixed community emerged at the turn of the twentieth century with a majority of coloured and a sprinkling of white and African squatters. Nevertheless, from the late 1930s, with the relaxation of pass laws and increasing poverty in the former 'homelands' of Ciskei and Transkei, African squatters rapidly became the majority in Windermere. While Windermere was economically poor, it had vibrant cultural formations such as shebeens, dance venues, bazaars and even a gravel horse racing track. The community faced sporadic forced removals and pass law raids throughout the 1940s and 50s. It was eventually erased between 1958 and 1963. African residents who received permanent residence rights were removed to the townships of Langa and Guguletu, and the remainder were 'endorsed out' to the distant 'homelands'. Most coloured residents received housing in Factreton and Kensington, which by the late 1960s covered the spatial area once occupied by Windermere (Field 1996).

Mr G.B. (classified 'African') and Mr A.O. (classified 'coloured') were childhood friends in Windermere.[4] In the aftermath of forced removals in 1963 they lived in separate, racially defined 'group areas'. But these men had hybrid cultural and linguistic histories. Therefore, within the apartheid context of state-imposed 'racial' identity labels, their struggle to construct a positive sense of masculine identity was hindered. While growing up in Windermere, their choices were restricted to the dominant masculine roles of 'the gangster', 'the sportsman' or 'the working man'. At various moments in their lives, they experienced degrees of disappointment when masculine myths of potency could not be attained through these roles.[5] Furthermore, during the telling of their life stories, they also experienced intense feelings of hurt, sadness and anger. On the one hand, these feelings of disappointment relate to external social events under apartheid, which thwarted them. On the other hand, they relate to an inevitable failure to 'match up' to the masculine myths they had internalised since childhood. These masculine myths were often forged around unfulfilled expectations and desires, but they also had an important self-sustaining function under unstable socio-political and economic circumstances.[6]

## Childhood stories

Mr A.O. was born in 1937 in District Six. In 1940, he moved to 10th Avenue in Windermere. For the 28 years that he lived in Windermere, he and his family lived opposite the notorious iron-shanty formation called the 'Timberyard'. His father was a violent man who worked as a labourer, and his mother was a housewife. His childhood friend, Mr G.B. was born in 1940 in a house in 10th Avenue, Windermere. He lived in Windermere until the age of 23 when his family was forcibly removed to Guguletu. His father owned a butchery in Ndabeni, and in the wake of removals from Ndabeni, this was transferred to Langa. His mother was a housewife. In contrast to Mr A.O.'s poverty-stricken circumstances, Mr G.B. was a member of one of the few middle class African families in the area. He had eight brothers and three sisters:

> And growing up in a coloured community, it never struck me that, I wasn't coloured, especially at Volkskerk School. My father was well known. The principal, the teachers, everybody knew him, so I didn't get any different handling from, from the principal and the teachers. So I found everything the same as anybody, any other child. So that's why I, I grew up not being aware of the fact that I'm, I'm African. And Xhosa is, is still new to me because I can't read or write Xhosa. . . . So growing up, starting from, from Volkskerk made life difficult. You know in-between. You don't fit with the Africans. You don't fit with the coloureds. You live a normal life. But, you know or you don't fit into everything, you know? . . . it's with apartheid and whatnot, you were forced in-between. (Mr G.B.)

Sean Field

Mr G.B. learnt how to speak Afrikaans and English before he learnt how to speak Xhosa. He talked about his sense of cultural ambivalence created through living between and across the classifications 'coloured' and 'African':

> When from, walk from school, then you get one or two silly children, silly boys like all boys. They say, 'This one thinks he's coloured and he's black'. The heh! So that's why I say you don't fit properly. The African children regarded you as, 'He thinks he's coloured', you know? And then the coloureds who say, 'What does you say?'

During his school days he excelled at sport, particularly rugby, and this is where he developed a positive sense of masculinity. He says, 'And it turned out that I was very, very gifted in rugby.' In contrast, Mr A.O. says, 'How can I play sports, life was too fast, there was no time for sports. As I told you about fifteen minutes ago, your life was worth a cigarette.' Mr A.O. and Mr G.B. lived in a part of Windermere where there was considerable cross-cultural interaction between African and coloured residents:

> . . . Africans and coloureds, now nothing was wrong. You know my mother, when my father went to war, we lived in a shanty and we were surrounded by Africans, but my mother could take a ash tray and knock it against the wall, you can hear the kierries going in the other side. 'Mama, are you alright?' Fucking hit those guys. Learning my Xhosa, no, I grew up in very poor, you know I used to bury African shit to get something in my stomach, listen my Xhosa is fluent, I can speak Xhosa, you know? (Mr A.O.)[7]

Mr A.O.'s life story is pockmarked with stories of violence and abuse both inflicted upon him and by him on others:

> AO: We used to sleep in the kitchen. In the front of the dressing table, still had a mattress, . . . you actually sleep on the floor. My sisters used to sleep in the dining room, my parents in the bedroom. Sunday mornings my father worked for Imperial Cold Storage, he would wake up at four o'clock in the morning. You still sleeping, this guy wants to get through to the kitchen dresser, but you sleeping against it. So what does he do, take a jug of cold water, 'Hey come on wake up!' I used to curse my father. Even up to today, I can't, you know I just can't take it.

SF:  A strict man?

AO: He was a hard bastard. When he came from war, he had a shell
shock, you know. Used to carry furniture out of the house, hit
my mother, until one day. I think I was about 16, 14 years of
age, hit my mother down. I said, 'Daddy, I am getting big
now, I think you can't do it anymore, hit my mother like that'.
'Bastard', he says, 'So you call yourself big! You want to stand
up against me'. He got hold of me, one sucker punch, there I
was laying next to my mother on the floor. Aaaag it wasn't easy,
but, thank God, what I got today I struggled and worked for,
you know, I have seen life. Human life was nothing for me.

His narration then jumped to his experiences as a gang member of the
Black Diamond Legion. Throughout the interview, without prompting,
he would return to his experiences under his abusive father but he would
repeatedly break off these stories and jump to other Windermere stories.
In contrast, Mr G.B. was never involved in the local gangs:

You had to grow up being able to defend yourself. As a result, I did
karate. I did wrestling. I did judo. So you had to unless you wanted
to be victimised. . . . It was actually the survival of the fittest. Not
unless you gonna be mommy's boy and stay at home. You had to
develop to defend yourself. It is interesting you know because, so
many survived, like myself. But you either had to join a gang or
you had to defend yourself.

Most young men in Windermere had to confront this choice, which was
also a choice between different forms of masculinity. Connell (1995) has
argued that there is no single or monolithic form of masculinity and
different forms of masculinity 'do not name fixed types but configurations
of practice generated in particular situations in a changing structure of
relationships' (81). The 'gangster' or 'sportsman' were the salient masculine options in Windermere. Mr G.B. constructs the former form as
'aggressive' and the latter as 'defensive'. Both these forms of masculinity
laid claim to 'respectability' and a 'potent' way of surviving tough social
circumstances. However, in this predominantly working class squatter
community, the dominant masculinity for young men was the heroic
'gangster'.[8] Mr A.O. and Mr G.B. faced a series of situations where they
either took decisions or had decisions forced on them. Their 'decisions'
not only impacted on their sense of masculinity, but also affected inter-
twining identities such as culture, 'race' and ethnicity. One such watershed

in their transition from adolescence to adulthood was the Xhosa circumcision ritual.

## Circumcision, masculinity and ethnicity

Mr G.B. described the circumcision ritual as lasting approximately six weeks, and usually happening around the age of 18. For Windermere men, the ritual usually happened in an adjacent bush area called, 'Graafse bos'.[9] Dikeni described the ritual as,

> A foreskin is removed while the initiate watches. And when the blood flows, the initiate asserts his sexual identity by uttering the words of which every man is proud: '*Ndiyindoda!*' ('I am a man'). The moment is unforgettable, because of blood. Blood is something we seldom forget; that is why blood rituals are so important. (*Cape Times*, 29 January 1999)

On return from circumcision the initiates wear a blanket and

> . . . wash thoroughly to get the lime out, the alkaline out of your skin . . . to get that balance, they put a lot of fat or vaseline or something then a person develops a beautiful complexion, you look changed, you know a person, you can see he's changed. There's a difference in what you were before, and what you are now, a person can straight away see. He is a man now, his circumcision, a sort of beautiful, nice complexion. (Mr G.B.)

In this passage, the entry into adult masculinity becomes associated with a particular aesthetic. This is an image understood by others to be the mark of a man. But this ritual is not simply about circumcision:

> . . . you are trained you know for the first week, you don't drink water, it's just to discipline you. For instance let me tell you right away, the difference between circumcised and the un-circumcised, boys or youngsters. When you get youngsters, he will straightaway, pull up his guard and fight. But when [he's] a man now, he will ask you, why are we doing this, you know you are prepared now for, you are doctrined, you are lectured for to be tomorrow's father, that's the difference, now between the boys and the men. The boys always get in fights and are undisciplined and doing wrongs. Where a man will think, you must think something over three, four times. (Mr G.B.)

215

Here masculinity is associated with discipline and reason, whereas those who are uncircumcised fight without reasonable cause. Mager concurs with Mr G.B.'s description of circumcision, 'Circumcised bodies signaled a change in personality, manliness and identity. Circumcision signified masculine identity and male power, constructed over and against boys and women. It was a rite of passage that placed young men on the path to marriage, homestead, headship and fatherhood . . .' (1998: 660). The form of the Xhosa circumcision ritual gradually changed within the urban context. However, there is little doubt that what Mager describes as culturally significant in the rural context of the 1940s to 60s was also pervasively in force in Windermere during the same period. These rituals were reinforced in Windermere by the homeboy networks that were maintained. Boys and men from the same area kept in touch with one another , providing one another with identity, support and protection. As Mager argues, the Xhosa circumcision ritual was the '. . . touchstone of Xhosa masculinity' (1998: 625); or as Mr G.B. puts it, 'I didn't know what it meant to be African until I went to the circumcision ritual.'

In contrast, Mr A.O. explains why he became immersed in African culture:

> . . . let me tell you another thing, why I went to the African culture, they even want to send me to the bush, to have myself circumcised, and my mother stopped me. She said, 'Not a fuck further, you are still my child'. You know my father was a drunkard, hit my mother. . . . I was about ten years old. I don't know what make that man want to have a shit in the night or to have a pee, when he came to the toilet door, he found it close, so it might be somebody inside, he bang the door open, he found a small little boy myself, myself sitting on the toilet. What he do to me, that guy nearly killed me, he kicked myself blue and black, 'What are you doing on the fucken toilet!' I had to run to a African, and he loved me so much, when I came there I was full of blood, I was wet with rain. He opened the door and he said to me, 'Here my child, he put me next to his wife, you go sleep there'. And there's my wife, I hate coloured people, I didn't like them. Why must I run away from my own people, to get comfort from a African.

Mr A.O. asserts that due to his abusive father he 'fled' culturally, linguistically and literally into African culture. Not only did his father abuse him but he also failed him in the educative parental role that Mr G.B. described as a central part of the African circumcision ritual. Mr A.O.'s legitimate anger at his father is also directed at 'coloured people'. It is as if all 'coloured people' and coloured identity have failed him because his father failed him. There is also a sense that his mother let him down on a personal level by blocking him from being circumcised and in gendered, cultural terms, she policed the boundary between 'African' and 'coloured' identity. The decisive action of his mother also conforms to the matrifocal form of patriarchal relationships prevalent within working class households in this community (Field 1990). Mr A.O. turned instead to gang rituals to fulfil his needs for affirmation and identity. Where Mr A.O.'s father failed him in an abusive manner, Mr G.B. had a distant, semi-absent father.

> Often there is an unspoken sense of disappointment and a yearning for contact that rarely seems to come. Boys in different generations have had to learn that their fathers had to work so that the family could survive. So it is that boys from diverse class and ethnic backgrounds have had to learn to expect very little from their fathers.   (Seidler 1997: 162)

## Disappointed men

Mr G.B. and Mr A.O. spent their formative years living across and through apartheid's boundary between 'African' and 'coloured'. For the apartheid state one of the central goals of the category 'coloured' was to use it as a symbolic and literal dumping ground for the hybrid peoples, who did not quite 'fit into' other pure apartheid classifications (Field 1996). The lives of Mr A.O. and Mr G.B. make the painful consequences of drawing such a boundary explicit.

> GB: If you grew up in a coloured community, you end up being lost in-between. If I grew up in an African environment, I would have gone to an African school. I had the ability at school, I would have had a profession. I grew up and I knew I was coloured, most probably I would have been a teacher or a social worker where I [would] work amongst the community, be busy in the community. You can't be busy in the coloured community and entirely busy, not being coloured. Same as I can't read or write, so I wouldn't be able to do door-to-door work in the African community, you end up, it deprives you of a positiveness in your life.
>
> SF: How did you overcome that?
>
> GB: That's a guess, well mostly, you know, because I was good at

sport and I, became known, became like[d] and that's how I did it.

Caught in this 'in-between' position, Mr G.B. grew up questioning and doubting his masculinity and whether he was 'man enough' (Seidler 1997). His sense of marginalisation from both communities evoked uncertainty about his place in a masculine world where certainty and assertiveness are prized qualities. When he told his story, Mr G.B. often constructed himself as loner who had difficulty with socialising with others, but he also repeatedly returned to heroic stories of being a 'gifted scrum-half'. Messner argues that, 'For the boy who seeks and fears attachments with others, the rule-bound structure of organised sports can promise to be a safe place in which to seek non intimate attachments with others within a context that maintains clear boundaries, distance and separation' (1992: 169). Mr G.B. wanted to play rugby for 'the Springboks' and, in his view, if it had not been for apartheid he would have been chosen.[10] In a symbolic sense, he was *dis-appointed* from a position he felt he had earned, and in an emotional sense, he felt *disappointed*. In the one activity where he experienced a potent masculinity, he was thwarted by the racist exclusions of the apartheid system. Apartheid also interfered in other areas of Mr G.B.'s life:

> Well I married very late in life, everything of mine was late in life, I never had a positiveness in life. I married late, and of the marriage, I got two children. . . . I got married late in life, only after my mother passed away, to maintain the house, otherwise I would have been kicked out of the house, if, if your parents die you can't occupy a house in the location. That used to be the law, you quickly had to get married . . .

There is both a hint of disappointment about having 'married very late in life' as well as resentment at again being threatened with forced removal.

Mr A.O.'s sense of self and masculine identity was clearly hurt through his physically abusive father. As a working class youth, Mr A.O. had fewer social options and joined a gang. He described the masculine rituals, codes and activities with a paradoxical mixture of pride and anguish. The desire for, and fear of, attachment also seems to be evident here. Whereas Mr G.B. constructed meaningful masculine relationships within organised sport, Mr A.O. achieved this through the neo-military organisation of gangs. In response to a request for final thoughts, Mr A.O. said:

Are you a man? *Pêl.* [Pal.] I know the only time I feel like a man is when somebody draw a knife on me, and I can take out my own knife out of my pocket, and say okay *pêl*, come on! Then I am a man, because I know, I got two alternatives now, either you or me. But I have to out think you, very quickly, and the moment I get my knife into your body I am a great guy. When I go for the jugular vein first, kill you, not today. Anyway, thank you very much for the interview, I really enjoy it. You know at least it's a outlet for my feelings and emotions, I like that, because it's been sitting in me all these years, as a little boy, growing up in poverty, knowing now what I know, thank you very much.

In literal terms, Mr A.O. reduced his sense of masculinity to the one-on-one knife fight. The symbolic framework of gang culture and traditions gave him a sense of potent masculinity. But this potency was often challenged and/or reinforced in dangerous life-threatening situations. Mr A.O. narrated several events where he claimed to have killed people and was involved in a gang rape. These stories were narrated with a nostalgic framing of how 'beautiful' life in Windermere was. It was as if the violence he inflicted on women and the emotions Mr A.O. felt about these events were avoided through removing women – as real emotional actors – from his life story. While I have no doubt that these events happened, what is significant is how he drew on the mythology of the heroic but civilised gangster to service his sense of masculinity in the present. As Rutherford puts it, 'the solitary male hero is a nostalgic longing for "the organised self". . . . What is an attempt' to hold onto a sense of self is translated into an attempt to master others' (1992: 130).

In the first half of our interview Mr A.O. presented a macho image and was aggressive towards me when my questions seemed naïve to him. At this stage in the interview, anger was openly expressed at his father, poverty and the apartheid system and there was clearly no problem (for him) in expressing these emotions. However, as the interview progressed, his attitude softened as other emotions surfaced. While the oral historian is not a psychotherapist, it is imperative that the interviewer listens empathetically and reflects back to the interviewee that his or her emotions are appropriate to their life experiences. When I switched off the tape-recorder, he asked me to replay parts of the interview. While listening to his own stories, he began crying profusely. Feelings of vulnerability and sadness were difficult for both interviewees to admit to. In Mr A.O.'s case, when he openly revealed his feelings of hurt and sadness he 'perceived' this as a sign of weakness and unmanliness.

> As men grow up to deny their emotional needs, as they learn to live
> out myths that we have absorbed about 'how men are supposed to
> be', we hardly appreciate the injuries we do to ourselves through
> being cut-off from our emotional lives. We learn to *present* our-
> selves as we are 'supposed to be' and we learn to conceal any
> emotions that might bring this ideal into question.   (Seidler 1997:
> 50)

I maintained an appropriate composure during the interview situation
but while driving away I found myself overcome by sadness.[11] Qualitative
interviewers have a responsibility for their own feelings, and more crucially for the feelings their questions evoke in interviewees. Furthermore, I
think it is crucial for researchers to explore ways to interpret the feelings
that people invest in their sense of self and identity as an integral part of
the discursive movements of memory, myth and identity. The interpretations of the researcher are more likely to be 'accurate' if he or she is both
self-reflexive and open to listening for the emotions and emotional signals
within themselves and the interviewee.

Throughout both interviews, these men used nostalgic forms of myth
making. As I have argued elsewhere, this form of myth making tends to be
shaped by defence mechanisms or the need to protect a fragile, ageing self,
struggling within the present (Field 1998).

> Nostalgia makes life narratable, representing what is hard to speak
> of. . . . There is a specifically masculine form of nostalgia, which
> addresses the problems of men's historicity. Problems which are
> products of a transitional loss of cultural authority and a psycho-
> logical feeling of loss. . . . the function of nostalgia is to evade
> anxiety and the effect of predicaments within male subjectivity.
> (Rutherford 1992: 126–7)

The rigid cultural boundaries that these men lived across created uncertainty and doubt over their sense of self and masculinity. Their hybrid
cultural identities was not only an anathema to apartheid ideology, but
also seemed to contradict puritanical masculine myths about being 'man
enough'. The myths of complete 'purity' and 'potency' are intimately
related, and do not coexist easily with the diversity of cultural and linguistic hybridity. In contrast, myths constructed in the form of nostalgia
provided a comfort zone split off from these agonising tensions and the
potentially distressing feelings related to disappointment. The comfort
zone of masculine nostalgia can also involve the 'fulfillment' of omnipo-

tent needs at a level of fantasy. The relationship between myths that have punitive consequences *and* myths which are comforting are best captured in Mr A.O.'s repeated shifts between life in Windermere as being either 'not worth a cigarette' or 'it was beautiful'. In a similar vein, Mr G.B. said:

> I was fortunate that I was the outgoing, outdoor living, type of person. You know, I was a home-loving child, I stayed in the house. When I started training, I saw that it was the survival of the fittest, I started training judo. . . . Staying in Windermere was a pleasure, because number one a person can do what you feel like doing, if you feel like staying at Constantia you will stay there, if you can afford it . . . That's how South Africa is going to develop to be again. A man stays where he want to stay, he has a friend he feels like having. He will associate with people he feels like associating with.

In this final interview response from Mr G.B. there is a contestation between 'the home-loving child' and 'the outdoor person'. In addition, there are contrasting images of Windermere as 'rough and unsafe' versus the Windermere 'where you could do as you pleased'. The past and the future are made more manageable through a masculine nostalgia for a world of free-thinking and freely associating men. A significant emotional consequence of masculine myths rooted in restrictive social circumstances is that these men live with the inevitable disappointment of not fulfilling their own, and others, expectations of themselves. Irrespective of context, the myth of a complete and full masculinity will always be unattainable. However, the disappointment of these men was both due to the 'failure' to meet omnipotent expectations of themselves *and* to effectively resist the disempowering practices inflicted upon them by the apartheid system. While both men had been involved in anti-apartheid political organisations, this did not help them resolve these painful feelings and memories. In addition, their disappointment was constructed by the degrees of appropriate and inappropriate parenting they received during childhood. It was especially evident in Mr A.O.'s life story that abusive or inappropriate parenting is itself a form of loss and disappointment that has to be 'managed' throughout the stages of life.

It is important to note that while the working lives of Mr G.B. and Mr A.O. had difficult beginnings, they ultimately have had successful careers in small business, and today they live in middle class homes with relative economic security. It is precisely the mythical, totally masculine, heroic figure, of 'the gangster' or 'rugby player' that has helped these men to negotiate their uncomfortable emotions and oppressive social contexts. The mythical roles, which they reconstructed in memory, from their experiences, helped these men find a meaningful path in a world where they saw their own lives as either 'not being worth a cigarette' or always 'lacking in positiveness'. However, these mythical roles and nostalgic stories were only partly self-sustaining for these men, and in the process an emotional cost was incurred. The cost of unresolved feelings and unacknowledged needs means that for all the success of their social and working lives, these men remain disappointed.

NOTES

1. Many thanks to Ian Craib, Rob Morrell and Jane van der Riet for their constructive comments on an earlier draft of this chapter.

2. The term 'myth' is not defined as a commonsense falsity. Rather, myths are metaphors, symbols, themes or stories that people internalise as 'truths' for themselves or 'truths' to be lived up to. See Samuel and Thompson (1990).

3. I wrote this chapter about these two men because they are intelligent, engaging storytellers with a shared past. A pivotal moment of intersection in their life stories was around being circumcised or not being circumcised. The decisions they took in response to this and other events provide revealing insights into the construction of masculinity and cultural identity.

4. These are invented initials. The correct names and initials have been withheld so that anonymity and confidentiality are maintained.

5. I have not applied any psychoanalytic model. Rather, I use psychoanalysis as a 'sensitising theory' in interpreting oral narratives. See Craib (1994) and Frosh (1994).

6. For a general discussion on self-sustaining myths, see Laubscher and Klinger (1997); and for specific analysis of myth and memory under violent social conditions, see Field (1998).

7. Mr A.O. worked under 'the bucket system'. He would earn 'a sixpence' for burying a drum of faeces.

8. For discussion of youth gangs in the Western Cape, see Pinnock (1984).

9. 'Graafse bos' was a bush area dominated by Port Jackson trees and owned by Sir De Villiers Graaf.

10. For interpretations of South African rugby and masculine identity, see Grundlingh, Odendaal and Spies (1995) and Van der Riet (1996).
11. There are several reasons why this interview evoked sadness in me. Mr A.O.'s stories of physical abuse and violent incidents reminded me of my father and the physical abuse that he suffered as a child. Just as I was unable as a child to help my father, there was little more that I could do as the researcher in relation to the interviewee. However, after the interview was completed I did spend another hour listening to Mr A.O.

BIBLIOGRAPHY

Connell, R. 1995. *Masculinities*. Cambridge: Polity Press.

Craib, I. 1994. *The Importance of Disappointment*. London: Routledge.

Field, S. 1991. 'Sy is die Baas van die Huis: Women's Position in the Coloured Working Class Family', *Agenda* 9.

————. 1996. 'The Power of Exclusion: Moving Memories from Windermere to the Cape Flats, 1920s–1990s'. Unpublished Ph.D. thesis. Essex: University of Essex.

————. 1998. 'From the "Peaceful Past" to the "Violent Present": Memory, Myth and Identity in Guguletu'. In D. Howarth and A. Norval, eds., *South Africa in Transition*. London: Macmillan Press.

Frosh, S. 1994. *Sexual Difference, Masculinity and Psychoanalysis*. London: Routledge.

Grundlingh, A., A. Odendaal and B. Spies. 1995. *Beyond the Tryline, Rugby and South African Society*. Johannesburg: Ravan Press.

Laubscher, L. and J. Klinger. 1997. 'Story and the Making of Self'. In C. de la Rey, N. Duncan, T. Shefer and A. van Niekerk, eds., *Contemporary Issues in Human Development, A South African Focus*. Johannesburg: Thomson Publishing.

Mager, A. 1998. 'Youth Organisations and the Construction of Masculine Identities in the Ciskei and Transkei, 1945–1960', *Journal of South African Studies* 24(4).

Messner, M. 1992. 'Boyhood, Organised Sports and the Construction of Masculinity'. In M. Kimmel and M. Messner, eds., *Men's Lives*. New York: Macmillan Press.

Pinnock, D. 1984. *The Brotherhoods*. Cape Town: David Philip.

Rutherford, J. 1992. *Men's Silences, Predicaments in Masculinity*. London: Routledge.

Samuel, R. and P. Thompson. 1990. *The Myths We Live By*. London: Routledge.

Seidler, V. 1997. *Man Enough, Embodying Masculinities*. London: Sage.

Van der Riet, J. 1995. 'Triumph of the Rainbow Warriors: Gender, Nationalism and the Rugby World Cup', *Agenda* 27.

# CHAPTER 12

# 'The Beer Drinkers Say I had a Nice Prostitute, but the Church Goers Talk about Things Spiritual'
## Learning to be Men at a Teachers' College in Zimbabwe

ROB PATTMAN

## Introduction

In 1991 I was recruited by a British developmental agency, International Co-operation for Development (ICD), to lecture in Theory of Education at Masvingo Primary Teachers' College in Zimbabwe. The only other whites at teachers' colleges in Zimbabwe were expatriate lecturers like myself. With the ending at Independence (1980) of separate schools for blacks and whites and the introduction of free primary education, whites overwhelmingly withdrew from the government sector and chose to send their children to private schools with fees way beyond the reach of most black Zimbabweans. White teachers also moved from the state to the private sector. Institutions of higher education became almost exclusively black as young whites went to pursue their studies abroad – usually in South Africa – or did not bother with higher education, proceeding instead to work in their family businesses.

There were about one thousand students at Masvingo College taking the three-year course to become qualified primary school teachers. Those who qualified were virtually guaranteed teaching positions, but were usually required to teach in the rural areas for the first two years. This helped to stem the movement of qualified teachers from Zimbabwe to neighbouring Botswana and South Africa where remuneration for teachers was considerably higher. Competition for places at colleges was intense. In my last year (1993) there were about forty thousand applications for three hundred places at Masvingo College. The basic entry requirement was five 'O' levels but successful applicants were usually expected to have more, or some years' experience as 'temporary' unqualified teachers. Because positive discrimination was practised in favour of female applicants, the ratio of male to female students at all teachers' colleges in Zimbabwe was about 50:50, in spite of the higher numbers of men applying for places. This was sometimes alluded to by male students when trying to position themselves as intellectually superior to women. About two-thirds of the staff at Masvingo College were men, and, as in schools, men dominated the high status positions.

The campus was ten kilometres by road from Masvingo, the local town and capital of a predominantly rural province. Four kilometres of dirt track connected it with the main road. It was therefore quite isolated and felt cut off. The campus was a wide grassy expanse with eight hostels (four men's and four women's) situated opposite each other, teaching blocks, a dining hall, staffroom, various staff houses, and a dry, hard stoney football pitch. It was surrounded by bush. On a Friday afternoon and at the weekends, streams of students could be seen pouring along the well-trodden short cuts through the bush which led to Masvingo. They went there to buy academic utensils such as pens and paper, newspapers and magazines, to visit the beer hall (if they were men), to see friends and relatives, or to catch long distance buses to take them to their homes. Usually students went around in single-sex groups, with men sometimes in quite large groups and the women in twos or threes.

Much value was put on education as a vehicle for intellectual, material and cultural development. Given the competition for places at teachers' colleges and the guarantee of employment, a relatively affluent life style and social status at the end of the course, students tended to consider themselves lucky to be at College. Yet there were recognised hardships. All spent time away from their families. While some went 'home' at weekends, for those who lived further afield the cost of going home was equivalent to a whole term's grant and they therefore seldom were able to make this trip. The academic workload was considered heavy – there was at least one assignment per term in each of the ten subjects taken. In addition, the food was poor and students complained particularly about the monotony of the food – usually meat and *sadza* (maize meal), and the lack of vegetables, as well as about their hunger working late into the night, having had their last meal at 17h00. However, these hardships were rationalised by many students and were felt to be necessary sacrifices, associated with investing in themselves.

Rob Pattman

The Theory of Education department was by far the biggest department in the College, comprising ten lecturers with interests in the sociology, psychology and philosophy of education. The senior lecturers and Heads of Department, across the College curriculum (with the exception of Home Economics) were usually men. In Theory of Education, the male lecturers were predominantly the senior ones, and also tended to be louder and more 'charismatic' than the women when they lectured, walking up and down the stage, telling anecdotes, making jokes and 'taking questions'. Theory of Education was understood by lecturers to be a particularly important part of the curriculum, closely associated with the social and intellectual development of students. It was the only subject which was taught to all the students in a particular year at the same time, and, unlike other subjects, it was taught (twice-weekly) in the lecture theatre which could accommodate the large numbers (over three hundred).

If College life was understood as promoting cultural advancement and modern ways of thinking and behaving, that very accomplishment was seen as presenting particular problems and challenges for female students. Female students, and especially women from urban backgrounds, were the ones made out to be most susceptible to 'cultural' amnesia. They were blamed for 'prostituting' themselves and emulating whites by wearing trousers, short skirts or going to the disco. They (not men) were frequently warned in College lectures preparing them for their year's teaching practice in the rural areas to 'observe the values of the community' by not going out at night or wearing 'provocative', 'modern' clothing. By contrast, the status of men students was often linked to their perceived level of 'cultural development'.

Men experienced the College education of women as a threat to male dominance – a threat manifested, and to some extent defused in discursively constructing particular women students as 'prostitutes' and Western. 'Prostitute' was a broad category, used against women for wearing trousers or mini skirts or speaking in class or going out with older, richer, more powerful men. In terms of this discourse at the College, the term 'prostitute' connoted a woman violating her culture as well as her body. Following Connell (1995) who makes clear that masculine identities are constructed in relation to femininities, this chapter focuses on the various ways men learn to be men by eroticising and policing women students. Though Connell argues that ('hegemonic') masculinities are also produced through the repudiation of ('subordinated') gay masculinities, I suggest that homophobia was not significant in the making of men at Masvingo College. However, in the light of President Robert Mugabe's recent attacks on homosexuality, I argue that it may have become more significant.

Student gendered identities were being constructed in a context in which sexuality was frequently inferred and connected (problematically) with women's bodies. Whereas female students' appearances were subject to public scrutiny, masculinity was taken for granted. By investigating the forms that masculinity took in the College, I am addressing them as social constructions rather than essences, and as moralistic and hedonistic identities whose construction are bound up with the eroticisation and problematisation of women. My focus is on discourse as the medium through which masculinities and femininities are produced as particular relationships (Foucault 1979).

## Interviewing students

As I was lecturing on the sociology of education, gender and culture in Zimbabwe to students who were much more knowledgeable than I was, I used them as resources. Usually I split them into single-sex groups and gave them, as topics to discuss, extracts from popular cultural texts and interviews I had conducted with some of them about their experience and understanding of education, culture and gender. This was followed by feedback and discussion in a plenary session. In doing this, I wanted not only to avoid being an 'expatriate expert', but also to encourage women, who were usually very quiet in the lecture theatre, to speak. A difficulty with this approach was that vocal female students were seen by the men present as violating 'culture'.

I felt quite nervous about asking students to be interviewed because I feared they might think that they were, in Western eyes, problematic or unusual, and I stressed that a key aim of the research was to give them a voice (which, given the hierarchical nature of the College, was rarely heard). Initially the volunteers were mainly men, but more women came after their women friends had been interviewed.

I interviewed students in single-sex groups. I interviewed the men in their rooms in the hostels, but because the women's rooms were off-limits to men, I had to find a relatively quiet public place – usually in the hostel common room, if no-one else was present, or on the grass outside – to interview the women. Interviews conducted in public places were often interrupted, since they tended to draw the curiosity of other students. Sometimes students – always men – would say 'hello' and ask me what I was doing. This made me feel rather defensive, as if I was doing something I should not. I felt this especially when I was interviewing female students, because their behaviour was subject to public scrutiny in ways which male's was not.

Rob Pattman

## Beer drinkers and church goers

The male students whom I interviewed identified themselves as beer drinkers or church goers, or as people without a specific group identity who might mix with beer drinkers and church goers but who did not feel committed to either group. I was made aware of the significance of beer drinking and church going in the construction of male identities when I was asked, when declining to drink alcohol, whether I attended church regularly.

Fadzai, a popular student, elaborated upon the differences between the beer drinkers and the church goers. He mixed with both groups though he was more drawn to the beer drinkers:

> Fadzai: It's easy to mix with beer drinkers. They just enjoy. They've got nice stories to tell when they're drunk.
>
> RP: And the church goers are less friendly to you?
>
> Fadzai: They try and convert you. They say you can join with us to Church.
>
> RP: Is there a conflict between church goers and beer drinkers?
>
> Fadzai: It doesn't go into conflict. They don't mix. Those who go to church don't want to mix with people who do bad things.
>
> RP: Such as?
>
> Fadzai: Drinking beer and falling in love. The beer drinkers say I had a nice prostitute, but the church goers talk about things spiritual.

When Fadzai spoke of the beer drinkers a malevolent grin appeared across his face. He found their enjoyment in 'bad things' funny and endearing, and he could not stop laughing when he pointed out that the 'old men' (the older married students) 'are the worst'. He found this particularly funny because of cultural associations between ageing, responsibility and exemplary behaviour. It was always men who presented themselves as giving in to temptation, as being slightly naughty and irresponsible for being hedonistic. The 'bad things' which Fadzai said the church goers refrained from doing – getting drunk and being with prostitutes – were things which real men did.

When I asked some 'church goers' how their attitudes and relationships to women compared with those of beer drinkers, they spoke about 'refraining' from the 'scramble for women'. But their animosity was directed at 'loose women' for tempting men, including themselves, and for violating culture.

Paradoxically, church goers identified with 'traditional' cultural values. These were presented as raising sexual abstention and fidelity to the status of virtue. As writers like Shire (1994) have observed, however, sex in pre-colonial religions in Zimbabwe was regarded as pleasurable. The distortion of 'traditional' culture by modern-day Christians can be explained by the contemporary tendency to highlight the similarity between traditional and Christian values. Christianity was originally a colonial discourse which rendered blacks childlike and uncivilised as compared to the civil-ised colonist. Contemporary Christian discourses about 'traditional African values', however, now counterpose fundamental values about the sanctity of sex as observed by Christian and African traditional religion alike and the debasement and corruption of sex associated with modernisation and westernisation.

Christianity had presented itself as a civilising force, partly, indeed, by constructing the black population as being promiscuous and lacking cultural and moral values about sex. But in this contemporary discursive alignment between Christianity and African traditional religion, the latter was reinvented as primarily concerned with the sanctity and purity of sex. A statement on AIDS by the Zimbabwean Christian Churches in 1992 called for a reassertion of traditional values against modern hedonism and promiscuity. Young people were urged to 'resist the fashion of the day in matters of sexuality', and return to 'traditional African culture'.

According to the moral frame used, the behaviour of men towards 'bad women' or women who 'violated culture' could be judged in dif-ferent stereotypical ways. On the one hand, being a man might mean being moralistic, becoming a spokesperson for 'culture' and criticising women for prostituting themselves. Or, on the other hand, it might mean glorifying in the transgression and enjoying 'prostitutes', at the same time making it clear, through laughter and 'entertaining' stories they told other men, that they were not 'in love' with these women and were only 'using' them to gratify hedonistic desires. While the male beer drinker could laugh about being tempted at the disco, the woman who 'tempted' him was derided and could become the object of insulting graffiti in the lecture theatres. Although these two positions – moralistic and hedon-istic – were represented by the categorisation of men into church goers and beer drinkers, they were by no means mutually exclusive in terms of how they were lived. For, in constructing women as prostitutes, men were simultaneously making them the objects of their desire and contempt. Thus beer drinkers were also critical of the College as a potentially westernising and corrupting influence upon the women students they 'used'.

There was a third category of men which some students mentioned in the interviews – 'punky men'. Punky men had 'punky' hair and earrings, lived in the cities, and were likened to the 'bad' women in the College as denigrators of culture. They were despised and ridiculed for looking effeminate – when the men students spoke about their earrings there was much laughter. None of these men were said to be in the College. But 'punky men' were symbolically significant in the construction of male students' identities. In differentiating themselves from 'punky men', they could be spokespeople for culture and assert themselves as 'real' men. The 'beer drinkers' revelled in being 'naughty', but their naughtiness was distinguished from the ways punky men subverted culture. The former was regarded as 'funny' and hedonistic and as representing a particularly masculine way of being, while the latter was seen as absurd, not masculine and Western.

Though male students learnt to be men in stereotypically different ways in relation to 'bad' women and, less apparently, 'punky men', there appeared to be little conflict between 'different' male students. Focusing on relations between men as constitutive of masculinities, I want to turn to the following discussion with a group of beer drinkers. This is particularly interesting because one man criticised the other black Zimbabwean men, and not 'bad' women. I asked them if they were attracted to women in the disco, whom they called 'loose':

Jacob:  Definitely – most proposals emanate from discos. We're attracted by the way a woman dances. We're encouraged.

Chris:  I'd say men are of loose morals. If you know you're not looking for such type of woman, why do you propose love to her?

Anyway:  I'm totally against what's being said here. When we look at man, man is quickly attracted by sight. Just seeing for a man, I need it now.

Chris:  You can't expect yourself to be attracted just because you've seen someone dancing, just because you've seen a lady's thighs. It means you've got loose morals yourself.

Jacob:  We're looking at culture. According to the culture of the Shona people, the girls are assumed to have low morals.

Chris:  What about men who dress in black punky dress? Why do you blame ladies only?

Jacob:  In that case men are to be blamed. But in our culture men may have ten wives. Is that loose morals?

Chris:    No because he looks after the family. But the man of today, you impregnate one and another one and you dump her. Who is to be blamed – the lady or man?

Jacob:    Both.

Chris:    Both? Are you sure? So you mean to say our old people used to impregnate then drop a woman. Today the blame is on men.

Jacob:    I don't think so, because women are looked at as mirrors of culture. They're supposed to control themselves. They're not to accept every man on the street. So therefore they've got to guard against these temptations themselves. The men are set free.

Anyway:    Man is prone to temptation because of his nature. He's so fast. So we must blame women for not withholding their emotions.

RP:    (to Chris) Do you accept that?

Chris:    No, if he finds his child is playing with fire, he'll let the child continue to play and burn himself. The College is letting the woman do something bad and he'll join in instead of correcting the person.

Like Anyway and Jacob, Chris presented men as subjects with desires. But while Anyway and Jacob blamed women for provoking men's desires, Chris stressed the vulnerability of women (to men's desires), and compared women who did 'bad' things with children playing with fire, as if they were not really the authors of (and accountable for) their own actions. The problem with modern society, according to Chris, was men 'joining in' and not correcting 'bad' women, as if the alternative to exploiting women was looking after them like children, as in his construction of traditional polygamous culture. Chris challenged double sexual standards in a way which reinforced the cultural stereotype of men as subjects of desires and drives, putting the onus on them to control these, and, indirectly, the behaviour of women.

When Chris inquired why men in black punky dress were not also blamed, Jacob argued that they were as culpable as particular women. This was not because Jacob saw such men as hedonistic, for he maintained men were 'free'. Rather, as I discovered in other interviews, punky looking men were criticised for looking effeminate. In mixed gender interviews some women suggested these men with permed hair, earrings and jewellery, and not women wearing trousers and short skirts, should be blamed. Hegemonic masculinity (Connell 1995) was constructed in opposition to

Rob Pattman

women and punky men and, like particular women, punky men were positioned as violating culture.

## Masculinities and homophobia

Recent research in educational institutions in England has pointed to the significance of homophobia in the construction of young male identities (for example, Mac an Ghaill 1994; Nayak and Kehily 1996; Epstein 1997). The importance of homophobic 'performances' in the cultures of young English boys, indicates that their identities are produced through constant policing and the public repudiation of versions of the subordinate and effeminate Other. Men at Masvingo College in Zimbabwe constructed themselves as moralistic and hedonistic, as spokespeople for culture, and as subjects of the (heterosexual) sex drive. However, I want to argue that these identities were achieved and maintained through misogyny rather than homophobia.

While men with perms and earrings may have been ridiculed by students for appearing feminine, this ridicule did not seem like a homophobic response in that no references were ever made to these men's sexuality. They were despised for being like women but it was not assumed they were gay. When I asked whether some people at the College were sexually attracted to people of the same sex, all the students I spoke to looked puzzled and suggested that this was not a Zimbabwean or African phenomenon. Of course that was how many men students described women wearing trousers and men with perms. But same sex sexual attraction was never mentioned. In contrast, many men were obsessively concerned with women wearing trousers, and in some of the interviews they ridiculed men with perms for not looking like 'proper' men, but never for being gay. Raising the topic of same sex sexual attraction seemed to confirm my status as an outsider.

The 'insignificance' of homosexuality in students' accounts contrasts with recent well-publicised government tirades against gays and lesbians. In 1995 President Mugabe denounced 'sodomists' as 'behaving worse than dogs and pigs' (*The Herald*, 12 August 1995), and as a threat to 'culture' and 'tradition'. 'We have our own culture, and we must reeducate ourselves to our traditional values that made us human beings' (*The Citizen*, 12 August 1995). As in discourses which sexualise and problematise black women, 'tradition' and 'culture' were invoked against 'homosexuals'. Phillips points out that the 'President's attack on sodomists' has been delivered in 'the same context' as a critique of 'white economic power', and that its aim has been to create 'a new sense of Africanism' (1997: 485). Ironically, it may be that a consequence of the

233

government's anti-colonial attack on 'homosexuals' has been to make homosexuality less distant and detached for black College students. A feature of the government's moral panic is the assumption that black Zimbabweans may become homosexual and thereby violate their culture and traditions. It may be that the issue of homosexuality has become of increased significance in the construction of College students' identities, and in the shoring up of hegemonic symbols of masculinity (the beer drinker and church goer) constructed around heterosexual desire.

## Assertive masculinities and threatening women

It was in relation to women students who threatened them that men most passionately asserted themselves as spokespeople for culture by stigmatising the women as prostitutes. These women were often from urban areas, wore Western clothes, went to the College disco, and spoke out in the lecture theatre. One woman I interviewed who was particularly confident and articulate in English, was often ridiculed by men sitting at the back of the lecture theatre. Her appearance – she regularly wore trousers, a shiny jacket and large earrings, her hair was straightened and the backs and sides were shaved – accent, intonation and fluency in English were interpreted, especially by men, as signs of arrogance. She told me that some men sitting near her in the lecture theatre muttered 'nose', 'nose' when she spoke. 'Nose' referred to 'nose brigade', a derogatory term for black Zimbabweans who were thought to be emulating Western nasal patterns of speaking. Usually it was applied to women students, and only rarely to men. In her study of student politics and gendered identities in the University of Zimbabwe, Rudo Gaidzanwa (1993) also found that middle class and urban women were constructed as 'nose women' and 'stigmatized as wanting to be like Whites'. They were experienced as undermining the authority of men, especially by those men from rural and working class backgrounds who, themselves, aspired to middle class lifestyles. As in Masvingo Teachers' College, these women were criticised for their 'Western' and 'provocative' clothes, though, Gaidzanwa argues, 'it was not so much what these women wore but their self-confidence, their independence . . . . that had to be dealt with' by men who were identified, in opposition to them, as cultural loyalists and arbiters (28).

'Modern looking' women were often the subjects of Sugar Daddy stories which reflected and quelled men's anxieties about being rejected by women for more powerful men. The most popular Sugar Daddy stories centred on love relationships between men in their third year of study and women in their first year. Being 'educated', 'modern' and relatively affluent (having completed their year's teaching practice for which they were paid) was how third-year men presented themselves to impress and attract first-year women. The first-year men were highly critical of affairs between third-year men and first-year women. In an AIDS drama, improvised and performed by first-year students, which focused on such a relationship, the first-year men in the audience jeered when the third-year man offered to help the first-year woman with her assignment, as if this was for them a familiar bone of contention.

These Sugar Daddy stories seemed like tales of retribution: women were attacked in them for their arrogance and promiscuity, ending up as 'stale' and rejected, having been used by third-year men. The power of men (first-years) was affirmed, women were presented as manipulative – exploiting their bodies – and also as passive victims. Even though the first-year men were critical of the third-years who 'took their women', they did not demonise them like their 'taken' women. First-year women were understood not only as deserting them (first-year men), but also deserting their 'culture'.

## Conclusion: making culture and masculinities

How the men spoke in the interviews about women was never just a description of actual relations but a staking out of identities. They positioned themselves as particular kinds of men in relation to versions of femininity. Men constructed themselves as free and active subjects selecting, testing, being attracted by and 'protecting' the gendered Other. These positions *depended upon* men breaking the rules they set for women – going to discos, dancing, drinking, and making sexual overtures.

The kinds of identities men students adopted and inhabited were racialised. As young, black male intellectuals in the making, they constructed themselves not only in relation to women but also in relation to gendered versions of culture. They kept referring to 'culture' to explain their relations with women. Often they laughed when they invoked 'culture', recognising an anomaly between the veneration they accorded 'culture' and the licence it gave them to be 'naughty'.

Frantz Fanon argues that:

> the passionate search for a national culture which existed before the colonial era finds its legitimate reason in the anxiety shared by native intellectuals to shrink away from that Western culture in which they all risk being swamped. (1990: 168–9)

In accord with Fanon's argument, students did express anxieties about becoming westernised and detached by virtue of their education from their African roots. By 'roots' they usually meant the rural areas from whence the majority of the students came and to which even those from towns had close ties and attachments. In the post-colonial context, marked as it was, in the aftermath of the Rhodesian settler state, by a heritage of continued racism and segregation, black students were powerfully attracted to the notion of an essential or traditional African 'culture', because having such a 'culture' affirmed the identities of black Zimbabweans as independent and dignified human beings.

What Fanon's view does not lead us to expect, however, is the way that 'culture' was mobilised against 'modern' female students. Labelling these women as 'prostitutes', men asserted themselves in various ways, quelling their anxieties about the perceived threat posed by educated women. It was female students who were exhorted not to abandon 'culture'. The reification and romanticisation of a traditional culture was linked, on the one hand, with the idealisation of rural women as repositories of culture and, on the other hand, with the demonisation of women influenced by modernity, with the West (Molara Ogundipe-Leslie 1994; Burke 1996: 191). Even beyond the College, and more generally in the literature on modernity in Zimbabwe, the colonial and post-colonial anxieties black men experienced about their status were linked to the perceived threat posed by 'modern' women (Schmidt 1992; Shire 1994; Phillips 1994; Burke 1996). It was against this threat that men constructed themselves as arbiters and spokespeople for culture.

When the students graduated, they were thanked by government ministers and high-ranking local politicians for their hard work and sacrifices, and were addressed as people of high status who would be looked up to by the community and whose behaviour should accordingly be exemplary. These messages were gendered. It was really the men who were being asked on graduation day to demonstrate a sense of responsibility appropriate to their positions as qualified teachers. Those with the highest standing in the community were likely to be men – almost all head teachers and senior teachers in primary and secondary schools were men, and men were much more likely to teach, what were commonly construed as, the more demanding older years. Furthermore, as we have seen, many men identified as, and revelled in, being 'naughty' and 'irresponsible'. Tales of senior male teachers getting drunk and being 'promiscuous' were legion among students and lecturers at the College, and were told by men, often with a mix of disdain and a great deal of laughter.

Becoming a qualified teacher meant, for many men, being both 're-sponsible' and 'naughty'. But, as mentioned earlier, it was women not men who were problematised in College lectures preparing students for

Rob Pattman

their roles living and working in the rural communities. While women may have been constructed as more responsible than men, they were also seen as likely, because of their College education, to forget 'traditional cultural, rural values' and to become too Western and modern – too 'proud', 'independent' and also morally 'loose'. College educated men were not blamed as their fellow women students were for violating 'culture'. Indeed, these men could be both naughty and upholders and arbiters of 'culture'.

BIBLIOGRAPHY

Burke, T. 1996. *Lifebuoy men, Lux women*. Durham and London: Duke University Press.

Connell, R. 1995. *Masculinities*. Cambridge: Polity Press.

Epstein, D. 1997. 'Boyz own stories: masculinities and sexualities in schools'. In C. Griffin and S. Lees, eds., *Gender and Education*. Special issue of *Masculinities in Education* 9(1).

Fanon, F. 1990. *The Wretched of the Earth*. London: Penguin Books.

Foucault, M. 1979. *The History of Sexuality: Vol. 1 An Introduction*. London: Allen Lane.

Gaidzanwa, R. 1993. 'The Politics of the Body and the Politics of Control: An analysis of class, gender and cultural issues in student politics at the University of Zimbabwe', *Zambezia* 20.

*The Herald*, 12 August 1995. Harare, Zimbabwe.

Mac an Ghaill, M. 1994. *The Making of Men: Masculinities, Sexualities and Schooling*. Buckingham: Oxford University Press.

Nayak, A. and M. Kehily. 1996. 'Playing it straight: masculinities, homophobias and schooling', *Journal of Gender Studies* 5(2).

Ogundipie-Leslie, M. 1994. *Re-creating Ourselves, African Women and Critical Transformations*. New Jersey: Africa World Press.

Phillips, O. 1994. 'Censuring Sexuality in Urban Zimbabwe, Moments of Crisis'. Unpublished paper presented at British Sociological Conference on Sexuality.

———. 1997. 'Zimbabwean Law and the Production of a White Man's Disease'. *Social and Legal Studies* 6(4).

Schmidt, E. 1992. *Peasants, Traders and Wives*. Harare: Baobab Books.

Shire, C. 1994. 'Men don't go to the Moon: Language, space and masculinities in Zimbabwe'. In A. Cornwall and N. Lindisfarne, eds., *Dislocating Masculinity: Comparative Ethnographies*. London: Routledge.

# CHAPTER 13

# Between 'Ouens'
## Everyday Makings of Black Masculinity

KOPANO RATELE

## Introduction

If, in 1995, it could be declared that the African-American male was both the most visible and least understood figure of all sex-race groups in the United States of America (Blake and Darling 1995; Staples 1982), what can one say about the black man in South Africa today? For a start, one could say that he is yet to receive any serious attention by scholars, and that such attention should form part of the recent attempts to understand local masculinities and male behaviours in general (for example, see *Agenda* 37, 1998). In addition, one could say that these attempts should be located systematically in a bigger project to research and theorise identities and subjectivities in a changing South Africa (see Mokgatlhe and Schoeman 1998; Ratele 1998a; Stevens and Lockhat 1997).

This chapter focuses on how black South African masculinities are constructed in everyday interactions between black males. It does this by examining the discursive experiences of a number of black men. The approach adopted should be read as an attempt to reject efforts that want to fit the experiences of black males into foreign or pre-existing frames. In other words, by making black males heard, the trap of measuring them against white males is avoided.

The men who are the subjects of this chapter are all black professionals. They are young (between 24 and 30) and have a tertiary education. While all of them grew up in African urban townships, some have moved to previously white suburbs. Their outlook reflects the material ambitions of a new middle class, but they still have strong connections with an apartheid past. Not only were their formative life experiences framed by apartheid, but they remain immersed in a symbolic and cultural world that was, until recently, distinct from the white world of business and other professions. This cultural and class mixture can be clearly heard in the language they choose to speak amongst themselves.

The term 'ouens' is derived from the noun/adjective 'ou', meaning 'chap', 'guy', 'fellow'. It is a common manner of address or reference to a man or boy. As an adjective it is used affectionately in the sense of 'dear' (Branford 1975; Brown 1993). Ouens could also be translated in African-American slang to 'home-boys', or 'my men'. It is part of a language variation spoken in South African townships known as *tsotsitaal*, which is a blend of languages dominated by Afrikaans. *Tsotsitaal* tends to be spoken mostly by relatively older black males from or with ties to (a tradition of) Sophiatown, District Six and places like these which were (to a greater or lesser degree) centres of black progressive life in the 1960s.

The use of the word 'ouens' is not restricted to the above group but may also be found in another slang known as *S'Camtho*. This slang is spoken mostly by young black African males and tends to be dominated by *isiZulu*, although this depends on the region and degree of urbanisation. For example, around the Western and Eastern Cape the slang is dominated by *isiXhosa*. In the Free State as well as parts of Gauteng and Mpumalanga the dominant language is Sesotho. Outside KwaZulu-Natal, *isiZulu* is dominant in Soweto and other Gauteng townships. Along the same regional lines, black ouens can call each other *ama-gents, majita, ma-authi, bafowethu,* or *magomosha*. All these terms signal that the speaker is 'with it', can speak the language, and is urbanised. Young black people, mostly males, then tend to '*camtha*' (verb) to communicate among themselves. There are many reasons for the choice, some historical, others psychological and about identification, and others subcultural and about being seen as 'in'.

This chapter analyses constructions of gender subjectivities and identities in language. The analysis is based on ten recorded interviews conducted with black men in Johannesburg and Pretoria in 1995 on, among other things, their constructions of achievement. Since 1998 these interviews have become less structured. That is, while achievement is still one of the subjects that may get spoken about, the aim of the more recent interviews has been to talk as naturally as possible about things other than achievement, with particular themes being raised if they did not come up spontaneously. These interviews usually occurred at the homes of the interviewees, although others were held elsewhere.

Following the sorts of reasoning common among discursive psychologists – that the acquisition of language involves the acquisition of psychological processes (see, for example, Antaki 1994; Billig 1996, 1998;

Kopano Ratele

Edwards 1996) – I have been trying to understand how black masculinities are made in everyday conversations between peers. I take language to be productive. Ouens who are engaged in a conversation must not be thought of as merely talking to each other about the subject of females, or blackness, for example – and that's the end of it. They should rather be thought of as transacting back and forth constructions of gendered and racialised identities. The conversation itself is also actively (re)producing those identities, and to a greater or lesser degree the identities of the male speakers as well (see, for example, Burman and Parker 1993; Macnaghten 1993; Potter and Wetherell 1987; Stenner 1993).

One of my major concerns with these interviews has been to explore the intersection of race and gender subjectivities: to study how, for instance, girls and women are located in the way in which black males view, project, and understand themselves; as well as how ouens engage masculinity and take up social positions. The concern, conduct of the interviews, analysis, as well as the interpretations that are made are guided by three assumptions. Firstly, it is assumed that there are particular ways to understand the things said by young black men to other young black men, as opposed, for instance, to parents, or females (even close ones), or researchers. Secondly, it is assumed that unique meanings of black masculinities will be found in things said 'just between ouens'. Unique because they are perhaps less guarded, unrehearsed, so more revealing, and thus more 'real' because the speakers (and interviewer) assume (sometimes wrongly) that they share a reality. Thirdly, it is assumed that the everyday things spoken about between ouens should be seen as playing an important part in the making and remaking of black masculinities.

In the various interviews with the men, two questions were asked directly: 'What does it mean to be a black man in South Africa today?' and 'How does one become a black man?' The first question contains one way in which masculinity can be defined. Contained in this question is an attempt to understand a configuration of the practice of masculinity (Connell 1995): how men think of theirs and others' lives *as men*, in their 'taking up of an enunciative position and social gender' (Bhabha 1995: 58). Consequently, contained in the responses to this question will be what masculinity means to the individual men.

The responses are written in the original language for a number of reasons. One important reason is that the languages used by the speakers are integral to the purposes of the study. As mentioned above, how ouens speak to each other is different and, one could even argue, more frank, from how an ou speaks to others such as family members, women, and so on. This has to be so since it is tied to their identities as males. It is

241

intended, not always deliberately, to include some and exclude others from the social group of black males. In addition, with regard to research processes, transcripts of interviews conducted with second-language speakers, or those with lesser fluency in the language of the audience/readership for which work is intended, often betray a certain clumsiness. What is said can easily be misunderstood. Language in this case may hinder rather than aid our understanding of what is happening.

## Ways of being a man and black

In attempting to understand black men *as males* our analytical tools should at the same time be focused on the behaviours of men that are usually explained away as part and parcel of being a real man (be he white or black). This may be contrasted with another kind of man who Ricky – one of the interviewees – in a slightly disparaging tone, refers to as 'a man of the nineties'. Only by problematising the notion of black masculinity can one avoid unwittingly perpetuating the domination of one group over another – men over women, one version of oppressive masculinity over another.

In everyday language it is quite possible to reproduce repressive male identities and practices even when one's engagement with black masculinity is underlined by the scholarly attitude of sympathetic understanding. For example, Ricky, who elsewhere lamented the lack of control that young black boys have in African townships, also gave an indication of his power when claiming access to 'the right black woman' for himself:

> And then, hayi, ukufeba ke nje, it's a no-no, uyabo. You can't ukuthi uthi uyafeba, uthi ujola nami uyintombazani. But at the same time mina I do accept ukuthi you must understand, if you do catch me, ukuthi ngiyafeba, 'uthi no, it's a man's thing, uyabon'.

> [And then, no, as to promiscuity, it's a no-no, see. You can't go on and be promiscuous, while saying you have a thing with me as a girl. But at the same time, me, I do accept that you must understand, if you do catch me, that I'm promiscuous, 'say no, it's a man's thing, see'.]

Which black men are being referred to and who is being represented in Ricky's words? Whose blackness and whose masculinity is contained here? Is it only Ricky's own, or does it cover other ouens? These questions are the very ones that the approach here tackles head on, the very thing Bulelani is trying to describe, with much difficulty, in the extract below.

242

Kopano Ratele

Bulelani is a 28-year-old professional nurse working at Groote Schuur Hospital in Cape Town. He grew up in Kwamashu (in KwaZulu-Natal). For him, who gets to be a black man boils down to the way one gets accepted among black males which makes a man see himself as a black male because he is welcomed among them:

Awusasiyona lapho idarkie, yabona. Usozonikezwa le'nyi ilokhuza-na manje, itag yabona . . . mhlambe ubizwa ngemulti, or whatever. Zeningi i'ndlela okubizwana ngazo. So, ja, mina ah think, i . . . ilokhuzana, indlela, indlela wena oaccepteka ngayo kuma-authi a-amadarkie, yabona . . . at large . . . e'kwenza ukuthi uyibone ukuthi uyidarkie, because you welcomed kubona. But once k'wenzeka lento be ngi ighaza manje, ngeke usabizwa ngedarkie, yabona. So nawe ngeke u . . . nawe ngeke u . . . uzoba ioutcast, yabona. So it's, it's not ehm, ilokhuzana, icolour of your skin kakhulu ya-bona. Well, nayo, i . . . inayo ilokhuzana, ipart yayo, uyabona. But njengobangisho kuthi ene even iskin colour, ak'sona es' . . . es' . . . esdifaina ilokhuzana yabona, eh, lento yobodarkie completely, but kufanele kube nezinye izinto ozenzayo ezik'wenza ukuthi ube idarkie, yabona. Yona ayilula lento ukuy' iqhaza, yabona.

[Then you're no longer black, see. You will be given another, what do you call it, a tag see . . . perhaps you'll be called by 'multi' or whatever, there many things you could be called by. So, ja, me, ah think, what do you call it, the way you are acceptable to black brothers, see . . . at large . . . that's what makes you see yourself as black, because you welcomed to them. But once what I explained now happens, you can't be called black, see. So you won't also . . . you won't, you'll be an outcast, see. So it's, it's not so much, what do you call it, the colour of your skin. Well, it too, it . . . it has, what do you call it, a role, see. But like I'm saying, even skin colour is not what defines, what do you call it, see, eh, this thing of blackness. There has to be other things that make you black see. This is not an easy thing to explain, see.]

According to Bulelani, there are certain things other than skin colour which define one as a black man, and which, if absent, make one something else. When the borders and practice of black masculinity are thus policed, what one should be out to do, to paraphrase Fanon (1987) rather badly, is set the black 'boy' free (see also Morrell 1998). How does one achieve this goal, and is this what one should aim to do? The first part of the question is the burden of this chapter, and the response is an urgent and resounding yes. Against the sentiments expressed above, one has to surface the varied blacknesses and masculinities for their liberatory possibilities, as well as being a way of militating against the patriarchal power of black males over black females. In other words, there is a need to reveal the available repertoire of gendered and African stylistic options that are, or should be, open to every African male and female in South Africa (see West 1994). One way of doing this is to show how Ricky's view (from the first extract) on male–female sexual relationships exemplifies the double standard and one way of being black which is tied to *one type* of dominant black masculinity.

## The making of black men

When asked, what does it mean to you to be a young black man, TwoBoy, a 20-year-old prospective Master in Clinical Psychology degree student in 1998, answered, 'to be a black person is very difficult'. This is what he said later:

> And, if ubuya edladleni uzofika kungena muntu endlini, abantu bayespani, you have to clean, kethina akunama-cherie ekhaya . . . ucleane, upheke, udl' isinkwa, uthole ukuthi akuna nebutter, akuna vokol, nedrink, mara uzoshaya amanzi ufake ushukele, uphuze . . .

> [And, if you return home there would be no one in the house, the people gone to work, you have to clean, as there were no girls at home . . . you clean, you cook, you eat bread, and you find there's no butter, no nothing, even a drink, but you'll mix water with sugar, and drink.]

Before the above response, TwoBoy had been telling of the time he and his friends went hungry in high school. The boys would write the homework for their female classmates who came from relatively well-to-do families in exchange for the girls' packed lunches. I suppose at other times when there was no homework to be done, or maybe they were too hungry to bother, they would simply steal the lunch boxes or money from the female students. When they were found out and punished by the school principal, they decided to bring a soccer ball to school with which they would fill in their lunch breaks. TwoBoy said he didn't know whether this was deliberate, but the soccer games became an everyday thing following the punishment, and made them forget their hunger.

These words may reasonably be taken as an attempt by TwoBoy

to explain the difficulty of being a black person. This difficulty has to do with having little to eat and doing chores. TwoBoy uses his own childhood experience in Mdantsane (in the Eastern Cape) to exemplify what it means to be black. It could be argued that his words could be spoken by any member of the underclasses anywhere in the world and, further, that there is nothing inherently black about poverty, nor anything legitimate in equating the poor with the black. Although these are sound arguments, they do not help when one wants to understand what a person is doing with words. The arguments rightly call one's attention to things that are about the larger political economy, but do not elucidate the subjective experience of the speaker. That emerges in the kind of after-thought that TwoBoy tacks on to why he had to clean: 'there were no girls', he says.

Masculinity is, of course, not only about male things, and it is not only about men's relationships to their bodies and sexuality. Masculinity also constructs the social reality of institutions and the identities of women. That is one reason why in the middle of a response indicating how one had to suffer as a black person, drinking what is called in some locales 'starch water', and eating unbuttered bread, TwoBoy slips us a particular construction of masculine identity. This he sets up against what it means to be female: girls clean. Our minds then spring back to the response at the beginning of this section where TwoBoy innocently (or blindly, or arrogantly) replaces 'black man' in the question I asked of him with 'black person'. It is as though the black man is equal to the black person. In this regard, Ramphele has referred to the honorary male status accorded to black women in the Black Consciousness movement (see Yates and Gqola 1998).

Yet one has to be cautious, since TwoBoy might actually be saying that the difficulties faced by black males and females are generally the same. However, if that is the case, the idea that girls (naturally) do the cleaning undoes this assumed similarity. In fact, when asked about these habits and his relationship, this was TwoBoy's response:

Lento lena apha esgele ayi-applayi kuthi abodarkie, in most cases, lento yokuthi iequality nani ... because even the very same ma-cheri, because icheri yami erumini, if sihlezi, uthole ukuthi ngizoya edining-hall mhlambe, ngiyoland' ukudla, sidle ... masigqed' uku-dla, without ukuthi engibuze, mhlambe 'kuthi ngisarileksile, uzothat' izitya azihlambe, and then athi, TwoBoy phakama, sukuma, a'ume eceleni, acleane ... and then ... I never said ukuthi makayenze lento mina, and then she doesn't feel bad, ukuthi hayi.

[This equality thing and whatnot doesn't apply to black people, because even the very same girls, because my girlfriend, if we're sitting, and you'll find that, I go to the dining-hall, to fetch food, we'll eat, and when we're finished eating, without asking me, maybe I am relaxing, she'll take the crockery, wash them, and then she'll say, 'TwoBoy, get up, stand aside'. She'll clean. I never say she should do those things. And she never feels bad, that, no . . .]

Obviously, what happens in TwoBoy's relationship with his girlfriend doesn't necessarily happen in all black heterosexual relationships. But that's exactly what one is asked to make of the story: these things and whatnot don't apply to *us blacks*. The upshot is that the principle of gender equality does not hold for black males and females because females like cleaning up and they do not even complain about it. In fact, TwoBoy is arguing that he never says his girlfriend should do the housework. How can he be oppressing her?

## The futures of black boys

When one asks 'What does it mean to be a black man in South Africa today?', the kinds of responses given include themes such as: to be a black man . . . 'means the same thing as it always has'; 'is very difficult' (TwoBoy, Bulelani and Mandla); 'is to be strong because it is not easy to be a *black person*' (Ricky); 'confusing'; 'to feel proud especially now because it is as if you have a chance to show whites something'; and so on. In view of the themes of writing on the problems of black manhood (for example, Gary 1981; Hunter and Davis 1994), and given the history of racism and the politics of South Africa, one tends to expect these sorts of responses. However, one should be careful of what has been called 'the imperative of affirmation' (see Jackson 1990). One cannot accept uncritically that 'things are so', 'life is hard', 'there's no other way'. This is very easy to do if one is influenced by, for example, the fact that the speakers might have suffered political oppression, or that what they are is framed by white racism and so misinterpreted and misunderstood.

The responses to the question 'How does one become a black man?', and how these responses relate to the first question, are more illuminating in this regard. The men's answers here are often slow in coming. It seems as if the question needs a little more thought. The responses are accompanied by pauses, there's a change in tone, perhaps some hesitation, and even questions such as, 'what do you mean?' It is often at this stage that a personal life event is told or a story is related. It is at this point that an occurrence thought of as significant is recalled from the memory of a childhood.

Why is the question 'How does one become a black man?' answered, when it is, in this manner? I wish to argue that it is an indication of the difficulty in grasping what masculinities are by those who do not theorise or research these things. This difficulty is, in any case, reflected in the many definitions of masculinity (see, for example, the multiplicity of definitions within one theoretical position, in Berger, Wallis, and Watson 1995; see also Brod and Kaufman 1994; Kimmel 1987). The hesitant responses to how one raises a son into a black man may signal a continuing crisis, a dispersal of hegemonic masculinity, a grappling with the 'manly ideal', or the old male-sex role identity.

The roundabout way the males interviewed had of responding to this question is particularly interesting when one notes that the 'how' question is in fact part of the 'what' question. Perhaps it is because the development of a masculine identity implies a pre-existing meaning (or version) of masculinity.

To illustrate, when TwoBoy says he cleaned as there were no girls, he is simultaneously confirming a particular version of masculinity. He is staking a claim about what black men and women are and should be, and indicating how male and female children are (to be) brought up. This is also what makes someone like Mavula say, 'I am atypical', because he cleans, cooks, and likes helping his girlfriend, and his mother at home. Therefore, in both the questions posed to the interviewees and in the males' responses to them, can be found attempts at how masculinity is both *understood and routinely constructed* by black males. One finds here not just the way things were or are, but also the reproduction or performance of masculinities. In other words, one is able to interpret what the interviewees are saying as to how black boys are to be raised in a society and culture, how they should come to understand themselves as part of a group of males in that culture, and how they are to measure up to prevailing images of manhood.

Ricky was born in Umlazi (KwaZulu-Natal) 28 years ago. His mother tongue is *isiZulu*. He has lived around Cape Town for ten years after completing a BA Law from the University of Cape Town. He works as a marketing manager in an international company. Ricky related a number of events from his childhood, from picking up a man's heavy corpse with his now-retired labourer father, to random chases by strangers with knives. Some of the stories were less dramatic:

Amabra amadala, hei baba, they rough you up, they send you

anywhere. So, you got no control elokshini. It was even worse ke mina ekhaya, because enext door yasekhaya kwa kuyispoti, itavern. It was one of the hottest taverns zaseMlazi.

[The older brothers, hey baba, they rough you up, they send you anywhere. So, you got no control in the location. It was even worse for me at home, because next door to us was a drinking spot, a tavern. It was one of the hottest taverns around Umlazi.]

In considering the words of both Ricky and TwoBoy it must be recognised that these men – who tell us about how difficult being a black child is, and what little control black children (and, by implication, themselves) have over their own lives – exercise very real power in their adult lives. Ricky has power in his relationships with black women, and he speaks of this as though it is the natural order of things. The phrase (taken from the passage below) 'big daddy, the right thing, the . . . is a person who listens to you' may also be taken to mean the proper or correct thing. The way Ricky says the words also functions to separate him from the nature of his relationships: it is not his doing, but it's the proper thing, the way things should be. That 'the right thing' merges into 'a person' can be analysed to show how this slippage on Ricky's part functions and is significant. What needs emphasis is that the speaker has power which he takes for granted. He presents himself, even though it might be unconsciously, as if he has no power to speak of. His power, in fact, extends over uneducated blacks, the unemployed, and over younger males (which is similar to the kind of power the 'older brothers' in Umlazi were exercising when they roughed up youngsters like him).

Here is the extract from Ricky's interview that demonstrates the paradoxes of power felt by black men:

'Yabona baba, int' eright, inte . . . umuntu olalela wena, at the same time, ongakulaleli kakhulu, you understand what I'm saying. For instance mina baba, I'm not a man of the nineties, uyabon'. Umfazi uyapheka, uyawasha, uyakuhlonipha, uyabon'. Angifuni umfazi oquestion' ukuthi why ubuya ngo 2, why ubuya ngo 4, uyabona . . . Ngi fun' umuntu one-independence but at the same time ozoba nami, uyabon'. So what 'am saying is you must have your own friends, me ngibe namafriends wami, but sazi ukuconnekta sonke, instead of ukuthi wena maubuy' emsebenzini awunayo indawo ongaya kuyona. So if mina ngijwayele okufika ngo6 sengifika ngo7, it's a big story, ngik' hlalise wedwa, uyabo'. So what 'am saying, you must have your own life, nami ngibe nelife yami but siconnekte. So umuntu oright kimina umuntu onjalo.

[See, baba (*roughly, father, or used between peers, old man or big daddy*), the right thing, the . . . is a person who listens to you, at the same time, who doesn't listen too much, you understand what I'm saying. For instance, me baba, I'm not a man of the nineties, see. A woman cooks, does the washing, respects you, see. I don't want a woman who ask questions about why you come in at 2, why you come in at 4, see . . . I want someone with independence but at the same time who'll be with me, see. So what 'am saying is you must have your own friends, and I have my own friends, but we should be able to connect, instead of you coming back from work and with nowhere to go. So if I am used to coming in at 6 and I come in at 7, it's a big story, I kept you on your own, see. So what 'am saying, you must have your own life, and I must have my life also but we should be able to connect. So the right person to me is that kind of person.]

It was once held – and perhaps may still be so – that the concerns of black men are not towards relinquishing male privilege. One of the reasons given for this view is that black males have (had) to deal with what in the language of the struggle against apartheid was termed 'the bread and butter issues'. Poor black men do not have the luxury to forge new concepts of masculinity. It was sometimes said ('on the ground', that is, 'in everyday society') that the use of any means to attain status and power among black youths was because of their perception that the opportunity structure remains blocked. Although surely not meant to support violence, these were reckless views which had the effect of leaving communities steeped in violence.

The context for such views can be found in Steve Mokwena's (1991) study on the violent masculine black youth subculture of the 1980s. In that study Mokwena argues convincingly that the crisis of racist capitalism resulted in the marginalisation of great numbers of black youth. The crisis created social conditions which spawned a survival-oriented, violent subculture. These conditions included the collapse of civic culture, high levels of youth unemployment, high drop-out rates in the schooling system and high failure rates, as well as the breakdown of the community fabric. When one observes that the meaning of manhood and masculinity has traditionally been largely of men as economic providers, a great many young black males must (have) look(ed) to their futures and their own sense of fulfilling their perceived male roles with a sense of desperate manhood. It might then be said that these social conditions were not conducive to a (re)negotiation of male power vis-à-vis black females or the production of open, multiple understandings of what it means to be a black man.

While there can be no question that conditions in apartheid South Africa have affected constructions of masculinity, it is dangerous to view such conditions in a determinist way. Examining male power or reworking masculinities is urgently required. It is now critical to go further and analyse how violence has become integral to the idea of what it is to be a real man and what the effects of such a construction are. In this investigation it may be shown that, far from being free of the structures of apartheid, black men are still caught up and support oppressive discourses which that structure also supported.

The real point is that ignoring how race intersects with other nexuses of social power (such as gender, class, and heterosexual masculinity) provides at best an incomplete vision of social reality. At worst, concentrating on racial oppression while glossing over sex hierarchies can hurt people, who are usually those with less power such as black women and children. Black males as subjects of both gender and race should be sites for interrogating contradictions of power and connections among gender, age and sexuality, of accent, race and class.

It is against the backdrop of a culture and society which espouses attaining a specific sort of power, a certain kind of masculinity, that one should understand TwoBoy. He was saying that many of his childhood peers never finished school because they didn't have money, but maybe they also lacked perseverance, which he had, and so they turned to crime, and he didn't.

TwoBoy: Maar apha esgela, ja, inasmuchas sikhuluma nga macherie, maar no Mongezi, ifriend yam', we fantasise a lot naleauti leyo

Kopano: Ngani? Ni fantasiza ngani?

TwoBoy: Eish, about getting money, making lots of bucks, before the age of 35.

Kopano: Ngizwile, wakewangitshela ukuthi, one time, ukuthi ufun' ukuba imillionaire wena.

TwoBoy: Mmh

Kopano: Why maara, why kahle kahle?

TwoBoy: I believe it's high time nabodarkie be'nze a lot of money. Because we were made to believe thina we're the second best, yabona.

> [TwoBoy: But here at school, yes, inasmuchas we talk about girls, but with Mongezi, a friend of mine, we fantasise a lot with that brother
>
> Kopano: About what? What do you fantasise about?
>
> TwoBoy: Eish, about getting money, making lots of bucks, before the age of 35.
>
> Kopano: I heard, you told me once that, one time, that you want to be a millionaire
>
> TwoBoy: Mmh
>
> Kopano: But why, why really?
>
> TwoBoy: I believe it's high time darkies start making a lot of money. Because we were made to believe we're the second best, see.]

TwoBoy's concerns are still about money. And for him, the concern with making money is connected to being black. Once again the identity is not of black people but black males, who, in their fantasies, go beyond females to dreaming about making money and being millionaires. It is even clearer when one hears Ricky saying something like,

> girls are generally opportunistic. If you're not all right, they don't want you. So what I'm trying to say, it's not about love now, it all revolves around what you have, or what you can give, see. You with me? If you don't have the money you can't access a certain type of girls. If you don't have a car you can't access a certain type of girls. But the more you become successful the easier it gets to get the girls.

## Conclusion

This chapter has argued three major points. Firstly, there is a need to examine the subjective lives of black African men *as men*. A focus on the gender of black males is a deliberate move to disturb the often taken-for-granted connection of race and gender subjectivities, and to unconsciously consider all black people as men. Secondly, it may be preferable for such examinations to use the method of discourse analysis as in this way the unique meanings of black masculinities, as well as how masculinity and blackness are policed and practised become evident. Thirdly, although one might want to study the subjective experiences of black males within a framework of sympathetic understanding (because one identifies with the political struggle of black people against racial oppression), there is the constant risk of simply confirming oppressive experiences from the side of black males. It is necessary, then, to remain vigilant against this. For example, when as a black male one studies other black men, one may be tempted to say something like, *'I hear what you're saying, I had a similar experience'*. It is critical to cultivate reflexivity or else one may simply be bracing up black males' sense of a lack of power with all its contradictions, as well as the violent consequences that may and do follow from these felt contradictions.

BIBLIOGRAPHY

Antaki, C. 1994. *Explaining and arguing*. London: Sage.

Bhabha, H.K. 1995. 'Are you a man or a mouse?' In M. Berger, B. Wallis, and S. Watson, eds., *Constructing Masculinities*. New York: Routledge.

Berger, M., B. Wallis and S. Watson, eds. 1995. *Constructing Masculinities*. New York: Routledge.

Billig, M. 1996. *Arguing and thinking*. Cambridge: Cambridge University Press.

————. 1998. 'Rhetoric and the unconscious', *Argumentation* 12.

Blake, W.M. and C.A. Darling. 1994. 'The dilemmas of the African-American male', *Journal of Black Studies* 24(4).

Branford, J. 1975. *A Dictionary of South African English*. Cape Town: Oxford University Press.

Brod, H. and M. Kaufman, eds. 1994. *Theorizing masculinities*. Thousand Oaks, California: Sage.

Brown. 1993. *The New Shorter Oxford English Dictionary*. Oxford: Oxford University Press.

Burman, E. and I. Parker. 1993. 'Introduction – discourse analysis: the turn to the text'. In E. Burman and I. Parker, eds., *Discourse analytic research: repertoires and readings of texts in action*. London: Routledge.

Connell, R.W. 1987. *Gender and power: society, the person and sexual politics*. Stanford, California: Stanford University Press.

————. 1993. 'The big picture in recent world history', *Theory and Society* 22.

————. 1995. *Masculinities*. Cambridge: Polity Press.

Edwards, D. 1996. *Discourse and cognition*. London: Sage.

Fanon, F. 1986. *Black Skins, White Masks*. London: Pluto Press.

Gary, L. 1981. *Black men*. Beverly Hills: Sage.

Hunter, A.G. and J.E. Davis. 1994. 'Hidden voices of black men: the meaning, structure, complexity of manhood', *Journal of Black Studies* 25(1).

Jackson, D. 1990. *Unmasking masculinity: a critical autobiography*. London: Unwin Hyman.

Kimmel, M.S., ed. 1987. *Changing men: new directions in research on men and masculinity*. Beverly Hills: Sage.

Macnaghten, P. 1993. 'Discourses of nature: argumentation and power'. In E. Burman and I. Parker, eds., *Discourse analytic research: repertoires and readings of texts in action*. London: Routledge.

Mokgatlhe, B.P. and J.B. Schoeman. 1998. 'Predictors of satisfaction with life: the role of racial identity, collective self-esteem and gender-role attitudes', *South African Journal of Psychology* 28(1).

Mokwena, S. 1991. 'The era of the jackrollers: contextualising the rise of youth gangs in Soweto'. Paper presented at Project for the Study of Violence Seminar. Johannesburg: Wits University.

Morrell, R. 1998. 'Of Boys and Men: Masculinity and Gender in Southern African Studies', *Journal of Southern African Studies* 24(4).

Potter, J. and M. Wetherell. 1987. *Discourse and social psychology*. London: Sage.

Ratele, K. 1998a. 'The end of the black man', *Agenda* 37.

———. 1998b. 'Relating to whiteness: writing about the black man', *Psychology Bulletin* 8(2).

Staples, R. 1982. *Black Masculinity: the black males' role in American society*. San Francisco: The Black Scholar Press.

———. 1986. 'The political economy of black family life', *The Black Scholar* 17(5).

Stenner, P. 1993. 'Discoursing jealousy'. In E. Burman and I. Parker, eds., *Discourse analytic research: repertoires and readings of texts in action*. London: Routledge.

Stevens, G. and R. Lockhat. 1997. '"Coca-Cola kids" – reflections on black adolescent identity development in post-apartheid South Africa', *South African Journal of Psychology* 27(4).

West, C. 1993. *Race matters*. New York: Vintage.

Yates, K. and P. Gqola. 1998. 'This little bit of madness: Mamphela Ramphele on being black and transgressive', *Agenda* 37.

# CHAPTER 14

# 'Simply the Best'[1]
# The Soweto Flying Squad, Professional Masculinities and the Rejection of *Machismo*

JOAN WARDROP

## Introduction

Police are often popularly constructed as exemplars of an almost-Ramboesque *machismo*. This image is derived from endless television cop shows and movies in which the likes of Mel Gibson, Don Johnson or Sean Penn play policemen who are steel-cored, super cool, and profoundly invulnerable. This is a seductively monolithic image that is, at one and the same time, both consciously appropriated and systematically rejected by operational members of the Soweto Flying Squad, the major-crime emergency-response unit for Soweto, Lenasia and Eldorado Park.

Soweto is a densely populated agglomeration of townships and shack settlements to the south-west of Johannesburg. Its actual population is unknown, but the figure that the emergency services (including the police) work to is five million, in an area of about three hundred square kilometres. The streetscape has changed very rapidly during the 1990s. Residents have been able to buy the properties they previously were forced to rent, and have rebuilt, very often converting the tiny three or four-room 'matchbox' houses into substantial dwellings (often of two stories). A significant addition to the streetscape has been what Sowetans call a 'stop nonsense': high walls and fences designed partly for privacy but partly as a defence against significant rates of personal and property crime (both reported and unreported).

For police, as for residents, Soweto is a uniquely complex mix: a city of ordinary people leading ordinary lives, using any one of a dozen or more languages, weaving multifaceted social webs of ties and interactions; and a city of grinding daily awareness of the threat of violent crime, of theft or robbery, attack, rape, and/or murder. South Africa now has the highest per capita rate of reported rape in the world, and the highest rate of police killed (on and off duty). Of the 275 police who were killed in 1998, more than 60 were killed in Soweto alone.

This chapter draws on material collected in a longitudinal ethnographic study of high-intensity policing in a period of rapid political and social change. Between March 1994 and 1999 I spent nearly 250 shifts (each 12 to 14 hours long) as a participant observer with the Soweto Flying Squad and police from other Soweto units. In addition, I conducted many hundreds of hours of interviews with various police.[2]

The Soweto Flying Squad consists of nearly 250 policemen and women as well as associated administrative and control room staff. These staff are divided into four reliefs (or shifts) and a Highway Patrol section of two reliefs. 'Working Flying Squad' in Soweto, and dealing constantly with major-crime incidents such as murder and rape scenes, fighting complaints and shooting incidents, means working in an intensely threat-filled environment. The stresses are not only the immediate threats to the individual, but also the injuries to and death of other police, as well as members of the public.

With very few exceptions those who 'work outside' are male. Of the women who have worked outside during the period of this study, none have worked as drivers and several have expressed a specific disinclination to take on such responsibility under the extremely difficult conditions of police driving in Soweto. Numerous men also expressed the same reluctance, while others have ambitions to become a regular driver but are prevented from doing so because they are not considered by their peers and the officers of their relief to possess the levels of skill and judgement that will allow them to drive at very high speeds to reach urgent complaints quickly or to chase stolen (hijacked, stolen with violence) vehicles. There is a widely expressed view on the unit that women are capable of learning to shoot very well but are not good at judgement calls (that is, when and when not to shoot), and are incapable of 'driving' by Flying Squad[3] definitions of what 'driving' is.

While the capacity to perform a core element of the work such as driving is clearly gendered and might seem, superficially, to contain indicators of notions of *machismo*, this link is rejected by the men (and women) themselves. Oddly, the feelings that often are manifested during high-speed driving, such as the sense of control and focus, the adrenaline rush and the exhilaration that everyone in the vehicle experiences, are not

Joan Wardrop

specifically gendered, or thought of as having macho connotations, nor generally are they read in such a way by members of the unit. Rather they are deciphered and described as having a universality that links all of those who experience them, on cross-gendered lines. Despite this affective reading of the effects of the intensities of some elements of the work, however, an overwhelming consensus remains about the specifically gendered roles that police on the unit can and should assume, both in terms of technical skills such as driving and in terms of tasks requiring physical strength, such as the restraint of recalcitrant, struggling suspects. Here, the construction of utilitarian masculinities can be seen most starkly.

This chapter makes the proposition that Flying Squad notions of masculinity are more deeply grounded and more subtly crafted than superficial appearances would suggest. Far from there being a single construction of masculinity on the unit, let alone one which unreflexively buys into conventional notions of *machismo*, the more-than two hundred men who 'work outside' are engaged in multiple presentations of finely-articulated masculinities which are painstakingly negotiated to achieve very particular outcomes. These multiple, utilitarian masculinities are situational in nature, derived from and dependent upon the very specific and highly pressured conditions of stress and threat of elite-level law enforcement in South Africa.[4] It is in this context of the construction of professional masculinities – and in direct contradiction of the popular stereotypes and their expression of an essentialised and undifferentiated 'toughness' in such conditions – that members of the unit, both implicitly in their style of work, and explicitly in discussion of their work, reject any notion of *machismo* or other overt displays of stylised masculinity which are intended for the ego enhancement of the individual.

### The denial of *machismo*

During a discussion of macho images of masculinity one senior non-commissioned officer (NCO) said, emphatically: 'Rather leave that shit (acting flamboyantly and dangerously) to Jo'burg [Johannesburg Flying Squad] – we'd be killed if we did.' Later in the same conversation, a more junior NCO vividly expressed the notion that macho attitudes were 'a fucking quick way to be shot'. In the eyes of experienced Flying Squad members then, rampant egos, macho attitudes and danger are often synonymous. The antidote is the construction of intensely-reflexive masculinities which enable the framing of multiple functional and externalised presentations of the self which are positioned in very particular circumstances.

Members of the unit express an awareness that the process by which

257

images of themselves as men, as police, and as policemen, are formed might take years on other less-pressured units. In the policing environment of Soweto, responsibility and exercising judgement comes early.

In theory it is the officers of the unit who determine who will work where, but in practice members of each relief self-select those who will regularly 'work outside' on patrol and answer complaints. Indeed, they select who will work with whom, and in which vehicles. Only under exceptional circumstances will a member of the unit be forced to work with a partner, either crew or driver, about whose capacities he has serious reservations.

The processes for uncovering those capacities involve testing newcomers with the unit's own unofficial battery of tests (both overt and covert). Within carefully constructed frameworks that will allow more experienced police to recover the situation should it go wrong, newcomers are deliberately and unpredictably placed in situations in which they will have to exercise discretion and judgement; in which they will be confronted with the often-horrific results of violent crime; in which they have to exercise massive self-control, over, for example, the adrenaline at the end of a high-speed chase, or the anger at a drunken rape suspect insisting on his right to fuck a small child; in which any images of themselves as 'tough guys' they may have brought with them to the unit will be disturbed and confused. In addition, they will be tested on the technicalities of the work and, most crucially, on their potential to learn the Flying Squad ways of doing things.

In pushing new members towards the point at which they might break ('lose it'), unit members gauge whether the new person is reliable, whether he can be trusted, whether his judgement is 'sharp' or 'cool', and whether he knows (or can learn) 'how to work safe' in a threat-filled environment.

All of the above elements are crucial to the confidence, usually quietly expressed (although it may have more vigorous manifestations), that lies at the core of the notion of the masculine self on whose existence and dependability the Flying Squad policeman and those around him will rely. It is within these images of self that some members of the unit explicitly recognise the 'real man', a 'strong man', a 'man who doesn't need to show anything'. These images represent shared notions of masculinity which are precisely drawn and clear to members of the unit. Despite their seemingly rigid boundaries, they can accommodate a wide range of behaviours which might in other circumstances be read as signs of 'weakness', such as weeping over a child's body or expressing unfocused anger.[5] 'He's my crew, he can do that shit of his,' a driver stated very firmly after his long-term partner had snapped at both of us in the aftermath of a very heated

Joan Wardrop

domestic fighting complaint. The policeman in question was 'having a bad time' (in his private life) and allowances must be made for him, even when he was being 'a child'.

By contrast, the behaviour of a member who allows his colleagues to see his need for his ego to be overtly massaged or boosted will be met with far less tolerance. Such behaviour might consist of a need to show off in public, to unnecessarily antagonise members of the public at an incident scene ('wanting to be Rambo', 'thinks he's *Miami Vice*'), or to brag or boast in a way that takes credit from other members. It will be read as having the potential to disrupt social interactions with colleagues, and as having the more extreme potential for 'making shit' at an incident and perhaps causing a small incident to spiral out of control into a major scene. If the behaviour persists or becomes a pattern, members will gradually isolate the offender and in some cases will cause him to be removed from the unit. The type of masculinity which is being presented by such individuals is clearly perceived and is articulated by unit members as flawed and, in the Soweto environment, as dangerous.

At the repeated points of interaction between police and public (whether suspects, incident participants, bystanders or witnesses), the particular manifestations of masculine self selected for presentation (consciously or not) are crucial in defining the shape and progress of the incident. The form of masculinity chosen is a critical element in determining whether or not an incident will progress smoothly. As police make clear in discussions of their colleagues and, more reflexively, of themselves, the professional persona might well be completely unlike that adopted off-duty, a condition which also applies directly to images of masculinity. Nonetheless, Flying Squad members who are recognised by their colleagues as 'good policemen' are recognised also as tending to demonstrate the same characteristics (restraint, self-control) in their personal lives and many of the men have expressed the notion that 'when you've worked Soweto you've done it all', saying that they feel no need to 'be macho' when off-duty.

What is suggested here is that these presentations of self are utilitarian in nature, designed for particular circumstances, but made possible only by control and knowledge of the self. Inherent in this is awareness of the particular articulations of masculinity/ies that will be most useful. 'Crime', 'criminal behaviour' and their 'consequences' (arrest, imprisonment, community service) might seem to be susceptible to very precise definition in legislation, the media or other public domains. In practice, however, policing is about blurred boundaries, about 'crimes' for which no one can be charged (for lack of evidence, for example); or which suddenly have not occurred (the witnesses evaporate, the complainant withdraws the complaint); about crimes which exist only as a plan in someone's head and which do not take place because police appear or intervene, patrolling or perhaps even on the track of a quite different incident. What seems clearcut and obvious to 'the public' (in calls for 'zero tolerance' policing, for example) is much less evident or defined on the ground, where what is demanded of police is a constant and subtle reading and re-reading of the social as well as the physical environment, of the particular circumstances of each complaint, and of the wider context of the area and its changing moods. To work constantly at a critical interface between the state and the public is to spend 12 hours at a time negotiating utilitarian personas, which can be effective only if the framing identities are sufficiently well developed to withstand the stresses which are imposed on them.

## Stop and search

Some elements of these personas are illustrated in the passage below (which is an expansion of my field notes of a small incident).[6] Such scenes represent what the police see as a vital component of their visible policing and crime prevention function. They occur very frequently and have the potential to be very dangerous since those stopped and searched, if they are actively engaged in criminal activity, will not infrequently draw firearms and use them. Building a method which would enable me to comprehend both the most minute constituent parts of the policing work and, just as importantly, the feelings and thoughts of the police doing the work, necessitated close contact, and the deliberate construction of an openness and even vulnerability to the experience. It was here, in an environment of physical and psychological pressure that the structure and solidity provided by an 'experience-near' perspective was invaluable, both in framing my own position and enabling the narrative recording of events as far as possible from the inside, from the police's point of view.

The police vehicle swoops off the road in Diepkloof zone 5, the driver using the handbrake to slow and turn the Golf sharply through 180°. Both he and the crew, riding in the front passenger seat, had seen something 'not right' about the Toyota Corolla parked on the opposite side of the road, and about its occupants, three young men, *tsotsis*, by their dress and demeanour. Two are out of the car, on either side of the engine, the hood just raised; the other is straddling the front passenger seat, one foot on the ground, fiddling with a very loud CD system.

After the noise and dust of the handbrake turn, the *tsotsis* stiffen, demonstrably aware of the arrival of the Flying Squad but

Joan Wardrop

pretending otherwise, the emotional temperature of the street visibly rising, the attention of a score or more people on the two
vehicles, the police driver nonetheless takes his time climbing out
of the vehicle. In dozens of emergency situations I have seen him
seem to fly out of the front seat, covering ten metres or more before
the vehicle has fully stopped. Now, though, he looks through the
side window at the *tsotsis*, taking off his sunglasses for a moment
before resettling them, bending forward slightly to take his 9 mill
automatic pistol from the holster on his left hip as he opens the
door, his eyes not moving from the Corolla.

Every move is deliberate – but can be so only because the crew
is already standing by the side of his own open door, a 9 mill
resting on the roof, aimed at the other vehicle. By staying back, he
provides the cover, the eyes that can scan a wider periphery while
simultaneously holding the movements and body language of the
*tsotsis* as his central focus, alert for any minute indication that one
of the young men might be about to go for a firearm, exercising a
different type of control over the scene.

The crew is tall and solidly built, the driver much shorter and
slighter. But, as he walks the fifteen feet across to the Toyota, he is
manifestly transformed: taller, broad shouldered, authoritative, slightly swaggering, using both his stance and his walk to change his
body shape and the way it is projected and perceived. Combined
with the inherent authority of the blue uniform, historically contested though that might be, the demonstration of confidence
displayed by the language of his body focuses the attention of all
three *tsotsis* on him: the direction and intensity of their gaze make it
evident that I, now out of the vehicle on the far side, and even the
crew and the 9 mill, are almost completely irrelevant to the small
theatrical exercise of question and answer, banter and counterpoint
that will be played out over the next few minutes.

The policeman, no older than the three *tsotsis*, and physically
smaller, will determine the parameters and rhythm of the scene,
performing a nuanced act of social control, discovering what he
needs to know about the ownership of the Toyota, working out the
limited probabilities of a charge of possession of stolen parts successfully negotiating the court system, walking a fine line between
dominance and empathy in order to do so, knowing that there are
many potentially hostile firearms within a usable radius, and that
overt challenges to the self-image of the *tsotsis* as 'big men' will
inevitably provoke potentially fatal violence – and knowing that

more members of Flying Squad have been injured and killed in such seemingly innocent stop-and-search incidents than in any other type of complaints.

A few minutes later, the police vehicle was *blomming*[7] again, and I was talking with the two policemen about their knowledge that two of the *tsotsis* had been involved in some serious vehicle robbery recently, involving the deaths of at least two people, but that there was not enough evidence for an arrest. The driver was laughing as he tried to find the words to describe how he felt as he sauntered across to the Corolla, taking charge even though he appeared so casual. For him, as for most other members of the Flying Squad, the key to control of an incident is control of the self, and that is almost always described as specifically including control of the body and its presentation.

He said, and the crew concurred, that 'knowing' the body is critical: being able to 'feel' individual muscles and their immediate potential for movement; aware of the muscles of the hands and arms and their line up through the shoulders and into the back, held loosely but a microsecond from tension; walking on the balls of the feet (not difficult in the soft-soled police boots), both poised for action; and stretching out the muscles of calves and thighs. The facial muscles too are crucial: to lock eyes and hold a stare, to project a carefully defined persona, to minimise vulnerability. Without an underlying psychological self-awareness and control, however, none of this physical control is feasible.

The development and maintenance of this reflexivity involve a complex of processes over time, including the deliberate (re)construction of images of the self, both psychologically and physically. Always implicit (and sometimes explicit) in this remodelling are multiple notions of masculine selves, which for most of the members of the unit come over time to frame all their notions of personhood. This degree of self-knowledge is not easily gained. For many it involves confrontations with their own lack of knowledge or technique, with physical pain, with the vulnerability of a fragile body, with fear, and with the imminent possibility of their own deaths.

Some do not manage a transition to 'manhood'. Of the last formal intake directly from the police college (in 1994, shortly before a moratorium on police recruitment was imposed), for example, half (six of twelve)[8] were no longer with the unit six months later. In some cases this was due to the informal testing processes that each relief imposes on newcomers. In other cases this was due to a recognition on the part of the individuals that they were not suited for policing at the extreme cutting edge at which the Soweto Flying Squad performs. One of the recruits

Joan Wardrop

falling into the latter category told me shortly before he applied for transfer that he was so continuously frightened that he had not slept through a night since he came to the unit several weeks before. He was drinking very heavily in an attempt to stop 'the nightmares'.

The first year with the unit involves intensive learning and equally intensive maturation, turning 'little boys into men' as one NCO told me during the initial intensive training period. He went on to say that he was embarrassed at describing the process that way because it seemed to put the recruits down, 'but that's how they are'.

The same NCO frequently talked to me about his and my observations of the recruits during the next year or so, with repeated references to the various ways in which the young men were becoming more effective as Flying Squad policemen out in the area and more competent (that is, mature) in their relationships on their various reliefs. Although he was less than ten years older than the recruits, he described himself as being 'another father' to them and to the other young men of his relief. He acknowledged such a strong sense of responsibility for their survival and sanity that on his rest days he would leave his police radio switched on and race the thirty kilometres from his home into Soweto if an incident occurred in which they were involved. For him, these attitudes represented a deep-seated notion of an important part of his own masculinity, which was connected both to his own father and other older males in his family, and also to older members of the police – in particular, men who had 'trained' him when he 'was learning'. Further, he (and other NCOs) expressed an awareness of 'family problems', both functionally in terms of having 'to sort out' intra-relief conflicts, and theoretically in that they would consciously think about internal relief or unit problems through the mirror of their own or other families.[9]

The simple force with which such attitudes of responsibility for the lives of others in these stressful and dangerous working conditions are expressed reaches back to a pre-modern understanding of the realities of men's friendships, an understanding in which 'The friends are heroes . . . who share danger, loyal to the death' (Hammond and Jablow 1987: 247). Critics argue that such male friendship is mythical and 'lacks relevance to modern times. . . . [and] is anomalous in a bureaucratized world' (Hammond and Jablow 1987: 255). While these critics debunk accepted views about male friendship, they also acknowledge the power of the pre-modern myths and narratives of male friendship, and of the literary/ textual descriptions of men at war or in other isolated or dangerous environments. Ultimately, however, they implicitly reject the experience (and its formative, affective qualities) that lies beyond the text, informing, constructing and shaping it. By contrast, the lived experience of policemen from the Soweto Flying Squad confirms the power and complex emotional forces which underpin the relationships of mutual trust and shared responsibility which make policing in Soweto possible.

## Inner spaces

Small scenes such as the stop and search described above are played out by Flying Squad police dozens of times in each twelve-hour shift that they work. At its most basic, their work is to determine if an illegal act has occurred and, if so, whether that act is susceptible to the processes of the formal legal system. However, enveloping that seemingly simple determination, each interaction with the public involves a complex of assumptions, understandings, assessments and negotiations. These cannot be achieved without the policemen reading the social environment of each incident: focusing on the core issue of a putative crime, but simultaneously being aware of the subtexts of the social interactions, both between themselves and the 'suspects' and others at the scene, and also the internal interactions of the non-police participants and observers. These often speak a verbal language with which individual police are not familiar.[10] Experienced Flying Squad police (the *oupas* or grandfathers) constantly reiterate to younger/newer members the importance of learning how to deal with the nuances and ambiguities of what would otherwise be meaningless babble. One of the hallmarks of a member of the Flying Squad, as perceived both by other members of the unit and by other police, is the conscious and active development of cross-cultural capacities to read intonation, facial expressions and body language, and always to take into account the manifestations of what are often deeply precarious (and therefore sometimes unpredictable and dangerous) masculinities on the part of those they have contact with on the streets, in the shebeens or at the site of a complaint.[11]

The initiated have developed or found a crucial inner space that members of the unit recognise as the mark of police 'who know how to work' and 'who work safe'. These are men (and, in some cases, women) who have faced the grinding fear of a major shooting incident, or of a solitary chase on foot in the dark after an armed suspect, and who have come out the other side of an inner experience whose psychological elements are as tangible as any physical experience. It is this that both underpins and permits the construction of the unmacho utilitarian masculinities that in their turn permit the performance of the work of policing in this type of environment.

The rejection of boasting or arrogant behaviours in the wrong contexts as 'that shit', as 'immature' and 'dangerous', is commonly expressed across

Joan Wardrop

the four reliefs (shifts) of the unit. It functions as one of the first tests for new members; to see whether they possess any of these dangerous characteristics, whether they can hold back and not allow their own egos to be threatened, whether they can work through a complaint without engaging the participants in ways that could have negative consequences. At their most obvious, these attitudes are articulated and developed through the workings of the various component small groups/teams ('the vehicle', 'the relief', 'the unit') of the Squad. The formation and studied construction of the bonds between partners and between relief members parallels the development of technical skills (driving, negotiation, questioning, shooting) and is viewed by senior members (in particular) as being of equal importance. 'All *I* need to know is my crew is with me', expresses the trust that in practice transcends both race and gender boundaries, and goes to the darkest moments of policing, those of terminal threat to police lives.

The crucial subtext here is threat assessment and the competence (in the eyes of fellow police) with which it is handled. Police in Soweto are often injured or even killed in the course of their work. Being able to read both the physical environment (the hiding places where an attacker might wait, the cover if an attack does occur) and the social/psychological environment (which individuals in a group are distressed, angry or hostile, who might use a knife, a broken bottle or a firearm against police) is defined by many police as the most significant skill acquired by members of the Flying Squad after they join the unit. Paradoxically, however, while helping to keep the numbers of deaths lower than those of many other police branches and units, it is a knowledge which almost certainly increases the injury rate because unit members take on responsibility for very violent complaints that police from, for example, a local police station will not or cannot handle. Implicit in this is a strong (and at times specifically articulated) sense of what the unit's internally-agreed 'story' sees as the essential connections between high levels of technical competence, psychological stability, quickness of reflex, soundness of judgement, and responsible attitudes in crucial situations. These characteristics are what make up 'a good policeman' in Flying Squad terms and reflect the ways 'a good man' can be defined.

## Street theatre

A developed ability to read the social environment underpins the Flying Squad conception of 'a good policeman' and hence of 'a good man'. Incident scenes are often chaotic, violent and disordered, both physically and psychologically. In the following narrative example (again adapted from my field notes), a situation that had the potential to explode was defused by the actions of a policeman who seized the leading role in the scene and held on to it.

Taking the taxi roads from west to east, heading towards Meadow-lands, early in the afternoon, traffic heavy and slow-moving, taxis swerving in to the side of the road, stopping too quickly for the vehicles behind them, pulling out again without any check on the road. Passing PP shopping centre, rundown, barely open for business, a sudden coagulation of vehicles and the police vehicle stops dead in the centre of the road, two taxis in the other lane, a group of seven or eight men are punching one another. As the two policemen approach, the victim falls and is kicked, hard, the sound of boots thudding against flesh audible above the noise of the gathering crowd.

I stand by the rear of the vehicle watching as the police begin to push back the attackers, remonstrating with them, preventing them from continuing to punish the man groaning on the road. One shoves through the circle and aims a flying kick at an already bleeding head, the man on the ground shudders and recoils. A dozen or more taxis are banking up in the T-junction, passengers pointing and shouting and whistling as the police begin to take charge. A young woman is bumped, gently, from behind by a Toyota trying to get through and I am feeling insecure by the vehicle, taxis coming within inches of me as they make another lane to get past the disturbance, heedless of the danger to pedestrians. As I cross towards the police one glances at me, frowning, obviously worried. The other is being confronted by a much taller man, in his face, shouting, pushing. The aggression is being transferred from the victim on the ground to the police, and I hesitate, knowing I have done the wrong thing in leaving the vehicle. I confirm that quickly with one of the police and move back again, out of the circle of hostility that is eddying around them.

Without looking down at what he is doing, one takes a cigarette from his top pocket and lights it, breathing the smoke in hard, watching intently as his partner stands face to face with the most aggressive of the attackers, refusing to back off from the confrontation. The partner is someone I have worked several shifts with. I have seen him in a number of situations, but not before directly physically outnumbered and confronted like this. He seems to be growing taller and I realise that he is refusing to look up at the other man. Instead he has squared his shoulders, underneath his

Joan Wardrop

jacket he is using all the muscles of his upper body to appear larger, and he has swayed back an inch or two, not enough to seem threatened or give a cue that he is going to back off, just enough to give him space to look directly at the eyes of the other man.

But the body is only part of the armoury he is using to gain psychological control of the scene: suddenly and unexpectedly he shouts, loudly, a sound rather than a word, and the taximan flinches, jerking his head back. Several of the others react physically, wary because an element of unpredictability has entered what they had been assuming was an incident they controlled.

More than a hundred people are crowded around, on foot and hanging out of vehicles, noisy, intent on the small, crucial drama being played out between the blue uniform and the garish colours of a handknitted jersey. The police are greatly outnumbered. Even with the use of the long guns they would have no chance if the crowd turned against them. No firearms are visible but in a crowd of this size, with so many taxis, it is inevitable that there will be *tipas*, knives, *pangas*, and many handguns. But the delicate balance of the scene is passing to the police. The moment in which the taximan flinched was crucial, the two policemen are facing down the group of attacking taxi drivers, using their body language and their voices to establish a sense of dominance that can control the tempo and rhythm of the incident.

The cigarette is thrown away with an abrupt movement that spells readiness to act physically, and the final components fall into place. Control has been established and the incident is over. The man on the ground drags himself up, using the side of his taxi to support himself. He sits for a moment, slumped over the steering wheel and then smiles at the police. They watch till he has driven his passengers away, and warn the rival drivers not to follow him. They are using their discretion: with a full-scale taxi war brewing, endless conferences of rival taxi association leaders being brokered by the senior officers at the police base, it is not the time for mass arrests for what remained a relatively trivial beating. No firearms or knives had been used, the crowd had remained neutral.

## Conclusion: utilitarian masculinities

What is illustrated in the two vignettes of 'working outside', is the externalised notion of masculinity that was posited at the beginning of this chapter. This is a persona which is made manifest through the body and the voice, which is projected onto and into the interface between police and 'the people',[12] and which is used as an essential component of the mechanisms by which social control is exerted by the police. The persona is deliberately constructed and assumed, becoming over time an integral part of the presentation of self of individual policemen. It is crafted to suit particular circumstances and particular people, and depends heavily on the capacity of the policeman to read the social environment and to be able to convert his reading into an appropriate response. Some of its elements are drawn from the models of older or more experienced Flying Squad members, while others are derived from a more generalised set of notions of how 'men' can and should conduct themselves.

In appropriating these other images of masculinity, from media depictions in particular, police are using (often consciously) modes of behaviour that they know will be recognised and taken seriously by the people with whom they deal. Their understandings and projection of these images are grounded in knowledge and control of the professional self and are pragmatically directed to specific purposes. A 'good policeman' in Flying Squad terms is someone who knows 'instinctively' (as a result of years of training and reflexive experience) precisely what attitudes and personas, what masculinities, to select and use for each circumstance he encounters. A 'good policeman' in Flying Squad terms is not someone who needs to play Rambo, not someone whose ego is needy in that way, and not someone therefore who plays back into the common media stereotypes of 'masculinity', of 'macho', of 'what a policeman is'. As the examples above demonstrate, those stereotypes are considered by members of the Flying Squad to be pointless and even dangerous in the particular policing conditions of Soweto. Nonetheless, their rejection of the stereotypes is not total. Aspects of the stereotypes are appropriated and incorporated (in body language, for example) where they are perceived to have utility, with the constant caveat that they be used subtly and reflexively – for to assume them unconsciously is to increase the level of risk to potentially intolerable levels.

In the study of the ways in which this small group of men working in such specific circumstances form their constructions of masculinities, I suggest that the capacity that these men demonstrate in selecting and developing utilitarian professional masculinities is conditioned by the environment in which they work. Equally importantly, it is framed by the self-conscious reiteration on the Soweto Flying Squad of a particular set of understandings of masculine behaviours. The comparatively closed nature of the social institution then encourages the transmission of these masculinities within the group, restraining and redirecting behaviours which stray from the frame established within and by the group.

268

Joan Wardrop

NOTES

1. A slogan much used on the Flying Squad, often with a sense of irony and awareness that becoming complacent 'can get you killed'.

2. I wish to express my thanks to the Soweto Flying Squad, and to the police from other Soweto units, for their wholehearted participation in this project.

3. The use of Flying Squad in this chapter always refers to the Soweto Flying Squad. No description or interpretation should be extrapolated from this chapter and applied to any other Flying Squad.

4. The difficulty for any outsider in being able to move past the assumptions and 'commonsense' preconceptions of policing and police towards a type of understanding which permits the construction of even a minimal grammar of the meanings that the police themselves find and make in their lives and work, is both substantial, and also frequently recognised and articulated by the police themselves (Burke 1969). As a consequence, in seeking to understand and to describe these social interfaces and the modes of self-presentation used by the police of this unit, and after much discussion with members of the Flying Squad about the problems of representation, I have chosen to go back to Clifford Geertz and his seminal evocation of Heinz Kohut's notion of the 'experience-near' perspective (Geertz 1983: 57). This provides a means both of overcoming at least some of these difficulties, and also of constructing textual representations of incidents, moods and feelings through vignettes of experience which illustrate the points made here, expressed in my words but which remain recognisable to the police involved in those events.

5. Similarly, McElhinny has developed the idea of an 'economy of affect' within which police 'do express positive affect on the job, but they choose the situations in which they do so carefully . . .' (1994: 165).

6. As part of the field method drafts of what I write about policing have been circulated around the unit. Any member of the unit can comment and discuss the work with me. Police involved in specific incidents have often enabled me to avoid mistakes of fact and to expand my representations of the events through this process. However, my interpretations remain my own.

7. This is unit parlance for patrolling. From the Afrikaans *blom* ('flower'), metaphorically to open up an area as a flower's petals might open.

8. The twelve included two men who came from other units and so had some field experience. They both continued with the unit.

9. For a problematised notion of the 'family' and its internal competitions and conflicts in the athletic world, see Messner (1992: 219–22).

10. At any incident any combination of the 11 official South African languages, as well as *fanagalo* (the lingua franca developed on the mines of the Witwatersrand; multilingual in origin) or *isicamtho* (an informal, constantly evolving township lingua franca, drawing on elements of a variety of languages) might be used.

11. Township life under apartheid has been a debilitating experience psychologically for many men, their sense of self negated by the constant petty humiliations of the system. For the police, it is particularly the 'youth' (the ANC Youth League includes people up to 35 years of age, for example), many of whom were involved as shock troops in the liberation struggle but who now find no role, and who remain uneducated and unemployed, whom they encounter.

12. As the Soweto public is usually referred to by members of the Flying Squad.

BIBLIOGRAPHY

Burke, K. 1969. *A grammar of motives*. Berkeley: University of California Press.

Geertz, C. 1983. *Local knowledge. Further essays in interpretative anthropology*. New York: Basic Books.

Hammond, D. and A. Jablow. 1987. 'Gilgamesh and the Sundance Kid: the myth of male friendship'. In H. Brod, ed., *The Making of Masculinities: The New Men's Studies*. Boston: Allen & Unwin.

McElhinny, B. 1994. 'An economy of affect: objectivity, masculinity and the gendering of police work'. In A. Cornwall and N. Lindisfarne, eds., *Dislocating Masculinity: Comparative Ethnographies*. London: Routledge.

Messner, M.A. 1992. 'Like family. Power, intimacy, and sexuality in male athletes' friendships'. In P.M. Nardi, ed., *Men's friendships*. Newbury Park, California: Sage.

# PART FOUR

Sexuality in South Africa has been placed under the spotlight by the AIDS pandemic. Those most affected are young, sexually-active, heterosexual Africans. The racially skewed nature of infection rates can be explained by examining constructions of masculinity. Young African men living in townships to a large extent construct their masculinity around sexual prowess. Having several girlfriends establishes a young man's masculinity. The heavy emphasis on heterosexuality is largely a result of the decline of work opportunities, traditionally the major arena where the credentials of masculinity could be established. Young African girls are the major (but by no means unwitting) 'victims' of this sexually assertive male behaviour but the young men are not free from the consequences of their choices. Their need for sexual affirmation makes them vulnerable to the machinations of rivals and to the rejections of women.

The way in which context influences forms of sexuality is particularly clear in closed institutions. South Africa's gold mines have historically been the largest employer of labour and remain significant because of the large numbers of African men who work together. The dangerous nature of mine work gives some workers a devil-may-care attitude to sex. They insist on unprotected sexual intercourse because it is a pleasure that makes them feel masculine in a context where that masculinity is under threat and their very lives are constantly at risk in a dangerous working environment. Another response is for older men to find 'wives' amongst the younger miners. In these relationships the need for intimacy is met though the heterosexual orientation of masculinity is not challenged as wives and families remain the focus of procreative sex. Nevertheless, the sharp distinction between gay and heterosexual sexuality is blurred.

Although South Africa is a very homophobic society there have been times when gay relationships have been, within limited and defined social boundaries, visible and accepted. Some African men in urban areas were able to construct a sexually liberated zone within the metaphorical apartheid prison camp. Space for gay relationships has since grown under the new South African Constitution. Protection from discrimination is guaranteed and consensual homosexual acts have been decriminalised. Despite these developments sexuality remains a contested site.

# Sexuality

# CHAPTER 15

# 'Going Underground and Going After Women'
## Masculinity and HIV Transmission amongst Black Workers on the Gold Mines

CATHERINE CAMPBELL

## Introduction

The South African gold mines currently employ about 350 000 black male workers. Ninety-five per cent are migrants who come from rural areas within South Africa and from surrounding countries such as Lesotho, Botswana and Mozambique. The vast majority of these black workers are housed in single-sex hostels close to their workplaces. A recent study of levels of HIV in the mining area of Carletonville suggested that levels of HIV infection amongst mineworkers are in the region of 25 per cent (Williams 1999). While migrancy certainly played a key role in HIV transmission early on in the epidemic (Hunt 1989; Jochelson et al. 1991), the extent to which migrant workers continue to have higher levels of HIV than non-migrant men is not firmly established. Thus, for example, in the survey mentioned above, Williams found that levels of HIV amongst migrant workers in the mine hostels were similar to levels amongst men in the townships.

This chapter seeks to explain how large numbers of men become HIV positive by examining the work and living contexts in which their sexual appetites are formed. From the start it should be noted that despite living in single-sex compounds, transmission occurs almost exclusively in heterosexual relations.

This chapter argues that the particular way in which masculine identities are socially constructed amongst miners explains why infection rates are so high. The ways in which men understand their masculine identities play a key role in shaping how they seek sexual satisfaction and intimacy.

This chapter was written within the context of the Mothusimpilo HIV-prevention project, co-ordinated by Professor Brian Williams, of the Council of Scientific and Industrial Research in Johannesburg.[1] This study was conducted on a Johannesburg gold mine in 1995 under the auspices of the Epidemiology Research Unit, and involved semi-structured, open-ended interviews with 42 Zulu-, Xhosa- and Sotho-speaking underground mineworkers.

Interviews were conducted by the author, together with a multilingual team of interviewers. The interviews were on average three hours long, and aimed to elicit informants' life histories with a particular focus on their experiences and perceptions of health, healing, sexuality and HIV/AIDS.[2]

This chapter has two sections. The first presents an account of underground miners' working and living conditions in the interests of portraying the broad contextual backdrop within which their sexual relationships are conducted. These conditions provide limited opportunities for social support and the development of emotionally sustaining intimate relationships. The second section seeks to examine the way in which such working and living conditions interact with a particular concept of masculinity to undermine the likelihood of safe sexual behaviour by mineworkers.

## The social context of identity formation on the mines

The process of social identity construction is context-dependent and situation-specific (Campbell 1995). In the interviews conducted, factors such as the general working and living conditions on the mines, the ever-present danger of accidents, and mineworkers' perceived lack of control over their health and well-being repeatedly emerged as important features of the world in which mineworker identities were fashioned. In an extremely dangerous environment, sex is regarded as one of the most easily available recreational activities at the end of a stressful and exhausting day – with a range of factors undermining the likelihood of condom use.

This chapter seeks to illustrate the ambiguous role played by the construction of masculine identity in relation to the well-being of underground workers. On the one hand, male identities serve as a key coping mechanism for dealing with high risk working conditions, through encouraging men to be brave and fearless in the interests of supporting their families. On the other hand, such identities simultaneously place workers at particular risk of contracting HIV through perpetuating the view that

Catherine Campbell

'real men' have insatiable urges to seek pleasure through unprotected sex with large numbers of women. There is a corresponding macho lack of concern for the consequences.

Living and working conditions on the mines are dangerous and highly stressful (Leon, Davies, Salamon and Davies 1995; Molapo 1995). The majority of mineworkers live some distance from their homes and families, in large single-sex hostels, with up to 18 people sharing a room. Informants described compound life as dirty and overcrowded, with no space for privacy or quiet. While some facilities exist for wives and families to visit, informants said that these were extremely limited. Opportunities for leisure are few. Some workers spend time in the African townships near to the mines, but others avoid them as dangerous places. From the accounts of our informants, drinking and sex appeared to be two of the few diversionary activities easily available on a day-to-day basis.

Even more stressful than life outside of work, however, was the time spent underground in the mines. Miners' accounts of their working conditions varied widely according to their specific job and the demands of particular production team leaders, but there were also several common themes. Many men said that they were expected to engage in physically taxing and dangerous work for up to eight hours with infrequent breaks. Sometimes they had minimal access to food or water, and worked under conditions of tremendous heat, often with unpleasantly noisy machinery. In addition, the air was frequently stale and dusty.

In talking about the stresses of daily life on the mines, the issue of rock-falls was the central concern of most of the informants. They reported living in daily fear of fatal, mutilating or disabling accidents. This fear is well-founded. The South African mining industry has been characterised by an alarming accident rate.[3]

[In the following extracts from various interviews the abbreviations 'Inf' (for 'Informant') and 'Int' (for 'Interviewer') have been used.]

Inf 1: Everytime you go underground you have to wear a lamp on your head. Once you take on that lamp you know that you are wearing death. Where you are going you are not sure whether you will come back to the surface alive or dead. It is only with luck if you come to the surface still alive because everyday somebody gets injured or dies.

Int: Do you worry about death from accidents, working underground?

Inf 2:  This thought scares us when something has happened – maybe to a person one knows, or even a person one does not know. You might hear that so-and-so has gone (in an accident) and you think: 'Eish! our brothers are passing away,' that's all. We cannot know, maybe we are also on the way, and we live in hope – and with the knowledge that it will happen to everyone sooner or later. We live for dying, no one lives forever. Every day people lose their arms and legs and we just live in hope.

Many workers have witnessed accidents in which friends and co-workers were either killed or injured, or have seen the dead or injured being brought above the ground after accidents. The stress and distress caused by such incidents cannot be underestimated. The psychologically disabling effects of being subject to life-threatening or shocking incidents are well-documented in the literature on post-traumatic stress. Also well-documented is the fact that while some individuals are able to make a quick recovery, others suffer the after-effects for varying periods of time after an incident. Members of the latter group were amongst our interviewees. They spoke about the classic symptoms of post-traumatic stress disorder: social withdrawal, problems in concentrating, as well as flashbacks or nightmares in which they re-lived the shocking incident. Such flashbacks or nightmares sometimes troubled them for months or even years after an accident. Several informants talked about the disturbances at night caused by the screaming of men suffering nightmares, who would then be woken up and comforted by their room-mates.

Informants referred to accidents in a fatalistic way:

Inf 1:  The rock can just fall anytime and we try not to think about that. A rock can fall and kill someone while you are working with them, it has happened to me before . . . last week someone in my team met his fate that way and we had to pull his corpse from under the stones.

Int:  Are there any religious measures that people take before starting to work?

Inf 1:  No one prays or does such things – because when a rock is going to fall it just falls anytime and there is nothing that can be done about it.

Int:  Is there any form of traditional protection that people seek out – to try to protect themselves against falling rocks?

Catherine Campbell

Inf 2: There are those that seek help from traditional healers for protection, but when the rocks fall, they fall all over, and it does not matter whether you are protected or not – they fall on those with and without the protection.

This sense of powerlessness is an important feature of the contextual backdrop in which miners' sexual identities are negotiated. Self-efficacy (or the degree to which a person feels that she/he has control over important aspects of her/his life) is an important determinant of health-related behaviour. The greater a person's sense of self-efficacy, the more likely that person is to engage in health-promoting behaviours (Bandura 1996).

It was not only in relation to accidents that informants referred to a sense of powerlessness. In the interviews, they repeatedly spoke about their lack of control in a range of contexts. For example, virtually every interviewee said that he hated his job, but that he had no choice given his lack of education, the high levels of unemployment, and the chronic poverty in his rural place of origin.

Int: Is your job easy or difficult?

Inf: The work is heavy but I have endured it because I have no education. It's risky – every time I go down I am not sure if I will come back. But I have no choice. I am forced to do it.

Int: Would you say that this is a source of pride for these men that they do this dangerous and difficult job?

Inf: Facing such struggles is not a source of pride. It is because of frustration and poverty that men do this job.

Many commented on their powerlessness to avoid a range of health problems. Tuberculosis (TB) was one problem mentioned. The incidence of TB on South African gold mines increased from 620 per 100 000 workers per year in 1988, to 1 070 per 100 000 workers per year in 1992 (Packard and Coetzee 1995), so it is a very real concern for mineworkers. One 25-year-old man said that he would inevitably get TB if he stayed on the mines for 20 years, no matter how much he tried to avoid it. A 41-year-old man, who looked considerably older than his years, appeared depressed and apathetic. Telling us about his recurrent bouts of TB he said that he doubted he would ever be in good health again:

Int: Given the situation you working in, are there any attempts that you make to improve your health?

Inf: There is nothing that I try because I don't have that privilege. Where I am living on the mines, I don't have any choice on how to conduct my life, it is imposed on me. Most of my life that I have spent here has not been so fruitful and when I look ahead, I don't see myself having a long life.

Int: Why do you say that?

Inf: Because of my ill health and I don't spend a year without visiting a hospital.

Int: Do you not feel that this negative attitude might encourage you to be lazy about looking after yourself?

Inf: I care about my life very deeply but I can really feel that I am suffering with my health – I feel that my life won't last for much longer, and that due to my working conditions I am prevented from prolonging it.

While people spoke with feeling about frightening working conditions and poor living conditions, they had little faith in their ability to bring about improvements. Complaints to unions or indunas (senior black officials on the mines) seldom bore fruit. As one man commented wryly in response to a question about channels for complaint:

Int: Is there any way you can complain about things you do not like?

Inf: There are several channels for complaints but we are never considered. So, we just complain for the sake of complaining.

One informant commented that the risk of HIV/AIDS appeared minimal compared to the risks of death underground, and suggested that this was the reason why many mineworkers preferred flesh-to-flesh sex:

Int: Why is it that men think about pleasure first before thinking about their health?

Inf: The dangers and risks of the job we are doing are such that no one can afford to be motivated with life – so the only thing that motivates us is pleasure.

These accounts highlight features of the social context within which mineworkers construct their identities. Now let's turn our attention to the interpretative repertoires drawn on by mineworkers in presenting their health-related life histories, with particular emphasis on the role played by masculinity in structuring these accounts.

## Masculinity, sexuality and intimacy

Much has been written about the creative and innovative way in which mineworkers have responded to the alienation and danger of their working lives, constructing personally meaningful identities despite massive social constraints.[4] Particularly evident in the interviews was the way in which masculine identities had been shaped and crafted by workers as a way of dealing with the fears and struggles of their day-to-day working lives.

Men frequently spoke of their terror the first time they entered the 'cage' (lift) that would carry them to their work sites up to three kilometres underground. They recounted how more experienced workers would encourage them by urging them to remember that they were men. A man was someone who had the responsibility of supporting his family and therefore he had no choice but to put up with the risks and stresses of working underground. A man was someone who was brave enough to withstand the rigours of the job:

> Int: How did they console you when you entered the cage?
> Inf: They told me that in this situation you must know that now that you are on the mines you are a man and must be able to face anything without fear.
> Int: Is this theme of being a man common in the mine?
> Inf: To be called a man serves to encourage and console you time and again . . . You will hear people saying 'a man is a sheep, he does not cry'. I mean this is the way to encourage or console you at most times.
> Int: Can you explain more about the metaphor of 'a man being a sheep'?
> Inf: . . . I can explain it this way: no matter how hard you hit a sheep or slaughter it you will not hear it cry. The animal that can cry is a goat. So, that is a comparison that whatever pain you can inflict on a man you will not see him cry.

Thus the notion of manhood plays a key role as a coping mechanism which men use to overcome their daily fears of injury and death as well as the exhausting demands of the work. As one informant told us: 'We commit ourselves as men because if we don't do it our children will suffer.' Another commented:

> You show your manhood by going underground, working in difficult conditions – this shows that you are man enough to accept

that if you die you are just dead. Once you go underground you are a man and no longer a child.

This notion of masculinity brings together the concepts of bravery, fearlessness and persistence in the face of the demands of underground work. Closely intertwined with this is a macho sexuality, which was captured in the comment: 'There are two things to being a man: going underground, and going after women.' Linked to this masculine identity were the repertoires of insatiable sexuality, the need for multiple sexual partners, and a desire for the pleasure of flesh-to-flesh sexual contact.

In response to questions regarding their reluctance to use condoms, informants repeatedly reiterated their desire for flesh-to-flesh contact. When asked specifically about the reasons for this desire, informants referred to pleasure, and also to the fact that this was simply something that men needed. 'A man must have flesh-to-flesh' was something of a cliché in the interviews.

All these are factors that put mineworkers at risk for contracting HIV/ AIDS. Ironically, the very sense of masculinity that assists men in their day-to-day survival also serves to heighten their exposure to the risks of HIV infection.

Int: Why do you think that men have sex on their minds?

Inf: I think that is the way men were made, that is to always have a desire for a woman.

Int: You have a family that you love and support but on the other hand you behave in a way that can make you vulnerable to diseases. Why should men behave like that?

Inf: The truth is that 'a man is a dog' meaning that he does not get satisfied. That is why we come across such things. Because when a man sees 'a dress', meaning a woman, he follows her.

Int: Why do people think about pleasure before they think about their life which is at risk?

Inf: The truth is that we are pushed by desire to have sex with a certain woman. We do not think about AIDS during that time but about it when we are finished. It is a matter of satisfying your body because of someone beautiful. Basically it is the body that has that desire.

Informants made a strong link between sex and masculinity in relation to their general physical and mental health and well-being. Several men commented that sex played a key role in the regulation of a balanced

Catherine Campbell

supply of blood and sperm, and that regular sex was essential for the maintenance of a man's good health. A range of possible ill-effects of poorly regulated bodily fluids resulting from prolonged celibacy were mentioned.

Informants dwelt the most on mental ill-effects: depression, short-temperedness, violence, and an inability to think clearly. Less frequently mentioned were physical ill-effects such as pimples and obesity. Behavioural ill-effects included recklessness and impulsive behaviour. A normally prudent and responsible man who had been celibate for too long might, it was claimed, be unable to control his desire for sex when he encountered a commercial sex worker in the street, even if he did not have a condom with him.

The other side of the coin, the role of women, should also not be ignored. In a companion paper (1998) to this chapter, I provide a detailed account of the way in which the social construction of women's identities militates against condom use by female sex workers selling sex to gold mineworkers, despite the women's fear of HIV infection and their desire to use condoms. Women who are economically dependent on men, and who are socialised to 'over-respect' men, lack the psychological or the material resources to insist on condom use in the face of reluctant clients.

Lengthy celibacy might also lead a man to consider homosexual relationships which he would not have considered in other circumstances. While homosexual relationships in the form of 'mine marriages' were a common feature of life in the mine hostels until the 1970s these are no longer common. Dunbar Moodie (1994) provides a fascinating historical account of the way in which the popularity of such interactions arose, flourished, and later declined, this process being shaped by the changing face of the social and economic contexts of people's lives on the mines and in the countryside. Our own informants echoed Moodie's findings, saying that homosexual relationships were not as common as they had been in the past.

Unrequited sexual urges might also lead a man to take unnecessary risks in the African townships near the mines, by seeking out women whose friends or brothers might beat him up or steal his money.

The continued practice of dangerous sexual behaviours by mineworkers must also be located within a context that provides limited social support and scant opportunities for intimacy. Research in both Europe and America has found a significant correlation between levels of social support and safe sex. Thus, for example, gay men in Norway were far less likely to engage in unprotected sexual intercourse if they lived in a supportive social environment. In conditions where they felt lonely and isolated, flesh-to-flesh sexual contact came to symbolise a form of emotional intimacy that may have been lacking in other areas of their lives (Prieur 1990). Amongst American adolescents, safe sexual behaviour is predicted more by teenagers' perceptions of how much their parents care for them, than by the frequency of health warnings, social class or parents' health status (Mechanic 1990).

This correlation between social support and risk-taking behaviour provides an interesting framework within which to consider the high levels of unsafe sexual behaviour practised amongst mineworkers. Informants spoke at length about the loneliness of being away from their families. They spoke of anxieties that their distant rural wives or girlfriends might be unfaithful; of worries about their children growing up without a father's guidance. They also talked about their own guilt about money they might sent to their families, but instead wasted on drink and commercial sex. These absent families were never far away in their accounts of their lives and their health. Some spoke with dread of fears that they would die underground, and that their bodies might not be returned to their families for proper funeral rites. This was a particularly frightening prospect in a context where deceased ancestors often play a pivotal role in peoples' lives.

While hostel room-mates, underground team-mates, and men from the same home village appeared to constitute support systems in certain contexts, informants were adamant that male friends could not make up for the loss of female partners and children within a homely domestic setting. The youngest of our informants (aged 19), also the most sexually active and least interested in condoms, spoke wistfully of his close relationship with his parents in rural Lesotho. The 41-year-old interviewee referred to earlier who had been plagued by recurrent attacks of TB for five years, ascribed his distance from his wife as one of the main reasons for his poor health: 'There is no one who can help me here and it is quite impossible for me to know all my needs. If I was nearer to my wife, she would take care of me, look after me.'

## Conclusion

Black mineworkers' social and sexual identities are forged in response to the life challenges of the mining context in a manner that makes them particularly vulnerable to HIV infection. In a context where employment is scarce and where mineworkers' earnings support large numbers of people, masculinity is an important coping device. It assists these men in the daily challenge of having to repeatedly place themselves at physical risk in order to earn a living. However, the very concept of masculinity

Catherine Campbell

that enables men to cope with their life-threatening working conditions, simultaneously serves to endanger their sexual health.

The task of changing mineworkers' sexual behaviour, and persuading them to use condoms, for example, cannot be achieved without attention to the broader context of sex and sexuality, including the symbolic role of flesh-to-flesh contact in the face of general loneliness and reduced opportunities for intimate social relationships.

## NOTES

1. Thanks to Social Science and Medicine for permission to use some material from Campbell (1997) in this chapter.
2. See Macheke and Campbell (1998) for a detailed account of the research methodology.
3. Based on the average fatality and reportable injury rates published by the South African Chamber of Mines for the ten-year period 1984 to 1993, an underground worker has a 2,9 per cent chance of being killed in a work-related accident, and a 42 per cent chance of suffering a reportable injury in a twenty-year working life (Chamber of Mines 1993).
4. Sitas (1985) has written of the 'defensive combinations' of rural, urban and protest identities that mineworkers have creatively integrated in the task of dealing with the day-to-day stresses and indignities of their lives. Moodie (1994) speaks of the 'integrity' and 'character' of such coping mechanisms.
5. See Moodie elsewhere in this collection for more on this topic.

## BIBLIOGRAPHY

Bandura, A. 1996. *Self-efficacy in changing societies*. Cambridge: Cambridge University Press.

Campbell, C. 1995. 'The social identity of township youth (part 1): An extension of social identity theory', *South African Journal of Psychology* 25(3).

————. 1997. 'Migrancy, masculine identities and AIDS: The psychosocial context of HIV transmission on the South African gold mines', *Social Science and Medicine* 45(2).

————. 1998. 'Representations of gender, respectability and commercial sex in the shadow of AIDS: A South African case study', *Social Science Information* 37(4).

Chamber of Mines. 1993. *Statistical Tables 1993*. Johannesburg: Chamber of Mines.

Hunt, C. 1989. 'Migrant labour and sexually transmitted disease: AIDS in Africa', *Journal of Health and Social Behaviour* 30(4).

Jochelson, K., M. Mothibeli and J-P. Leger. 1991. 'Human immunodeficiency virus and migrant labour in South Africa', *International Journal of Health Services* 21(1).

Leon, The Hon R., A. Davies, M. Salamon and J. Davies. 1995. *Commission of inquiry into safety and health in the mining industry*. Pretoria: Department of Mineral and Energy Affairs.

Macheke, C. and C. Campbell. 1998. 'Perceptions of health on a Johannesburg gold mine', *South African Journal of Psychology* 28(3).

Mechanic, D. 1990. 'Promoting health', *Society* January/February.

Molapo, M. 1995. 'Job stress, health and perceptions of migrant mineworkers'. In J. Crush and W. James, eds., *Crossing boundaries: mine migrancy in a democratic South Africa*. Cape Town: Creda.

Moodie, T.D. 1994. *Going for Gold: Men, Mines and Migration*. Johannesburg: Witwatersrand University Press.

Packard, R. and D. Coetzee. 1995. 'White plague: black labour revisited: TB and the mining industry'. In: Crush and James, eds., *Crossing boundaries: mine migrancy in a democratic South Africa*. Cape Town: Creda.

Prieur, A. 1990. 'Norwegian gay men: reasons for the continued practice of unsafe sex', *AIDS Education and Prevention* 2(2).

Sitas, A. 1985. 'From grassroots control to democracy: a case study of the impact of trade unionism on migrant workers' cultural formations', *Social Dynamics* 11(1).

Williams, B. 1999. 'The Carletonville Baseline Survey: age prevalence by housing type and gender'. Unpublished mimeo, Mothusimpilo Project Evaluation. Johannesburg: Council for Scientific and Industrial Research.

CHAPTER 16

# Mkhumbane and New Traditions of (Un)African Same-Sex Weddings[1]

RONALD LOUW

## Introduction

More than twenty years ago in a village some distance from Durban in KwaZulu-Natal a young African man by the name of S'bu got married in front of a small circle of friends. What made this otherwise everyday event unusual was that, firstly, he was marrying another man, secondly, the wedding took place in the home of the local Methodist minister, and thirdly, he was marrying the minister! S'bu, a waiter living in Pinetown told me the story as follows:

> When I was 18 years old (in about 1972) the minister called me to stay behind in church one Sunday to count the collection. After everyone had gone he called me into the vestry and told me that he liked me very much and wanted me to be his wife. I was shocked at first but I also liked him. He was about 55 at the time. He had a four-roomed house in the township and I used to spend a lot of time there looking after him and the house. I used to cook and clean and was very happy. After a couple of years he said we must get married. We then had a big party where we invited about 20 guests who were living the same type of life as we were. I had to cook all day for the party in the evening but I had a bridesmaid to help me. Then I got dressed in white: white trousers and a white shirt with big cuffs and I also carried some flowers. I had many necklaces on as well. One of the older people in the church, an old man who was also gay, married us. He also made a speech and said a prayer. We had a wedding cake and people brought presents for me. I also had a wedding ring.

The story of S'bu is one of the many fascinating episodes that I stumbled across in my study of the unresearched history of same-sex desire among African men in KwaZulu-Natal. In this chapter I trace back the origins of the wedding to a moment and a place (Mkhumbane, near Durban), and I argue that specific circumstances made possible new and public expressions of sexuality amongst African men.

It is impossible to talk of homosexual identity in South Africa as a single stable entity (De Vos 1996). Rather, a variety of homosexual identities have been and still are produced by a set of power relations within the contexts of neo-colonialism, capitalist development, and racial domination. Within these same relations constructions of masculinities have been forged. Homophobia frequently prevented the emergence of alternate masculinities, but it was not all-pervasive or uniform. In specific circumstances and communities homosexual identities could and did emerge. The new spaces of desire had a powerful liberatory capacity for masculine identities.

Contrary to dominant images of African masculinity, there emerged in Mkhumbane a thriving and celebrated identity of same-sex relationships. This was unusual in the context of the times and owed much to the structure of Mkhumbane. Epstein argues:

> [W]ithin any ethnic group there is a range of ways of being a man or a woman, from those who are heavily invested in the dominant ethnically or racially marked form to those whose identities are constructed in opposition to dominant forms in a variety of ways (gay masculinities in all groups, for example).   (1998: 52)

With regard to African men, Kopano Ratele argues that there is no 'coherent and stable black manhood'. Rather, there have always have been 'queer and straight black men, modern and traditional black men, professional black men and unskilled black men' (1998: 62).

## New masculinities in Mkhumbane

The origins of Mkhumbane, on the fringes of the port city of Durban, can be traced back to the mid-1940s. The land, hilly and fertile, was agricultural and owned largely by Indian market gardeners. Some African-owned cattle herds also grazed on the land. Throughout South Africa Africans left their rural farmsteads in search of employment in the rapidly growing white towns and cities. Although it was largely the men that left the farms for the towns, the gender composition of African settlements in Durban was nothing like that of the single-sex mine compounds. In the case of the latter, the men were migrants, while in the former the men were relocating to the city even if they may have retained a farmstead in the countryside and left behind a wife and family. In 1944, Mkhumbane consisted of only 27 shacks but by 1948 its population had reached approximately 29 000 people. Although some of the inhabitants had moved to Mkhumbane from elsewhere in Durban, the vast majority had been in the city less than five months (Edwards 1989: 57).

The residents of Mkhumbane were quick to assert their new proletarian consciousness to the point of militant rebellion. In Durban, the African National Congress, the Natal Indian Congress and the South African Communist Party were all active. A government official noted, albeit paternalistically, that politically Mkhumbane 'was a melting pot for any number of agitators, self-appointed leaders, grafters, cliques and factions'. The militancy of the inhabitants erupted in rioting in 1949 and in 1959. Even by 1952 Mkhumbane 'was a virtual no-man's land' for government officials. Socially new opportunities were developing. It was a 'hotbed of prostitution' and 'every imaginable vice or illicit undertaking' (Edwards 1989: 12). The unstable but dynamic society of Mkhumbane was a fertile ground for new identities of challenge. These were asserted, established and even accommodated.

One of the people who moved to Durban was a man by the name of Khumalo, then in his early thirties. Shortly thereafter he was introduced to the homosexual community living in Mkhumbane beneath the affluent, white, hilltop suburb of Berea. The community was divided into the gendered stereotypes of *iqenge* and *isikhesana*. The former term as used in Mkhumbane in the 1950s refers to men who adopt a male homosexual gender, or who are the 'active' participants in sexual relations. This is a term still occasionally used today and has retained its specific gender reference. *Isikhesana* describes men who adopt a female homosexual gender. The term is still used today but its meaning has changed in that it may now be gender neutral.[2]

The *iqenge* and *isikhesana* of Mkhumbane were concentrated in the section known as Esinmanyeni or Place of Darkness, so named for its lack of street lighting. The spirited character of Khumalo soon provided a leader for the *isikhesana* and *iqenge* and he later moved to the area, building a wood and iron hall in Esinmanyeni for *isikhesana* and *iqenge* celebrations. In using the tradition of Zulu dancing, Khumalo organised the *isikhesana* into dressing up as Zulu maidens so they could openly celebrate their sexuality.

The act of dressing up and dancing in traditional women's clothing by African men was not confined to the 1950s. Similar participation in dances seems to have a long history. Moodie (1988: 231) notes that in 1916 a mine compound manager reported that he had 'recently seen heavily scented young Mozambicans at a dance "wearing imitation breasts"'. Khumalo also refers to a man much older than himself who had participated in such dances:

> When I first came to Durban, I stayed in Botanic Gardens. Also staying there was an old man, Alfred Mkhize, a big *isitabane*, like a king or a chairman of the gays. He stayed in the backyard of Mrs Cohen's house. Everybody came to him and phoned him there. Mrs Cohen knew what Alfred was because he also worked in the house. She would take his calls and so knew about us. Mrs Cohen was also my friend. We used to dress up in Alfred's room with skins and titties and go to Mkhumbane by car. Mrs Cohen is dead now. Alfred is also dead.

Typically a wedding would start on a Saturday afternoon and invited *isikhesana* and *iqenge* would attend a night of partying in the hall which could take up to one hundred people. The wedding ceremony would commence on the Sunday afternoon, after everybody had slept off the effects of the previous night's party. The wedding ceremony could follow the style of a traditional Zulu wedding with the husband and wife wearing customary attire. In later years, Western styled weddings also took place with the husband wearing a suit and the wife a white dress and veil accompanied by her bridesmaids. The traditional wedding would include the slaughtering of a goat to feed the guests. A member of the Esinmanyeni community would act as the *induna*, or tribal elder, in order to perform the marriage ceremony which would take place outdoors. The rest of the Mkhumbane community would be welcome, sometimes attracting several hundred people who would be offered food and beer. Weddings occurred approximately monthly for at least ten years up until 1961 when the government's apartheid policy brought about the destruction of Mkhumbane.

Marital bliss did not always follow the wedding. If accommodation could be found, the new couple might live together with the newly-wed wife having to perform all domestic chores for her husband. Some marriages lasted, some did not. In other instances, after the weddings, the husband and wife returned to their respective families perhaps only seeing each other over weekends, a situation not uncommon for heterosexual African couples, where the wife might be a live-in domestic worker at her employer's residence. But it was also possible that either the *isikhesana* or *iqenge* or both were already married and would return home to their respective spouses after the wedding!

Interesting forms of polygamy also arose in Mkhumbane. A common form was one where the *iqenge* was married to a woman who might still live on the family farm. But when she came to town, she might meet her husband's *isikhesana* wife. The latter was usually considered the second or junior wife and would need to show respect and deference to the senior wife in order to gain her respect. While the *isikhesana* wife might be dressed up to look like a woman, and might in fact pass unnoticed by some as a woman, if the female wife knew of this, she kept quiet, now in deference to her husband.

The second form of polygamy was in the instance where an *iqenge* would take on more than one *isikhesana* wife. This, according to Khumalo, was an institution he introduced. According to him, some *iqenge* were not being faithful to their *isikhesana* wives but were indulging in secret relationships outside of marriage. Realising that that it would be futile to enforce monogamy, the unfaithfulness was institutionalised in polygamy!

The responses of the Mkhumbane community to the homosexual community in general and the weddings in particular varied from enjoyment to derision, but not to harassment. This instead came from the police who sometimes raided the dancing ceremonies fining the *isikhesana* two rand each for dressing in women's clothing. Khumalo sought the legal advice of an attorney, Wiggins, and obtained official permission to organise Zulu dancing through the then Bantu Affairs Office in Durban (at KwaMuhle). The official, one Anderson, who forwarded the request to Pretoria apparently knew that the dances were a disguise for the weddings and same-sex parties and supported Khumalo's application. Rather than being remarkably progressive, he apparently would rather have had somebody in charge of the occasion than not. However, the Durban Municipality also benefited financially. Visitors and apparently also tourists would be charged 25 cents to attend the dances held in the hall. The Municipality then collected half the proceeds. Thus it is not surprising that when Mkhumbane was demolished and the inhabitants relocated to the apartheid-created dormitory towns of Umlazi and KwaMashu, the Municipality offered Khumalo the opportunity of rebuilding his hall in one of these towns.

My recounting here of events some forty years ago is not an unproblematic retelling of those events. Time, memory, language, and culture have all impinged on the process. No written or photographic documentation of the events exists of which I am aware. Little work has been done by any other researchers. Much of my information comes from Khumalo, who is now well into his eighties. His English is not fluent and much of my interviews were done via an interpreter. Some things I may have misunderstood, some he may have embellished. The generalisations should also be approached cautiously. All these interruptions necessarily distort the narrative. There has, however, been some corroboration by other informants.

Given the paucity of resources and relative lack of corroboration of the above, the account needs to be treated with some caution. For example, Edwards (1989) suggests that the homosexual community (he refers to the *izitabane*) was divided into three hierarchical groups: 'professional homo-sexuals' or *ungqingili* at the apex, followed by lovers coming from domestic workers (or kitchen boys), and finally lithe, young stevedores who also took the role of lovers. I found no reference to the above, but rather only a gendered hierarchy of *iqenge* and *isikhesana*. Here Edwards's sources of evidence may constitute part of the problem.

A number of terms are used by Africans to describe same-sex desire. The meanings of these terms are neither fixed nor do they have uncon-tested English translations. The term 'gay' with its Western origin is both culturally and historically specific and cannot be uncritically used to describe same-sex desire among Africans. Although the term has been appropriated by Africans and is currently used widely, it may only be a poor translation of some of the terms indicated below and not always appropriate. Some terms may either be known generally to Zulu speakers as part of the formally recognised Zulu language and other terms belong to a homosexual argot (referred to as *isingqumo* from the Zulu word *ukungqumuza* meaning 'to speak quietly so that others about do not hear of important matters'). Terms generally known include *isitabane* which is a derogatory word (except where it has been appropriated by those whom it describes). It refers to men who are effeminate in manner and who may or may not prefer sexual relations with other men. It is also used to refer to hermaphrodites as does the more specific, archaic and also derogatory term *ungqingili*. (It is a commonly held myth among heterosexual Af-ricans that homosexuals are hermaphrodites).

As both the terms *isitabane* and *ungqingili* are derogatory, Edwards's information might have come from outside the homosexual community. It would appear, perhaps, from his hierarchy that the *ungqingili* are the *iqenge* and the domestic workers and stevedores the *isikhesana*. Why the former should be considered 'professional homosexuals' is unclear. Finally, it was reported to me that domestic workers could comprise either *iqenge* or *isikhesana*. Perhaps we might only, but importantly, conclude that any attempt to impose too rigid a structure will fail to take account of the fluid nature of the social sexual relations in Mkhumbane in the 1950s. This might also question the gendered and oppressive hierarchy that I have suggested, except that the latter would be a reflection of existing social relations and therefore more likely to have been recreated by the homosexual community.

## Same-sex marriage in South Africa and constructions of desire

The episode of same-sex marriages in the 1950s between African men that I recount here is built on a history going back to at least the end of the nineteenth century. In the context of this chapter, the term 'marriage' is employed to refer to same-sex relationships that have appropriated to varying extents the discourse of marriage. The first recorded incidents occurred amongst a gang known as the Ninevites. The gang originated as a band of brigands operating in the hills south of Johannesburg but later spread to Zululand. With inevitable convictions following their criminal activities, the gang also began operating in the prisons under the name of the 28s. Under the leadership of Nongoloza, born in Zululand in 1867, the gang openly engaged in sodomy. It was in the prisons that the discourse of marriage became institutionalised. Gang members were divided into two groups, the fighters and the wives or 'wyfies'. It was this practice of taking wives that primarily distinguished the 28s from other gangs. Achmat (1993) points out that 'The Ninevites are the only prison gang in South Africa who consciously adopt homosexuality as a creed, and who have a set of laws governing their sexual relations' (99). The 'wyfies' are, however, not only sexual partners who are protected from other gangs, but are also subject to the domestic drudgery of marriage of having to wash and care for their fighters.

The same-sex sexual practices of the gang have been disingenuously explained away by various social historians. Haysom (1981) argues, 'The practice of sodomy is not perhaps so strange given the institutions and laws which kept men in all-male institutions and excluded women from the cities' (3). Likewise, Van Onselen (1984) comments:

> Pointing to all women as the source of the 'poison' of venereal disease, the 'King of Nineveh' [Nongoloza] instructed his troops to abstain from all physical contact with members of the opposite sex. Instead the older men of marriageable age within the regiment – the *ikhela* – were to take younger male initiates in the gang – the *abafana* – and keep them as *izinkotshane*, 'boy-wives'. (15)

However, as Achmat points out, Van Onselen significantly fails to refer to the recorded statement of Nongoloza: 'Even when we were free on the hills south of Johannesburg some of us had women and others had young men for sexual purposes' (1993: 99).

Other recorded incidents of same-sex marriage among African men occurred on the gold mines. Towards the end of the nineteenth century South Africa developed a booming gold mining industry located initially in the city of Johannesburg. Through a process of various land acts the South African peasantry was forced off the land into wage labour on the mines. Movement to the cities was, however, regulated through influx control laws. Only men with labour contracts were allowed into the cities. Furthermore, they were compelled to stay in single-sex hostels or compounds on the mines and were allowed little freedom of movement. It was in the compounds that there developed the practice of what has become known as 'mine marriages'. Moodie records that the men or husbands were older men with mine experience who would take a young, new recruit to be their wives. As with the prison 'wyfies', the wives were not merely sexual partners but would also carried out domestic chores for their 'hubbies'.

Why did homosexual relations in Mkhumbane take on such an unusual form? The answers are to be found in locating the episode in its historical context. For decades prior to these events, Africans in South Africa had been subjected to European colonial expansion and land dispossession. Traditional lifestyles were severely disrupted, and a relatively stable peasantry was forced into wage labour both on white-owned farms and in the cities. In the latter very little of a once more autonomous life remained. Achmat points out that early accounts of same-sex desire among Africans did not develop the notion of a discontinuity giving rise to new sexual practices. He views the emergence of new homosexual practices as ruptures of former social formations which created new historical possibilities and produced new discourses of masculinity. These discourses had their own rules of formation. Achmat argues further that 'the compound represented a new space of desire and that it fostered a number of practices, including male homosexuality – practices which irrevocably disrupted social relations in the countryside. In terms of the appropriation of pleasure in the body, a new freedom was created' (1993: 106). Could Mkhumbane too represent 'a new space of desire'?

## Conclusion

With the forced removals by the nationalist government in the 1950s and 60s the people of Mkhumbane were scattered into far-flung apartheid townships. Although shebeens and other informal structures developed in these townships, nothing as cohesive as Mkhumbane emerged. The demise of racially based group areas in the late 1980s created inner city spaces for black homosexual men and women, freeing them from the confinements of the townships.

The weddings documented in this chapter have not ceased. Durban is still nationally identified as the place (though not exclusively) of black gay weddings. Although with less frequency, these continue today and have developed further interesting forms including inter-racial and lesbian weddings.

The break-up of apartheid in the 1980s and the creation of a democratic society in the 1990s produced the political and social space for new expressions of sexuality and constructions of masculinity. In 1990 South Africa's first Gay Pride Parade was held through the streets of Hillbrow in Johannesburg. Significantly the Parade was organised by the late Simon Nkoli and the organisation he led, the predominantly black Soweto-based Gay and Lesbian Organisation of the Witwatersrand.

The growing public display and wider acceptance of homosexuality culminated in 1994 in an explicit constitutional prohibition of discrimination on the ground of sexual orientation. This has again created a space for new identities to emerge. It is in this inclusive space that the government could appoint an openly gay man, Edwin Cameron, to be a judge of the High Court and enable gays and lesbians to rally and organise under the banner of the National Coalition for Gay and Lesbian Equality. The Coalition has been able to shift gays and lesbians from racially restrictive organisations to an inclusive movement that has as one of its founding aims the development of a black and lesbian leadership. The transformed nature of gay and lesbian politics in South Africa was most evident when, in 1998, the usually quiet Constitutional Court was packed with enthusiastic and predominantly black gays and lesbians who came to hear the triumphant decriminalisation of gay sex. The confidence and energy of the gay and lesbian movement challenges existing, narrow and prescriptive ideas of what it means to be a man. This may result in a more tolerant society where men can choose their identities with greater freedom than ever before.

NOTES

1. This chapter is dedicated to Philani Nyanisa.
2. The origin of the word is unclear and has no other meaning in Zulu. In Nanda's study of *hijras* in India, he refers to the term *zenana* describing 'effeminate males who are assumed to play the passive role in homosexual relationships'. The homophonic similarity between *zenana* and *isikhesana* (pronounced s'kesana) is obvious. What makes the similarity in meaning more intriguing is that Durban is also the home to a large Indian population who originally came to South Africa as indentured labourers and later immigrants, many of whom lived in the racially mixed Mkhumbane. In some Hindu weddings held in Durban (also in the 1950s) men dressed in Indian female clothing gave performances. Whether the men were *hijras* or *zenana* or otherwise is uncertain. The possibility, however, is that *isikhesana* has its etymological roots in the term *zenana*.

BIBLIOGRAPHY

Achmat, Z. 1993. '"Apostles of Civilised Vice": "Immoral Practices" and "Unnatural Vice" in South African Prisons and Compounds, 1890–1920', *Social Dynamics* 19.

De Vos, P. 1996. 'On the Legal Construction of Gay and Lesbian Identity and South Africa's Transitional Constitution', *South African Journal on Human Rights* 12.

Edwards, I. 1989. 'Mkhumbane: Our Home: African Shantytown Society in Cato Manor, 1946–1960'. Unpublished Ph.D. thesis. Durban: University of Natal.

Epstein, D. 1998. 'Marked Men: Whiteness and Masculinity', *Agenda* 37.

Haysom, N. 1981. *Towards an Understanding of Prison Gangs*. Cape Town: Institute of Criminology, University of Cape Town.

Moodie, T.D. 1988. 'Migrancy and male sexuality on the South African gold mines', *Journal of Southern African Studies* 14(2).

Nanda, S. 1993. 'Hijras as Neither Man Nor Woman'. In H. Abelove, M.A. Borale and Halprin, eds., *The Lesbian and Gay Studies Reader*. New York: Routledge.

Ratele, K. 1998. 'The End of the Black Man', *Agenda* 37.

Van Onselen, C. 1984. *'The Small Matter of a Horse': The Life of 'Nongoloza Mathebula 1869–1948*. Johannesburg: Ravan Press.

# CHAPTER 17

# Black Migrant Mine Labourers and the Vicissitudes of Male Desire

T. DUNBAR MOODIE

## Introduction

In 1982, Vivienne Ndatshe, who had been collecting life histories as a research assistant for my wife's Ph.D. in psychology, returned to her home in Pondoland in the eastern Transkei. Since her father had been a mine-worker, I suggested that she might collect life histories for me there. Six weeks later, she sent me forty extraordinary accounts of men's lives. Fifteen of them contained material on what would nowadays be called 'homosexuality'.[1] These Mpondo life histories marked the beginning of a remarkable joint research effort which continues today. I have myself been to Pondoland and have tramped the hills with Ms Ndatshe, who has served as interpreter for dozens of interviews with ex-mineworkers in which they cheerfully confirmed her initial accounts of sexual relations on the mines, their friendships with their age-peers, their relationships with women and their deep commitment to rural life-worlds. As I listened to the stories of these old men about youthful experiences, I found myself contrasting them to my own schoolboy experiences. These included my terror of erotic violence, my gratitude that I was not a boarder and hence subject to sexual assault by senior boys, and my closeness to a couple of boys (and my slightly younger brother) whose fellowship I still remember as much more meaningfully 'loving' than the girls whom I objectified romantically, narcissistically, and (usually without practical success) exploitatively.

I grew up voraciously reading Rudyard Kipling, John Buchan, G.A. Henty, A.E. Marshall and other middle class celebrations of imperial responsibility. I have been struck by the contrast, despite their common patriarchal assumptions, between the tortuous and incipiently violent (against both self and others) psychological justifications set forth by

Kipling and his successors for the British colonial order and the unem-
barrassed straightforwardness of discussions Vivienne Ndatshe and I had
with traditional South African migrants about sexuality. Indeed, this African material casts serious doubt on the universality of Freudian models
that usually inform discussions of sexual desire. That is the theme of this
chapter – to cast light on the emotional integrity of traditional South
African migrancy (and on the implications of its disappearance) and to
evoke more general scholarly discussion on the social structuring of male
desire.[2]

## Masculinity and desire: the 'ruling passion' in the West

In his brilliant critique of liberalism, Roberto Unger (1975) argues that an
antinomy between reason and desire is central to modern Western thought.
Desire is seen to be arbitrary and beyond the control of reason. Such an
assumption is implicit in Freud's distinction between the pleasure principle and the reality principle and is fundamental to a long Western
tradition about sexuality that Foucault (1997: 121–280) has traced back
to late pagan antiquity as well as Christianity. Here I shall focus attention
on the late Victorian and Edwardian period which is in many ways
archetypal for contemporary Western masculinity.

With enormous industry, Ronald Hyam (1990) provides multiple
examples of how in British imperialist practice 'desire' frequently overwhelmed 'reason'. Lane (1995) theorises this tension along Lacanian lines.
British imperialism saw itself on a civilising mission, to bring reason, to
establish legal order and to replace despotic barbarism with the rule of
resolute masculine integrity. In the words of imperial administrator, James
Fitzjames Stephen:

> The sum and substance of what we have to teach them [amounts
> to] the gospel of the English. . . . It is a compulsory gospel which
> admits of no dissent and no disobedience. . . . If it should lose its
> essential unity of purpose, and fall into hands either weak or
> unfaithful, chaos would come again like a flood.   (Lane 1995: 16)

Precisely because they so deeply feared the seductiveness of their self-
indulgent (implicitly feminine and erotic) subjects, the administrators of
Empire could brook no unmanly weakness in their ranks. The British
imperial economy of desire was structured firmly upon a conception of
masculine integrity, and respect for reason and order (forcibly imposed),
encapsulated in social networks of closely bonded white men. Eroticism
was vehemently eschewed in this ethic, but it always haunted the imperial

mission. Lane (1995: 19) quotes Kipling: 'There are many lies in the world, and not a few liars, but there are no liars like our bodies, except it be the sensations of our bodies.' Homophobic anxiety shadowed these male exemplars of imperial order, as did fears of going native.

Freud distinguished between the aim of an instinct and its object. Instincts aim for satisfaction, but their objects are social and variable. Sexual desire finds satisfaction in available and socially acceptable objects whose identities are not necessarily fixed:

> In all of us, throughout life, the libido normally oscillates between male and female objects; the bachelor gives up his men friends when he marries, and returns to club-life when married life has lost its savour. (1963[1920]: 144)

It should thus not surprise us that the 'ruling passion' of the sexually segregated colonial ruling class, even when repressed entirely, tended to homoeroticism, especially when we consider the public school self-formation of most of these men.

Central to the ideology of public schools was commitment to manly love, 'passing the love of women', which institutionalised the tradition of 'strong non-sexual male friendships' so typical of upper middle class male club-life that Freud himself took for granted. Precisely because sexual aims are so variable and because in such circles men were the available sexual objects, while 'close noble friendships' were encouraged in public schools, 'beastliness' or 'unnatural vice' was equally adamantly proscribed with homophobic zeal (Richards 1987). The asexual integrity of men's friendships in this sort of social world would always be haunted by the spectre of homoeroticism. Structures of seniority (the prefect system) combined in public schools to exacerbate the tensions of this economy of desire, which was reproduced all over the Empire.

## 'Women with manhood' and male mine migration in South Africa[3]

For more than a century, migration to work on the South African gold mines has been the employment of choice for African men living in rural reserves with access to land. Migrant mineworkers lived in single-sex compounds, barracked together from eight to fifty to a room, away from their homes for months and often years at a time. Despite the violence and danger of the work (Breckenridge 1998) and the low wages, men who would inherit rights to an *umzi* (a rural homestead) preferred mining. In the early years of mine migration, cattle advances from mine recruiters (Beinart 1979) enabled young Mpondo men to make downpayments on their *lobola* (bridewealth payment) before leaving for work. Although mine wages were very low, the free food and accommodation enabled workers to accumulate cash which was paid out to them in a lump sum upon their return home.

Over the whole history of South African gold mining, the most continuous sources of migrant labour have been the Portuguese colony of Mozambique (whence came workers who were lumped together as 'Shangaans' on the mines and who worked the longest contracts), the mountains of the land-locked kingdom of Lesotho, and the Xhosa-speaking Transkei (especially Pondoland in the east which maintained its agricultural integrity much longer than western Transkei).[4] As long as homestead agriculture was possible in these areas, the survival of African kinship systems (however much transformed by migrancy) confirmed the masculine status of those who chose oscillating migration.

Kenelm Burridge (1969: 114) points out that for Melanesian men migrating to the white areas to work for money created irreconcilable contradictions:

> In the indigenous prestige systems of Melanesia, only mature men could have any influence. But when money appeared the young had the readiest access to it through their labour, and they could outbid their seniors. On the other hand, when a young man settled down and married he re-entered the traditional prestige system and could no longer earn money. . . Either [men] could return to their villages and become men of stature in traditional terms without the aid of money, or they could remain in the European settled areas, with money, and be considered men of small account.

For African men on the South African gold mines, participation in the migrant system overcame this dilemma, but it did so only because, despite undoubted generational tensions, the exchange of women through the bridewealth system redistributed wealth upward across the generations. Over several generations the traditional prestige system in which men exchanged bridewealth cattle earned by the labour of their own homesteads (Guy 1990) was modified to incorporate proceeds from migrant labour. Because older men controlled access to land, however, the young men could not 'outbid' their seniors, although households became more 'nuclear' as young men took on more responsibilities over the years. Young men were obliged to delay the gratifications of patriarchy until well into their maturity, but in the end they could look forward to the pleasures of seniority in an indigenous prestige system rooted in conceptions of mature manhood. Such manhood was manifested in just and generous homestead proprietorship, maintained by the labour of women and children and funded by cattle payments from a new generation of young men working on the mines.

Mpondo men maintained their commitment to the rural prestige system by importing to the mine compounds (conveniently insulated from the temptations of town) varieties of indigenous networks and practices which traditionally integrated them into rural society at home (Beinart 1991). Such networks, already homosocial, were modified on the mines in response to new exigencies such as the absence of young women and the influences of urban life, but they continued to maintain the commitment of young men to the rural life-world, and they bridged the cultural gap between mine and country life.[5]

Traditionally, young men and boys had always spent days away from home herding cattle. There, according to Coplan, for the Basotho (1995: 96–7):

> Older boys school the younger in rugged self-defence, stoic endurance, one-upmanship in securing the best grazing spots, hunting for wild rodents and edible plants, locating lost (and stolen) animals, and overall animal husbandry. . . . Their sport is the ancient martial art of stick-fighting. . . . Herding is regarded as a fundamental experience in the process of male socialization, inculcating comradeship and self-reliance, stoicism and aggressiveness, responsibility and independence, cooperation and wildness.

The same certainly applied to Mpondo mine migrants. As with public schools for British colonial officials, so herding prepared African youngsters for *their* migrant mission, to go to the mines in order to ensure manhood at home. However, traditional Xhosa youth cultures did not totally exclude women, unlike single-sex British schools, nor were they asexual. Young women joined the herdboys for all-night parties in the hills, where they danced and sang and where they practised *ukumetsha*, ejaculation by rubbing between the thighs, which both avoided pregnancy and assured sexual release, at least for the men (Mayer 1970).[6] Sex with penetration was reserved for marriage. Missionaries and their Christian converts were scandalised,[7] but, as traditionalists loved to point out, conversion to Christianity meant that young women got pregnant.

Country wives had always been important in a practical as well as a sexual and symbolic sense because without women the building of the homestead – and hence manhood itself – would have been impossible.

Exchange of women (and the children they would eventually bear) was also exchange of labour units (Guy 1990). Increasingly, as men were obliged to migrate to the mines during their early married years, and homesteads became more nuclear, women also began to take on typical male responsibilities for homestead administration. Women had always organised labour. Now, in the absence of their husbands, they were also obliged to settle disputes and distribute resources. In symbolic terms, a range of adjustments of basic notions of masculinity became necessary.

In our interviews in Pondoland with ex-miners (men who had worked on the mines during the 1940s, 50s and 60s), Ms Ndatshe and I asked them about the meaning of the Xhosa word *ubudoda*, usually translated as 'manhood'. Despite the Mpondo's reputation for belligerence on the mines, all the Mpondo men to whom we spoke denied that *ubudoda* had anything to do with warrior prowess. Instead, they said that *ubudoda*, the essence of manhood, had to do with competent and benevolent management of the homestead, aiding in homestead decision-making, settling disputes, and generous sharing of homestead resources with guests and neighbours. A second meaning referred to consistency, staying-power, strength in remaining true to one's purposes and in solidarity with friends and neighbours, although in the country that meaning was subsidiary to the broader idea of building up and administering the homestead which constituted the essence of manhood. On the mines, men migrated to work to earn wages which would enable them to 'build the homestead', but there they were subjected to all sorts of temptations to depart from truly manly ways and become *tshipa* (absconders), 'those who fail to return', so that the notion of male integrity as steadfastness was firmly emphasised and reinforced in close 'homeboy' networks.

Most interesting, however, was the men's response to the question of whether women could have *ubudoda*. Virtually all the retired miners to whom we spoke said that a woman could have *ubudoda*, although *ubufazi*, womanhood, was most proper for her. Since these non-circumcising Mpondo defined manhood morally rather than ritually, this was a logical inference. Sometimes, they explained, a woman would have *ubudoda* when the migrant male was away from home. They denied, however, that a man could have womanhood, except in an explicitly metaphorical sense that implied cowardice. In speaking of female 'manhood' traditional Mpondo men were not denying male power in the last instance. Migrant cultures clearly brought to the fore, however, the conception of male-female partnership which was always embedded in the notion of 'building the homestead'. This became obvious as the homestead became more nuclear. During the years of intensive Mpondo mine migration, women were left in charge, in fact if not formally, when married men left for the mines. If notions of 'maleness' necessarily imply 'femaleness' (however repressed or denied), in Mpondo migrant cultures awareness of the term's complementarity was very close to the surface. The conception of manhood that formed the basis of migrant cultures made no sense without a woman left at home building the homestead and presiding over it in the absence of the man. The migrant system modified patriarchal power and representations of manhood at the same time that it stressed the ambiguity of male-female complementarity.

For English public school boys sent out in the colonial service, any such suggestion of gender ambiguity would have been shocking. If Kipling believed that: 'East is East and West is West and never the twain shall meet,' he was equally sure that men were men and women women. The imperial mission was 'men's work'. Women, for Kipling, were a dangerous distraction from 'the austere love that springs up between men who have tugged at the same oar together and are yoked by custom and use and the intimacies of toil' (Lane 1995: 21). Home, which for Mpondo men justified and sustained their migratory mission and yoked them to 'women with manhood', in the colonial ideal always represented a temptation for men to abandon their civilising quest. Home, linked by Victorian and Edwardian Englishmen with femininity, had to be eschewed with fierce resolve, even as ideal Englishwomen, entirely other, presided over a completely other world than men. For all the hardships of traditional Bantu-speaking herdboys, growing up with cattle and toughness far from the *umzi*, but also playfully (and often roughly) 'proposing love to girls' there is nothing like the Victorian gendered separation of spheres. Indeed, especially with the coming of migrant labour, as we have seen, men and women needed each other. Migrant marriage as Coplan (1994) nicely puts it, was 'a crucial and precarious partnership'. The *umzi* gave meaning to traditional patterns of migration. What then of erotic desire?

## Men as other men's wives

An important aspect of the economy of African male desire on the mines was a set of practices by which young men on the mine compounds would become the 'wives' of more senior men, providing them with both domestic and sexual services in exchange for substantial and regular monetary rewards. One old Mpondo in 1982 was quite open with Vivienne Ndatshe about his affairs on the mines:

> There were *boss boys* who liked boys. I did that once myself. There were boys who looked like women – fat and attractive. My 'girl-

friend' was a Sotho young lad. I did not ill-treat him as other *boss boys* did. I was very nice to him.

He smiled while talking to Ms Ndatshe about this matter and asked her not to tell others at his home. She promised not to and asked him why he got involved with the boy. He replied:

> I felt very lonely for all the long period without meeting a woman. Because of boredom I needed someone to be with me. I was not doing that in public – not in the room but in the old section underground where people no longer worked. I proposed love to him in the compound – called on him in our spare time. I did promise to give him some of my pay, but not all of it as others did. Then he agreed. I warned him that everything was our secret because I did not want my home friends to know that I was doing that as they might tell people at home or girlfriends in the country. I loved that boy very much.

Ms Ndatshe asked whether the Sotho youngster didn't have feelings himself when they slept together. The response was revealing about the 'men's' expectations of 'women': 'He had quick feelings, but he had to control himself as he was my girlfriend.'

The type of sexual activity in these relationships on the mines corresponded to *ukumetsha*. Although these relationships for the Mpondo seldom extended beyond one contract and were never brought home ('it was only friendship on the mines'), and although Mpondo men preferred to conceal these liaisons from their home fellows, everyone knew that such affairs existed and joked with each other about them. According to Ms Ndatshe, old men, long since retired from the mines, sit around at beer drinks in Pondoland and talk of men who wanted to make love to them. They laugh because they know that 'among us there were those who practised it'. One man, when asked whether such homosexual relationships hampered a man's prospects as a lover of women back home, smiled quietly and told us, 'No, it actually helps because you understand the woman's point of view. You learn to be more gentle.'

In their sexual relations, the young men were expected to behave with womanly decorum. In the account above, although the Sotho 'wife' might have wished to respond ardently to his Mpondo husband, 'he had to control himself as he was my girlfriend'. A Shangaan informant expanded such hints, saying, 'Don't forget, the boy would never make a mistake of "breathing out" into the "hubby." It was taboo. Only the "hubby" could "breathe out" into the boy's legs.'

The implication is inescapable. Proper 'wifely' sexual behaviour was essentially receptive rather than intrusive. Boys might 'wish they were so-and-so's wife . . ., for the sake of security, for the acquisition of property . . ., and for the fun itself', but they were certainly subordinate, both socially and sexually. Although the relationships might end in 'divorce' after a quarrel or upon returning home, there was also a 'natural' point at which they could be terminated. As the boy became 'old enough', he might 'wish to start his own family' on the mine, becoming the senior partner. Nor could his partner refuse him that right, according to the Shangaan custom:

> When the boy thought he was old enough he would tell the 'husband' that he also wished to get himself a 'wife' and that would be the end. Therefore the 'husband' would have to get himself another boy. . . . As long as you are old enough there would be no problem. I mean that was the way of life. You would just have to explain that you are experiencing some biological problems at night. (It was not possible for the boy to penetrate [ejaculate with] the [senior partner], only the [senior partner] could.) You would then have to wait for newcomers where you could choose. After choosing you would just show him which bed was yours.

There was thus a 'biological' period (somewhere in his middle twenties, it would seem, but also depending on the extent of one's mine experience), when a 'boy' would become a man, unable to endure any longer his non-ejaculatory sexual role. That would be the end of it for the 'marriage'.[8] Thus men who were sexually active with senior men in their youth, themselves took 'boys' when they became senior black miners or 'boss boys'. Indeed, the entire system of mine marriages was thoroughly interwoven with the power structure of the mines themselves.

One Mpondo man told Vivienne Ndatshe that when he started at Daggafontein Mine in 1940, his '"boss boy," who was Xhosa, treated him very nicely because he was in love with him'. This man offered him all his wages. He agreed because 'he was on business' at the mine. 'He needed money desperately as he wanted to buy cattle and pay lobola for his wife and build his homestead.' Some boys reportedly had two or three lovers 'which was very dangerous because these men might kill one another'. They took chances because 'they only did that for money'.

So men became 'wives' on the mines in order to become husbands and therefore full 'men' more rapidly at home. Mine marriages were an integral part of traditional migrant cultures. While attraction was on only one

305

side in the beginning, in some cases affectionate mutuality might grow. This seems especially to have been the case for Shangaans from Mozambique who tended to serve much longer contracts on the mines. Harries's (1990: 330) Shangaan informants 'today remember the loving and deep ties that a husband often developed for his mine wife'. Indeed, Harries (1990: 327–8) suggests that, for Mozambican workers, mine marriage constituted an important aspect of a young boy's passage to full masculinity.

For Mpondo, the junior partner bore the initial indignity (as he saw it) of *ukumetsha* relations with senior men, partly out of necessity and partly out of interest in 'building a homestead' – the true goal to which every traditionalist Xhosa-speaker aspired. Being a 'wife' on the mine, for all its apparent gender reversals, eventually reinforced the potential for male hegemony at home by earning money for homestead-building. Senior partners in the mine marriage system were presumably quite well established at home by the time they undertook the responsibility of having a 'boy' of their own – or they were *amatshipa*, men who had absconded from country ways and become creatures of the mines and townships. At any rate, becoming a 'husband' on the mines was one of the accoutrements of seniority in the mine system, a perquisite of success in the mine world, making somewhat more comfortable the hardships of the migrant life. Certainly, that was the way Shangaans saw it – and that seems also to have been the point of view of most Mpondo.

However, this attitude was by no means universal amongst Mpondo. Some rejected sexual advances. Several Mpondo men interviewed by Vivienne Ndatshe stated that being on the mines was like herding or going to war. One simply abstained while away from one's girlfriend or wife, which implied that sexual activity was 'natural' in certain situations and abstention was 'natural' in others. While abstention was one way of dealing with migrant life, however, it was never exclusively the prescribed way. Sexual release in mine marriages was always available as an alternative organisation of libidinal aims for senior men. Indeed, Coplan (1995: 138) has a delightfully bawdy account of the *seakhi* dance (with its accompanying song), organised at midnight by the Sotho *induna* (the highest black official on the mines), 'where miners danced naked to be awarded [a] boy, who also danced, dressed in towel, earrings, and other ornaments to arouse the ardor of the competitors'.

## Town women

It is important to stress that 'mine marriages' and abstention were not the only sexual options for black miners. Compounds on the gold mines were never closed, so men who wished to leave on afternoons or weekends to shop or visit friends could always do so with a simple 'permission slip' from a clerk at the gate. Another important reason for leaving the mine was to visit women in town. These town women often entered into fairly long-term liaisons with miners, serving them alcohol and providing sexual services in exchange for gifts, monetary or otherwise. One old Mpondo who had been a mine 'wife' in his early years reported:

> I had an *induna* as my best friend who took me to the township. Again I had a boy, and the *induna* had one too. In the township we both had girl-friends. We left the boys in the compound when we went to town, but we never spent the night in the township. We just spent a few hours with our girl-friends and then returned to our boys. We loved them better.

This man, when Ms Ndatshe interviewed him in 1982, was married and living happily in a rural homestead with his wife and family. Why did he prefer 'boys' during his earlier years on the mines? That being so, why did he seek a town girlfriend at all? What did he mean when he said that they 'loved their boys better'?

On the basis of the statements of other migrants, part of the answer seems to lie in a deep-seated and ambivalent fear of town women. Some of this was the simple and quite legitimate apprehension of being robbed. Several of the old men with town lovers asserted that they dared not go to sleep with them lest their pockets be picked. Others feared venereal disease. A deeper fear than any of these, I believe, was that of a person losing his rural identity. The attractions of town women might seduce a person into forgetting his home, absconding, becoming *amatshipa*, or in Sesotho *lekholoa* ('the ones who stay a long time on the mines'). In a society where rural marriage established an economic base for retirement the dangers of going *tshipa* were the subject of many a cautionary tale. Every Mpondo boy who had grown up in the country would know of men who eventually returned home as paupers, totally without status in the rural community. Ms Ndatshe and I interviewed several of them, chastened and filled with deep regret. Indeed, this was truly the Mpondo 'heart of darkness'. Emotional parallels between black migrant concerns about becoming *tshipa* and imperialist fears of 'going native' are quite precise in the two economies of desire.

'Mine wives', after all, would always eventually 'grow up' and become men, so that there was a natural limit to mine marriage, a 'biological' terminus, as it were. Also important was the stability of mine marriage –

its integration into a well-ordered emotional regime. Part of the attraction of arrangements with 'boys' was surely their reliability, their assuredness as opposed to the heady but risky attractions of town women who might seduce one away from homestead-building at home. The 'wives of the mine' were on hand with their services on an everyday basis, very important in a society where older men have a basic right to the services and benefits of domesticity. Is it any wonder that senior men on the mines would return to their 'boys' because 'we loved them better'?

Finally, of course, some men may simply prefer sex with other men. Coplan (1995: 141) cites an evocative Sotho song:

> In such a way [how much] I love boys!
> Legs entwined in the bed,
> The fondling of small thighs is sweet.

Even so. In ancient Rome, for instance, where options were open, 'according to taste some chose women, some boys, some both' (Veyne 1985: 28).

## Economies of desire

Traditional African migrant men apparently saw no antinomy between reason and desire (except in the case of *ukutshipa*). Sexual desire was quite reasonable and deserved to be met. There was a certain modesty about public discussion of sex,[9] but little guilt or shame. The inherent male right to pleasurable sexual activity accommodated to migrancy with no apparent guilt about the shift in sexual object – although everyone seemed aware of the tremendous dangers of sex with town women. What seems to have mattered to these senior men in sexual relationships was the right and power to initiate and control sexual activity. When we asked old men in Pondoland in 1988 whether it was possible for women actively and verbally to 'propose love to men', even as men did to women, seizing them and telling them they wanted 'love' from them, they were puzzled by the question. Women could act seductively and so convey their availability, they said, but for women 'to propose love like men' was inconceivable. In this regard the receptive 'boys' in mine marriages were wives indeed.

Migrant life-worlds were profoundly homosocial and age-graded. Traditionalist young men on the mines spent their free time drinking together, socialising with one another, talking about home, remembering girlfriends and the battles of stick-fighting herdboys. Older, married men would discuss the intricate details of legal disputes at home, proper ways to maintain order, relationships with chiefs and fellow elders, offering sage advice to younger men. They would sing the songs of home together and celebrate country ways. Migrants watched over each other, lest anyone be seduced by the attractions of town women and town life. Such comradeship was asexual. Mine 'wives' were not included in such circles except as providers of domestic services. All juniors treated older men with respect, however, so domestic service did not necessarily imply sexual relations, and wives at home were similarly excluded from men's social circles. Sociality was strictly separate from sexuality and profoundly gender-based. A person found companionship with same-sex peers regardless of his or her sexual partners.[10]

Mine cultures were predicated upon patriarchal rights in land with the labour-power and means of production to work it. While women left behind at home could be perceived to have manhood and young men on the mines became wives, such variations of manliness all functioned to maintain an economy of desire that privileged senior men both at home and in migrant life-worlds. Ambivalence in such cathectic structures is to be found between men at different life-stages rather than within the individual male psyche. At home these age-related tensions were contained by the hardships of herding, the pleasures of *ukumetsha* with country girls, and, amongst the Xhosa and Sotho, by circumcision rituals.[11]

Mpondo accounts of the young man's part in mine marriages give little evidence of erotic pleasure on his part, stressing instead their monetary value. Indeed, Mpondo on the mines were legendary for their stinginess as well as their roughness. Mpondo men to whom we spoke were much more comfortable discussing relationships in which they were 'husbands'. However, Coplan's (1995: 140) account of the nude Sotho *seakhi* dance, whose name itself 'describes the flapping motion of a young boy's penis as he runs carelessly clad about the fields', captures some of the erotic excitement that must surely also have been conveyed to the boy at the centre of the dance. Moreover, for Shangaans, Harries (1994: 202–6) argues that mine marriages constituted a passage to manhood for inexperienced boys, a 'rite of sexual inversion' that softened the transition to the harsh work realities of the mine. Whatever the experiential reality, tensions between older and younger men were ultimately contained by the promise of maturity, of senior manhood on the mine, but, more important, of *umzi* proprietorship at home.

Thus, finally, for all their patriarchal overtones and their co-optative relationship with mining capitalism, it seems to me that migrant African economies of desire described in this chapter manifested an integrity and psychological coherence that disrupts the implicit essentialism of much contemporary gender identity politics and analysis. Was the sexual regime on the mines an example of 'sexual orientation', or inverted object-choice, for instance? Or both? Or neither? Indeed, the occidental boundaries of Freudian notions of sexual desire are stretched by these African men. For them, there was no sharp antinomy between reason and desire, reality and pleasure. Sexual acts were real, reasonable and pleasurable at the same time.

## Conclusion: contemporary transitions

It is sad to report that 'women with manhood' and 'mine wives' are now largely extinct even in Lesotho and Pondoland, as is teenage *ukumetsha*, broken by the same social, political and economic forces that have destroyed the rural homestead proprietorships that supported them.[12] There are few cattle to herd in the impoverished countryside and in most parts of Pondoland, herding and stick fighting has been replaced for boys by soccer and school-going. Young Xhosa-speakers both in Soweto and Pondoland have no conception of the moral meaning of *ubudoda*. They are embarrassed if I ask them the meaning of the word in the presence of women, reluctantly explaining its purely sexual meaning. When your fly is open, one explained to me, 'your *ubudoda* is showing'.

Moral injunctions against sexual desire have become common in life-worlds where, at least on the mines, migrant sexual practices consistently contravene them in an ambivalent double standard. It is inconceivable that women might have *ubudoda*. The old responsibilities of manhood have largely been reduced to the (hetero-)sexual and domestic needs of men and homophobia has returned in force. 'Manhood' now tends to mean simply the basic right of men to exploit women as sexual objects and to be exploited by the women in return. Country women migrate to town or settle around the mines, often seeking husbands who no longer remit money home to rural slums. The project of rural *umzi* proprietorship has largely vanished. As the men now say, 'Our families eat our money.' Appeals to 'traditional manhood' from dispossessed migrants lack the cathectic integrity of the old migrant system without its economic base.[13] Mamphele Ramphele's (1989 and 1993) findings from migrant hostels in Cape Town, demonstrate what Vivienne Ndatshe (Moodie and Ndatshe 1992) also found in townships round the mines. Town women are engaged in a desperate struggle with country wives for men's wages and urban accommodation. In Ramphele's words, 'relationships [between men and single women in the migrant hostels] are characterised by mutual abuse'. Indigent women manipulate 'sexual and reproductive capacities [as] a major part of [their] survival kit' (1993: 78–9). Many of the most moving songs in Coplan's collection are those of the town women, who often sing of exploitative men and the women's longing for their absent children:

> Oh, the young prostitutes,
> The young prostitutes, girls –
> We, the new recruits, live in difficulties.
> What kind of people are you [gangsters]?
> You fight each other each time you meet.
> I have left my poor child Thabang;
> Yes, I have left my sweetheart behind crying.    (1996: 152)

While many marriages do survive the stresses of migrancy, the old cathectic unity of reason and desire has been replaced by deeply ambivalent anger and sadness. Let me close this chapter by quoting from British Sibuyi's 1987 interview with a Shangaan man who no longer works on the mines but is now an urban migrant, living far from his family, alone in town. His combination of nostalgia for and ambiguity about the old practices reflects the breakdown of the old economy of desire. On the one hand, Philemon said: 'It was just for the sake of 'satisfying' one because really, what pleasure? I mean . . . it was just as good as making love to oneself.'

On the other hand:

> But anyway, one would get psychological relief because I mean . . . [being alone] was bad . . . [I]t was better [then] because the boy would look after your things, wash your clothes, and so on. It [was] unlike now, [because now] you spend all your money buying clothes and giving money to your wife [at your rural home] with whom you are not even staying. That's somehow a loss of money. I mean, she does not even wash your vest, while with those [mine wives] it was better because evenings were for 'legs'.

## NOTES

1. Two of these initial life histories have since been published in Gevisser and Cameron (1994).
2. For comment and thoughtful encouragement in revising this chapter,

I am most grateful to Lee Quinby, Robert Morrell, Bob Connell, and Meredith Aldrich.

3. The following descriptive sections of this paper will be familiar to readers of my earlier work which has been incorporated in *Going for Gold* (Moodie 1994). I have drawn on that work here to focus attention on the structuring of desire. I am now able also to draw support from the work of David Coplan (1995) and Patrick Harries (1994). A useful recent article by Marc Epprecht (1998) on Zimbabwe appeared too late to be used in this chapter, but largely confirms the argument.

4. My own work has been largely conducted in Pondoland (with the assistance of Vivienne Ndatshe) and Lesotho (with the help of Palama Lelosa and Puseletso Salae).

5. For similar patterns in Lesotho, see Coplan (1995: 118–49). For Mozambique, see Harries (1982).

6. I asked one old woman who had given me a graphic description of the process of *ukumetsha* (secret assignations in the bush, washing in the stream afterwards) what pleasure girls found in it. 'We enjoyed it', she said, 'because it was the right thing to do.' Since the young women wore a beaded triangle between their legs to prevent penetration, there was probably clitoral stimulation as well.

7. Christian reactions to *ukumetsha* and traditionalist (*amaqaba*) young people's parties were astonishingly similar to those of high-minded boarding school boys in England. For example, Jeffrey Richards (1987: 113) cites J.A. Symonds as follows:

> The talk in the dormitories and studies was incredibly obscene. Here and there one could not avoid seeing acts of onanism, mutual masturbation, the sports of naked boys in bed together. There was no refinement, no sentiment, no passion; nothing but animal lust in these occurrences. They filled me with disgust and loathing.

8. This account of course evokes Foucault's (1985) account of ancient Greek sexuality where the achievement of full citizenship denied to young men the receptive role. Note, however, the 'biological' nature of the Shangaan explanation of this essentially political shift.

9. For a beautiful discussion of sexual modesty in Lesotho, see Murray (1975). For Zimbabwe, see Epprecht (1998).

10. Mamphela Ramphele (1993: 69) follows Goran Hyden speaking in this context of an 'economy of affection'. Such homosocial bonds are much easier to sustain, of course, if there are other available objects for erotic satisfaction.

11. It is surely significant that the Mayer's (1972) African research assistant was shocked by traditional Mpondo young men's lack of respect for their elders when he moved from studying young men and women in Xhosaland to observing Mpondo youth. Mpondo young men might even engage in physical altercations with their fathers, he reported. Such disrespect was never seen amongst the Xhosa, where circumcision rites enforced a much stronger sense of age order.

12. Anne Mager's (1998) article addresses transformations in masculine identities of Xhosa-speakers between 1945 and 1960. In my opinion she needs to pay more attention to differences between regions (change came more slowly to Pondoland and it was quite effectively mediated by *iindlavini* groups) but her general conclusions are well taken.

13. Robert Morrell (1998) addresses some of these changes by making a conceptual distinction between 'African' and 'black' masculinities.

## BIBLIOGRAPHY

Beinart, W. 1979. '*Joyini Inkomo*: Cattle Advances and the Origins of Migrancy from Pondoland', *Journal of Southern African Studies* 5(2).

———. 1991. 'The Rise of the Indlavini'. In A.D. Spiegel and P.A. McAllister, eds., *Tradition and Transition in Southern Africa*. Johannesburg: Witwatersrand University Press.

Breckenridge, K. 1998. 'The Allure of Violence: Men, Race and Masculinity on the South African Goldmines, 1900–1950', *Journal of Southern African Studies* 24(4).

Burridge, K. 1969. *New Heaven, New Earth*. New York: Schocken.

Coplan, D. 1995. *In the Time of Cannibals: The Word Music of South Africa's Basotho Migrants*. Chicago: University of Chicago Press.

Epprecht, M. 1998. 'The "Unsaying" of Indigenous Homosexualities in Zimbabwe: Mapping a Blindspot in an African Masculinity', *Journal of Southern African Studies* 24(4).

Foucault, M. 1985. *The Use of Pleasure*. New York: Random House.

———. 1997. *Ethics, Subjectivity and Truth: The Essential Works of Michel Foucault, 1954–1984*. New York: The New Press.

Freud, S. 1963(1920). 'The Psychogenesis of a Case of Homosexuality in a Woman'. In P. Rieff, ed., *Sexuality and the Psychology of Love*. New York: Collier.

Gevisser, M. and E. Cameron. 1994. *Defiant Desire: Gay and Lesbian Lives in South Africa*. Johannesburg: Ravan Press.

Guy, J. 1990. 'Gender Oppression in Southern Africa's Pre-Capitalist Societies'. In C. Walker, ed., *Women and Gender in Southern Africa to 1945*. Cape Town: David Philip.

Harries, P. 1982. 'Kinship, Ideology and the Nature of Pre-colonial Labour Migration from the Delagoa Bay Hinterland to South Africa up to 1895'. In S. Marks and R. Rathbone, eds., *Industrialization and Social Change*. London: Heinemann.

———. 1990. 'Symbols and Sexuality: Culture and Identity on the Early Witwatersrand Gold Mines', *Gender and History* 2(3).

———. 1994. *Work, Culture and Identity: Migrant Laborers in Mozambique and South Africa, c.1860–1910*. Portsmouth, N.H.: Heinemann.

Hyam, R. 1990. *Empire and Sexuality: The British Experience*. Manchester: Manchester University Press.

Lane, C. 1995. *The Ruling Passion: British Colonial Allegory and the Paradox of Homosexual Desire*. Durham: Duke University Press.

Mager, A. 1998. 'Youth Organisations and the Construction of Masculine Identities in the Ciskei and Transkei, 1945–1960', *Journal of Southern African Studies* 24(4).

Mayer, P. and I. Mayer. 1970. 'Socialization by Peers: The Youth Organization of the Red Xhosa'. In P. Mayer, ed., *Socialization: The Approach from Social Anthropology*. London: Tavistock.

———. 1972. 'Self-Organization by Youth among the Xhosa-speaking Peoples of the Ciskei and Transkei: Volume Two' (typescript). Grahamstown: Institute for Social and Economic Research.

Moodie, T.D. 1994. *Going for Gold: Men, Mines and Migration*. Berkeley: University of California Press.

Moodie, T.D. and V. Ndatshe. 1992. 'Town Women and Country Wives: Migrant Labor, Family Politics, and Housing Preferences at Vaal Reefs Mine', *Labor, Capital and Society* 25(1).

Morrell, R. 1998. 'Of Boys and Men: Masculinity and Gender in Southern African Studies', *Journal of Southern African Studies* 24(4).

Murray, C. 1975. 'Sex, Smoking and the Shades'. In M. Whisson and M. West, eds., *Religion and Social Change in Southern Africa*. London: Rex Collings.

Ramphele, M. 1989. 'The Dynamics of Gender Politics in the Hostels of Cape Town: Another Legacy of the South African Migrant Labour System', *Journal of Southern African Studies* 15(3).

———. 1993. *A Bed Called Home: Life in the Migrant Labour Hostels of Cape Town*. Cape Town: David Philip.

Richards, J. 1987. '"Passing the Love of Women": Manly Love and Victorian Society'. In J. Mangan and J. Walvin, eds., *Manliness and Morality: Middle-Class Masculinity in Britain and America, 1800–1940*. New York: St. Martin's Press.

Unger, R.M. 1975. *Knowledge and Politics*. New York: Free Press.

Veyne, P. 1985. 'Homosexuality in Ancient Rome'. In P. Aries and A. Bejin, eds., *Western Sexuality: Practice and Precept in Past and Present Times*. Oxford: Basil Blackwell.

# CHAPTER 18

# 'Dangerous' Love
## Reflections on Violence among Xhosa Township Youth

KATHARINE WOOD and RACHEL JEWKES

I must keep my heart from falling for this girl, I must study my books, fight for my own future, just because love is a dangerous thing to us. I could kill myself about my girlfriend.   (young man, Ngangelizwe)[1]

He beat me with a stick as if he has no feelings for me.   (young woman, Ngangelizwe)

## Introduction

A critical challenge in doing ethnographic work on violence practised by men against their female partners is to problematise the connections between violence and masculinity. Much popular discourse as well as socio-biological, evolutionist, and (some) radical feminist and psychological writings on male 'aggression' have reduced this relationship to one of monolithic essentialism. While male dominance is likely to be one consequence of violence against women, explaining its cause solely in such terms radically 'over-simplifies the processes involved in the constitution of masculinity, and may even take at face value some of the representations of masculinity as '"naturally" aggressive' (Wade 1994: 115). In this chapter, we draw on empirical data in which young African men living in a working class Eastern Cape township discuss their experiences of practising violence, in particular assault and coercive sex, against their sexual partners, in order to explore connections between this kind of violence

317

and the notions of masculinity that are predominant among local male youth.[2] This data was collected using rapid ethnographic methods with Xhosa-speaking youth in and around Ngangelizwe (Wood and Jewkes 1998).[3]

Ngangelizwe is the oldest township in Umtata, which is the main town (population c.100 000) of the former Transkei region of the Eastern Cape. Like most townships in South Africa, Ngangelizwe is characterised by various levels of housing development, ranging from middle class households in Kwezi Extension to the squatter camp located on its southern periphery. Umtata is a town without industry, where there are few job opportunities or recreational facilities for young people. Unemployment and its ramifications are widespread. Ngangelizwe police report escalating levels among local youth of illegal fire-arm possession, alcohol abuse, as well as hard-drug use and dealing (cocaine and mandrax). Young men whose families are without the means to further their education have few options, and frequently drop out of school to 'hang around' the streets of Ngangelizwe and central town, begging for money, harassing schoolgirls and other township residents, and committing petty crimes. Echoing a discourse which has been prominent in regional ethnographies since the 1930s (Wilson 1979[1934]; Pauw 1962), elders complain that their children are 'out of control', disrespectful and idle. In this context, poverty, mind-numbing boredom and the lack of opportunities or prospects for advancement contribute to young people investing substantial personal effort in the few arenas where entertainment and success are achievable, most notably their sexual relationships. These become an important vehicle for gaining (or losing) respect and 'position' among peers, as well as for material benefit: many teenage girls engage in a variety of sexual exchanges for money, often with older men or 'Sugar Daddies'. About half of the informants participating in this study came from backgrounds of poverty: in particular, some of the young women lived in the squatter camp and were more recently urbanised than other township youth, with many of them recently having come from rural areas with members of their families seeking employment.

Fieldwork in Ngangelizwe revealed violent male practices, in particular, assault, forced sex and verbal threats, to be a common feature of young people's sexual relationships. These findings reflect other work, both qualitative and quantitative, which has been carried out in diverse parts of the country, including Khayelitsha (Cape Town), Durban and Gauteng (Wood et al. 1998; Vundule et al. n.d.; Varga and Makhubalo 1996; NPPHCN 1996). In one epidemiological study, 60 per cent of teenage girls reported having experienced physical assault by boyfriends (Jewkes 1998). Patterns

Katharine Wood and Rachel Jewkes

of sexual practice among the youth, including assault, poor interpersonal communication, multiple partners and high levels of 'risk'-taking, are of particular concern in a country which has one of the fastest spreading HIV/AIDS epidemics in the world.

Most of the young men who participated in the research in Ngangelizwe reported that they and most of their male acquaintances had 'beaten' their sexual partners on a varying number of occasions (cf. Wood et al. 1998). Violence lay on a continuum which included such diverse acts as slapping, 'persuading' a woman to have sex, threatening to beat, hitting with sticks and other objects, pushing, assaulting with fists, violent rape, stabbing with a knife, and public humiliation. Much of the violence was of a less severe kind, such as slapping and issuing threats. Nevertheless, many young women described having been visibly injured on various parts of their body at some point in their sexual histories. In terms of frequency, violence appeared rarely to be a one-off occurrence, with male and female youths reporting recurrent events within relationships. In explaining their violence, the men frequently referred superficially to a 'loss of control' caused by anger (described as 'high' or 'rising' temper) or 'mood changes' exacerbated by the use of alcohol and *dagga* (marijuana). *Prima facie*, physical beatings appeared to be a common means by which young men enforced discipline and control over their female partners when they perceived them to have broken certain (often implicit) 'rules' underlying the relationship, or to have resisted male attempts to enforce these 'rules' and control their behaviour. Thus, most reported violence was associated with girls' rejection of a male 'proposal' to become involved in a 'love affair', their actual or suspected sexual 'infidelity', their attempts to end relationships, their sexual refusals, their acts of resistance to boyfriends' attempts to dictate the terms of the relationship, and their efforts to undermine their boyfriend's sexual success with other women.

This chapter presents the broader contexts in which assault in relationships occurs. In writing about these contexts, we attempt to demonstrate that young men (in particular) are intensely invested in their sexual partnerships. Gaining and keeping sexual partners, often described in terms of a 'game' or 'competition', were highly preoccupying activities for Ngangelizwe youth. Notions of 'successful' masculinity prevailing in the streets were partially constituted through sexual relationships with girls and deployed in struggles for position and status among male peers. Thus, on one level, 'successful' masculinity was defined in dominant peer culture in terms of a young man's number of sexual partners, his choice of main partner (and related to this, the sexual desirability of his partners to other men) and his ability to 'control' girlfriends. In attempting to understand young men's violence against sexual partners in this chapter, we focus on their discussions of the *sexual* aspects of their masculinity, although we acknowledge that violence in sexual relationships is far from being exclusively bound up with sexuality. Yet while local criteria for 'successful' masculinity or 'real manhood' are clearly multiplicitous, context-dependent and disputed, and include a wide range of qualities and practices, the particular salience of sexuality to young men's sense of their own and others' masculinity was obvious.

Violence by young men against their girlfriends cannot be understood without a recognition of broader attitudes towards different types of violence in this and surrounding communities. Violence against sexual partners among the youth was widely tolerated in Ngangelizwe: by boys who continued to deploy it as part of their behaviour; by girls who perceived that they could do little to change it and more often than not failed to leave abusive boyfriends; by parents in not taking action to advise their children; by elders in attributing violence to boyish behaviour; by the police who tend to be disinterested in perceived 'domestic' cases; and by some teachers who participated in sometimes coercive sexual relationships with female pupils. The fact that a variety of different players turned a blind eye to young men's violence against girlfriends, thus giving out a message that it was tolerable, evidently contributed to a perception among young men that certain forms of violence, particularly mild 'disciplinary' forms deployed in specific circumstances, were acceptable. This tolerance was further made possible by prevailing patriarchal ideas about male entitlement to women and the importance of men asserting hierarchy in their sexual relationships.

## Investing in sex: struggling to get and keep sexual partners

Describing the extent to which young men were invested in their sexual partnerships helps to set the scene for understanding the dynamics of their violence. Young men spoke explicitly about the importance of their sexual relationships in enabling them to access 'position' and respect among their male peers. The salience of sexuality as an arena for intense male competition had particular implications for the kinds of behaviour which men expected of their girlfriends. For young men, celibacy was unthinkable, to the extent that the strategic acquisition of other girlfriends to offset the possibility of their main relationship ending was reportedly common practice. In the narratives this was linked to male 'sex drive' (which was also a rationalisation for forced sex) and intense pressure from male peers. Competition for sexual partners, either in the form of struggle for possession or 'revenge' for a 'stolen' girlfriend, often resulted in physical violence

Katharine Wood and Rachel Jewkes

between same-gender peers, with fights among young men often involving knives (and among *tsotsis*, the 'bad boys' of the streets, guns), and becoming group or street gang events.[4] As one informant explained:

> it's because there are two groups and these girls are liquors [drinkers] and started sleeping with me and then with another guy in a different group, and we start fighting just because other guys provoke us, and then we in my group provoke them, we start fighting, we start killing each other. They all have knives, we open our knives and each one goes to each one in pairs, and then we stab each other.[5]

Fighting back was perceived to be a sign of bravery which reflected another aspect of successful masculinity as one young man explained: 'I am not a coward. You see I can't shut up when a person tries to kill me or shoot at me.' This type of street-fighting partially represented a means of establishing group and individual hierarchy, and has a well-documented historical trajectory: ethnographic sources report that stick-fighting rituals (an activity exclusive to uncircumcised boys in the past) 'allowed for hierarchies among boys to be constantly challenged, tested and re-established', with rival peer groups regularly being ascribed 'enemy status' (Mager 1998, citing the Mayers' unpublished documents). It is clear that social and sexual prestige has long been attached to being a 'good fighter' (Glaser 1998).

For the young men, acquiring a girlfriend was not necessarily enough. The actual number of partners acquired was also important in their 'positioning' processes among peers. Multiple sexual partners, by all accounts virtually universal among boys, was said to be an important defining feature of 'being a man'. The usual male practice was said to be to have a '5-60' ('five-sixty'), 'named after the Mercedes-Benz, the top range of cars', and described as 'the one you really love and want to be with all the time' and, in addition to this, several partners 'just for sex' ('cherries' or one-night stands). Informants explained that having many girlfriends brought recognition from other men that they were a 'playboy' and a 'real' man: 'it's to show my status to men . . . they start respecting you . . . we say it's the difference between boys and men: I'm a big boy, I can do all those things, I have a way with women'.

In addition, competition among male peers constituted a powerful motivation for young men's actual *choice* of their '5-60', with sexual access to partners defined by consensus as 'desirable' (to other men) being seen as a criterion of 'successful' masculinity:

she was so beautiful . . . I thought 'let me protect this'. . . . I always felt we should be close together because I wanted to portray that image . . . most of the other guys wanted her but they couldn't get her, so I had to show the boys that I'm the man here. Basically I think that relationship was power.

'Taking' the partner of another boy (an expression which explicitly denies female agency, or else advocates male irresistibility) involved acquiring a woman who by definition was desirable to other men, an activity used to assert superiority over rivals and in some cases friends. There were clearly 'rules' about whose girlfriend it was acceptable to 'take'. One boy pointed out that the '5-60s' of men in rival groups were seen to be a fair target 'to tamper with' 'just for sex', often simply to 'prove' superiority. Thus rivalry within the male peer group was so strong that it could become the driving force for having an affair with a particular girl: 'this kind of relationship is not love-oriented. He just wants to prove it to the other guy: I'm a lot better than you. . . . there are no feelings there'. In contrast, an affair with a friend's '5-60' would cause him 'to hate you and fight with you': 'there are lines you don't cross if you know how he feels about someone – you can not tell him, you tell him it was another girl'.

While the importance of relationships in influencing male positioning among peers was salient, on another level the men were evidently invested emotionally in their '5-60s'. Men spoke about their intense feelings for particular women, enjoyed listening to soul and romantic pop music (idealistically relating it to their own relationships) and described their sense of vulnerability in relationships. Sexual relationships and their conflicts were said to be significant sources of emotional stress and disappointment, with persistent references made to love being a 'dangerous' game, and epic-romantic notions of revenge, betrayal, pain and deceit being evoked in the language of Mills-and-Boon and television soap operas to illustrate this. At times, love was perceived to act as a disease, which would 'work into' one's heart and destroy it. However, this discourse was usually only applied to a man's '5-60', as opposed to the 'cherries' who were 'just for sex'. The particular 'dangerousness' of relationships with '5-60s', which seemed to be ascribed a quasi-married status, was reflected in the fact that violence was reportedly more likely to occur in these partnerships.

The environment of competition rendered the men inherently vulnerable, both to the emotional vicissitudes brought by relationships and to threats to their 'position' among peers. Vulnerability also arose from another important source, which was poverty. Although violence, as

Katharine Wood and Rachel Jewkes

everywhere, cuts across all social classes, interviews and participant observation in this study suggested that the young men from working class backgrounds were more likely to report having practised regular violence against (potential or actual) sexual partners than those from wealthier families. Likewise, poorer women from the squatter camp were more likely to have been assaulted more regularly and violently by a series of partners, than those from evidently middle class households. In a place where wealth is an important feature of success and where many young women actively choose partners who are able to provide them with food, money and clothes, the poorer boys faced particular difficulties in acquiring partners and gaining status with peers. For example, male informants who came from much poorer backgrounds and those who were still at school expressed their feelings of vulnerability in the face of girls' preference for wealthy partners with cars, who were said to enable them to 'boast' and compete with other girls. For these young men, it was not just love that was 'dangerous' but life itself, with status precarious and hard to come by and maintain. This is perhaps reflected in their being more ready to resort to violence as a strategy to keep the upper hand in relationships. Thus one young man whom the first author first encountered while he was begging in the township, who lived with seven family members (most of whom were unemployed) in a dilapidated mud-brick house and who had a history of dropping out of school to 'hang around' the streets, explained:

> Because of hunger and all those problems I have got nothing, and that other guy has a car and everything . . . it's that problem, because girls are interested in . . . having money, beautiful dresses. It's a competition: may be one girl says 'my guy has a BM' and another girl also wants to be like that. If you find a beautiful one you want to try to have her the whole of your life, but after that they disappoint you by having sex with another guy. You see we do not have any status. I think in my life I have lost six girls to other men. I think it's because I've got nothing. Even you can see I am living in a house of damp, when it is raining water enters the room, may be she is not satisfied because I'm not even eating good stuff. We are competing with clothes, we are competing with money, status. If I was not patient . . . I could kill myself about girls.

## Violence, 'successful' masculinity and controlling women

Violence usually occurred in situations where the girlfriend was perceived to be stepping out of line by behaving in ways which threatened men's sense of authority in the relationship and undermined their public presentation of themselves as 'men in control'. That 'successful' masculinity was partially defined in terms of young men's capacity for controlling their girlfriend(s) was particularly prominent in the narratives. Underlying this construction were explicit notions of hierarchy, 'ownership' of women, and 'place' within sexual relationships, reflecting a patriarchal discourse institutionalised in traditional practices such as bridewealth (*lobola*) (Wilson 1979[1934]). In Ngangelizwe, sexist notions about the importance of men asserting their dominance and authority in relationships were expressed by the young men, though often half-jokingly and in a depersonalised manner, in the form of one-off phrases such as: 'regret is a woman's natural food' (which seems to suggest that women are controlled for their own good), and 'everyone thinks men have the right to use'.[6] The fact that patriarchal discourse about gender relations was appropriated (partially, at least) by young men was indicated more broadly by their notions about male 'rights' in certain situations,[7] which included expectations of male sexual entitlement and female sexual passivity.

Attempts to control girlfriends and assert hierarchy were manifested in sometimes petty ways. In particular, dictating which friends were suitable associates and which 'bad influences' for their girlfriends; and attempting to control their physical movements around the township. Male expectations were often that their girlfriend should await their visits in her home; and not finding her there could lead them to conclude that she was seeing another boyfriend (one of the most common catalysts for assault). Some men considered that receiving uninvited visits from their girlfriends was grounds for assault, especially if they were with another girlfriend at the time, as they interpreted this as a deliberate attempt to 'thwart' their success with other women.[8]

Most controlling strategies revolved around men's perceived need to control the sexual behaviour of their girlfriend(s), in particular their '5-60s' (as opposed to 'cherries'), and were frequently enforced through threats of or actual assault. In fact, proof of sexual 'infidelity' on the part of a girlfriend was not needed for violence to take place. 'Jealousy' (often worsened by alcohol) was often said by female informants to lead men to beat their girlfriend if she was seen even talking to, or walking with, another man in the street. On one level, beating in these circumstances was perceived positively: the words of some young men suggested that they regarded violence to be an indication of depth of feeling; 'you beat her to try to stop her concentrating on the other guy because you're serious about her, so you grab her to make her scared and to make her tell you the truth'. This reasoning, which was said to be shared by many girls,

Katharine Wood and Rachel Jewkes

was based on the perception that intense male jealousy was an explicit sign of love (hence the view held by some young people that beating itself indicates love).

Actual sexual relations between established partners constituted one of the most important areas of conflict in relationships. Young men and women described sex in multiple ways: as an inexorable physical need (a perception illustrated with reference to slang food metaphors such as 'tasting', 'chowing' [literally: eating] and 'cherry'); as a strategy to acquire 'position' and prove sexual desirability (particularly among same-gender peers); as a weapon of revenge; as a resource exchanged by girls with middle-aged men popularly known as 'Sugar Daddies' (including teachers) in return for money, clothes and exam passes; and (occasionally) as an expression of romantic feelings. While having multiple sexual partners was widely represented by men to be a defining feature of 'successful' masculinity in street discourse, young women with more than one partner were perceived by the overwhelming majority of young men to be breaking a rigid social 'rule'. The unfairness of this double standard was acknowledged by some.[9] One young man, for example, expressed discomfort with dominant notions of hierarchy when he said, 'it's bullying, treating someone as if you are the boss, controlling her life while you don't want to be controlled by her . . . it's not right, you have to control each other'.

Sexual 'infidelities' of a '5-60' were described as particularly ignominious and threatening, and represented the most prominently reported cause of violence in relationships. Such a young woman was extensively criticised for 'playing' with her man and, in some cases, the girl was said to be badly beaten by both boys with whom she was involved, who 'made a plan' to punish her (usually through assault) on discovering the deception.[10]

> I mean, what would other people start thinking about me? That she's bullying you, you have no control over her. . . . it starts to demote you completely, and that's where you start to hit her because she's making me a fool in front of everybody. Frustration starts, some go and drink, full of rage . . . . if your friends hit their girlfriends and you don't, they question why you let her control you, so you want to show that you are a man and hit her.

In their own relationships, young men's insecurities about their girlfriends having sex with others were exemplified by the comment that it made them 'feel small'. The young men repeatedly cited specific examples of

325

situations in their relationships in which the actions of their girlfriends had caused them to feel acutely vulnerable, and in so doing used their feelings of insecurity to justify their violent or 'promiscuous' behaviour. One justified his affairs with reference to female infidelity: 'you see that this girl is playing with you, you must do your own things with your own life and your own body; I expect to have many girlfriends just because a girl can disappoint you by proposing to another guy, and she can leave you for that'. Similarly another, expressing his own vulnerability from past disappointments, said: 'when I'm alone I think: no, man, I've been trying to give my heart for nothing, I've wasted my time. Then I think: let me just hit and run.'[11]

At other times, the young men's insecurities were intensified by their own attempts to present themselves as 'macho' in public, such as by boasting to peers about their ability to control their girlfriends, only to find that the woman involved wanted to end the relationship. Controlling the beginning and end of sexual relationships was widely represented by men to be a male prerogative. The young men clearly tried to counteract their vulnerability and retaliate in cases where it was the woman who wanted to leave. Their strategies included physical assault; attempts to humiliate the girl by telling others that she was not 'good in bed'; emotional manipulation; and continuing to 'use' the girl for sex, as one girl described, 'as in just sleep with you, no feelings involved. He'll continue having a relationship for the physical pleasure, not because he still loves you, because now he knows you have other guys, you are sharing with other males and he doesn't like it. It's some sort of revenge.'

Controlling strategies were visible in the manner in which many young men attempted to dictate the terms of sex with their partners. By all accounts, coercive and physically forced sex, and assault to enforce sexual co-operation,[12] were a particularly common manifestation of violence in youth relationships (cf. Wood et al. 1997), and a major source of resentment for girls:

> One day I was on my way home from school and I stopped at my boyfriend's place. We talked and talked and then he suddenly said to me that we had to have sex. I refused and he forced himself onto me until I couldn't overpower him. I hated him from that day; a person must talk to you if he wants something.

This kind of narrative was common. On a certain level, prominent constructions of 'love' espoused by young men tended to reflect a particular idea of exchange, involving notions of female duty which resonate with

Katharine Wood and Rachel Jewkes

ethnographic descriptions of traditional bridewealth systems (Wilson 1981). Thus if a girl accepted a male 'proposal' to love, she would be expected to have sex whenever he wanted it in return for presents, money, being visited frequently and taken out to parties and films. Thus sexual refusal on the part of girls, which contradicted this 'contract' as well as challenging dominant ideas about (male) sexual entitlement in relationships and female sexual availability, was an important catalyst for assault and was seen (by some men) to legitimise the 'taking' of sex, by force if necessary.[13] Most male informants believed that if girls did not want sex they should not have accepted the 'love' proposal at the outset; and said they were suspicious about a girlfriend's motivation for refusing sex, with their most prominent explanation for a girlfriend's refusal being that she had another partner: 'having sex is a moment of truth: if you are honest enough to share everything with your boyfriend you must have sex, or he'll get suspicious that you are having an affair'.[14] At the same time, some men admitted to feelings of insecurity about their sexual capabilities. Interviews with young women confirmed this ('either they can do it or they fail; some of the guys don't know how to [have] sex really, or else I can say they don't know how to satisfy you'), and revealed that female sexual dissatisfaction was seen (by some women) to justify their acquiring a second boyfriend, even if it exposed them to the risk of being beaten for 'infidelity'.

## Explaining violence in Ngangelizwe

This data indicates the significant extent to which young men become invested in their sexual relationships, particularly those with '5-60s', which represent critically important arenas for the playing-out of their struggles to gain male 'prestige', respect and self-esteem. The fact that 'successful' masculinity was partially constructed through the young men's ability to access and control the 'right' women made them vulnerable as they were dependent on their sexual partners submissively following the 'rules' or being effectively coerced by their strategies of access and control. In turn, achieving female compliance with these rules formed an essential part of notions of 'successful' masculinity as defined by dominant (male) peer culture. This resonates with Mager's discussion of the Mayers' 1950s data: '[hegemonic] masculinities were constructed around a desire to assert control not only over male rivals but also over young females' (Mager 1998: 654). On one level, violent practices constituted critical strategies for young men in their attempts to maintain particular self-images and social evaluations, in particular those reflecting 'successful' masculinity. Assault was one means of dealing with those aspects of their girlfriends' behaviour which threatened to subvert the young men's living-out of particular notions of successful masculinity.

These findings are resonant of the ideas of feminist anthropologist Moore (1994a, 1994b), who suggests that a critical link exists between violent practice and the 'thwarting' of investments in various subject-positions, particularly those based on gender:

> Thwarting can be understood as the inability to sustain or properly take up a gendered subject-position, resulting in a crisis, real or imagined, of self-representation and social evaluation . . . Thwarting can also be the result of contradictions arising from the taking up of multiple subject-positions, and the pressure of multiple expectations about self-identity or social presentation. It may also come about as the result of other persons refusing to take up or sustain their subject-positions vis-à-vis oneself and thereby calling one's self-identity into question.   (1994b: 66)

Holloway (1984), elaborating on the question of what makes people take up some subject-positions and not others, posits a notion of 'investment' (seen as a combination of emotional commitment and vested interest), in order to explain this 'taking-up' process in terms of the relative 'power' (or 'pay-off' [Moore 1994a, 1994b]) promised, but not necessarily provided, by a particular subject-position. Moore (1994b) takes this notion further to suggest that fantasy – in the sense of a person's notions of how he wants to be and be seen by others to be – plays a critical part in motivations for the taking-up of specific subject-positions. The process of taking-up of positions cannot be seen as one of simple choice, for the obvious reason that all discourses have social histories which ensure that some subject-positions contain much more social reward than others, which may be negatively sanctioned.

Moore (1994b) suggests that particular acts of a man's girlfriend or wife (such as engaging in sexual relations with other men) might threaten his self-representations as well as jeopardise the social evaluations held of him by others (in whose achievement he may have invested great effort), particularly those concerning his sense of masculinity. The process is often not simply reactive to actual events. Common too is the scenario where a man produces a 'manufactured crisis' through imagining that his sexual partner has actually had sex with another man (when this is not the case) or claiming to foresee the occurrence of such an event (cf. township boys beating their girlfriends for simply talking to other men). According to this argument, these crises of representation produce feelings of 'thwart-

Katharine Wood and Rachel Jewkes

ing', which bring a man to use violence against his partner as a strategy of struggle in the maintenance of his particular invested-in 'fantasies of identity'. Moore (1994a) further broadens her perspective to recognise the links between violence, a sense of powerlessness and multiple structural factors (poverty, ethnicity) which produce varying forms of vulnerability outside the immediate arena of gender.

Notions of 'thwarting' and vulnerability (produced along multiple axes) are useful starting-points for elucidating the connections between masculinities and violence against women and for understanding on one level why some men practise violence against their sexual partners in particular situations. Yet while perhaps explaining men's perceived need to take some sort of action, Moore's idea of 'thwarting' as a stand-alone explanation neither addresses the question of why it is violence which is often readily deployed in response to 'thwarting' as opposed to any other strategy, nor is it able to do justice to the always multiplicitous meanings which are attached to violence in social relationships and conflict situations in specific communities. It also fails to give due acknowledgement to violence deployed in anger, disappointment and resentment, reflecting young men's emotional attachments to the women in question.

Young men in Ngangelizwe had access to a variety of alternative discourses about 'manhood' which explicitly rejected essentialist notions that violence and aggression were the exclusive domain of males. One of the most prominent of these was the traditional teaching delivered by community elders to male initiates in the bush, which teach that non-violence, social responsibility, fewer sexual partners and respect for elders are defining characteristics of 'manhood': 'if you are a man, you must not force things, you must not fight, use guns and all that'. Through initiation (the ritual of circumcision), male youth[15] are provided with alternative constructions of masculinity to those commonly displayed on the township streets. These teachings have some effect on practices, although in the longer term many young men revert to some of their pre-circumcision ways. While there is little historic-ethnographic data on the extent and nature of such reversion in traditional Xhosa societies, the overall decline of elder patriarchs' influence over young men has been documented (for example, Mager 1998) and is likely to be a contributing factor, alongside multiple others, to contemporary reversion. In Ngangelizwe the extent to which reversion occurred varied between individuals, but it seems likely that peer surveillance mechanisms were more effective in reinforcing changes in 'public' practices such as drinking excessively and fighting other men with knives, than more 'private' ones, including relations with women.

Ironically, these images of manhood are constructed in parallel with a notion of 'normal boyish behaviour' which, while not necessarily conveying full approval for 'boyish' practices, may lend legitimacy to actions abusive to women when undertaken by uncircumcised boys. Thus it was argued that if boys go to be circumcised too young, initiation will not have a long-term impact on behaviours as they were not 'ready' to change and be responsible, because they had not had enough time without responsibilities. A corollary of this is that actions taken by boys in this age group are not regarded as serious, even if they are not liked. These findings resonate with ethnographic reports from earlier this century which indicate that in traditional Xhosa-speaking societies uncircumcised boys were expected to engage in pugnacious behaviour, and that the period prior to male initiation was seen as a time of fighting and sexual experimentation, tolerated and even encouraged in the name of self-expression (Glaser 1998; Mager 1998).

On no occasion did the young men of Ngangelizwe present violence against women *per se* as a necessary part of 'successful' masculinity, yet they did suggest that the use of certain forms of violence against girl-friends in particular situations was entirely right because they perceived it to be enacted as part of a defensive rather than offensive strategy (which might also entail other tactics such as 'talking' to a partner or walking out of a situation). This was based on a notion of honour: that taking action is honourable if somebody has 'wronged' you. Violence of varying severity was clearly a common strategy for taking this action. This idea of honour is reflected in the reports that some men deliberately get drunk before beating their partners, in order to take action which they perceive to be appropriate[16] and the 'right thing' to do, the assumption being that consuming alcohol enabled them to work up a violent temper and carry out action which they would not otherwise carry out.[17] Evidently this raises further questions, but it is clear that on a certain level, taking action against a 'misbehaving' girlfriend – though not necessarily by means of assault – was condoned by male peers and this perception may have contributed to the tolerance of violence (particularly in its milder forms, such as slapping), as one strategy to achieve this. More severe violence against girlfriends was not generally condoned, and indeed was often said to be morally unacceptable by young men who recognised the 'unfairness' of the physical 'one-sidedness' of beating (as opposed to slapping) women, and who reported that they sometimes attempted to persuade male friends who were assaulting their sexual partners on a regular basis or in a manner which resulted in injury that this was not acceptable behaviour.[18] One young man (who was feared as a *tsotsi* by some peers) explained how he was chastised by elders for assaulting his girlfriend:

Katharine Wood and Rachel Jewkes

> I felt sorry for [my girlfriend] and I asked myself: why did you do this wrong. I didn't think I would grab her like that . . . Here were the parents and neighbours and I feel for that, I feel guilty. I don't think it's right to beat a girl, that's why I feel guilty, and even grabbing her . . . [trails off] . . . if she's doing wrong I must sit and talk to her. The words of her grandmother are affecting my heart. She said I'm a rascal, and I've got no discipline, that I could kill somebody if I see it as important to kill somebody . . . and those words make me sad.

The question of severity has clearly been an important one for local people in judging what kinds of violent action are acceptable. For example, Mager (1998) in her revisitation of the Mayers' unpublished data on youth organisation in the former Transkei and Ciskei, reports that during the period 1945 to 1960 boys annoyed elders not for (stick) fighting *per se* but for 'fighting too much' or for engaging in violence 'for its own sake'. This issue of degree of violence is further reflected in ethnographic reports that the distinction between 'playful' violence and violent action between boys was regularly blurred in the past, with competitive tensions often erupting into 'lethal war' in which from time to time individuals lost their lives (as they continue to do in contemporary street-fights) (Mager 1998; Broster 1976; Wilson 1979[1934]). Yet it is unclear how excessive violence by young unmarried men against their girlfriends was dealt with in traditional arenas. Among married couples, the woman who had been 'marked' in a marital assault was entitled to return home to her own family and her guilty husband was widely reprimanded (Wilson 1979[1934]). There are suggestions, however, that from the 1950s, young men in particular were beginning to assert new oppositional masculinities of which the increasing and 'excessively aggressive' 'surveillance' of girls' behaviour (including the enforcing of female obedience with the traditional stick) in the former Ciskei and Transkei was one manifestation (Mager 1998). This brought about a widening gulf between the cultural ideals of elders and the practices of the youth.

As other writers have noted, the use of violence is often condoned and legitimated in South African communities as a first-line tactic in resolving conflict and gaining ascendancy (Simpson 1991). This is evident in ethnographic data collected in the 1950s, with reports of civil society widely condoning corporal punishment and penal violence (Mager 1998). In Ngangelizwe, beating was reportedly used in a variety of contexts as a strategy for punishment, and as a way of gaining the upper hand over others. Many young people had witnessed violence at home between their parents, experienced the use of force against them by parents, teachers and (among boys) by elders at circumcision school, witnessed (or been the target of) violent bullying by *tsotsis* on the streets of the township, and observed or participated in physical fights between same-gender peers and neighbours. In this context, it is important to be cautious about interpreting the violent acts of young men against their girlfriends as particularly unusual or 'misogynistic'. Further, while aspects of male violence against women evidently relate to young men's struggle to be successful men in the eyes of significant peers, interpreting it solely or primarily in terms of sexual aspects of (heterosexual) gender identity would be simplistic. It would ignore the existence of assault in a wide range of social relations, including non-heterosexual sexual relationships (violence has been shown to occur in many lesbian relationships), and professional ones, as demonstrated by Jewkes et al.'s (1998b) work on nurses hitting their obstetric patients in a Cape Town township.[19]

This chapter is a preliminary discussion of ongoing ethnographic work and is limited by the short-term nature of the fieldwork thus far conducted, its reliance on what people said to the first author and its lack of attention to female agency. Long-term ethnographic work based on participant observation and grounded in subtle historical and politico-economic analyses is needed to provide a more complex and nuanced picture of violence, by focusing on micro-level constellations of action and exposing the contradictory, multiplicitous and shifting ways in which people 'live' their gender and class (Cornwall and Lindisfarne 1994; Loizos 1994).

NOTES

1. Interviews with the young men were conducted in English, tape-recorded and fully transcribed.

2. This research was funded by the National Innovation Fund of the Department of Arts, Culture, Science and Technology as part of the South African government's National Crime Prevention Strategy. Special acknowledgement is due to the many informants who spoke about difficult issues; to Asandiswa Nkohla; to Nokwanda Ntshukumbana; to Nolwazi Mbananga; and to Albertina Makalima of Ngangelizwe Clinic.

3. The first author (a medical anthropologist) carried out participant

Katharine Wood and Rachel Jewkes

observation and in-depth interviewing on violence in youth sexual relationships over a period of six weeks with 30 young Xhosa-speaking men and women aged between 16 and 25 years, and with parents of youths. In addition, discussions were held with young women who talked about their boyfriends and male acquaintances. The young men who were interviewed were circumcised (initiated into 'manhood') but unmarried, and schoolgoing. About half had working class backgrounds.

4. Physical fights between women over boyfriends were regarded by some young men as a legitimate way of resolving disputes about whom they should have sexual involvement with, reportedly often 'taking the winner'. Others would choose whichever girl they wanted, and one boy said that 'some leave them to fight and go with a third so they can both see how stupid they are'. These latter two reactions were related to boys' perceptions that they had a 'right' to propose 'love' to whomsoever they wanted and that girls should not interfere with these processes. Some men said that they perceived such fights to be 'ego-boosting': 'you think "I'm the man" when they start to fight'.

5. This almost choreographic description of fighting is reminiscent of ethnographic accounts of stick fights, a traditional pursuit for young unmarried men in the region; cf. Broster (1976) on the sometimes fatal axe- and assegai-fighting which occurred between factions of male Tembu youth during the traditional *umtsotsho*, a 'tribal gathering' for adolescents characterised by dancing and courtship rituals.

6. 'Using' is also an idiom for sexual intercourse.

7. There is regional evidence that many women too have sympathy for patriarchal ideas. A 1998 survey of domestic violence in the Eastern Cape (Jewkes et al. 1998a), for example, found that 59 per cent of participating women agreed with the statement that 'culture gives a husband the right to punish his wife'.

8. On another level, however, some men were positive about their girl-friends' jealousy and associated attempts, though clearly not actual successes, to 'possess' them (for example, through physically fighting with female rivals) as it gave them status by indicating that several women 'desired' them.

9. On an abstract level, the most common 'official' argument against a girl having multiple partners was that if she were to become pregnant, she would not know who the father was, although the fact that 'promiscuous' girls are called insulting names by peers indicates a moralistic dimension too.

10. Despite male attempts to control them and the risk of assault, having

more than one sexual partner was common practice among the girls, and motives for this included: unwillingness to end one relationship out of fear of violence; taking on boyfriends in the township and in rural areas at the same time; 'revenge' for their boyfriend's infidelities; out of a continuation of their search for their 'real lover'; sexual dissatisfaction with their main partner; the need 'to explore'; for 'fun'; for financial or material benefit; to offset the possibility of being without a partner if another left; and competition with other girls to prove beauty through sexual desirability.

11. This is a metaphor from the armed struggle.

12. Forced sex in relationships was never described as 'rape' by the girls, as 'it is with your boyfriend'.

13. While many young women experienced coercive sex as a brutal and undermining process which often involved physical assault, the men perceived 'forcing' to be played out in variant ways, attaching different meanings according to context. The subtleties of these sexual dynamics need further exploration.

14. This suspicion was so acute that some men at times checked up on the validity of female excuses. One girl said, 'sometimes you say to your boyfriend that you can't sleep with him because you are menstruating, and he will demand to see the blood'.

15. Amongst the people of the former Transkei, male circumcision is virtually universal. The young men who participated in this research had all been circumcised.

16. Being under the influence of alcohol, and therefore not being in control, was also a common excuse for assault used by men when apologising to their girlfriends in the days after the event.

17. Cf. in a focus group with coloured men in Cape Town, one participant explained that he took alcohol before he beat his wife in order 'to get a sparkie-some steam', and that this was necessary because when 'sober it is almost like I am a lamb' (Abrahams and Jewkes 1997).

18. It is likely that minor forms of assault may have been regarded as so 'normal' and commonplace as to not even warrant appearance in young men's narratives or merit their interpretation as 'violence'.

19. In discussing why nurses abuse patients Jewkes et al. (1998b) also draw on Moore's notion of thwarting.

**BIBLIOGRAPHY**

Abrahams, N. and R. Jewkes. 1997. 'Men on violence against women', *Urbanisation and Health Newsletter* 34. Cape Town: Medical Research Council.

Broster, J. 1976. *The Tembu: their beadwork, songs and dances.* Cape Town: Purnell.

Cornwall, A. and N. Lindisfarne, eds. 1994. *Dislocating Masculinity: Comparative Ethnographies.* London: Routledge.

Department of Health. 1999. *1998 National HIV sero-prevalence survey of women attending public ante-natal clinics in South Africa.* Pretoria: Health Systems Research and Epidemiology, Department of Health.

Glaser, C. 1998. 'Swines, hazels and the dirty dozen: masculinity, territoriality and the youth gangs of Soweto, 1960–1976', *Journal of Southern African Studies* 24(4).

Holloway, W. 1984. 'Gender difference and the production of subjectivity'. In J. Henriques, ed., *Changing the subject: psychology, social regulation and subjectivity.* London: Methuen.

Jewkes, R. 1998. 'Promoting adolescent sexual and reproductive health'. Keynote address. Fifth Reproductive Health Priorities Conference, Vanderbijlpark.

Jewkes, R., L. Penn-Kekana and J. Levin. 1998a. *Gender violence in South Africa: an emerging public health issue.* National Conference of the Epidemiological Society of South Africa, October 1998.

Jewkes, R., N. Abrahams and Z. Mvo. 1998b. 'Why do nurses abuse patients? Reflections from South African obstetric services', *Social Science and Medicine* 47.

Loizos, P. 1994. 'A broken mirror: masculine sexuality in Greek ethnography'. In A. Cornwall and N. Lindisfarne, eds., *Dislocating Masculinity: Comparative Ethnographies.* London: Routledge.

Mager, A. 1998. 'Youth organisations and the construction of masculine identities in the Ciskei and Transkei, 1945–1960', *Journal of Southern African Studies* 24(4).

Moore, H. 1994a. 'The problem of explaining violence in the social sciences'. In P. Harvey and P. Gow, eds., *Sex and violence: issues in representation and experience.* London: Routledge.

———. 1994b. 'Fantasies of power, and fantasies of identity: gender, race and violence'. In H. Moore, *A passion for difference.* Cambridge: Polity Press.

National Progressive Primary Healthcare Network (NPPHCN). 1995. *Youth speak out for a healthy future.* Johannesburg: NPPHCN/UNICEF.

Pauw, B. 1962. *The second generation: a study of the family among urbanised Bantu in East London.* Cape Town: Oxford University Press.

Simpson, G. 1991. *Explaining sexual violence: some background factors in the current socio-political context.* Johannesburg: Project for the Study of Violence.

Varga, C. and E. Makubalo. 1996. 'Sexual (non)-negotiation', *Agenda* 28.

Vundule, C., R. Jewkes, F. Maforah and E. Jordaan. n.d. 'Risk factors for teenage pregnancy amongst African adolescents in metropolitan Cape Town: a case-control study'.

Wade, P. 1994. 'Man the hunter: gender and violence in music and drinking contexts in Columbia'. In P. Harvey and P. Gow, eds., *Sex and violence: issues in representation and experience.* London: Routledge.

Wilson, M. 1979(1934). *Reaction to conquest: effects of contact with Europeans on the Pondo of South Africa.* Abridged version. Cape Town: David Philip.

———. 1981. 'Xhosa marriage in historical perspective'. In E. Krige and J.L. Comaroff, eds., *Essays on African marriage in Southern Africa.* Cape Town: Juta.

Wood, K. and R. Jewkes. 1998. *'Love is a dangerous thing': micro-dynamics of violence in sexual relationships of young people in Umtata.* Pretoria: Medical Research Council.

Wood, K., F. Maforah and R. Jewkes. 1998. '"He forced me to love him": putting violence on adolescent sexual health agendas', *Social Science and Medicine* 47(2).

# Afterword

MICHAEL KIMMEL

'The fish', a Chinese proverb has it, 'are the last to discover the ocean.' To be inscribed as the norm against which 'others' are measured often obscures the processes to those who are cast as 'generic'. So it was the pioneering efforts of women who first made gender visible as both a category of identity and as a set of institutional and interpersonal processes that reproduced power relations. And so too it was the efforts of people of colour and those from the economic South who first understood the distorting social and disfiguring personal impact of racism and uneven global development.

Today we know that gender, class, and race are fundamental axes around which social, economic, political and personal power is organised, axes along which identities are placed. And while those nations that bear the scars of racism as official policy have long been aware of both 'whiteness' and 'blackness' and have begun the arduous processes of reconfiguring their meanings in a more egalitarian society, gender remains relatively invisible to those who are privileged by it. Thus while the investigation of women's experiences and the interrogation of femininity has been a staple of academic discourses for three decades, we are, today, only beginning to understand masculinity.

Take, for example, the world of development studies, in which the essays in this book are partially situated as a bridge to gender studies. We understand that women and men are differently situated culturally and economically with unequal access to material and cultural resources, different and unequal relationships to the provision and consumption of material goods, and different and unequal access to the political process that guides economic development. Thus we speak, for example, of the global 'feminisation of poverty', when we acknowledge that women represent approximately 70 per cent of the 1,3 billion poor people in the world. But why not speak of the 'masculinisation of wealth'? When men's wages are the norm against which others are measured, we speak of women in the United States being underpaid, earning 70 per cent of what men earn. But is it not equally true that were we to use women's wages as the standard then men are *overpaid* by about 40 per cent?

The essays in this volume address the previous invisibility of masculinity in the gendered processes of historical development and change. They both simplify and complicate our understanding in bold new ways by bringing the obvious to our attention for the first time and by adding new elements to an analytic mix that had previously included colonial status, race and class. Perhaps most centrally, by using feminist-inspired analytic frames, these essays examine the construction of masculinities at the local level. Rather than force our understanding through universalising theoretical models that posit 'manhood' as some timeless, transcendent essence, the authors here examine the construction and articulation of different masculinities as emergent local processes.

The use of the plural – masculinities – acknowledges that masculinity means different things to different groups of men at different times. Within any society at any one moment there are multiple meanings of manhood. Men's experiences depend on class, race, ethnicity, age, region of the country and location in the global economy. A 75-year-old white rural gay Boer in the Northern Province would have a very different notion of masculinity to a young, heterosexual Zulu man in Durban.

These essays also recognise that to pluralise the term does not mean that all masculinities are equal. Typically, each nation constructs at least one model of masculinity against which each man measures himself and against which other men measure him. This hegemonic image of manhood is 'constructed in relation to various subordinated masculinities as well as in relation to women', writes sociologist R.W. Connell (1987: 183).

In each society, then, there are multiple definitions of masculinity, some more valorised than others. In all cases, masculinities are constructed in relation to femininities and express the multiple ways in which gender identity is articulated through a gender *order*, in which gender is not only a property of individuals but a process of institutions and a dynamic of power relations between groups. That is, the gender order expresses men's power over women (male domination) and the power of some men over other men (by race, sexuality, ethnicity, age, able-bodiedness).

The construction of masculinities in southern Africa is both a local and a global process. On the one hand, globalisation reconfigures and reshapes the arena in which these national and local masculinities are articulated, and transforms the shape of domestic and public patriarchies.

Michael Kimmel

Globalisation disrupts and reconfigures traditional, neo-colonial, or other national, regional or local economic, political and cultural arrangements. In so doing, globalisation transforms local articulations of both domestic and public patriarchy. Thus, for example, globalisation includes the gradual proletarianisation of local peasantries as market criteria replace subsistence and survival.

Local small craft producers, small farmers, and independent peasants traditionally stake their notions of masculinity in ownership of land and economic autonomy in their work; these are increasingly transferred upwards in the class hierarchy and outwards to transnational corporations. Proletarianisation also leads to massive labour migrations – typically migrations of *male* workers – who leave their homes and populate migrant enclaves, squatter camps, labour camps.

Globalisation thus presents another level at which hegemonic and local masculinities are constructed. Globalisation was always a gendered process. As Andre Gunder Frank pointed out several decades ago in his studies of economic development, development and underdevelopment were not simply stages through which all countries pass. There was no single continuum along which individual nations might be positioned. Rather, he argued, there was a relationship between development and underdevelopment, that, in fact, the development of some countries implied the specific and deliberate underdevelopment of others. The creation of the metropole was simultaneous and co-ordinated with the creation of the periphery.

As with economic development so too with gender, with the historical constructions of the meanings of masculinity. As the hegemonic ideal was being created it was created against a screen of 'others' whose masculinity was thus problematised and devalued. Hegemonic and subaltern emerged in mutual but unequal interaction in a gendered social and economic order. Thus, for example, colonial administrations often problematised the masculinity of the colonised. For instance, in British India Bengali men were perceived as weak and effeminate, though Pathans and Sikhs were perceived as hypermasculine – violent and uncontrolled (see Sinha 1995). Similar distinctions were made in South Africa between Hottentots and Zulus, and in North America between Navaho or Algonquin on the one hand, and Sioux, Apache and Cheyenne on the other (see Connell 1998: 14). In many colonial situations, the colonised men were called 'boys' by the colonisers (see Shire 1994).

At the same time, the construction of masculinities in southern Africa responds to a historically specific collection of local conditions, circumstances and struggles. One cannot impose meanings on these particularities. Rather, as the authors in this collection remind us, we must allow these meanings to emerge through their local circumstances. It is from these local and national studies that the larger regional and international theories of gender construction will be built.

Thus in many ways these gender scholars – historians, sociologists, anthropologists, legal and medical experts – are closer to archaeologists of gender, carefully extracting artefacts, discursive and practical, that enable them to build understandings of how masculinity is experienced at the local level. Ever mindful of larger structural processes that constrain, distort, and often over-determine these local constructions, they are equally aware of the ways in which individuals and groups can modify, reconfigure these macro-level processes at the local level. Forests are not missed because of trees; equally, individual trees are carefully and thoughtfully discerned in their particularities.

In that sense, these essays are exemplary both conceptually and methodologically. Conceptually, they limn the boundaries between global and local, ever mindful that people make meaning locally, but the materials from which they do so are not always found in their backyards. And methodologically they remain attuned to the subtle ways in which the micro and the macro may be fruitfully examined simultaneously. In that they remain true to the cardinal rule of the historical method, articulated by the great French historian Marc Bloch: they have learned 'not to attach too much importance to local pseudo-causes'; while, at the same time they are always 'sensitive to specific differences' (Bloch 1967: 73).

BIBLIOGRAPHY

Bloch, M. 1967. *Land and Work in Medieval Europe*. New York: Harper and Row.

Connell, R.W. 1987. *Gender and Power*. Stanford: Stanford University Press.

———. 1998. 'Masculinities and Globalization', *Men and Masculinities* 1(1).

Shire, C. 1994. 'Men Don't Go to the Moon: Language, Space and Masculinities in Zimbabwe'. In A. Cornwall and N. Lindisfarne, eds., *Dislocating Masculinity: Comparative Ethnographies*. New York: Routledge.

Sinha, M. 1995. *Colonial Masculinity: The Manly Englishman and the Effeminate Bengali in the Late Nineteenth Century*. Manchester: Manchester University Press.

# Appendix
## Biographies of Contributors

**Catherine Campbell** is a South African psychologist, lecturing in the Department of Social Psychology at the London School of Economics, where she is also the Associate Director of the Gender Institute. She studied at the Universities of Natal, Stellenbosch, and Bristol (UK), and worked as a journalist and then a clinical and community psychologist in South Africa prior to becoming an academic. Her research interests lie in the area of the social psychology of health, with a particular interest in community development and health promotion. She is currently pursuing these interests in research projects focusing on the psycho-social context of HIV-transmission in southern Africa, and on community-level determinants of health in multi-ethnic communities in England.

**Benedict Carton** received his Ph.D. in History from Yale University in 1996. He teaches in the Department of History and African American Studies Programme at George Mason University. He is the author of *Blood from Your Children: The Colonial Origins of Generational Conflict in South Africa* (Charlottesville/London/Pietermaritzburg: University Press of Virginia/University of Natal Press, 2000) and several chapters in edited volumes. In 1992 and 1993 he was a Fulbright Scholar at the University Natal, Pietermaritzburg. The research for this chapter was gathered over ten years of fieldwork in rural Natal and KwaZulu.

**Jacklyn Cock** is a professor of Sociology at the University of the Witwatersrand, Johannesburg. She has written extensively on militarisation, gender and environmentalism in southern Africa. Her books include *Maids and Madams: The Politics of Exploitation in South Africa* (Johannesburg: Ravan Press, 1980; London: The Women's Press, 1989); *Colonels* *and Cadres. War and Gender in South Africa* (Cape Town: David Philip, 1991). She has been a visiting scholar at the University of Oxford, the Institute for Advanced Study in Princeton, the Woodrow Wilson School, Princeton University, and the Center for Historical Analysis at Rutgers University.

**Kobus du Pisani** is the chair of the Subject Group History in the School for Social Studies at the Potchefstroom University for Christian Higher Education. His research interest up to 1990, when he obtained his D.Phil. in history at the University of the Orange Free State, was contemporary South African political history, particularly during the Vorster years (1966–1978). He switched to the topic of gender history, and since 1996 has presented papers and written articles on the construction of Afrikaner masculinities. Currently he is involved in research projects in the field of environmental history.

**Sean Field** is the co-ordinator of the Western Cape Oral History Project at the University of Cape Town (UCT). He obtained initial degrees at UCT, which were followed by a Ph.D. at the University of Essex in England. His Ph.D. was based on oral history interviews with former residents of the Windermere/Kensington community of Cape Town. This study also developed a narrative analysis of memory, myth and identity. Telling stories and eating chocolate are just two of his many passions.

**Crispin Hemson** works in the Centre of Community and Adult Education at the University of Natal, Durban. He is an organiser for the Thekwini Surf Lifesaving Committee and runs a development programme in the sport of bodyboarding. Crispin was previously a city councillor in Durban and the director of the School of Education. He is presently engaged in developing a programme of social justice education in collaboration with the University of Massachusetts.

**Jonathan Hyslop** is a senior lecturer in Sociology at the University of the Witwatersrand, Johannesburg. He is the author of *The Classroom Struggle* (Pietermaritzburg: University of Natal Press, 1999), a history of social conflicts over African Education during the apartheid period. He has edited *African Democracy in the Era of Globalization* (Johannesburg: University of the Witwatersrand Press, 1999), a collection of papers on the issues facing attempts at democratic renewal in Africa. His current work concerns white responses to the political transition in South Africa. He is also working on a historical project on Scottish migrants in southern Africa.

**Rachel Jewkes** is the co-ordinator of the Women's Health Research Focus of the Medical Research Council of South Africa. She is a medical doctor, who has trained as a specialist in Public Health. She has a particular interest in medical anthropology and her research interests include gender violence, health promotion, community participation in health, and aspects of reproductive health, in particular, abortion and youth sexuality.

**Björn Lindgren** is a research associate at the Department of Cultural Anthropology and Ethnology at Uppsala University in Sweden. He has conducted research on journalism, ethnicity, and gender in Zimbabwe since 1993. He received a BA in Journalism at Stockholm University in 1991 and, after having studied Zulu at the University of London, an M.Phil in Cultural Anthropology at Uppsala University in 1996. He is currently working on a Ph.D. thesis in Cultural Anthropology on Ndebele identity.

**Ronald Louw** has an LLM degree from the University of Cape Town. He is a senior lecturer in the School of Law at the University of Natal, Durban, where he teaches Criminal Law and Criminology. He was a founder member of the KwaZulu-Natal Provincial Coalition for Gay and Lesbian Equality and is a co-convenor of the national Coalition for Gay and Lesbian Equality. He has published several articles on the topic of sexual orientation and the law, as well as having delivered conference papers on the topic both nationally and internationally.

**Gerhard Maré** is an associate professor at the University of Natal, Durban, teaching in Sociology and Industrial and Labour Studies. He has published extensively on issues of ethnicity and ethnic mobilisation for political purposes, with a specific focus on the Inkatha movement. His publications include two books: one co-authored with Georgina Hamilton entitled *An Appetite for Power* (Johannesburg/Bloomington and Indianapolis: Ravan Press/Indiana University Press, 1987); and the other published locally as *Brothers Born of Warrior Blood* (Johannesburg: Ravan Press, 1992) and internationally as *Politics and Ethnicity in South Africa* (London: Zed, 1993).

**T. Dunbar Moodie** is a professor of Sociology at Hobart and William Smith Colleges in Geneva, NY and director of the Fisher Centre for the Study of Women and Men. He has taught at the University of

Natal and the University of the Witwatersrand, where he was professor and head of the Department of Sociology. His book, *Going for Gold: Men, Mines and Migration* (Johannesburg/Berkeley and Los Angeles: Wits University Press/University of California Press, 1994), on black migrant miners, deals with the profound impact of their changing perceptions of themselves as men upon all aspects of their work and social lives. Recently, as a consultant for the United Nations, he conducted a series of workshops on 'Mainstreaming Gender' for the Department of Peacekeeping Operations.

**Robert Morrell** is a professor in the School of Education at the University of Natal, Durban. He has been studying masculinity in South Africa for ten years. In 1998 he was guest editor for special issues on masculinity of the *Journal of Southern African Studies* and *Agenda*. He is a member of IASOM, the International Association for the Study of Men. He has edited two books entitled *White But Poor* (Pretoria: UNISA, 1992) and *Political Economy and Identities in KwaZulu-Natal* (Durban: Indicator, 1996).

**Rob Pattman** describes himself as a 'British man, white and came out as straight. Lived and taught in Zimbabwe 1991–93, wrote Ph.D. on Gender, Identity and Sex education in Post-colonial Zimbabwe.' As a researcher at the Birkbeck College, University of London, he recently finished a three-year project researching the identities of 11- to 14-year-old London boys from different ethnic and social class backgrounds. He has just moved to the Department of Sociology at the University of Botswana, and hopes to research gendered identities and schooling in Botswana.

**Kopano Ratele** lectures in the Psychology Department at the University of the Western Cape. He is the convenor of the Masters Programme in Research Psychology. He previously worked as a Researcher and Head of Training and Development at the Human Sciences Research Council (HSRC). His doctoral work is on the sexuality of apartheid.

**Sandra Swart** is from Durban, where she completed her MA degree at the University of Natal on the 1914 Rebellion. Her broad interests include the construction of identity, gendered history and the creation of a synthesis between constructionist and evolutionary theories of gender. She believes the best research is done in bars. She is currently working on her doctorate on the creation of Afrikaner identity through the writings of Eugene Marais at Magdalen College in Oxford.

**Glen Thompson** is currently a director of T Minus One Consulting (Pty) Ltd, engaged in digital business strategy in Cape Town. He has lectured in Economic History at the University of Natal, Durban, and in History at the University of Durban-Westville, and has held the position of Cato Manor Researcher in the KwaZulu-Natal office of the Commission on Restitution of Land Rights. He has written on aspects of South African history including charismatic Christianity, surfing, and restitution, and assisted in the establishment of the Timewarp Surfing Museum in Durban.

**Thembisa Waetjen** teaches Political Sociology and Feminist Theory at the University of Oregon in the United States where she received her Ph.D. in Sociology in 1997. She conducted research for her dissertation on gender and ethnic conflict in KwaZulu-Natal and, during that time, taught at the University of Natal, Durban.

**Joan Wardrop** is a senior lecturer in History in the School of Social Sciences and Asian Languages, at Curtin University of Technology in Perth, Western Australia. Her research for the past five years has been focused on an ethnographic study of some aspects of elite-level policing in Soweto, and her current interests include the transforming politics of masculine identities in southern Africa.

**Katharine Wood** is a medical anthropologist affiliated to the Women's Health Research Focus of the Medical Research Council of South Africa. She is a doctoral candidate at the London School of Hygiene and Tropical Medicine, and is currently conducting ethnographic fieldwork with township youth in the Eastern Cape. Her research interests include youth sexuality and violence, reproductive health, and the anthropology of southern Africa.

**Thokozani Xaba** is a research fellow at the School of Development Studies at the University of Natal, Durban. He previously served as Co-ordinator of Projects within the Research Capacity Development division of the Human Sciences Research Council's Centre for Science Development. Prior to this he was a researcher at the Institute for Social and Economic Research at the University of Durban-Westville. His research interests include African traditional and Roman-Dutch conceptions of justice, as well as the dialogue between feminism and masculinity.

# Index